Springer
Berlin
Heidelberg
New York
Barcelona
Budapest
Hong Kong
London
Milan
Paris
Santa Clara
Singapore
Tokyo

Jörg R. Mühlbacher   Bernhard Leisch
Brian Kirk   Ulrich Kreuzeder

Oberon-2 Programming with Windows

With 66 Figures

Springer

Jörg R. Mühlbacher
Bernhard Leisch
Ulrich Kreuzeder

Johannes-Kepler-Universität Linz
Forschungsinstitut für Mikroprozessortechnik (FIM)
A-4040 Linz, Austria

Brian Kirk
Robinson Associates
Red Lion House
St. Mary's St.
GL6 6QG Painswick, Glos., UK

Library of Congress Cataloging-in-Publication Data
Oberon-2 programming with Windows / Jörg R. Mühlbacher ... (et al.).
      p.   cm.
   Includes bibliographical references and index.
   ISBN 3-540-62522-4 (alk. paper)
   1. Oberon.   2. Object-oriented programming.   3. Operating systems
(computers)   I. Mühlbacher, Jörg, 1946-   .
   QA76.76.O63O24   1997
   005.13´3--dc21   97-8043
                                                                        CIP

ISBN 3-540-62522-4 Springer-Verlag Berlin Heidelberg New York

Cover Design: d&p, Heidelberg,
Typesetting: Camera ready by authors
SPIN 10561309   45/3142 – 5 4 3 2 1 0 – Printed on acid-free paper

Preface

This book is aimed at students who need to learn the basics of programming or who are studying computing. It is a "hands on" book containing many examples which start by illustrating basic Oberon-2 language features and gradually increase in scope to cover object-oriented programming concepts and constructs. Oberon-2 is a successor to the language Pascal, which was also designed by Prof. N. Wirth [Wir71]. It has quickly become a major language used for teaching purposes. The only thing you need for successfully working through the book is to have access to a computer running Windows 3.11 or Windows 95. The material in the book is useful to students of schools, colleges, and universities for teaching Oberon-2 and programming at an introductory level.

The scope of the book is not focused on software engineering or object-oriented technology; other books mentioned in the reference section already cover these topics in much greater depth. However, the examples in the book have been designed with these topics firmly in mind. Currently the term "object-oriented" is very much in fashion, having taken over from structured programming of the 1970s and '80s. In this book we have taken the view that a structured programming approach can be used to teach the fundamentals of programming algorithms. The object-oriented approach is then brought in as a complementary way to think, analyze, design and program. It also provides richer techniques for achieving encapsulation and reuse of program implementations. Oberon-2 is often referred to as a hybrid language as it provides elegant support for programming using either structured or object-oriented programming, or indeed any practically useful combination of these two approaches.

A CD-ROM containing *POW!* software for Windows is provided with the book. It consists of a programming support environment including an Oberon-2 compiler, libraries, and the source code for the examples. The software is royalty free for educational use and so may be freely used within educational establishments. The first two chapters of the book describe the installation of the *POW!* Borland-like environment and how to work with the integrated text editor, which includes many features to support the development of programs written in Oberon-2. The facility for creating and linking Windows DLLs (Dynamic Link Libraries) makes it possible to use existing DLL based libraries and to interoperate with other Windows programs written in languages other than Oberon-2, for example C and C++.

In the text each Oberon-2 language construct is described using text, syntax diagrams, and also EBNF. This semi-formal definition of the language syntax can be skipped on first reading; full definitions and the syntaxes of the Oberon-2 and EBNF languages are given in the appendices.

We would like to encourage you not just to read the book but to use the *POW!* system and the examples on the CD-ROM to work through the book.

This way you will gradually gain confidence and ultimately be encouraged to start designing and writing your own object-oriented programs.

POW! and Oberon-2 for Windows originate from a joint project between FIM and the Johannes Kepler University, Linz, Austria, and Robinson Associates in the UK. This book evolved from an earlier work of three of the now four authors [MLK95].

We would like to thank the following people for their advice and contributions to *POW!* and the production of this book:

Rudolf Hörmanseder and Peter Dietmüller for their comments and suggestions on the manuscript.

Professor Hanspeter Mössenböck for permission to include the Oberon-2 Language Report as an Appendix and for his valuable contributions.

Günther Schwarz and Ernst Unger from the Federal Institute for Teacher Training for encouraging the use of *POW!* Oberon-2 in schools.

Students of computer science at the University of Linz who have used *POW!* widely and provided feedback which has contributed to many improvements.

J. R. Mühlbacher
B. Leisch
B. R. Kirk
U. Kreuzeder

Linz
Painswick
1997

Table of Contents

1. Introduction

There are many similarities between learning to drive a car and learning to program. Reading about it is fine for a while but there is no substitute for getting into a car and actually trying to drive. That's when you gain the experience that is needed to make the car actually useful to you and which can't be written down in books. In other words learning requires reading *and* doing. It's the same with programming; to learn a practical skill like programming requires practice. This book and the *POW!* software that comes with it provide a very easy way to learn to program in Oberon-2. The Programmers Open Workbench (*POW!*) provides the car and a safe and simple environment to drive in. Oberon-2 provides the rules of the road and a route for getting to the destination you want, i.e., writing programs which provide solutions to problems. *Learning by doing*

With *POW!* and Oberon-2 working in a Windows environment we have tried to minimize the difficulties of getting started without limiting how far you can go in the future. The *POW!* environment was inspired by the enormously successful Borland Pascal development environment. The Oberon-2 compiler from Robinson Associates has some special additions which make writing Windows programs very straightforward for a beginner. Together they provide a productive set of tools designed specifically for students and software engineers who are learning to program in Oberon-2. *Getting started*

Why Oberon-2?

Oberon-2 is almost ideal for use as an initial language for teaching programming because *Oberon-2*

- it is a small language so you can learn it and use it effectively in a relatively short time

- all the concepts of structured and object-oriented programming can be expressed clearly and naturally

- it contains no "archaic" remnants from past languages such as the *GOTO* statement or unnecessary *BEGIN* and *END* brackets

- there is a clear separation between the program itself and specific details about the system environment (input, output, etc.)

- the syntax is clearly specified using EBNF (Extended Backus-Naur Form) and fits on a single page

Oberon was kept as small and simple as possible deliberately so that the programmer can concentrate on the essentials when describing algorithms. The facility for partitioning programs into separately compilable modules together with interface consistency checking, which has also been introduced subsequently by some manufacturers in Pascal, is very important for software design. It also has a teaching benefit as in small training groups it becomes possible to discuss and work out quite demanding and motivating projects by simply providing clearly defined interfaces and some modules which are already programmed and tested. This makes it possible to set projects with reasonable and controllable workloads and also to avoid burdening students with irrelevant details.

The evolution of Oberon-2

Pascal Oberon-2 is the latest in a family of languages designed and developed by Prof. Niklaus Wirth of ETH Zurich. The first member of the family was Pascal [Wir71] which was designed as a teaching language based on experience gained from ALGOL-W. It quickly became used for teaching purposes on a world-wide basis and variants of it are still widely used today, for example Borland Pascal.

Modula After Pascal came Modula and Modula-2 [Wir82] which added the concept of separate compilation of software components (*modules*) whilst retaining the concept of data type checking within the whole program. A decade later came Oberon which resulted from Project Oberon, designed by Prof. Wirth and Prof. Gutknecht and described in [WG89] and [Rei91].

Oberon The design of Oberon was firmly based on Einstein's dictum "Make it as simple as possible, but no simpler". All redundant features of the previous languages were stripped out to yield the small yet powerful language Oberon. Oberon already contained the essential basis for object-oriented programming based on the concept of type extension, further details of which are given in Chapter 5.

Oberon-2 The language Oberon-2 [MW91] was based heavily on Oberon but with some minimal extensions which introduce concepts similar to classes and methods more explicitly using "type bound procedures".

The development of *POW!*

POW! Originally Oberon-2 only existed as a part of the ETH's Oberon System [Rei91]. Although the Oberon System is available hosted within many other operating systems many computer users with PCs wished to work within the familiar environment of Windows and to be able to create programs that would run in Windows. Also the popularity of Borland Pascal has shown how important and helpful a development support environment could be, particularly for students learning to program. The authors felt that it would be very helpful to make the benefits of Oberon-2 available to the PC community and especially for Windows. This may irritate some Oberon purists; however, with the ever wider use of C++ as a teaching language we felt justified in offering Oberon-2 as a simpler and clearer alternative.

The development environment *POW!*

POW! offers the usual functions of an integrated development environment: a multi-document-editor, embedded compiler and linker, project management with integrated Make and Build, and on-line help with information about interfaces and the programming language.

Apart from these well established functions *POW!* offers an interface for the embedding of additional software tools. Each tool can be called by either a menu entry in the "Tools" menu or by pressing a button on the button bar. The tools may take the form of a program, a Windows dynamic link library, or a dynamic data exchange server. In this way *POW!* itself is extensible.

Another feature and innovation in comparison to other environments is a concept for the production of *templates* (meta-projects), from which new projects can be derived and maintained very easily. This makes it easy for teachers, lecturers, and students to organise their projects.
Templates

As a support for the development of Windows programs with the Oberon-2 compiler the **Oberon Portable Applications Library** (**OPAL**) has been developed. This is a collection of modules for user interaction, floating point operations, file handling, strings, etc.
OPAL

A further library called OPAL++ is currently being developed based on object-oriented principles; updates are available from the FTP server mentioned at the end of this chapter.

Structure of the book

The book is split into several parts, each focused on a different aspect of learning to program with *POW!*, Oberon-2, and Windows. In effect it contains a User Manual for *POW!*, a programming test and reference guide for Oberon-2, and a detailed description of the *OPAL* programming library.

Chapter 1,
which you are reading, sets the scene and along with the preface describes the scope and purpose of the book.

Chapter 2
shows you how to install *POW!* on your computer and presents the development environment. With the help of an initial example it shows you how to get to an Oberon-2 program running quickly, step by step.

Chapter 3
provides complete documentation of the development environment and explains the integrated editor, the project management, the embedding of tools, and the system configuration.

Chapter 4
provides an introduction to Oberon-2 based on examples which can be found on the CD-ROM and run within *POW!* It uses a structured programming style and includes graded exercises for further study at the end of the chapter.

Chapter 5
introduces the concepts of object-oriented programming and again working through examples builds up to a larger scale program of more

realistic size for a student project. A set of graded exercises is provided for further study.

Chapter 6

is a reference for the programming library *OPAL* and shows its use in example programs.

Chapter 7

describes how to write programs in Oberon-2 which directly access individual functions of Windows.

Appendix A

provides a quick introduction to Oberon-2 for Pascal users.

Appendix B

contains the original Oberon-2 Language Report written by Prof. N. Wirth and Prof. H. Mössenböck at ETH. It includes an additional section with the minimal language extensions needed for programming in a Windows environment.

Appendix C

contains the ASCII character set code definition.

Literature

is a list of closely related and more advanced literature.

Typographic conventions

Items with particular significance are marked in the text as follows:

Identifiers, program code, product and file names *(example.mod)* within descriptions of programs are shown in *italic*. Important parts of the text are additionally printed bold.

Keyboard Key combinations are printed **bold**. A plus sign between two keys indicates that the first key should not be released until the second key is pressed. The order of release is not significant. An example: **CTRL+Y** means press the keys **CTRL** (control) and **Y** at the same time.

Program code is printed in a special fixed pitch character set to preserve the indentation of the text:

```
PROCEDURE Hello (name: ARRAY OF CHAR);
BEGIN
   Out.WriteString("Hello ");
   Out.WriteString(name);                              (*who?*)
END Hello;
```

System requirements

POW! operates with the graphic user interface MS Windows Version 3.1x or higher, Windows 95, and Windows NT. It requires at least 4 MB main memory and a 80386/486/Pentium CPU or equivalent.

For programs using floating point arithmetic (e.g., the data type *REAL* or the module *Float* of the *OPAL* library) a mathematics coprocessor is required (already integrated in the Intel 80486DX and Pentium processors). Otherwise, such programs can be neither compiled nor executed. Note that some examples on the CD-ROM also make use of the data type *REAL*! *Coprocessor*

Licensing

A license for the *POW!* system is included with this book. This version of the development environment is fully working.

The user license covers educational and private use and for these purposes the software may be reproduced and distributed without any restrictions.

You can request further copies of the educational version of the system from: *Educational license*

Forschungsinstitut für Mikroprozessortechnik (FIM)
Johannes-Kepler-Universität
A-4040 Linz
Austria

Phone:++43 (0) 732/2468-440
Fax: ++43 (0) 732/2468-559
E-mail: pow@fim.uni-linz.ac.at

For commercial licensing, please contact *Commercial license*

Oberon Product Group
Robinson Associates
St. Mary's Street
Painswick
Glos. GL6 6QG
United Kingdom

Fax: +44 (0)1452 812912
E-mail: oberon@robinsons.co.uk

Electronic Services

The latest educational version of *POW!* is always available on the Anonymous FTP-Server *ftp.fim.uni-linz.ac.at* in the directory *\pub\soft\pow-oberon2*. *FTP*

If you register on the *POW!* mailing list you will be able to communicate with other users of the programming system and will be informed about news *E-mail list* and extensions. Simply send an e-mail containing the text "subscribe pow-list" to *majordomo@fim.uni-linz.ac.at*.

WWW   On the world wide web (WWW) you will find the official *POW!* pages at the address *http://www.fim.uni-linz.ac.at/pow/pow.htm*. You can get the latest information about the system and also access additional electronic services.

2. First Steps

2.1 Installation of *POW!*

Installing *POW!* is very simple because a utility executes all the operations that are necessary to install the development environment on your computer.

Start the program *install.exe* on your installation disc (e.g., with the program manager) and indicate the directory where you would like to have *POW!* installed (the suggestion is *c:\pow*).

Install.exe

As soon as the installation program has copied all files to your computer it creates a group named *POW!* for the program manager of Windows 3.1. There references to the Oberon development environment and a *ReadMe* file containing information about the latest version of *POW!* are generated. Under Windows 95 a submenu *POW!* is created in the menu *Programs* together with the corresponding entries.

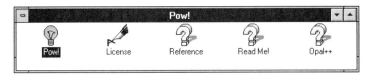

Fig. 1: POW! program group (Windows 3.1)

Please read carefully the information given in the *ReadMe* file and then start the Oberon-2 development environment with the *POW!* Icon.

ReadMe

When you start *Reference* you will be shown the on-line help for the programming language Oberon-2 and the library *OPAL* (which is equivalent to the command **Compiler** of the menu **Help** in *POW!*).

Reference

The document *License* contains the regulations of the licensing of the *POW!* system.

2.2 Operating the system

After the development environment has been started the configuration is restored automatically to the way it was when you quit the program the last time. When you start *POW!* for the very first time a demonstration program *Hello1* is opened:

Configuration

Just let *POW!* make the program! You can either choose the function **Make** from the menu **Compile** (key **F9**) or press the *Make* button ▦ on the button bar: a simple click on the mouse will do.

Make

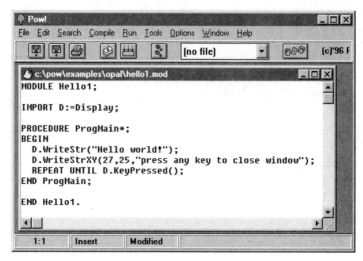

Fig. 2: Demonstration program hello1.mod

Message window The development environment automatically executes all the operations needed to generate the program. These steps are displayed in a message window.

Fig. 3: POW! message window

If no error occurs the program is created and can be started with the function **Run** of the **Run** menu, the key combination **CTRL+F9** or, again quicker, by clicking the *Run* button [icon]. After only a few seconds ...

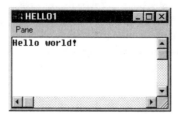

Fig. 4: Output of hello1.exe

The example program opens a simple output window, displays a short welcome message, and can be terminated with a key stroke.

Browsing through the example programs

POW! gathers information to support the further development of programs in   *Projects*
project files. However, for simple examples it is not necessary to open a
project file. In this case, a default project is predefined.

We will learn later how to create project files and how to generate them much
more easily from existing basic projects (called *templates*).

First let us take a look at a slightly more complex program which calculates
and displays a fractal fern.

1. Open the source file *fern.mod* with the function **Open** of the **File** menu.
   To do so, change to the directory *examples\opal\fern* in the dialog box
   and choose the file *fern.mod* (with a double click of the left mouse button
   or by selecting the file name and pressing the *OK* button).

2. Use the procedure already described (*Make* and *Run* buttons) to generate
   the program and then execute it. You can do this even more quickly by
   pressing the *Run* button because *POW!* knows whether a program is ready
   for execution or, as in our case, has to be generated first. In the case of the
   fern example a new window appears into which the fern is drawn. The
   program runs until it is terminated with the function **Close** of the system
   menu or the key combination **ALT+F4**.

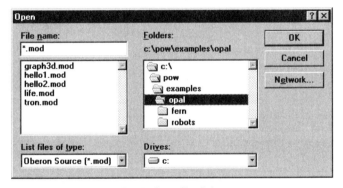

Fig. 5: Open file dialog

You can go through all the example programs provided just as you have done
with the fern program: generate the program and watch the output. By doing
so, you will gain an impression of the possibilities that will be available for
your own programs later. At the same time, you will get some valuable
experience in using the programming environment.

Most of the enclosed examples are designed to illustrate typical programming
problems that you may encounter later. You will also find some more
attractive graphics examples (*graf3d.mod*).

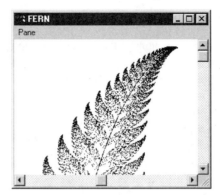

Fig. 6: The fern program

Example programs with project files

Most example programs work with the default project file. For certain problems where Oberon-2 source files and other files are used it is more convenient to define a customized project file. An example for this is the program *Bitmap*:

Opening a project
1. First open the project definition *bitmap.prj* of the example with the function ***Open Project*** of the ***Compile*** menu. In the dialog box choose the project file *bitmap.prj* of the directory *examples\winapi\bitmap*.

Creating a project
2. The further steps are identical to the ones used before, and the functions *Make* and *Run* may be used here as well.

3. If you want to work with the default project again, you must close the current project file with ***Close Project*** of the ***Compile*** menu. This function is executed automatically each time a new project file is opened.

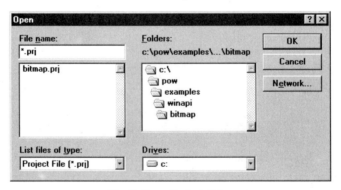

Fig. 7: Open Project dialog

2.3 A first program

You have learned so far how to select existing programs and project files. Now try to write your own program for the first time, or adapt an existing one if you prefer.

Generating a program from the default project

To get started use the default project as this will be easier; in any case close any open project so that you may be sure the default project is used. You can see that very easily from the title of the *POW!* window as the name of the currently used project file is displayed there.

1. Open a new file with the function *New* of the *File* menu.

2. Save the file under a name you like (with the function *Save As* of the *File* menu).

3. Enter your program, which should look like the following (you can make up your own text between the quotation marks):

```
MODULE Myfirst;
IMPORT Out;

PROCEDURE ProgMain*;
BEGIN
   Out.String("Is anybody there?");
   Out.Ln;                         (*new line*)
   Out.String("Close the window, I am freezing!");
END ProgMain;

END Myfirst.
```

You can operate the editor exactly the same way as you would do the Windows text editor *Notepad*. In addition, it offers some features that make a programmer's life easier, e.g., an automatic indent (for more detailed information about the editor see Chapter 3). *Editor*

If you have done everything correctly you can now let *POW!* generate and also execute your program. The example given waits for a key to be pressed and then prints the text.

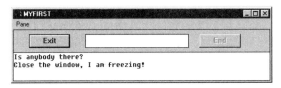

Fig. 8: Output of the program MyFirst

As an alternative to the example described above you may of course take an existing program, save it under a new name (*File/Save As*) and then make all your desired changes and extensions.

Generating a program with your own project file

Templates   As mentioned above, programs developed with *POW!* are built within project files. You do not need to generate a new project file for every program. The development environment provides a way for you to make new projects out of predefined *templates*.

POW! contains a series of templates for the most important types of programs (depending on the output library used). But you can also create templates from each of your own projects which you can use as a basis for your further projects. This is particularly useful if you have your own library of functions that you would like to use in all your programs, or if programs are structured according to a regular pattern (for more information about templates see Chapter 3).

Inout.tpl   For your first example use the template ***Inout*** from which simple projects using the modules *In* and *Out* can be generated. The templates can be reached by the menu commands ***Project/New*** or ***File/New/Project***. Select the menu entry *Use template "Inout"* for creating a new project based on the *Inout* template.

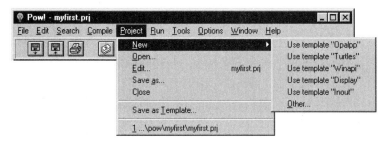

Fig. 9: Selection of a template

Once you have decided on a template you must tell the development environment the name of the new project and the directory in which you would like it to be generated and stored.

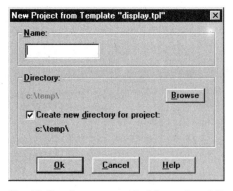

Fig. 10: Creating a new project from a template

Enter the name of the new project (not more than 8 characters), select the destination directory, and state, if a subdirectory has to be created for the new project.

When you press the **Ok** button after these settings, *POW!* immediately generates the desired project framework: the required directories are created, a project file with the name you have given is generated from the template, and the source files defined in the template are copied to the destination directory. Moreover, the main module of the template is automatically given the name of the new project.

Creating a project

After this step, our project *myfirst* looks like this:

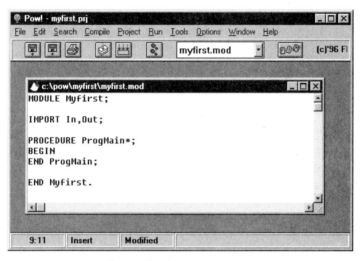

Fig. 11: The first project created

The generated project already contains a complete program which opens an output window and then closes it immediately. You can check that easily by running it.

Now when you want to write your own program you only need to extend the created program framework *myfirst.mod* in the function *ProgMain*.

Move the cursor in front of the keyword *END* and make the changes just described.

Example program

By repeating these steps you can create as many projects as you like from the template and avoid a great deal of typing.

3. The Working Environment of *POW!*

3.1 Basic ideas

A brief introduction to the development environment *POW!* has already been given in Chapter 2. This chapter presents a complete description of the functions which *POW!* offers to support quick and simple development of Oberon-2 programs and projects.

Each of the following sections covers a specific topic of the environment. Section 3.10 provides a summary of all the functions that can be accessed from the main menu.

3.2 Editor

The editor is the part of the programming environment that a software engineer uses most of the time. In *POW!* the editor is an extended standard edit control of MS Windows and so provides a familiar set of facilities. It edits text files using the keyboard settings from Windows, with the tab and line feed as the only control keys used.

3.2.1 Keyboard settings

For fast access to important functions you may use the following *accelerator keys*:

Accelerator keys

SHIFT+Ins	Insert from the clipboard
CTRL+Ins	Copy to the clipboard
SHIFT+Del	Copy to the clipboard and delete in the text
CTRL+Del	Delete selection
ALT+BkSp	Undo last change
CTRL+Y	Delete current line
F1	Help: Index
CTRL+F1	Help: Topic search in compiler help
SHIFT+F3	Find text
CTRL+F3	Replace text
F3	Repeat last find/replace action
ALT+F4	Exit *POW!*

SHIFT+F4	Arrange edit windows in cascade layout
SHIFT+F5	Arrange edit windows in horizontal tile layout
SHIFT+F6	Arrange edit windows in vertical tile layout
F7	Show previous compile error
F8	Show next compile error
F9	Compile files of project (equivalent to Compile/Make)
CTRL+F9	Run executable program (equivalent to Run/Run)
ALT+F9	Compile active edit file (equivalent to Compile/Compile)
SHIFT+F12	Save file
CTRL+F12	Load a file
CTRL+Pos1	Jump to the beginning of the text
CTRL+End	Jump to the end of the text
CTRL+Left	Jump to previous word
CTRL+Right	Jump to next word

3.2.2 Clipboard

In *POW!* the clipboard may be used to rearrange parts of the source code in a window or to move it from one edit window to the other. Text may also be transferred from or to other programs (e.g., word processors, mailing software) These commands are available in most Windows programs and so should be familiar.

Copy, Paste Use the command ***Edit/Copy*** (or **CTRL+Ins**) to copy the selected text to the clipboard. With the command ***Edit/Paste*** (or **SHIFT+Ins**) you can insert this text at the cursor position into your active document.

Cut The command ***Edit/Cut*** (or **SHIFT+Del**) both moves the selected text to the clipboard and deletes it in your document.

3.2.3 Text search

Search The editor can search for a piece of text in the active document. The function ***Search/Find*** (short cut **SHIFT+F3**) opens a dialog window to search for a string.

Starting at the cursor position *POW!* searches for the string *WriteStr* in the active document. If the string is found this part of the text is selected.

If the option ***Case Sensitive*** is active then the search treats upper and lower case characters as being different.

The switch *Whole Word only* enables the search for whole words. The search will only be successful if the right and left adjacent character is neither a digit nor a letter.

Fig. 12: Dialog for a text search

The direction of the search can be reversed by switching the option *Direction* to *Up* (from the cursor to the beginning of the text).

Direction of search

POW! retains the strings that are searched during a session and offers them in a list from which you can simply select the desired item. So there is no need to enter a search string twice.

This list can be reached by clicking the mouse on the small down arrow to the right of the Find data entry box shown in Figure 12.

Replace

Fig. 13: Dialog for replacing a text

If you want to both search for a string in the text and replace it by another one, use the command *Search/Replace* (short cut **CTRL+F3**):

If the switch *Replace All* is on, every occurrence of the search string is re-placed by the new text, starting from the cursor position down to the end of the text (or up to the beginning, if the *Direction* is *Up*).

Note: the previous search or replace action may be repeated with the command *Search/Search again* (short cut **F3**).

Repeat Search

3.2.4 Tab stops

Conversion of tabulator

The editor replaces tab stops by a number of blanks if this presetting is selected (*Options/Editor,* option *Replace Tabs*, see 3.6). This number can be changed using the option *Tab size* of the presettings dialog. A tab size of 2 is recommended for programs.

Note: A conversion of tabulators to blanks can only be made when you enter the text! If a file already contains tabulators, they will not be replaced automatically, even if the switch *Replace Tabs* is on.

3.2.5 Message window

POW! routes output from the compiler and the linker to the message window. This window is created and opened automatically by the development environment.

Error message

If you double-click an error message in the message window, *POW!* will open the corresponding source file and automatically position the cursor where the compiler found the error.

Next error

If you do not want to switch to the message window to view an error, you can display the previous and the next error using the commands *Search/-Next error* (key **F8**) and *Search/Previous error* (key **F7**).

The programming environment distinguishes between errors and warnings from the compiler. If the option *Search/Ignore Warnings* is not active, only errors (and no warnings) will appear in the message window, but this is not recommended for beginners.

3.2.6 Status bar

The bottom part of the main window of *POW!* is reserved for the status bar. The bar is divided into four regions:

Fig. 14: Status bar

Cursor
- The first region shows the line and column number of the cursor in the active document.

Insert Mode
- The second region indicates if the editor is currently working in the insert mode (new text is inserted) or in the overwrite mode (new text overwrites existing text). You can change from one mode to the other by pressing the **Ins** key.

- The third region shows *Modified* if the active file has been modified since you saved it last time.

- The fourth region is used for the output of information without having to open an additional window. Here you may find some information about the selected command, the error message for the current error, etc.

3.2.7 Help on keywords

If the option ***Topic Search*** in the presettings of the editor (***Options/Editor***, see 3.6) is active, you can get some help on a particular topic from the compiler by simply clicking a word with the right mouse button.

Right mouse button

So, for example, if you have forgotten the necessary parameters of a library function, you only need to click the function and you will get the relevant help text at once.

Example

The following help text was obtained by clicking the word *Out* in the program text with the right mouse button:

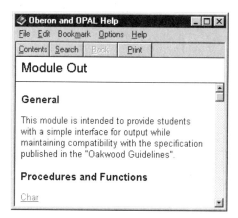

Fig. 15: Help on the module Display

3.3 Project management

A project is a framework which contains information about a program. Consequently *POW!* can automatically generate the current version of the program.

3.3.1 The default project

POW! always uses the default project if no other project file is active. This project file is named ***pow.prj*** and is located in the Windows directory. The only exception is that the active editor window is regarded as the main pro-

Default project

gram of the future program and all its parts (i.e., its modules) are also intended to belong to the project.

In the case of the default project, the development environment gathers all the necessary information about a program by itself. Additional information may be given by modifying the definition of the default project, just as in normal projects (file list, compiler settings, etc.; see below).

You will reach the limits of usefulness of the default project if a program consists of parts with source code not written in Oberon-2, e.g., resource files, object files that have already been compiled, or libraries.

When you initially install *POW!* on your computer, only the *OPAL* library will be on the file list of the default project.

3.3.2 Contents of a project file

Project file Project files are created and managed by the development environment. The following elements are always stored:

Typical • file names of the files needed to generate the program
contents • compiler settings
   • linker settings
   • directory settings
   • size, position, and contents of open editor files
   • size and position of the *POW!* window

POW! always keeps project files up to date. They are saved automatically and immediately upon any modification of any of the settings.

3.3.3 Establishing a project file

New projects Project files can be opened with the command **Compile/Open Project**. If you enter the name of a file that does not exist yet, *POW!* asks if you want to create a new project:

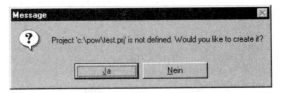

Fig. 16: Establishing a new project file

The extension of the file name for project files is ".prj" and is automatically appended to the file name by *POW!*

3.3.4 Update of a project definition

You can tell *POW!* the files belonging to a project using the menu command   *File list*
Compile/Edit Project. The appropriate dialog also appears if a new project is
created.

In this dialog, all the files needed to make a program have to be entered. In
general, these are all the source files and all the referenced libraries (e.g., the
OPAL library or import libraries for dynamic link libraries that will be
embedded).

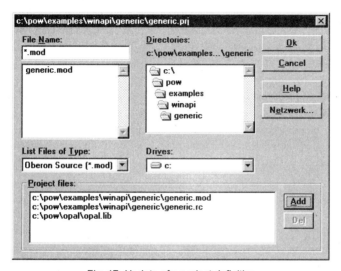

Fig. 17: Update of a project definition

The program *Generic* from the examples of *POW!* only consists of the
Oberon-2 program *generic.mod*, the resource definition *generic.rc*, and the
library *opal.lib*.

You may add further files to the file list with the button *Add File.* If you want
to delete a file of the project, select it on the project list and press the
Delete File button.

The Oberon-2 development environment works with the following file types: *File types*

".mod"	Oberon-2 source program
".obj"	object file in Microsoft's OMF format
".sym"	symbol file, automatically created and managed
".lib"	Library
".rc"	source file for the mini-resource compiler
".res"	resource file, automatically linked to the program

POW! knows how to handle the different types of files: Source files are compiled as necessary; object files, libraries, and resource files are linked to the program.

3.3.5 Producing a program

The benefit of having defined the elements of a project is that *POW!* can now make a program when you simply press a button.

Make When you use the command ***Compile/Make*** *POW!* compiles all source files that have been modified since the last compilation. If no error occurs then the object files and the libraries stated in the project definition are linked to a program. The only parts of libraries that are linked are those actually used in the program.

Build If you want to compile all source files without exception, you need to use the command ***Compile/Build***.

POW! finds the correct order of compilation of the referenced modules itself. Note that sometimes a module which has not been edited may need to be recompiled. This is because certain modifications of the interfaces to modules referenced by it affect its own interface (e.g., because of type extensions).

3.3.6 Running a program

Run Once a program has been through the "build" or "make" stage it can be started with the command ***Run/Run.*** The result of the program execution is immediately displayed on the status bar (not to be confused with values returned by the program).

Runtime error If a program causes an error which is detected by the Oberon-2 runtime system (array index is out of range, range violation with an assignment, etc.), then the runtime system indicates this error with a message such as

"index out of range in line 15 of module myprog".

It then terminates the execution of the program. Because of this precise feedback of the location of problem errors like these can easily be located and corrected.

Program termination The situation is more complicated with errors which are not detected by the runtime system (for example, because the compiler options for generating the check code were not set and a runtime error has caused an "unexpected application error" [MS Windows error text]). In such a case, Windows displays an error message, containing the name of the program in which the error occurred and an error address. If the error happened in the Oberon-2 program you can find out the module name and the line number of the program crash using the *Find Error* tool (menu ***Tools/Find Error***) and entering the error position. The line number can only be located if the object file belonging to the module is found and if it was compiled with the option ***Debug Symbols.***

For further information concerning the handling of the *Find Error* tool see Section 3.11.

Find error tool

3.3.7 Moving projects

The project definitions contain references to the project files. If these references were file names together with the complete path name you would have difficulties when moving a project to another computer. There, you could only run the project properly if you had exactly the same directories and all the files stored the same way as on the source computer.

Path information

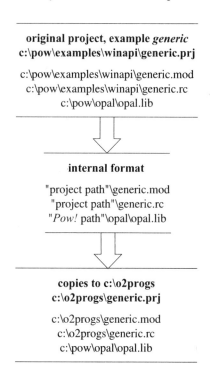

original project, example *generic*
c:\pow\examples\winapi\generic.prj

c:\pow\examples\winapi\generic.mod
c:\pow\examples\winapi\generic.rc
c:\pow\opal\opal.lib

internal format

"project path"\generic.mod
"project path"\generic.rc
"*Pow!* path"\opal\opal.lib

copies to c:\o2progs
c:\o2progs\generic.prj

c:\o2progs\generic.mod
c:\o2progs\generic.rc
c:\pow\opal\opal.lib

Fig. 18: Internal representation of project files

This is the reason why *POW!* stores the path information of the files *relatively* to certain directories (see Figure 18):

- If a file is located on the same drive as the project definition, the path will be stored relatively to the directory of the project definition.

- If a file is situated in the *POW!* directory or in a subdirectory of it, the path will be stored relatively to the *POW!* directory.

- In all other cases the complete path name will be stored in an absolute rather than relative way.

With this mechanism you can copy your projects easily if you stick to the rule of always storing your own files for a project in the directory of the project definition or in a subdirectory of it. The advantage of this procedure is that you can simply copy a project and *POW!* is able to work with it on computers with a different directory structure without requiring any modifications.

3.3.8 Symbol files

Module interface The programming language Oberon-2 does not require the separation of modules into definition and implementation modules as is the case with Modula-2. In order to check the module interface efficiently during the compilation, the compiler generates symbol files that define the export interface of a module (apart from the object files containing the program code).

POW! stores object files as well as symbol files in the same directory as the active project file. If you do not want this, you can define a different directory using the dialog *Options/Directories*, and your files will be managed there.

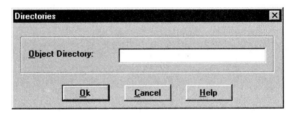

Fig. 19: Directory of the object and symbol files

3.4 Templates

From each project definition there is always exactly *one* particular application generated. Often different project definitions have many characteristics in common: they may have a similar program structure, use the same libraries, or work with the same compiler and linker settings.

Templates To benefit from these similarities between projects you can design templates from which you can derive as many project definitions as you like.

Generating templates You can generate a template easily by calling the command *Compile/- Save Project as Template*. By doing so, the active project definition will be saved under a new name with the extension ".tpl". In order not to affect the automatic derivation of the directory names (see Section 3.3) a template should always be saved in the directory of the project file. It is then possible to move or copy it together with the corresponding files.

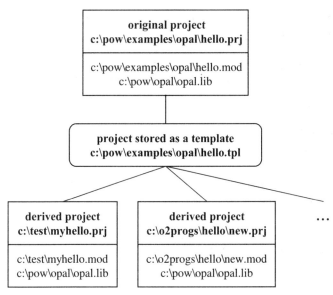

Fig. 20: How project names are derived

3.4.1 Templates as project models

In most cases you will use a template as a model framework for each new project. You can derive a new project from a template by selecting the menu entry of the template in the menu *File/New/Project* or *Project/New*.

Generating projects

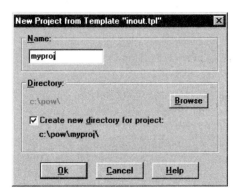

Fig. 21: Creating a new project from a template

A new project is saved in the selected directory under the stated name with the file name extension ".prj". If the field *Create new directory for project* is enabled, a subdirectory will be generated with the selected path and the new project will then be stored there.

After you have pressed the *Ok* button *POW!* generates the necessary directories, sets up the project definition and copies all the source files that are part of the project to the project directory. No libraries are copied as they are only referenced in the project definition.

Main module If a module exists with the same name as the template, the module name in its source code is changed to the name of the new project. Neither the runtime system nor the operating system requires such a measure, but this facilitates work with projects because it makes it easier to find the main module of a project quickly.

3.4.2 Templates for version management

Program versions Another way of using templates is a simple method to achieve version management of applications.

- When you have finished your work on a new version of a program you can generate a template from this current project (preferably with a version number in the file name). This, in effect, provides a snapshot of the current state of the program's development.

New version - From this last template you now generate the project definition for the next version of the application. So, all source files are copied for the new version whereas the old application remains untouched. Of course you must enter a new directory for every new version.

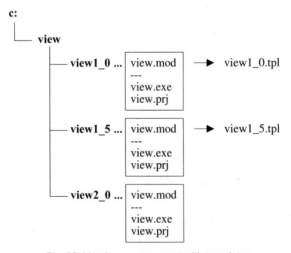

Fig. 22: Version management with templates

Figure 22 shows the management of a project *view* with the version numbers 1.0, 1.5, and 2.0. Note that from version 2.0 no template has been generated yet, as it is still being worked on currently. A new template has to be created only after the release of a version.

This use of templates for version management is fine for small projects but tends to take up more data storage space than absolutely necessary. For larger and more complex projects an additional version management utility could be used. However, the simple scheme described above is adequate for most projects.

3.5 Button bar

Functions of *POW!* which are very frequently used are arranged as buttons directly below the menu bar for fast access.

Fig. 23: The button bar

For fast access you can press one of these buttons instead of selecting the equivalent command from the menu.

The function of these menu command buttons is: *Menu*
shortcuts

🖫	*File/Open*	Selection of a file for editing
🖫	*File/Save*	Saves the text of the active edit window
🖨	*File/Print*	Prints the contents of the active edit window
🗇	*Compile/Compile*	Compiles the file in the active edit window
⌗	*Compile/Make*	Compiles all necessary source files of the project and links the object files and libraries to an executable program or a DLL
🗔	*Run/Run*	Starts the generated program. The function *Make* is called beforehand, if necessary

3.5.1 List of the source files

In the file list of the button bar you will find all source files of the active   *File list*
project. You can open a file by simply activating it on the list. If the editor is
already working on the file, the relevant window is put in the foreground.

This list has also a second useful feature. If a window that is part of the
project is in the foreground, the file name (but not the path) appears on the
button bar. When the active file is not part of the project, the text "(no file)"
appears instead. So you can see at a glance whether a file already belongs to
the active project or not.

3.5.2 User-defined buttons

Tools   Apart from the predefined elements of the button bar you can use the remaining unused space for your own buttons. These buttons may be linked to executable programs, functions of dynamic link libraries, or DDE connections. Using a utility (*RunMenu*) you can also shortcut other menu commands with your own fixed buttons in the button bar.

You will find further information about how to do this in Section 3.8.

3.6 Configuration

Preferences   In *POW!* the configuration of the development environment is set up using the presettings dialog which you can reach with the menu command *Options/Preferences*.

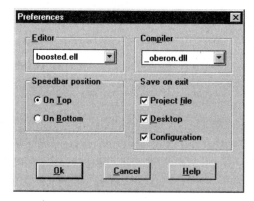

Fig. 24: Dialog for the presettings

Used editor (Editor)

The editor provided with *POW!* may be replaced by another one if a precisely defined interface is strictly adhered to. (If you are interested, the specification is available from the authors at the addresses given on p. 6) In this field you can choose one of the editors currently available. The default editor is "boosted.ell".

Position of the speedbar (Speedbar position)

The button bar is usually situated just below the menu bar of the main window. By activating the option *On bottom* you can instruct *POW!* to place the button bar at the bottom edge of the window (above the status bar).

This option has been introduced mainly to support overhead projection, because often it is not possible to project the whole screen, and by moving the button bar down to an undisplayed area more program code can be made visible.

Programming language (Compiler)

The development environment offers the opportunity to work with programming languages other than Oberon-2, or even with different Oberon
compilers. A compiler can be embedded into *POW!* with *Compiler-Interface DLLs*. The standard package contains exactly one interface library, i.e., the
interface for the Oberon-2 compiler you are working on.

Compiler interface

If you are interested in embedding other compilers into *POW!* please contact
the authors.

Automatic save (Save on exit)

Here you can indicate the information that you would like to have saved
automatically on exiting *POW!*

Pow.dsk

Project file *(default=on)*	If this option is active *POW!* will automatically open the project definition that you worked on when you exited the last time.
Desktop *(default=on)*	This switch instructs the environment to restore the windows and positions when you exit *POW!* The settings are stored in the file ***pow.dsk*** in the local Windows directory (so in a multi-user session each user may have his/her personal desktop).
Configuration *(default=on)*	If this option is switched on *POW!* automatically saves the current configuration at the end of the program when you exit.

Configuration files

The settings of the *Preferences* dialog can be saved as configuration files
(extension ".cfg"). The default file name for this is ***pow.cfg***.

Pow.cfg

Configuration files are usually stored in the local Windows directory. In this
way users having access to *POW!* over a network can create their own
configurations.

If the option ***Save on exit: Desktop*** is set in the presettings the most recently
used configuration file is loaded automatically. Otherwise *POW!* loads the
default configuration of *pow.cfg* when you start it.

You can use the following menu commands when working with configuration files:

Options/Open	Loads a configuration file
Options/Save	Saves the configuration in the current configuration file
Options/Save as	Saves the configuration in a new file

In addition to the settings of the Preferences dialog the defined tools and the current setting of the menu switch *Search/Ignore warnings* are also stored in the configuration file.

Editor settings (*Options/Editor*)

The following features relate to the editor installed in the standard package (*boosted.ell*):

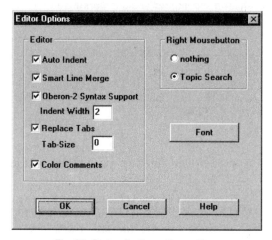

Fig. 25: Dialog for the editor settings

Auto Indent *(default=on)*	If this option is active and you are entering a new line of source text, this text will be indented to the starting column of the preceding line.
Smart Line Merge *(default=on)*	The editor reduces leading white space to a single character, whenever two lines are merged.
Oberon-2 Syntax Support *(default=on)*	This option results in easier input of Oberon-2 programs. The editor then generates the END parts for IF, WHILE, REPEAT, FOR, WITH, and PROCEDURE statements.
Replace Tabs *(default=on)*	Indicates whether the editor works with tabs (fixed tabstops in every eighth column) or replaces the tabs by blanks during the input.
Tab-Size *(default=2)*	Here you can tell *POW!* the number of blanks by which the tabs are replaced if the option *Replace tabs* is active.
Color Comments *(default=on)*	If this option is active, then comments in Oberon-2 programs are displayed in a different color (green).

Character set (Font)

After clicking this button you can select a new font. If you change the font, *Font* windows that are already open are not affected. So it is possible to have several windows with different fonts open.

Function of the right mouse button (Right mouse button)

If you select the option *Topic search* you can get information from the on-line help about the keyword the mouse pointer is pointing at by clicking with the right mouse button.

In case no direct help on the keyword exists a search window is opened within which a word is already selected. This is the word that is apparently the most similar to the one you are searching for.

This option is active automatically after the installation of *POW!*

Topic search

3.7 Working with windows

If there are several windows open in the development environment, you will come to the point where you would like to have them clearly arranged. *POW!* offers the following standard functions for the automatic arrangement of windows:

Arrange windows

Cascade	*POW!* sizes all sub-windows about 2/3 of the size of the main window. Then they are arranged in the main window in an overlapping way, starting from the left top, so that each window just leaves enough space for the preceding one to show its title. So you can access each window at any time, although they overlap, at least one corner of each window remains uncovered (see figure).	
Tile horizontal	The whole area of *POW!* is split horizontally. The several windows do not overlap.	

Tile vertical	The whole area of *POW!* is split vertically. Again the windows do not overlap.	
Arrange icons	Iconised windows are arranged at the bottom edge of the main window. This function is additionally carried out by each of the methods described above.	

Panes

Using the *Tile* functions you may create a clear arrangement of the windows very easily. However, in practice, you often do not wish to have all the windows to have equal sizes. The message window should for example be smaller than the windows of the files you wish to edit.

Non-overlapping windows   With *POW!* you can make such adjustments very simply with the help of an integrated mechanism (*Panes*). This technique ensures that non-overlapping windows remain non-overlapping, even if you have changed the size of a single window.

Right mouse button   In order not to affect the usual working methods of MS Windows this function has been assigned to the right mouse button: a change of a window size executed with the right mouse button automatically resizes all the other affected windows.

If for example you enlarge one window, the size of the·neighboring windows is reduced automatically. The advantage is that the windows do not overlap after the operation, guaranteeing that the whole contents of the windows remains visible.

Tolerance   The pane mechanism has a threshold of tolerance as far as its sphere of action is concerned. It is only effective for windows whose frames are adjacent or very close together, for example when comparing files.

Some examples of how the pane method works (the arrows always symbolize the moves of the mouse with the right mouse button pressed down):

before	*after*

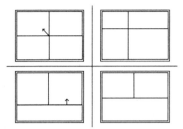

3.8 Tools

The predefined features of the development environment may be extended by some additional ones. These extensions *(tools)* can be configured as either menu commands or buttons of the button bar.   *Button bar*

When you install *POW!* a tool is included automatically which can locate the source code position of program crashes in Oberon-2 applications *(finderr.exe)*.

Tools can be added by the *POW!* developers or third-party suppliers. New tools can also be created with *POW!* and then added to it.

3.8.1 Types of tools

POW! supports tools packaged in three different ways: *Types of tools*

Programs	MS-Windows or MS-DOS EXE programs are called directly. These tools are controlled by parameters in their command line.
Dynamic link libraries (DLLs)	The development environment can call functions of dynamic link libraries. These functions may have either precisely one parameter (a pointer to a command string) or none.
DDE-server (dynamic data exchange)	*POW!* can send commands of the type *XTYP_EXECUTE* to DDE servers.

3.8.2 Embedding of tools

First we will describe the embedding of normal Windows and DOS programs. The calling of dynamic link libraries and DDE communication will be discussed in Section 3.12.   *Programs*

For the configuration and installation of tools you can use the menu command ***Tools/Options***.

Tool list   The left top list of the dialog shows the names of the tools already installed (in this case Find Error and Browse). All other settings refer to the one tool which is currently selected on the list.

The environment accepts any modifications of the settings automatically when either the active tool on the list is changed or the dialog is quit with **Ok**.

Menu entry   By activating the options **Menu Entry** or **Speed-button** you can add a tool to the menu bar as a command of the menu **Tools** or as a button of the button bar (both at the same time is also possible).

Options for   If the switch **Ask for Arguments** is active *POW!* asks for additional program
tools   arguments before it executes a tool. The option **POW! Window On Top** puts the window of the programming environment automatically in the foreground after you have started the program, and with the setting **Automatic start at POW! start-up** you can instruct *POW!* to run certain tools automatically when the environment is started (and to close them after *POW!* has been quit, if they are still active).

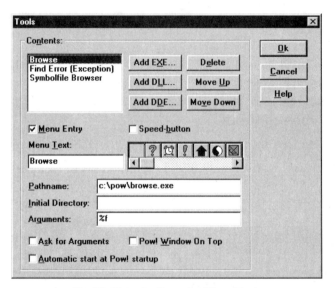

Fig. 26: Dialog for the embedding of tools

Icons   The text of a menu command is suggested by *POW!* and can be modified by editing the field **Menu Text**. There is a variety of graphics available which you may use as icons for tools to go onto the button bar.

3.8.3 Installing tools

New tool   The button **Add EXE...** starts a file selection in which a new tool can be looked for and from which it can also be selected. Then *POW!* generates a new entry for the tool on the tool list.

The entries in **Pathname**, **Initial directory**, and **Arguments** only refer to program tools: **Pathname** indicates the name of the program to call, an entry in *Initial directory* instructs *POW!* to change to the stated directory before it calls the program. With *Arguments* the tool can be started with command line parameters.

3.8.4 Command line parameters

In order to enable tools to integrate in specific ways with elements of the development environment, *POW!* defines several variables which are replaced by current values in the command line when programs are called.

Variables for tools

The following variables are replaced:

%a	by the handle of the active edit window (4 hex digits)
%d	by the path to *POW!*
%f	by the file name of the active edit window
%i	by the path to MS-Windows
%n	by the file name of the active edit window without path and file extension
%o	by the path to the currently active project
%p	by the active project name (without directory and file extension)
%r	by the full active project name
%w	by the handle of the main window (4 hex digits)
%x	by the name of the future application
%1	by the first program parameter of *POW!*
%2	by the second program parameter of *POW!*
%%	by a single percentage character

Examples

Some tools are added automatically when you install *POW!*:

Browse	Shows the export interface of a module
FindErr	Locates the position of a runtime error
RunMenu	Calls a menu command, e.g., with the parameters "*%w sf*" the dialog for searching a text is started (sf = Search/Find)

As an exercise, you can try to embed the calculator program of Windows *calc.exe* as a tool into the menu *Tools*. After having clicked the *Add Exe* button you can search and select this file in your Windows directory.

Embedding of calc.exe

3.9 On-line help

As already explained in Section 3.6 *POW!* can be used for any programming
language with the help of special dynamic link libraries. This is why the on-
line help is separated into two parts: a general help file showing how to
handle the environment and a more specific one on the compiler currently in
use.

3.9.1 Help on the environment

General help   The on-line help for the handling of *POW!* may either be accessed with menu
commands (see Section 3.10) or as more specific information using the help
buttons whenever they are included in dialogs.

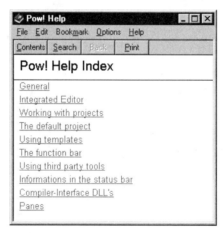

Fig. 27: Help on the handling of the environment

3.9.2 Help on the compiler

Help on   The on-line help on the Oberon-2 compiler contains the language definition
Oberon-2 and   of the programming language Oberon-2. It also describes the extensions to
OPAL   the language that are necessary to support the operating system MS Windows
and includes an on-line reference for the programming library *OPAL*.

Keywords   Apart from the menu command ***Help/Compiler*** you can also get compiler-
specific help on a keyword by clicking the word with the right mouse button
in the editor window (the presetting ***Right mouse button: Topic search*** must
be active for this facility to be active).

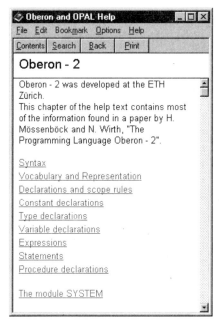

Fig. 28: Help on the programming language Oberon-2

3.10 Menu functions

Here is an overview of the default menu commands in *POW!*:

File	*New*	Generates an empty editor window
	Open...	Opens any text file for editing
	Save	Saves the active edit window
	Save as...	Saves the file under a new name
	Save all	Saves the contents of all edit windows
	Print	Prints the contents of the active edit window
	Printer Setup...	Starts a dialog for the selection and settings of a printer
	Exit	Quits *POW!*
Edit	*Undo*	Undoes the last edit command
	Redo	Revokes the *Undo* function
	Cut	Cuts out a selection of the edit window and moves it to the clipboard

	Copy	Copies the selected text to the clipboard
	Paste	Inserts text from the clipboard into the edit window
	Clear	Deletes the contents of an edit window
Search	*Find...*	Searches for a text in the edit window
	Replace...	Replaces strings in the edit window
	Search again	Repeats the last *Find* or *Replace* function
	Goto line...	Moves the cursor to a defined line number
	Next error	Moves the cursor to the next compiler error (and opens the corresponding file if necessary)
	Previous error	Moves the cursor to the previous compiler error
	Ignore warnings	If this option is active *POW!* ignores all warnings when you use the functions *Next error* and *Previous error*
Compile	*Compile*	Compiles the contents of the active edit window
	Make	Compiles the necessary files of a project definition and generates a program
	Build	Compiles all files of a project and generates a program
	Open Project...	Opens an existing project or generates a new one
	Edit Project...	Edits the definition of the active project (files may be added or taken out of the project)
	Save Project as...	Saves the active project definition under a new file name
	Close Project	Closes the active project file
	Create Project from Template...	Creates a new project from a template
	Save Project as Template...	Saves the active project definition as a template

Run	Run	Executes the compiled and linked project (*Make* will be called first, if necessary)
	Parameters	Defines the program parameters for *Run*
Tools	*xxx*	Menu entries defined by the user (selecting one of them executes the assigned command)
	Options...	Modifies existing tool definitions or adds new ones (an entry consists of the text of the menu entry, the command to be executed, and the parameters to be passed)
Options	*Editor...*	Dialog for setting the editor options (is provided by the editor interface of the editor used)
	Compiler...	Dialog for setting the compiler options (is provided by the compiler-interface DLL): this data is local to a project
	Linker...	Dialog for setting the linker options (also in the compiler-interface DLL)
	Directories...	Dialog for setting the paths for the compiler and the linker (from the compiler-interface DLL)
	Preferences...	Modifies the *POW!* settings: editor, compiler, etc.
	Open...	Loads a configuration file
	Save	Saves a configuration file
	Save as...	Generates a new configuration file
Window	*Tile horizontal*	Arranges the editor windows without overlapping by tiling the *POW!* window horizontally
	Tile vertical	Arranges the editor windows without overlapping by tiling the *POW!* window vertically
	Cascade	Cascades the editor windows
	Arrange Icons	Arranges the iconized edit windows in a queue
	Close all	Closes all edit windows
	c:\xxx\...	At the end of this menu you find the names of all open windows, which provides easier access to covered windows

Help	*POW!*	Show the index of the on-line help of the environment
	Compiler	Opens the help file on the compiler
	Compiler topic search	Searches for a keyword in the help on the compiler
	Editor	Opens the help file on the editor
	Using Help	Help on the on-line help
	About...	About-dialog of *POW!* and the compiler
	Bug Report...	Here you can note and evaluate errors that have occurred: *POW!* collects these comments in a text file *pow.bug* which can be passed to the authors to make corrections easier

3.11 Typical errors

In this section different methods and utilities are explained which may help you to locate errors in Oberon-2 programs and which have proved particularly effective when working with *POW!*

Case 1:   You want to make sure that variables in certain parts of the code contain correct values.

ASSERT   Use the function *ASSERT(boolean expression)*. If the passed expression has the value *FALSE*, the program execution is terminated and an error message is displayed, containing the module name and the line number.

Switch on the compiler option **Assert-Evaluation** for the check to be active, and switch it off if you want to have a program version without the check-code.

Case 2:   You want to find out if certain parts of the code are executed.

HALT   Insert the sequence *HALT(0)* into your code. When this command is executed, a message window appears showing the module name and the line number. You can now decide whether you want to terminate or continue the program. Values others than zero in the *HALT* command always terminate the program.

Case 3: **Your program is terminated with the message "unexpected application error" although you have not received an error message from the runtime system (*index out of range, arithmetic overflow, ...*). You want to locate the error position.**

This error message occurs if an exceptional situation has not been detected either because the corresponding compiler option is not active or because the program has accessed a memory region outside your program memory (memory violation).

Memory violation

In this case, Windows displays a message window containing the name of the faulty program and the error address (e.g., "memory violation in *hello.exe* at 0012:1234").

If the reported program is an Oberon-2 program you can use the command *Find Error* of the menu *Tools* to convert the error address to a combination of module name and line number, which is more helpful to you.

Find Error-tool

Find Error requires two or three parameters: first the file name of the program to be inspected, second a directory with the object files (which is an option and has to be led by a "-"), and third the error address reported by Windows.

The tool *Find Error* is configured so that usually you only need to enter the error address. Program name and the directory of the object files are provided from the project information.

Note that this tool can read line information only from programs that have been compiled with the option *Debug Information* switched on.

Case 4: **Your program reports a "wrong module version" when you start it.**

For each module the Oberon-2 compiler generates a unique identification key which is stored in both the symbol file (containing the interface definition of the module) and the object file. When you start a program *POW!* checks if the object files linked to the program are the same as the files from which the interface information was derived. The mentioned error occurs if there is an inconsistency.

Module versions

In such a case, the compiler has used a symbol file which does not correspond to the object file linked to the program. As a remedy, delete older object and symbol files of modules which are stored in the search area of *POW!* (directories of the project files) and execute a *Build* cycle which forces a recompilation of all modules in the program.

Warning: Do not delete the symbol files of the *OPAL* library under any circumstances (*POW*-subdirectory *opal*).

This error may also occur if you use a new version of the *OPAL* library without having recompiled your program.

Case 5:   Your program reports "undefined dynalink" when you start it.

DLLs This error may happen if a program uses a different version of a DLL than the one for which it was compiled and linked. As all Oberon-2 programs under *POW!* share the *OPAL* library in the form of a DLL this error can occur if you use a new version of this library.

Either make sure that the correct version of *opal.dll* is called or recompile your program.

Note that Windows searches for DLLs in the following order:

1. in the active directory,
2. in the Windows directory,
3. in the Windows system directory,
4. in the directory of the called program, and
5. in the directories of the environment variable *path*.

3.12 Advanced topics

The previous sections of this chapter have been dedicated to the most important features for using *POW!* efficiently. The remainder of the chapter consists of advanced topics which are more suited to advanced and experienced users.

If you are just learning about programming you are advised to go on straight to Chapter 4 and to reserve this section until later.

3.12.1 Compiler options

The project definition also contains the settings of the compiler. In *POW!* you can adapt them with the menu command ***Options/Compiler.:***

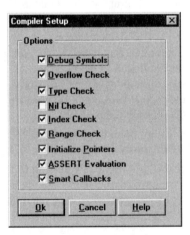

Fig. 29: Compiler settings

Additional code is generated for the activated compiler options. This results in slightly bigger program files and somewhat slower program execution. It is advisable to switch on all compiler options during the process of the development of an application, until the program is fully working, and then only switch them off when you generate the final version, if at all. As the compiler options have an influence on the generated code the program should then be tested again carefully in any case!

The options are:

Runtime checks

Debug Symbols *(default=on)*	The compiler generates line number information for working with a debugger or the *Find Error* tool
Overflow Check *(default=on)*	Every numerical operation is checked on overflow
Type Check *(default=on)*	The dynamic type of objects is checked during assignments and type guards
Nil Check *(default=off)*	At run-time check if a referenced pointer is NIL
Index Check *(default=on)*	When you access arrays the index is checked
Range Check	When an assignment is executed check to see if the range of the destination operand is exceeded
Initialize Pointers *(default=on)*	All pointers are initialized with the value 0 (*NIL*)
ASSERT Evaluation *(default=on)*	The expression in each *ASSERT* statement is evaluated: if the expression is *FALSE* the runtime system terminates the program
Smart Callbacks *(default=on)*	The compiler is forced to generate code, which allows other processes (like the kernel) calls to exported procedures without export declaration in the linker options dialog. This is also necessary for object-oriented programs, which use classes inside DLLs (like programs written for OPAL or our new object-oriented library OPAL++)

When one of the conditions above is violated and the relevant option is switched on, the application is terminated and the error position (module name and line number) is displayed.

Terminating a program

Example

The program section from module "MyFirst"

```
VAR i: INTEGER;
...
i:=MAX(INTEGER);        (*assign i the maximum integer value*)
i:=i+1;                              (*increment i by one*)
```

causes the program to terminate with the error message "arithmetic overflow in line 8 of module MyFirst" when the program is executed.

3.12.2 Linker options

Linker   The compiler always compiles precisely one source file into code that is executable by the processor. As described in the project definition a program usually consists of several source files. It is now the task of the linker to combine together all compiled files to one single program file and to resolve all the references between the parts.

The linker can be configured with menu command *Options/Linker.* The settings in this dialog box are stored in the project definition, too.

Export list   With the buttons *Add* and *Del* you can add or delete function names to or from the list. If you implement a DLL, all functions that will occur in the automatically generated import library must be listed here.

Resident,   The function names are sorted alphabetically. Function names that are
non-resident   supposed to be in the *resident-name table* in the generated program must be marked with an asterisk after their name. All other symbols are entered in the *non-resident-name table.*

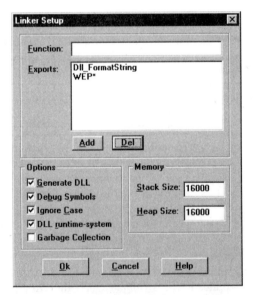

Fig. 30: Linker settings

DLLs   The meanings of the other settings are:

Generate DLL	A DLL is generated instead of a Windows EXE file.
Ignore case *(default=on)*	The linker ignores the case of identifier characters. This option must be switched on for Windows programs!

DLL runtime-system *(default=on)*	The generated program has no own runtime system, but shares a common runtime system with other Oberon-2 programs (e.g., *orts118.dll* for version 1.18).
	Advantage: The programs are smaller and their runtime system can be replaced without recompilation of the programs.
	Disadvantage: If you want to pass such a program to anyone else you always have to also send the runtime system DLL.
Stack size *(default=4096)*	Defines the size of the stack for the program. As DLLs have no stack of their own this value is of no importance if the option ***Generate DLL*** is active.
Heap size *(default=8192)*	This value indicates the size of the local heap assigned to the generated program. As programs created by *POW!* have independent self-contained memory management, this value does not need to be incremented even for large programs.
Garbage collection *(default=on)*	If this option is enabled, then allocated memory (via *NEW*) is removed automatically and need not be freed with *DISPOSE*. Programs linked with this option may stop for a short time now and then for garbage collection, depending on the amount of remaining heap memory.

3.12.3 Dynamic link libraries as tools

Functions of dynamic link libraries can be installed as tools using the button ***Add DLL...***. In the dialog shown in Figure 31 the following information is entered: the name of the DLL (searched for in the active directory, in the Windows directory, and in all directories of the environment variable *path*), the name of the function, and an optional string to be passed.

Fig. 31: Dialog for the embedding of a dynamic link library function

The settings of the options dialog of the tools are automatically changed to
DLL Name, **Function**, and **Arguments** for DLL functions. A call of the
function *Message Beep* of the *user*-DLL of Windows causes the output of a
sound over the loudspeaker.

DLL call Call conventions for DLL functions as tools:

Oberon-2	arguments	`PROCEDURE [WINDOWS] Name` `            (arg:Windows.LPSTR);`
Oberon-2	no arguments	`PROCEDURE [WINDOWS] Name*;`
C/C++	arguments	`Void FAR PASCAL name (LPSTR);`
C/C++	no arguments	`Void FAR PASCAL name (void);`

3.12.4 Dynamic data exchange (DDE) server

DDE tools With the button **Add DDE...** a dialog for the embedding of a DDE service is
started.

The entries in the dialog create a connection to the DDE server of the *POW!*
system. This connection is then used for sending a command "newfile" to
open a new file window. If you miss this functionality in the toolbar of *POW!*
then simply attach this service to a button and use it in the future instead of
the menu command **File/New**.

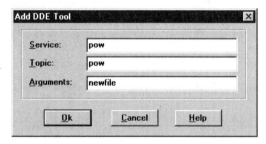

Fig. 32: Dialog for the embedding of a dynamic data exchange service

For programmers: The DDE command is of the type *XTYP_EXECUTE*.

3.12.5 Communication with *POW!*

POW! and The name of the DDE *service* is of course *POW*. As a **topic**, the handle of the
DDE   *POW!* main window can be used. In case of several instances of the environment it is therefore possible to establish which one is the receiver of the
command. If the name *POW* or no name at all is entered in this situation, the
instance of *POW!* to process the call becomes undefined.

The following commands of the type *XTYP_EXECUTE* are supported:

Remote control of POW!

OpenFile name	*POW!* opens a new window with the file *name*.
NewFile name	A new file for editing titled *name* is opened. If no parameter is entered a window without a title is opened.
SaveFile name	The active file in the editor is saved. If a parameter *name* is entered the file is saved under this name.
Activate name	The edit window titled *name* is put in the foreground.
AppendFile name	The contents of the file *name* is appended to the text in the active edit window.
AppendText buf	The text *buf* is appended to the text in the active edit window.
InsertFile name	The contents of the file *name* is inserted into the active edit window at the current cursor position.
InsertText buf	The text *buf* is inserted into the active edit window at the current cursor position.

The following items may be requested from *POW!* using commands of the type *XTYP_REQUEST*:

Data exchange

ActiveFile	The file name of the active editor file.
EditBuffer	The contents of the active editor file.

POW! also recognizes the *XTYP_POKE* command *EditBuffer* which replaces the contents of the active editor file by the transmitted text.

4. Introduction to Oberon-2

4.1 Introduction

This chapter provides a gentle introduction to the programming language Oberon-2. The approach is a very practical one and is based on the expressive quality of examples. After introducing the form (syntax) of the language and its basic constructs the theme moves to procedures, abstract data types and modules as the basic elements and the possibility of type extension and type-bound procedures. This brings us naturally to the world of object-oriented programming and, perhaps more important, an object-oriented way of thinking, so the introduction is evolutionary and aims to avoid any radical discussion of the pros and cons of introducing object-oriented programming (OOP) in the early stages of learning to program. The attractive thing about Oberon-2 is that the language is built on well-proven foundations and at the same time supports object-oriented programming with the help of simple but powerful extensions.

Readers who prefer an intensive training session on the programming language Oberon-2 and who have already acquired some experience in programming are referred to Appendix A.

Appendix A

4.2 Basics of a language

To write down a program you make use of a character set, an *alphabet*. In our case these are the characters {a,b,...,x,y,z,A,B,...,X,Y, Z,0,1,...9} as well as some special characters {<,>, {,},",..,=,:,(,),[,],~,+,-,*,/,&,|,^,;}.

Alphabet

When you join characters of the agreed alphabet in sequences you get *words*. A *phrase* consists of a sequence of words which are usually separated by blanks " " or semicolons ";".

Word, phrase

Example

"Oberon-2 is a modern object-oriented programming language; it is a worthy successor of Pascal and Modula-2"

are two English phrases, separated by ";" and " ". They have been built from a sequence of words like *modern, object-oriented.*

The grammar (*syntax*) of the English language defines the rules governing words which may be put together and additional rules which have to be adhered to (gender, tense, case etc.). There is no precise definition of what constitutes a word in the English language, but there are conventions saying that everything listed in an agreed dictionary belongs to an allowable set of words called a vocabulary. Numbers and special abbreviations also may be

Syntax

included. However, not every sequence of characters belongs to this diffuse vocabulary:

```
screenation, misrock, and95, turben, pascalatory
```

may sound familiar, but they are not words currently in the English vocabulary.

Vocabulary The *syntax* of a programming language has the purpose of precisely defining both the allowed and forbidden vocabulary. This partly happens by listing the words allowed (enumerating them) but mainly by stating rules according to which permitted words may be constructed from the given alphabet.

The syntax also determines the rules which determine how phrases may be composed in the programming language. In addition it may be worth considering whether all phrases that are composed according to the syntax make sense. We are already aware of this problem from our colloquial speech: for instance,

```
Heat is green
```

Semantics is a syntactically well-constructed phrase but it is doubtful whether it makes sense. By the "sense of a sequence of words" we understand the *meaning* of a phrase. In the world of computing we are talking about *semantics*.

When we discuss the syntactically correct vocabulary of Oberon-2 we first concentrate on the convention for which words may be used. These are defined partly by enumeration and partly by syntactic rules defining how they can be composed. The circumstances in which these words have associated semantics will be explained in the text.

Meta-language Software engineers use different methods when it comes to the definition of syntactic rules. First, there is the *description in meta-language*, where colloquial speech is used to describe a situation as precisely as possible. Also examples are used to make it more illustrative and therefore exclude other possible interpretations. This method is good for beginners because the descriptive method, the meta-language, is already familiar.

Examples for descriptions in meta-language are:

- A *letter* is one of the characters A-Z, a-z.

- A *digit* is one of the characters 0-9.

Name • A *name* is a finite sequence of letters or digits. This sequence must start with a letter.

   Examples: `start, end, three7`

String • A *string* starts with a simple (') or a double (") quote. The closing quote must be identical to the opening one and must not occur inside the string. In between there is a sequence of letters, digits, and special characters. If this sequence is empty (if it does not contain a character), we call the string *empty*.

Examples: `"Johannes Kepler"`, `'1571'`, `""`

Note that *'1571'* is a string constant and does not represent the number 1571!

In order to define the syntax of a language precisely and concisely a meta-language has been specially developed. It is called the "Extended Backus-Naur Form", in short *EBNF*.

EBNF

The EBNF

This language also needs to be defined! The following rules are valid:

1. A character between `" "` or `' '` means the character itself.

    Example

    ```
    full stop = ".".
    ```

2. If an element *A* consists of the element *B* followed by *C*, write *A=BC*.

3. If an element A consists either of the element B or C, you write *A=B|C*.

    Example

    ```
    Digit= "0"|"1"|"2"|"3"|"4"|"5"|"6"|"7"|"8"|"9".
    ```

4. If an element consists of a sequence of none, one or several elements *B*, write *A={B}*. Braces enclose expressions that may be repeated zero or more times. So this is the short form of $A=\varepsilon\ |B|BB|BBB|BBBB|...$, ε meaning an empty word.

    Example

    ```
    PositiveNumber= Digit {Digit}.
    ```

    Possible words of this syntax are 4, 23, 32767, etc.

5. If an element *A* is either empty or equal to the element *B*, write *A=[B]*. Brackets therefore enclose expressions that also may be optional, which is equivalent to $A=\varepsilon\ |B$.

    Example

    ```
    sign = +|-.
    number = [sign] PositiveNumber.
    ```

    The above rule defines that a word of the grammar "number" may optionally have a sign.

6. Parentheses are used for grouping expressions, using precedence to make the meaning clear.

    Example

    ```
    A= (B|C)(D|E).
    ```

    Here, the sequences *BD*, *BE*, *CD* and *CE* are allowed for *A*.

Initially you may have some difficulty with the EBNF, until you get used to it, then the advantages soon become obvious. It is useful to study grammar rules using colloquial descriptions and some examples at first and then go through these descriptions again with the help of the EBNF.

Syntax diagram   EBNF can also be visualized graphically using *syntax diagrams*:

EBNF	Syntax diagram
A = "*"	
A = BC	
A = B | C	
A = {B}	
A = [B]	

4.3 Basic language elements

Using EBNF we can now define the syntax of names, numbers, strings, operators, and delimiters as they occur in Oberon-2 programs in a simple and clear way.

Case sensitive   Oberon-2 programs consist of a sequence of characters from the alphabet of the ASCII code (see Appendix C). The language distinguishes upper and lower case; it is therefore *case sensitive*. From the alphabet the following rules are derived:

Letter= "A"|"B"|..|"Z"|"a"|..|"z".
Digit= "0"|"1"|..|"9".

4.3.1 Names

Names consist of a sequence of letters *(Letter)* or digits *(Digit)* starting with a letter. These names are *valid:*

    x, ch, FINISHED, String, firstSymbol, i1, i22, UpAndDown45

These names are *invalid:*

    3x, 6and45

Note that *POW!* allows the use of the character "_" (underscore) as an element of a valid name (as a contrast to some other Oberon-2 systems). This allows the embedding of all Windows identifiers which often have underscores in their names. The programmer should be aware of the consequences when it comes to transferring a program to other Oberon-2 compilers and therefore minimize the use of this option.

Because of case sensitivity the following names are different:

```
Newchar, NewChar, newchar.
```

It is usual to use the symbolic short form *Ident* (from *identifier*) for *Name*. This expresses the fact that names in programs have the purpose of naming single units, i.e., identifying them. Above all, it is vital to name the *variables* which contain data values in the program. Whenever possible the name should be "meaningful", that is it should describe the purpose of the variable's data.

Identifier

Examples: Altitude, StringLength, MaxCount

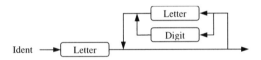

Ident= Letter {Letter | Digit}.

4.3.2 Numbers

In the Oberon-2 syntax numbers are unsigned integer or real *constants*. The sign of a number will be introduced later as a special single-character (*monadic*) operator which precedes a number (+, -).

Examples of *integer* numbers are

```
1571, 1946, 0, 32767
```

Integer numbers

and *real* numbers which always have a decimal point

```
3.14159, 0.004, 04.12
```

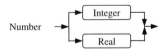

Number= Integer | Real.

The detailed representation of numbers in binary form in the computer memory is not discussed here; you can find more details in the compiler documentation.

INTEGER First let's concentrate on integer numbers. For the internal representation of an integer number you can use 1 byte, 2 bytes, or 4 bytes; this is a current standard. As a result you get the following value ranges:

Bytes	Type	Value Range (compiler dependent)
1	SHORTINT	-128 .. 127
2	INTEGER	-32768 .. 32767
4	LONGINT	-2147483648 .. 2147483647

Hexadecimal numbers It is also possible to represent number values in Oberon-2 programs using the hexadecimal system (radix 16) as an alternative to the usual decimal system (base 10). This convention uses the characters "A" to "F" to represent the decimal values 10..15.

In Oberon-2, numbers represented in base 16 are characterized by appending an "H":

21 represents $\quad 2*10^1 + 1*10^0 =$ $\qquad$ 21 decimal

21H stands for $\quad 2*16^1 + 1*16^0 =$ $\qquad$ 33 decimal

483 as a decimal number has the value $\qquad 4*10^2 + 8*10^1 + 3*10^0$

483H as a hexadecimal number has the value $\quad 4*16^2 + 8*16^1 + 3*16^0$

A character sequence like *A3H* is a syntactic problem. Is it a name or should it be understood as the number $10*16^1+3*16^0$? To prevent confusion there is another rule that every number must start with a decimal digit, which can also be a zero: *0A3H*. The string *A3H* therefore is a name.

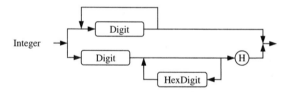

The definition in EBNF now is:

HexDigit=Digit|"A"|"B"|"C"|"D"|"E"|"F".
Integer= Digit {Digit} | Digit {HexDigit} "H".

Real numbers Real numbers can be represented in the form 3.14159, and also with scientific notation with a mantissa and exponent as in 0.314159E1 or 0.0314159E2 or 31.4159E-1. The letter "E" (or "D" for numbers with double precision) therefore indicates that the mantissa has to be multiplied by 10 to the power of the exponent, which is referred to in the syntax as the scaling factor.

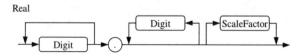

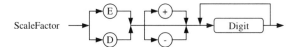

In EBNF we come to the following definition:

Real= Digit {Digit} "." {Digit} [ScaleFactor].
ScaleFactor= ("E"|"D") ["+"|"-"] Digit {Digit}.

Either 4 or 8 bytes can be used for the representation of different real number   *REAL*
ranges and precisions. So you distinguish between numbers of the type *REAL*
(e.g., 3.14 or 0.314E1) and of the type *LONGREAL* (e.g., 0.314159D1) by
means of the letter which separates the mantissa from the exponent value.

Bytes	Description of the type	Type	Range
4	Real number with single precision	REAL	+/- 3.40282E38
8	Real number with double precision	LONGREAL	+/- 1.79769D308

The stated ranges are not fixed in the definition of Oberon-2 but do conform
with the current conventions (and also with *POW!*). In general, double
precision real arithmetic is shown in operation, although it takes twice the
amount of memory for its variables compared with single precision.

4.3.3 Strings

We have already discussed at the beginning of the chapter what the term
string means and how one can be constructed. The EBNF and the syntax
diagram are:

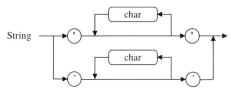

String= " ' " {char} " ' " | ' " ' {char} ' " '.

Char is a any character different from the opening quote and within the
predefined ASCII-character set.

Examples

```
"Oberon", 'Oberon', "It's nice", '3.5" diskette'
```

CHAR   The data type for a single character is *CHAR* and comprises the ASCII codes
0 to 127; the additional code values 128 to 255 are often used for specialized
extensions to the ASCII code standard, for example for graphic symbols or
accented characters. In Oberon-2 constants of this type are written in the
hexadecimal system followed by an "X". It is also possible to have a string of
length one.

Examples

```
23X, "A", '1', '#', 0FFX
```

4.3.4 Operators and Delimiters

Operators   Operators and delimiters have a special purpose in programs: *operators*
define arithmetic, boolean, or relational operations on data, whereas
delimiters separate single syntactic components of programs from each other.

In Oberon-2 there are the following special characters, character
combinations and keywords (we will discuss their meaning later):

+	:=	ARRAY	IF	RECORD
-	^	BEGIN	IMPORT	REPEAT
*	=	BY	IN	RETURN
/	#	CASE	IS	THEN
~	<	CONST	LOOP	TO
&	>	DIV	MOD	TYPE
.	<=	DO	MODULE	UNTIL
,	>=	ELSE	NIL	VAR
;	..	ELSIF	OF	WHILE
|	:	END	OR	WITH
(	)	EXIT	POINTER	
{	}	FOR	PROCEDURE	

Keyword   To avoid name conflicts, keywords must not be used as names. This also
applies to the following predefined names of built-in functions, types, and
values:

ABS	FALSE	NEW
ASH	HALT	ODD
ASSERT	INC	ORD
BOOLEAN	INCL	REAL
CAP	INTEGER	SET
CHAR	LEN	SHORT
CHR	LONG	SHORTINT
COPY	LONGINT	SIZE

DEC	LONGREAL	TRUE
ENTIER	MAX	
EXCL	MIN	

4.3.5 Comments

In Oberon-2, a comment is a sequence of any characters inside the parentheses (* and *). They have no semantic significance for a program, but are included in programs by the programmer for documentation purposes, in general to explain what the program is doing.

Comments may be put into programs anywhere where a delimiter can be used and even may be nested.

```
(* Johannes Kepler (*the famous astronomer*) lived
   in Linz from 1612 to 1628 *)
```

4.4 Oberon-2 programs under *POW!*

Oberon-2 programs can be separated into pieces, called modules, each dealing with a particular aspect of the problem. As *POW!* is embedded in *Windows* and the Oberon-2 statements written by the programmer will become part of an executable program, one module needs to play a special role as the *main module*. This contains a procedure called *ProgMain*, which is executed when the program starts.

Modules

This is different from the original language implementation under the operating system Oberon, where modules do not have to be linked to a program explicitly.

The main module under *POW!* therefore has the following form:

ProgMain

```
MODULE Ex1;                                    (*empty program*)
                                               Ex1.mod
PROCEDURE ProgMain*;                           (*exported*)
BEGIN
END ProgMain;

END Ex1.
```

This program probably doesn't make much sense to you yet, even though it is a complete program. The program does not do anything, which you can easily check by opening and running the file *\pow\book\ex1.mod*. The program will open a window and then close it immediately.

Like Modula-2, Oberon-2 can use already developed modules by declaring them in a list after the keyword *IMPORT*. We will discuss this mechanism later in detail once module interfaces have been explained.

In *POW!* there is a whole variety of modules available, collected together in the *OPAL* library file *opal???.dll*. The modules *In* and *Out* of this library for example provide procedures for input and output for windows (*In.String, Out.String, Out.Ln*, etc.).

Clipboard   In addition a menu entry *Pane/Copy* is provided. So the contents of a window can be copied to the clipboard very easily, and from there it may be transferred to an editor for re-editing or to a printer.

Alternatively, input can be read from file (menu entry *Pane/read input from file*) or written to a file (menu entry *Pane/save input to file*). Using this you can save your input once and load it later for testing newer versions of your program.

You may also use the module *Display* as an alternative to *In* and *Out* (see Chapter 5).

The above program was not very helpful because it was terminated immediately after it had been started. It was impossible to see what had happened during its execution. Now we will extend it a little with the procedure *Out.String* which writes a text. The program is now

Ex2.mod
```
MODULE Ex2;
(*print a text*)
IMPORT Out;

PROCEDURE ProgMain*;
BEGIN
    (*print text*)
    Out.String("This seems to be your first program!");
END ProgMain;

END Ex2.
```

The program now creates the following window on the screen and prints a text. Press the Exit button to close the window or click the Close button (⊠) to terminate the program:

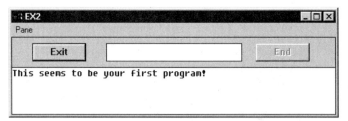

Fig. 33: Output of ex2.mod

Variables   For further examples we have to introduce the concept of *variable*. *Variables* are named storage locations in the program memory. A variable is always given a *type* to indicate the nature of the data values that may be stored in it. The type *INTEGER* describes numbers from the interval [-32768...32767].

The declaration

```
VAR num: INTEGER;
```

has the following effects:

- A variable is generated which can be referred to in statements with the name *num*.

- *num* stands for an integer number because it is of data type *INTEGER*.

- In the program's memory a sufficient number of bytes is reserved to store the variables value, which are all referenced as an entity. The position in the program memory at which the reserved bytes start is called the *address* of *num*. In the case of an *INTEGER* variable 2 bytes are reserved. *Address*

- An assignment *num:=7* stores the integer value 7 in the memory at the address of *num*, in other words "the variable *num* is assigned 7".

- Valid statements containing the *INTEGER* variable *num* conform with other types as the Oberon-2 compiler checks all the data types of variables for consistency.

- *num:=num+1* means the number 1 is added to the contents of the memory at the assigned address and the result is stored back in *num*.

- The statement sequence *num:=4; num:=num+2; num:=num-1* causes *num* finally to have the value 5. The semicolon ";" separates single statements from each other. *Semicolon*

- Given the additional variable declaration

  ```
  VAR
      c: CHAR;
  ```

  the assignments *num:=c* or *c:=num* would lead to an error which is detected by the Oberon-2 compiler because the incompatible data types would violate their *type safety*. *Type safety*

This leads to the question, what are the rules for deciding whether data types are compatible with each other?

Oberon-2 is a programming language which supports strong data-typing, in other words it checks the types of data and the operations on it at compile time. The benefit of this checking is that many programming errors can be detected before the program is executed. There are some pragmatic exceptions to the type checking rules which will be introduced later.

Now our Oberon-2 example can be expanded to include input and output functions.

```
MODULE Ex3;                                                      Ex3.mod
(*enter a number*)
IMPORT In,Out;                    (*use the In and Out modules*)  a)

PROCEDURE ProgMain*;
VAR                                (*variable declaration*)       b)
    n: INTEGER;
BEGIN                                                            c)
```

d)   `In.Int(n);`   *(*read number*)*

e)   `Out.String("The number was: ");`   *(*print text*)*

f)   `Out.Int(n,0);`   *(*output of the number*)*

g)   `END ProgMain;`

h)   `END Ex3.`

A description of its operation is as follows ...

In/Out,   a) The above program consists of the module *Ex3* and uses (imports) input
IMPORT   and output functions from the modules *In* and *Out* in the *OPAL* library.
             You can also say that the importing module is a *client* of the imported
             modules.

VAR   b) The declaration part for variables is introduced with VAR. Here the
             variable *n* of type *INTEGER* is defined.

BEGIN c) The program itself starts with *BEGIN*. It consists of single statements
             which are separated by semicolons. Altogether this is called a *statement
             sequence.*

         d) The function *Int* of the module *In* waits for the user to enter a number to
             be entered from the keyboard. The result is of type *INTEGER* and is
             assigned the variable *n*. In our initial example we omit the check about
             the success of the operation for the sake of simplicity.

         e) A text is printed with the function *Out.String*. The text must be enclosed
             by "".

         f) The number just read is printed with the function *Out.Int(n,0)*. The second
             parameter of this function indicates how many digits are used to display
             the number and it is right aligned. If the parameter is 0 the number is
             printed left aligned with as many digits as necessary for the
             representation.

         g) The program is terminated at the end of the *ProgMain* procedure.

END   h) *END Ex3* marks the end of the definition of the module *Ex3*, followed by
             a full stop.

4.5 Declarations

4.5.1 Declaration of variables

Oberon-2 compilers provide type checking and evaluate it at compile time.
This is why the type of the variables used must be *declared*.

In the previous sections some data types have already been discussed. We
now summarize these once again (for the POW! compiler implementation):

Integer numbers	*SHORTINT*	-128..127
	INTEGER	-32768..32767

	LONGINT	-2147483648..2147483647
Real numbers	REAL	+/- 3.40282E38
	LONGREAL	+/- 1.79769D308
ASCII-characters	CHAR	0X..0FFX
boolean expressions	BOOLEAN	TRUE, FALSE
Sets	SET	Sets of items from 0 to 31

These data types are also called *basic data types* as they are built into the language.

You should be aware that the typical ranges stated in the right column are not defined in the Oberon-2 language definition. These ranges are determined by the particular compiler and based upon the assumption that *INTEGER* requires 2 bytes, *REAL* 4 bytes, and *CHAR* 1 byte for the representation in the memory.

A d*eclaration part* in the program begins with the keyword *VAR* followed by names of the variables and the desired type, separated by ",". Several variables may be declared at once in a single declaration. In this case the variables must be of the same data type and are listed in the declaration before the data type, separated by commas.

Declaration part

```
VAR
    nodes: SET;
    ok: BOOLEAN;
    c,txt: CHAR;
    i,j: INTEGER;
    index: SHORTINT;
```

Operations are intimately associated with data types. Take numbers for example: for whole numbers (*SHORTINT, INTEGER, LONGINT*) as well as for real numbers (*REAL, LONGREAL)* the usual operators +,-,* and DIV or / and MOD may be used.

Operations

However, division is a special case which has different rules for integer and real numbers.

INTEGER division: *DIV*

8	DIV	2	equals	4		*DIV*
4	DIV	5	equals	0		
22	DIV	7	equals	3		
-3	DIV	2	equals	-1	*(* same as - (3 DIV 2) *)*	
(-3)	DIV	2	equals	-2		

For integer numbers there is also the modulo operator *MOD* which calculates the integer remainder after an INTEGER division:

MOD

| 8 | MOD | 2 | equals | 0 |
| 4 | MOD | 5 | equals | 4 |

```
22   MOD   7   equals     1
-3   MOD   2   equals    -1          (* same as - (3 MOD 2) *)
(-3) MOD   2   equals     1
```

Note that *i MOD j* is only defined for *j>0* in Oberon, so the result of *3 MOD -4* is not defined.

REAL division

Division   To divide data of the types *REAL* and *LONGREAL* the operator "*/*" is used:

```
22.0 / 7.0    equals    3.142857
0.0 / 1.0     equals    0.0
1.0 / 0.0     causes a program termination because the result of
              the operation is not a defined number which can be
              represented by the data type (division by 0 has the result
              infinity)!
```

Relations

< = > #   With the help of the relational operators $<$, $=$, $>$, #, $>=$, and $<=$ simple expressions can be formulated with a result of type *BOOLEAN*, which is *TRUE* if the relation is valid or *FALSE* if the relation is invalid. The character "#" for "unequal" replaces the usual sequence "$<>$" used in many other languages.

7	>	3	evaluates to	TRUE	(greater than)
1	>	4	evaluates to	FALSE	
2	#	3	evaluates to	TRUE	(not equal to)
1	#	1	evaluates to	FALSE	
2	>=	0	evaluates to	TRUE	(greater than or equal to)
1	<=	0	evaluates to	FALSE	(less than or equal to)

4.5.2 Declaration of constants

Named constants   Constants such as PI with a value of 3.14159 can be defined to improve the readability of programs. Doing this makes it easier to maintain programs. If the value of a constant is changed the whole program immediately works with the new value without any additional effort being necessary to search for each use of a particular instance of a value.

The declaration of named constants is made using a separate declaration part starting with *CONST*.

CONST   It is a convention in this book to write the names of constants using capital letters to distinguish them from variable names:

```
CONST
  PI= 3.14159;
```

4.5.3 Type declaration

In a declaration for variables of a basic data type the variable name is followed by the corresponding data type:

```
VAR
    i,j: INTEGER;
```

It is also possible to define additional data types in terms of data types already declared. A simple example:

```
TYPE
    IndexT= INTEGER;
    LabelT= SHORTINT;

VAR
    i,j: IndexT;
    label: LabelT;
```

TYPE

The fact that we have appended a "T" to the type name and given it an initial capital letter is a useful convention for marking the name of a data type defined as a *TYPE*. We have used this convention in all programs of this book.

4.6 Statements

Statements in programming languages can be compared to commands in the real world: they describe and cause actions. Statements can be elementary or structured, thus be composed of other statements. There are different kinds of structured statements, which cause sequential, iterative, or conditional execution of other statements. All these will be explained in the following pages.

Statements

Sequences of statements are separated by semicolons. A single isolated semi-colon is also allowed and is regarded as *empty statement*. There are other kinds of statements as well as assignments, which will be introduced in later chapters. The example

Empty statement

```
i:=0;
x:=i+1;
;
x:=x*i;
```

consists of a sequence (*statement sequence*) of four basic statements. The third statement is an empty statement and can be omitted without affecting the program.

Statement sequence

The syntax of statements in EBNF is:

StatementSequence = Statement {";" Statement}.
Statement = [Assignment | Procedure Call | IfStatement |
CaseStatement | WhileStatement | RepeatStatement |
ForStatement | LoopStatement | "EXIT" |
"RETURN" [Expression]].

4.7 Expressions and assignments

Expressions

Expressions consist of operators, operands, and functions which are evaluated to form a value.

Assignments

Assignments are basic statements and are used for assigning the result of an evaluated expression to a variable (the "designator"). The assignment operator ":=" is used to denote the assignment operation. The *designator* is the name of the program variable where the result of the expression will be stored.

```
i:=i+1;
```

The data type of the expression must be compatible with the data type of the variable it is assigned to (the *designator*). For example, this means that it is not possible to assign an integer value to a character variable.

The syntactic form of an assignment is:

Assignment = Designator ":=" Expression.

Type inclusion

Oberon-2 does not have hidden conversion rules that are applied during the evaluation of numerical expressions and assignments. Instead a practical hierarchy called *type inclusion* is introduced:

LONGREAL $\subseteq$ REAL $\subseteq$ LONGINT $\subseteq$ INTEGER $\subseteq$ SHORTINT

Type conversion

A "bigger" type may be used instead of a "smaller" type at any time. In the other direction an explicit conversion (using the *SHORT* function) must be carried out. Note that the value of the expression is checked against the range of the designator and the program is halted if a range violation is detected at runtime!

```
VAR
    i: INTEGER;
    l: LONGINT;
    s: SHORTINT;
BEGIN
    i:=1;
    l:=i;                   (*possible because of type inclusion*)
    s:=SHORT(i);            (*explicit conversion necessary*)
```

First we take a look at very simple assignments, such as

```
x:=(a+b)*c  or  x:=-(a+b)
```

For the moment we will only consider the arithmetic operators (+, -, /, *) leaving other operators (*OR*, &, *DIV*, *MOD*) and other advanced concepts until later. Then we get the following simple class of arithmetic expressions as a part of an assignment. To save space we use abbreviated names like *Expr* instead of *Expression*, etc., in the syntax diagrams:

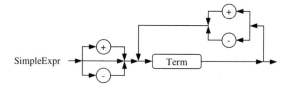

SimpleAddOp= "+" | "-".
SimpleMulOp= "" | "/".*
SimpleExpression= [SimpleAddOp] Term {SimpleAddOp Term}.

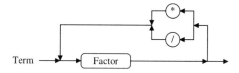

Term= Factor {SimpleMulOp Factor}.

This syntax has the consequence that the */ operators take precedence over (have a stronger binding than) the operators +-, just like in conventional arithmetic.

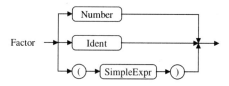

Factor= Number | Ident | "(" SimpleExpression ")".

Example

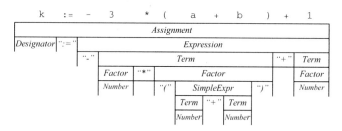

Expressions are not limited to arithmetic expressions, as we have already seen. The term

```
(a>1) OR (b<2)
```

for example is a *boolean expression*, its result is either *TRUE* or *FALSE*.

Furthermore, some operators may be applied to operands of different types and therefore have a different meaning, depending on the respective data type. An example for this is the addition operator "+" which can be used with integer, real, and *SET* datatypes, for example

```
VAR
    value,number: INTEGER;
    cluster1,cluster2,union,empty: SET;

(*arithmetic*)
value:=1;
number:=2;
number:=number+value;                              (*result is 3*)

(*SET+*)
cluster1:={0..2};                       (*cluster1 contains 0,1,2*)
cluster2:={1..3};                       (*cluster2 contains 1,2,3*)
union:=cluster1+cluster2;      (*union    contains    elements
0,1,2,3*)
empty:={};                                        (*empty set*)
```

A summary of all operators used in expressions is as follows:

Class	Operators	Result type
Arithmetic operators	+, -, *, /, DIV, MOD	numerical
Boolean operators	&, OR, ~	BOOLEAN
Relational operators	=, #, <, <=, >, >=, IN	BOOLEAN
Set operators	+, -, *, /	SET

Operations on sets

These operators work on sets:

- + ... *Union* (bitwise inclusive OR operator)

Sets
```
{0..1}+{4..6}  =  {0,1,4,5,6}
{0..3}+{4..5}  =  {0..5}
```

- * ... *Intersection* (bitwise AND operator)

```
{0..4}*{1..5}  =  {1..4}
```
Empty set
```
{0..4}*{5..9}  =  {}                              (*empty set*)
```

- - ... *Complementary set* (bitwise NOT operator)

The monadic operator "-" gives with -*y* the set of all numbers between *MIN(SET)* and *MAX(SET)* which are not contained in *y*.

```
y:={};
y:=-y;                          (*gives the complementary set {0..31}*)

y:={0..31};
y:=-y;                          (*gives the complementary set {}*)

y:={0..16};
y:=-y;                                    (*gives {17..31}*)
```

- - ...*Set difference (x-y = x * (-y))*

  ```
  {0..4}-{2..7} = {0..1}
  ```

- / ... *Symmetric difference (x/y = (x-y) + (y-x))*, bitwise exclusive OR operator

  ```
  {0..8} / {5..10} = {0..4, 9..10}
  ```

- *IN ... Set membership*

  The operator *IN* is used in expressions of the form *i IN s* and checks if bit *i* is set in the set *s*. The result is *TRUE* or *FALSE*.   **IN**

  ```
  3 IN {0..4}    (*TRUE*)
  3 IN -{0..4}                        (*FALSE*)
  ```

Predefined functions and procedures

Now the difference between functions and procedures needs to be defined   *Procedures*
and made clear.

Functions

Procedure calls are independent statements that work with and on the data passed as parameters (e.g., *INC(i)*) whereas *Functions* yield a results which can be used in expressions and consequently in assignments (e.g., *i:=ABS(j)*). In many ways they are like operators. In addition to the operators described so far, Oberon-2 contains the following predefined functions and procedures:

- *ABS(i)* ... calculates the absolute value of the numerical parameter *i*.   *ABS*

  ```
  VAR i,j: INTEGER;
  j:=-4;
  i:=ABS(j);               (*i now has the value 4*)
  ```

- *INC(i)* ... increments the value of the integer variable *i* by 1, and is   *INC*
  equivalent to the statement

  ```
  i:=i+1;
  ```

  Many microprocessors and computers have a built-in machine instruction for this special case which is why *INC(i)* should be preferred for speed reasons as it can give the compiler the hint to use the special increment instruction.

  There is an optional second parameter which defines the amount of the increment. Thus, you can write

  ```
  INC(i,2);
  ```

  instead of

  ```
  i:=i+2;
  ```

- *DEC(i)* ... is similar to INC and is equivalent to the statement   *DEC*

  ```
  i:=i-1;
  ```

SHORT • *SHORT(x)* ... returns value of *x* as of next smaller type (for the type hierarchy see earlier).

x	SHORT(x)
INTEGER	SHORTINT
LONGINT	INTEGER
LONGREAL	REAL

```
VAR
    l:  LONGINT;
    i:  INTEGER;
    s:  SHORTINT;

i:=SHORT(l);              (*converts LONGINT to INTEGER*)
s:=SHORT(i);              (*converts INTEGER to SHORTINT*)
s:=SHORT(SHORT(l));       (*converts LONGINT to SHORTINT*)
```

LONG • *LONG(x)* ... returns value of x as of next bigger type.

x	LONG(x)
SHORTINT	INTEGER
INTEGER	LONGINT
REAL	LONGREAL

HALT • *HALT(i)* ... terminates program execution

If the program is terminated by a HALT statement, then the module name and line number of the HALT statement are displayed to the user.

The interpretation of the parameter *i* is compiler dependent: *POW!* shows the number in the termination message. A value of zero brings up a message box, which lets the user decide whether to terminate the program or not. This can be used as a simple debugging technique to check if a code passage is executed.

CAP • *CAP(c)* ... returns the corresponding capital letter to the character given as an argument if it is not already a capital letter.

```
VAR c: CHAR;
c:="a";
c:=CAP(c);                (*returns the character "A"*)
```

CHR • *CHR(i)* ... returns the ASCII character corresponding to the number $0<=i<=255$. See Appendix C for a table of ASCII characters.

```
VAR c: CHAR;
c:=CHR(65);    (*returns the character "A"*)
```

Note that in effect this function converts from the INTEGER type of the parameter to the equivalent CHAR type for the result value.

- *ORD(c)* ... is the counterpart of *CHR(i)*.   *ORD*

```
VAR i: INTEGER;
i:=ORD('A');                            (*returns i=65*)
```

- *INCL* ... inserts an element into a set and is equivalent to *set:=set+{i}*.   *INCL*

```
VAR
   s: SET;
   i: INTEGER;
...
i:=5;
s:={};                                  (*s is empty*)
INCL(s,i);                     (*s contains element 5*)
```

- *MIN(T)* ... returns the minimum value of type *T*. This value is compiler   *MIN*
dependent (see table in 4.3).

```
VAR i: INTEGER;
i:=MIN(INTEGER);                   (*in POW!: -32768*)
```

- *MAX(T)* ... returns the maximum value of type *T*.   *MAX*

```
VAR i: INTEGER;
i:=MAX(INTEGER);                    (*in POW!: 32767*)
```

A complete list of the predefined functions and procedures can be found in Appendix C, Section C.10.3.

Example

To complete this section here is a small program which calculates the total number of minutes of a duration given in hours and minutes.

As structured statements have not yet been covered the program is rather simple.

```
MODULE Ex4;                  (*calculates number of minutes*)   Ex4.mod
IMPORT In,Out;

PROCEDURE ProgMain*;
VAR hours,minutes: LONGINT;
BEGIN
   In.Echo(TRUE);

   In.Prompt("hours: ");              (*get number of hours*)
   In.LongInt(hours);
   Out.Ln;

   In.Prompt("minutes: ");            (*get number of minutes*)
   In.LongInt(minutes);
   Out.Ln;

   minutes:=hours*60+minutes;      (*calculate total minutes*)
   Out.String("total minutes: ");          (*print minutes*)
   Out.Int(minutes);
   Out.Ln;
END ProgMain;

END Ex4.
```

4.8 Selection

The programs so far have all had a linear structure, each statement following one after the other in sequence.

In almost every practical program decisions have to be made which have an influence on the desired path of program execution. In most cases these are decisions which can be made upon a simple yes/no condition. To define such conditions we can use *boolean expressions* because their result can be described with the range of the data type *BOOLEAN* (*TRUE* if condition is valid, *FALSE* if condition is invalid).

BOOLEAN   The data type *BOOLEAN* is the result of the relational operators ($<$, $>$, ...) already discussed:

```
VAR
    test: BOOLEAN;       (*'test' can hold values TRUE or FALSE*)
    i: INTEGER;
    ...
    i:=4;
    test:= (i#5);  (*TRUE*)
    test:= (i>2) & (i<5);                                    (*TRUE*)
    test:= (i=4) OR (i<0);                                   (*TRUE*)
```

Our EBNF for arithmetic expressions can now be extended to include relational operators (the operator IS is used in connection with type checks and will be discussed later):

Relation= "=" | "#" | "<" | "<=" | ">" | ">=" | "IN" | "IS".
Expression = SimpleExpression [Relation SimpleExpression].

4.8.1 Boolean operators

The following operators are used in boolean expressions

- *&* ... boolean AND

  Only returns *TRUE* if both operands have the value *TRUE* (e.g., *(3>2) & (5<10)*, because both parts of the expression are *TRUE*).

- *OR* ... boolean OR

  Returns *TRUE* if either or both operands have the value *TRUE* (e.g., *(i=i) OR (i>5)* as *i=i* is *TRUE*).

- *~* ... boolean negation

  Returns *TRUE* if the operand has the value *FALSE* and vice versa.

Now we are able to build expressions like

```
((3*3)>13) OR ((3+4)=i) & test
```

This leads us to the question: in what order is such a complex expression evaluated?

4.8.2 Order of evaluation of expressions

The relative strength of binding between operators and operands is called precedence. High precedence operators bind more tightly than operators with lower precedence. If you have operators with identical precedence then the expression is evaluated from left to right.

Evaluation of expressions

highest precedence	Negation	~
	Multiplication operators	*, /, MOD, DIV, &
	Addition operators	+, -, OR
lowest precedence	Relational operators	=, #, <, <=, >, >=, IN, IS

Precedences

In order to clarify the readability and meaning of expressions it is recommended that parentheses are used to make the intended precedence of evaluation clear and unambiguous:

Short circuit evaluation

```
(((3*4)+1)=13) OR ~test;
```

Moreover, there is a convention in Oberon-2 called *short circuit evaluation*: This means that as soon as the result of a boolean expression is definitely determined, the rest of the expression is not evaluated because it is now irrelevant. As a consequence it is bad practice to include function calls in expressions if they have side effects!

Let us take a look at the expression

```
a & b
```

If *a* is *FALSE* the result of this expression *a&b* is *FALSE*, independently of the value *b*. In this case the evaluation of the expression stops once the value of *a* is known without taking into consideration the value of *b*.

It is important to keep in mind that the condition in an *IF* statement is a boolean expression and its evaluation may be short circuited. For this reason it is not advisable to include calls to functions with side effects in boolean expressions.

4.8.3 The *IF* statement

This statement provides alternative branches for program execution depending on the result value of a boolean condition ("*IF* condition *THEN* ... *ELSE* ..."). If the condition is valid (*TRUE*) all the statements of the *THEN* branch are executed, otherwise the statements of the *ELSE* branch are executed. The *ELSE* branch is optional and may be omitted. The *IF* statement must be terminated with an *END*.

IF

Examples

THEN   The following statement sequence writes "adult" only if the value of the variable *j* is greater than 18 (*THEN* branch).

```
IF j>18 THEN                          (*test for greater than 18*)
    Out.String("adult");
END;
```

ELSE   To react in the case that the condition (*j*>18) is not fulfilled an *ELSE* branch is included:

```
IF j>18 THEN                                  (*test for adult*)
    Out.String("adult");
ELSE
    Out.String("child");                              (*child*)
END; (*if*)
```

ELSIF   To check more conditions in one *IF* statement you can also work with additional *ELSIF* branches. In our example we now classify ages as "adult", "teenager" and "child":

```
IF j>18 THEN                                  (*test for adult*)
    Out.String("adult");
ELSIF j>14 THEN                             (*test for teenager*)
    Out.String("teenager");
ELSE
    Out.String("child");                              (*child*)
END;
```

Note that any *IF* statement of the form

```
IF a THEN
    val:=TRUE;
ELSE
    val:=FALSE;
END;
```

is equivalent to the much more concise assignment *val:=a*.

Similarily,

```
IF a THEN
    val:=b;
ELSE
    val:=FALSE;
END;
```

is equal to *val:=a & b* and

```
IF a THEN
    val:=TRUE;
ELSE
    val:=b;
END;
```

is equal to *val:=a OR b*.

So boolean expressions in assignment statements can often be used to write programs more clearly and concisely.

The syntax for the *IF* statement is

IfStatement

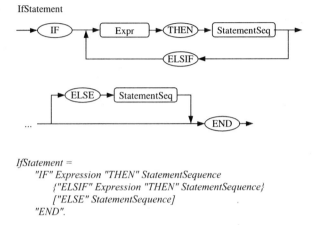

IfStatement =
>   *"IF" Expression "THEN" StatementSequence*
>   *{"ELSIF" Expression "THEN" StatementSequence}*
>   *["ELSE" StatementSequence]*
>   *"END".*

Example

The following example calculates the maximum of three numbers that are entered:

```
MODULE Ex5;                                                Ex5.mod
(*calculate the maximum of three numbers*)
IMPORT In,Out;

PROCEDURE ProgMain*;
VAR
    a,b,c,max: INTEGER;             (*declare the variables*)
BEGIN
    In.Echo(TRUE);

    In.Prompt("Enter number a: ");
    In.Int(a);
    Out.Ln;

    In.Prompt("Enter number b: ");
    In.Int(b);
    Out.Ln;

    In.Prompt("Enter number c: ");
    In.Int(c);
    Out.Ln;

    IF In.Done THEN                 (*check result of input*)
        (*calculate maximum*)
        (*Method: guess the result and then refine it,
          case by case*)
        max:=a;
        IF b>max THEN
            max:=b;
        END;
        IF c>max THEN
            max:=c;
        END;
```

```
        (*output of maximum*)
        Out.String("Maximum: ");
        Out.Int(max,0);
    ELSE
        Out.String("error in input!");          (*wrong or aborted*)
    END;
END ProgMain;

END Ex5.
```

4.8.4 The *CASE* statement

CASE The *CASE* statement is used to select between alternative statement sequences depending on the value of an expression. The expression may be either of type *INTEGER* or *CHAR*.

IF-Cascade For example, if we want to determine the nature of the character c we can write the following *IF*-cascade, which is based on the fact that the character constants defined by the ASCII codes are continuous as is shown in the following table:

Type of character	Range of characters	Range (decimal)
Digits	"0" to "9"	48 to 57
Upper case letters	"A" to "Z"	65 to 90
Lower case letters	"a" to "z"	97 to 122

```
In.Char(c);

IF    (i>='0') & (i<='9') THEN           (*check for digits*)
ELSIF (i>='A') & (i<='Z') THEN           (*check for upper case*)
ELSIF (i>='a') & (i<='z') THEN           (*check for lower case*)
ELSE                                     (*not a letter or digit*)
END;
```

Case distinction When discriminating between groups of values it is much easier and clearer to use the *CASE* statement instead of cascaded IF statement, for example an equivalent to the last example is

Ex6.mod
```
MODULE Ex6;
(*check the group of a character*)
IMPORT In,Out;

PROCEDURE ProgMain*;
VAR c: CHAR;
BEGIN
    In.Char(c);                             (*read character*)
    IF In.Done THEN                         (*check input*)
        CASE c OF                       (*classify the character*)
          '0'..'9': Out.String("digit");
        | 'A'..'Z': Out.String("upper case letter");
        | 'a'..'z': Out.String("lower case letter");
        ELSE Out.String("special character");
        END;
```

```
    ELSE
        Out.String("error in input!");              (*wrong input*)
    END;
END ProgMain;

END Ex6.
```

Depending on the value of the expression after the keyword *CASE* the *CASE*   CASE
branch associated with that value is executed. Note the following rules:

- The case values must contain constant expressions that correspond to the
  data type of the expression in question. Integer data types and the type
  CHAR are possible.

- Several values may be put together in ranges with the operator "..". (see
  program above).

- The several alternatives must be separated by the character "|". The first
  "|" is optional.

- The separately defined ranges must not overlap, to prevent ambiguity.

- If the value of the case variable does not equal any of the values in any of   ELSE
  the defined ranges then the *ELSE* branch of the *CASE* statement is
  executed. If no *ELSE* branch is defined in such a case, the program is
  terminated with an appropriate error message.

The syntax of the *CASE* statement is

CaseStatement

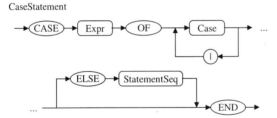

Case

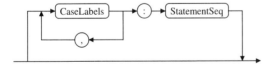

CaseStatement=
    "CASE" Expression OF Case {"|" Case}
    ["ELSE" StatementSequence] "END".
Case= [CaseLabelList ":" StatementSequence].
CaseLabelList= CaseLabels {"," CaseLabels}.
CaseLabels= ConstExpression [".." ConstExpression].

4.9 Repeated execution (*Iteration*)

One of the many reasons for the use of computer systems is the fact that they can be programmed to execute sequences of statements many times. Depending on the termination criteria four kinds of iteration statements are possible in Oberon-2:

Sorts of loops
- The iteration is repeated as long as an initial condition is fulfilled (*WHILE* loop).

- The iteration is repeated until a final condition is fulfilled (*REPEAT* loop)

- The number of iterations is fixed from the start and is counted during the execution. (*FOR* loop)

- A loop is stated without any termination criteria (*LOOP*), but has one or more termination conditions inserted anywhere within it (*EXIT*).

4.9.1 The *WHILE* statement

WHILE If you want to read and sum up a sequence of integer numbers, you can write:

```
VAR
    sum: LONGINT;
    i: INTEGER;

sum:=0;                                  (*initialize variable*)
In.Int(i);

(*click END button to end input*)
WHILE In.Done DO     (*termination condition at start of loop*)
    sum:=sum+i;
    In.Int(i)
END;

Out.Int(sum,0);
```

What happens if no number *i* is entered at all? The boolean expression *In.Done* is checked and evaluated before the execution of the *WHILE* statement, so the statements in the loop are repeated as long as the condition returns *TRUE* and this check is made before any repetition. It is therefore possible that the statement sequence inside a *WHILE* statement is not executed at all.

WhileStatement

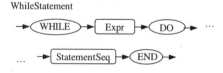

WhileStatement=
    "WHILE" Expression "DO" StatementSequence "END".

Example

The sum of digits of entered numbers needs to be calculated. The program runs until the END button is clicked. The example program is shown in Module Ex7 below.

```
MODULE Ex7;                                              Ex7.mod
(*calculate the sum of digits*)
IMPORT In,Out;

PROCEDURE ProgMain*;
VAR
   number,sum: INTEGER;
BEGIN
   In.Echo(TRUE);

   Out.String("Calculation of the sum of digits");
   Out.Ln;
   Out.String("Exit: click the END button");
   Out.Ln;

   In.Prompt("Enter number: ");
   In.Int(number);                     (*enter first number*)
   WHILE In.Done DO                     (*check if finished*)
      (*calculate sum of digits*)
      sum:=0;
      WHILE number#0 DO
         sum:=sum+(number MOD 10);
         number:=number DIV 10;
      END; (*while*)

      (*print sum of digits*)
      Out.String(" ... Sum of digits = ");
      Out.Int(sum,0);
      Out.Ln;

      In.Prompt("Enter number: ");
      In.Int(number);                  (*enter next number*)
   END; (*while*)
END ProgMain;

END Ex7.
```

4.9.2 The *REPEAT* statement

Here you start with a statement sequence and check at the end of the loop if the stated condition has the value *TRUE*. If not, the loop is repeated once again from the beginning, etc. The *REPEAT* loop therefore executes the statement sequence at least once, then the check for terminating the loop is made (after the keyword *UNTIL*).

REPEAT, UNTIL

The program fragment

```
VAR c: CHAR;

REPEAT
   In.Char(c);
UNTIL ~In.Done;
```

reads a sequence of characters until input is stopped. As the test of the termination criteria is at the end of the *REPEAT* loop, the procedure In.Char is called at least once!

RepeatStatement

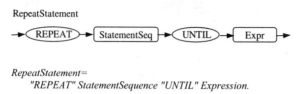

RepeatStatement=
        "REPEAT" StatementSequence "UNTIL" Expression.

Example

The digits of a number entered by the user shall be reversed.

Ex8.mod
```
MODULE Ex8;
(*reverse digits of a number*)
IMPORT In,Out;

PROCEDURE ProgMain*;
VAR
    n: INTEGER;
BEGIN
    In.Echo(TRUE);

    Out.String("Reverse digits of a number");
    Out.Ln;

    In.Prompt("Enter number: ");
    In.Int(n);                                  (*enter the number*)
    IF In.Done THEN
        Out.String(" ... ");
        REPEAT
            Out.Int(n MOD 10,0);                    (*write digit*)
            n:=n DIV 10;                            (*next digit*)
        UNTIL n=0;                       (*check loop condition*)
    END;
END ProgMain;

END Ex8.
```

4.9.3 The FOR statement (counting loop)

FOR Often you already know the precise number of times that a loop should be executed when you write the program. In this case a FOR statement can be used which increments a *control variable* from an initial value to a final value during each run. The statements in the loop are executed until the end value has been acted upon.

The program fragment

```
FOR i:=1 TO 5 DO
    Out.Int(i,0);
END;
```

for example prints out the numbers between 1 and 5.

The control variable (in the code above *i*) is usually incremented by 1 after each loop iteration; this value may optionally be modified by stating an iteration step (*BY n* for positive *and BY -n* for negative steps). The following loop, for example, counts from 100 down to 1:

Control variable

```
FOR i:=100 TO 1 BY -1 DO
    Out.Int(i,0);
END;
```

Instead of using the formula $n*(n+1)/2$ the numbers from 1 to 10 can also be summed up by the program

```
sum:=0;
FOR i:=1 TO 10 DO                    (*or: FOR i:=1 TO 10 BY 1 DO*)
    sum:=sum+i;
END;
```

or

```
sum:=0;
FOR i:=10 TO 1 BY -1 DO
    sum:=sum+i;
END;
```

By stating a step of 2 the control variable *i* of the following program is subsequently assigned the values 1, 3, 5, 7, and 9.

Step

```
FOR i:=1 TO 10 BY 2 DO
    ...
END;
```

The semantics of a *FOR* statement with the initial value *low,* the final value *high,* the step *step,* and the control variable *i* can also be expressed using equivalent *WHILE* loops [Moe93]:

```
temp:=high;
i:=low;

IF step>0 THEN
    WHILE i<=temp DO
        ...
        i:=i+step;
    END;
ELSE
    WHILE i>=temp DO
        ...
        i:=i+step;
    END;
END;
```

Therefore, in the program code with an implicit step of 1

```
FOR i:=4 TO 2 DO
    Out.Ln;
END;
```

the statement sequence between *DO* and *END* is not executed at all!

It is important to realize that inside the FOR loop the control variable may also be used for any statements:

```
FOR i:=1 TO 4 DO
   square:=i*i;
   Out.Int(square,0);
END;
```

So the value of this variable could also be modified inside the loop. This would reduce the readability of such a statement sequence, with the danger of violating the *FOR loop* termination. Finding such errors can be very difficult and frustrating. You should always keep in mind that the purpose of the *FOR* statement is to count!

```
FOR i:=1 TO 10 DO
   DEC(i);
END;
(*program will never terminate!*)
```

ForStatement

ForStatement=
   "FOR" ident ":=" Expression "TO" Expression
   ["BY" ConstExpression] "DO" StatementSequence "END".

Example

The indices of a two-dimensional matrix need to be produced and printed one after the other. For this purpose, two *FOR* loops may be nested:

Ex9.mod
```
MODULE Ex9;
(*print indices of a two-dimensional matrix*)
IMPORT Out;

PROCEDURE ProgMain*;
VAR
   lines, columns: INTEGER;
   c: CHAR;
BEGIN
   FOR lines:=1 TO 3 DO                          (*lines*)
      FOR columns:=1 TO 5 DO                     (*columns*)
         Out.Int(lines,5);
         Out.Char('/');
         Out.Int(columns,0);
      END;
      Out.Ln;
   END;
END ProgMain;

END Ex9.
```

4.9.4 The *LOOP* statement

The *LOOP* statement describes the infinite execution of a statement sequence   *LOOP*
which is only terminated when an *EXIT* statement is reached:

```
LOOP
    In.Char(c);
    IF ~In.Done THEN EXIT END;
    Out.Char(c);
END; (*loop*)
```

There may be several *EXIT* statements in different places inside *LOOP* ...   *EXIT*
END.

For simple loops with a single exit point the WHILE, REPEAT, or FOR
constructs are recommended. The LOOP construct is ideal for situations
where the natural structure of the solution has more than one exit point or an
exit point not at the beginning or the end of the loop.

LoopStatement

LoopStatement= "LOOP" StatementSeq "END".

Example

As an extension to the example discussed with the *CASE* statement (in 4.8.4),
characters need to be read and divided into categories (digits, upper and
lower case letters). Clicking the END button terminates the program.

```
MODULE Ex10;            (*determine the categories of characters*)   Ex10.mod
IMPORT In,Out;

PROCEDURE ProgMain*;
VAR
    c: CHAR;
BEGIN
    In.Echo(TRUE);
    LOOP
        In.Char(c);                                 (*read character*)

        IF ~In.Done THEN        (*user has entered a character?*)
            EXIT;                               (*no, exit loop*)
        END;

        CASE c OF                           (*case determination*)
        | '0'..'9': Out.String(" ... digit");
        | 'A'..'Z': Out.String(" ... upper case letter");
        | 'a'..'z': Out.String(" ... lower case letter");
        ELSE Out.String(" ... special character");
        END;
        Out.Ln;
    END; (*loop*)
END ProgMain;

END Ex10.
```

4.10 Structured data types

So far we have concentrated on the basic data types *SHORTINT, INTEGER, LONGINT, REAL, LONGREAL, CHAR, BOOLEAN* and *SET*. In order to model and represent the data in real-world problems more varied data types are needed. It is possible to combine basic data types together in the form of *structured data types* to achieve this. Once defined, these structured data types can in turn be used to create further more complex structured data types.

In practice there are two fundamental structured types:

Arrays • **Arrays**, which consist of a repeated instance of data of the same type (e.g. ten *INTEGER* values).

Structures • **Structures** (*records*), which consist of a collection of data of different types (e.g., a data type *person* which consists of name, address, and phone number).

In both cases, structured data types may be used in further type definitions to define structured data types (e.g., an array of the data type *person*).

4.10.1 Arrays

ARRAY In Oberon-2 arrays are defined starting with the keyword *ARRAY*.

Statically declared *ARRAY* variables consist of a fixed number of elements of a certain type, where each element is referenced by an index. Unlike its predecessors Algol, Pascal, and Modula-2, in Oberon-2 the index value of the first element is always zero.

The number of elements of a variable of type *ARRAY* is called the *length* of the array. Thus, the indices of an array may take integer values in the range[0,length-1]. A specific element of an array can be accessed by specifying its index value in square brackets.

The following statement defines an array *a* with three *INTEGER* elements *a[0]*, *a[1]* and *a[2]*:

```
VAR
   a: ARRAY 3 OF INTEGER;
```

In this case the variable declaration and the type declaration are combined into a single statement.

TYPE In Oberon-2 structured data types are declared with a new name after the keyword *TYPE*. For example an array "a" of type *VectorT* could be declared as follows:

```
TYPE
   VectorT= ARRAY 3 OF INTEGER;
VAR
   a: VectorT;
```

Given the following additional declarations

```
VAR
    i: INTEGER;
    b: VectorT;
```

the following assignments and expressions become possible:

```
i:=a[1]; (*assigns the second element of "a"*)
a[2]:=a[1]+a[0]+i;
b:=a;                       (*note: copies all three elements!*)
```

Assigning whole arrays is very convenient, particularly if it is an array of structured data types.

The predefined function *LEN* returns the number of elements in the array.   *LEN*

Multi-dimensional arrays

Arrays may also be multi-dimensional. In this case they have an index for   *Multi-*
each dimension. The declaration: *dimensional*

```
VAR
    m: ARRAY 3,4 OF INTEGER;
```

describes a 2-dimensional matrix *m* with the elements $m[0,0]$, $m[0,1]$, ..., $m[0,3]$, $m[1,0]$, the last element being $m[2,3]$.

In the general case multi-dimensional arrays such as

```
ARRAY L0,L1,…,Ln OF T;              (*where L0, L1 are indices*)
```

are an equivalent concise form of

```
ARRAY L0 OF
    ARRAY L1 OF
        …
            ARRAY Ln OF T;
```

The above matrix type could alternatively have been declared as

```
TYPE MatrixT= ARRAY 3 OF ARRAY 4 OF INTEGER;
```

Later on, we discuss procedure parameters and pointer types and also learn about *open arrays* which have their size specified at run-time rather than compile time.

Example program for arrays

This example solves a set of two simultaneous equations with two unknowns by applying Cramer's rule.

$a_{00}*x_0 + a_{01}*x_1 = d_0$	... equation 1
$a_{10}*x_0 + a_{11}*x_1 = d_1$	... equation 2
$det = a_{00}*a_{11} - a_{01}*a_{10}$	... determinant
$x_0 = d_0*a_{11} - d_1*a_{01}$	... solution for the first unknown
$x_1 = d_1*a_{00} - d_0*a_{10}$	... solution for the second unknown

Ex11.mod

```
MODULE Ex11;
(*solve two linear equations*)
IMPORT In,Out;

TYPE
    MatrixT= ARRAY 2,2 OF REAL;      (*data type for 2x2-matrix*)
    VectorT= ARRAY 2 OF REAL;      (*data type vector, length 2*)

PROCEDURE ProgMain*;
VAR
    a: MatrixT;
    d,x: VectorT;
    det: REAL;
BEGIN
    In.Echo(TRUE);

    (*read in the data values to solve*)
    In.Prompt("a00=");  In.Real(a[0,0]); Out.Ln;
    In.Prompt("a01=");  In.Real(a[0,1]); Out.Ln;
    In.Prompt("d0= ");  In.Real(d[0]); Out.Ln;
    Out.Ln;

    In.Prompt("a10=");  In.Real(a[1,0]); Out.Ln;
    In.Prompt("a11=");  In.Real(a[1,1]); Out.Ln;
    In.Prompt("d1= ");  In.Real(d[1]); Out.Ln;
    Out.Ln;

    IF In.Done THEN                              (*check input*)
        (*calculation of the determinant*)
        det:=a[0,0]*a[1,1]-a[0,1]*a[1,0];

        IF ABS(det)<(1.0/MAX(REAL)) THEN         (*is solvable?*)
            Out.String
              ("Not solvable, determinant is too small");
            Out.Ln;
        ELSE
            (*apply Cramers rule*)
            x[0]:=(d[0]*a[1,1]-d[1]*a[0,1])/det;
            x[1]:=(d[1]*a[0,0]-d[0]*a[1,0])/det;

            (*output of the calculated values*)
            Out.String("The solution is:");
            Out.String(" x0=");
            Out.Real(x[0],0);
            Out.String(", x1=");
            Out.Real(x[1],0);
            Out.Ln;
        END;
    END;
END ProgMain;

END Ex11.
```

Strings

ARRAY
OF CHAR
In Oberon-2 character strings are implemented using the structured type ARRAY OF CHAR.

A sequence of single characters can be stored in an *ARRAY OF CHAR* and manipulated as a variable. The end of a string is indicated by the terminal symbol *0X* which is stored at the end of the string as the last character (a "sentinel"). Thus, the array must be at least one character longer than the number of characters in the string. It is also possible to define a string constant.

```
CONST
   NAME = "POW!";

VAR
   txt: ARRAY 5 OF CHAR;
   detto: ARRAY 8 OF CHAR;
   illegal: ARRAY 4 OF CHAR;

txt:=NAME; detto:=NAME;      (*both are ok because the string
                          being assigned to is equal or larger
                               than the string being assigned*)
illegal:=NAME;                     (*error, no space for 0X!*)
```

Also note the source of mistakes in the following example:

```
detto:=NAME;
FOR i:=0 TO 3 DO
   txt[i]:=detto[i];
END;
```

Here, the 4 characters 'P', 'O', 'W' and '!' are copied correctly one after the other, but not the terminal symbol *0X*. A function for the output of strings that relies on the terminating zero symbol might read from the memory outside of *txt* until it detects a *0X*. In this case a runtime error would be reported and the program terminated.

To avoid such errors the predefined function *COPY* should always be used.   *COPY*
The statement *COPY(src,dst)* is directly equivalent to the statement *dst:=src*, where both the source operand *src* and the destination operand *dst* must be an array of characters (*src* may also be a constant). If necessary, the source operand will be truncated such that the character *0X* can be inserted into the destination operand. See Appendix B for a full explanation of *COPY*.

You will find more functions for the processing of strings in the module   *Module*
Strings of the OPAL library. The relational operators <, >, =, #, etc., also   *Strings*
work with strings but only if they contain the terminal symbol *0X*.

Example program for strings

In this program the procedures *Strings.Append* and *Strings.AppendChar* from the library module *Strings* are used. The names describe their purpose, but you can get more detailed information about their detailed operation from the *POW!* help file.

The following program composes a text from strings that are defined as constants. The resulting text is stored in an array and is then printed.

```
MODULE Ex12;             (*compose a string from text constants*)    Ex12.mod
IMPORT Out,Strings;

PROCEDURE ProgMain*;
CONST
   START= "Today is";
```

```
     FINISH= "a holiday.";
VAR
     line: ARRAY 100 OF CHAR;
BEGIN
     line:="";                        (*initialize the "line" string*)
     Strings.Append(line,START);           (*add the text to it*)
     Strings.AppendChar(line," ");
     Strings.Append(line,FINISH);
     Out.String(line);                            (*print it*)
END ProgMain;

END Ex12.
```

The syntactic form of arrays in EBNF is given below. This definition already
contains the case of an open array (the declaration contains no information
about the dimension). For a definition of *ConstExpression* see the full syntax
in Appendix B.

ArrayType

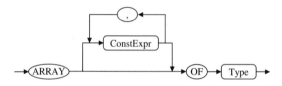

ArrayType = ARRAY [Length {"," Length}] OF Type ";".
Length= ConstExpression.

4.10.2 Structures

Record   Structures or records combine data items that need to be collected together
and referred to using a common name, allowing the selection and processing
of single components or the whole structure. In contrast to elements of arrays
the components of structures may be of different types.

Some examples of structure definitions are:

```
TYPE
    PersonT= RECORD
        name: ARRAY 32 OF CHAR;
        sex: CHAR;
        age: SHORTINT;
    END;

    TimeT= RECORD
        hours,minutes,seconds: SHORTINT;
    END;

    TimestampT= RECORD
        year,month,day: INTEGER;
        time: TimeT;                            (*declared above*)
    END;
```

If you define a variable *time* of the type *TimeT* the individual fields can be accessed with *time.hours, time.minutes,* and *time.seconds.* The same also applies to *VAR stamp:TimestampT.* Here, assignments of the form *stamp.year := 1946, stamp.time.hours := 12,* or expressions like *stamp.time.seconds := (stamp.time.seconds + 1) MOD 60* are possible. Note that structured type definitions can be nested.

Structures can also be assigned as a whole entity: *Assignment*

```
VAR
    oldStamp,newStamp: TimestampT;
...
oldStamp:=newStamp;
```

Here each of the values of the elements belonging to *newStamp* is assigned to its corresponding element of *oldStamp*; of course, the data types of the structures must be "assignment compatible".

Type extension of structures

The special thing about record data types in Oberon-2 is the possibility to   *Inheritance*
extend them. This leads us to a fundamental concept of object-oriented programming for the first time: *inheritance.*

If *BaseT* is a structure which is already declared as a type then you can define:

```
TYPE
    ExtenT= RECORD(BaseT)
        ...
    END;
```

The type *ExtenT* is called a *direct extension of the base type BaseT.* A   *Extension*
variable of type *ExtenT* then contains all elements of the data type *BaseT* and additionally those stated in the definition of *ExtenT.* In other words Extent *inherits* the elements of the base type BaseT and then extends them with additional elements.

Given the definition

```
TYPE
    PersonDataT= RECORD(PersonT)    (*PersonT is declared above*)
        salary: REAL;
    END;

VAR
    person: PersonDataT;
```

the variable *person* consists of the elements *person.name, person.sex, person.age,* and *person.salary.*

The concept "base type/extended type" may be applied more than once. For example the PersonDataT can itself be further extended to provide a new type PersonDetailedT.

```
TYPE
    PersonDetailedT= RECORD(PersonDataT)
        nationality: ARRAY 3 OF CHAR;
```

```
        birthtime: TimestampT;
      END;
```

The design of these extended types should naturally reflect the types in the problem and hence its programmed solution.

Type compatibility

It is important that an extended type is compatible with its base type. This is easily demonstrated by the example:

```
    VAR
      pers: PersonT;
      pdata: PersonDataT;
      pdetail: PersonDetailedT;
```

Projection   Now assignments of the form *pers:=pdata, pers:=pdetail* or *pdata:=pdetail* are possible. This always leads to a *projection* of the data: the contents of the elements of the extended type that are also part of the base type are the ones that are copied.

The assignment *pers:=pdata* has the following effect:

pers.name:= pdata.name, pers.sex:=pdata.sex, and *pers.age:=pdata.age.*

Similarly, *pdata:=pdetail* implies the assignments

pdata.name:=pdetail.name, etc., down to *pdata.salary:=pdetail.salary*.

The additional data of the variables of the extended type are lost. They cannot be copied because there are no corresponding elements contained in the base type.

It should now be obvious why an assignment in the reverse direction is not allowed. In this case, some elements would remain undefined and so would represent a vast source of potential errors. Therefore, the *statements* such as *pdata:=pers, pdetail:= pers*, and *pdetail:=pdata* are not allowed and are detected as invalid by the compiler based on data type compatibility rules.

There is a reason for the fact that Oberon-2 does not support types that are derived from more than one base type: the inheritance relation is strictly hierarchic. Multiple inheritance is not allowed, but can be easily simulated in Oberon-2 without suffering from the name clashes that generally arise in other languages such as SmallTalk and Eiffel.

Of course one base type can be used as a root for several different extensions:

```
    TYPE
      R0= RECORD ... END;
      R1= RECORD(R0) ... END;
      R2= RECORD(R0) ... END;
      R3= RECORD(R2) ... END;
```

Type hierarchy   In the above pattern, *R0* is the base type of both *R1* and *R2, R1* and *R2* are extended types of *R0. R3* is derived from *R2* (*R2* is the base type of *R3*). This principle is illustrated by a Venn diagram displaying the type hierarchies (it reads: every *R1* is a *R0*, etc.):

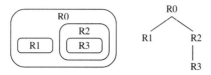

Fig. 34: Example of a type hierarchy

Example program of structures

In the program below, personal data are collected in an array and then sorted by surname. From this list of data a second, shorter table is generated.

For reasons of performance and simplicity the selected sorting algorithm is only suited for small amounts of data. There are much quicker methods available which we will not discuss here (see *MergeSort* algorithm in Section 4.13 for a more efficient algorithm).

```
MODULE Ex13;                      (*collect personal data in an array*)   Ex13.mod

IMPORT In,Out;

CONST
   MAXENTRIES= 10;

TYPE
   PersonT= RECORD                       (*the base record type*)
      name: ARRAY 40 OF CHAR;
      phoneNum: ARRAY 20 OF CHAR;
   END;

   PersonFullT= RECORD(PersonT)          (*a record extension*)
      address: ARRAY 80 OF CHAR;
   END;

PROCEDURE ProgMain*;
VAR
   short: ARRAY MAXENTRIES OF PersonT;
   full: ARRAY MAXENTRIES OF PersonFullT;
   temp: PersonFullT;
   num,min,i,j: INTEGER;
BEGIN
   In.Echo(TRUE);
   num:=0;

   REPEAT                              (*read the personal data*)
      In.Prompt("Enter new name: ");
      In.String(full[num].name);
      Out.Ln;

      In.Prompt("address: ");
      In.String(full[num].address);
      Out.Ln;

      In.Prompt("phone: ");
      In.String(full[num].phoneNum);
      Out.Ln;
      Out.Ln;
```

```
      IF In.Done THEN      (*user entered data for all fields?*)
         INC(num);                    (*yes, next array element*)
      END;
   UNTIL (num>=MAXENTRIES) OR (In.Done=FALSE);

   (*sort the directory*)
   FOR i:=0 TO num-2 DO
      min:=i;
      FOR j:=i+1 TO num-1 DO
         IF full[min].name>full[j].name THEN
            min:=j;
         END;
      END;
      temp:=full[min];
      full[min]:=full[i];
      full[i]:=temp;
   END (*FOR*);

   (*output of sorted directory*)
   FOR i:=0 TO num-1 DO
      Out.String(full[i].name); Out.Ln;
      Out.String(full[i].address); Out.Ln;
      Out.String(full[i].phoneNum); Out.Ln;
      Out.Ln;
   END;
   Out.Ln;

   (*generate a short table*)
   FOR i:=0 TO num-1 DO
      short[i]:=full[i];
   END;

   (*output of the pocket directory *)
   FOR i:=0 TO num-1 DO
      Out.String(short[i].name);
      Out.String(", ");
      Out.String(short[i].phoneNum);
      Out.Ln;
   END;
END ProgMain;

END Ex13.
```

4.11 Procedures

4.11.1 Procedures without parameters

Imagine the situation that you want to display five blank lines to make your program's output easier to read. Using the function *Out.Ln* of the *OPAL* library this problem can be solved as follows:

```
VAR i: INTEGER;
...
FOR i:=1 TO 5 DO
   Out.Ln;
END;
```

Of course you can insert these program lines with the editor each time they are needed but if one detail must be changed (e.g., only three lines are needed), all these occurrences would need to be found and corrected one after the other. This requires a lot of editing, and is also a potential source of mistakes. For example not all places may be found or an error could be introduced during editing.

Like all procedure-oriented programming languages Oberon-2 allows program fragments to be combined into procedures (subroutines). The benefit of this is that subroutines only need to be implemented and maintained in a single place. However, they can be called at runtime from many places in the program when needed.   *Subroutines*

The relevant program lines have to be introduced with the keyword *PROCEDURE,* and it is also necessary to name each subroutine so that it can be identified and therefore called unambiguously.   *PROCEDURE*

```
PROCEDURE PrintFiveLines;
VAR i: INTEGER;
BEGIN
   FOR i:=1 TO 5 DO
      Out.Ln;
   END;
END PrintFiveLines;
```

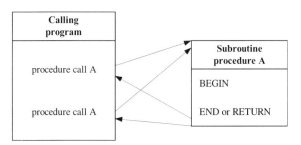

Fig. 35: Procedure call

Note that subroutines can be called from anywhere in the program (it is also possible to call the subroutine from itself if it is designed in a special way, see the section on *Recursion*).   *Recursion*

Once the procedure has been called and its statements executed or a RETURN statement is executed, control is automatically returned to the next statement after the original procedure call statement. In order not to make the program too complex and easier to understand it is advisable to use the *RETURN* statement fairly economically.   *RETURN*

```
PROCEDURE MyProc;
BEGIN
   ...
   IF x=esc THEN
      RETURN;
   END;
   ...
END MyProc;
```

In the procedure *PrintFiveLines* a variable *i* was declared. Some questions spring to mind:

- Is *i* known in the calling program?

  No, it's only defined in the procedure!

- If *ProgMain* contained a declaration like *VAR i: INTEGER*, would these two variables *i* refer to the same memory address?

  No, because there is no connection at all between the two declarations of *i*, other than the fact that they have the same name, which is itself rather unfortunate and potentially confusing.

We define the procedure *PrintFiveLines* inside *ProgMain* as follows:

Ex14.mod
```
MODULE Ex14;
(*nested procedures*)
IMPORT Out;

(*main procedure*)
PROCEDURE ProgMain*;
VAR i: INTEGER;

   (*nested procedure, local to ProgMain*)
   PROCEDURE PrintFiveLines;
   BEGIN
      FOR i:=1 TO 5 DO
         Out.Ln;
      END;
   END PrintFiveLines;

BEGIN
   PrintFiveLines;                          (*procedure call*)
   Out.String("five empty lines");

   PrintFiveLines;                          (*procedure call*)
   Out.String("five more empty lines");
END ProgMain;

END Ex14.
```

In the example Ex14 the single same variable *i* can be declared and used globally in *ProgMain* and also locally in *PrintFiveLines*. If *i* would be declared separately in each of these procedure declarations two different variables *i* were created, one in each. Variables within procedures are only created when the procedure is called and then cease to exist when the procedure returns control to its caller.

The following EBNF definition shows various possibilities for procedure declarations, including procedures with parameters and type-bound procedures which will be discussed in the following sections.

You will have noted that it is possible to define a procedure within an existing procedure definition. This "internal" procedure can only be called by the procedure which encloses it or by itself.

Procedures in procedures

```
PROCEDURE Outer;

    PROCEDURE Inner;            (*nested procedure declaration*)
    BEGIN
        ...
    END Inner;

BEGIN
    ...
    Inner;                      (*call to procedure Inner*)
END Outer;
```

IdentDef

ProcedureDeclaration

ProcedureDeclaration= ProcedureHeading ";" ProcedureBody IdentDef.
ProcedureHeading= "PROCEDURE" [Receiver] Ident [FormalParameters].
ProcedureBody= DeclarationSequence ["BEGIN" StatementSequence] "END".
DeclarationSequence =
    {"CONST" {ConstDeclaration ";"}
    | "TYPE" {TypeDeclaration ";"}
    | "VAR" {VariableDeclaration ";"}}
    | ProcedureDeclaration ";"}.
ForwardDeclaration =
    "PROCEDURE" "^" [Receiver] IdentDef [FormalParameters].

4.11.2 Procedures with parameters

The procedure *PrintFiveLines* already implemented can be called as often as desired and always shows the same behavior: it prints five blank lines.

Parameters Now we would like to change the way the procedure behaves so that the number of blank lines to be printed can be defined each time the procedure is called. The mechanism for passing information to procedures is the *parameter list* of procedures.

The parameter list is written in parentheses just after the definition of the procedure name and contains the names and data types of the values expected by the procedure. The values are then passed to the procedure when it is called. In our example we define a parameter *i* which stands for the number of blank lines:

```
PROCEDURE PrintLines (i:INTEGER);
BEGIN
    WHILE i>0 DO
        Out.Ln;
        i:=i-1;
    END;
END PrintLines;
```

Call When the procedure is called the parameter(s) must exactly match the original procedures parameter list in both number and order. A possibility would be:

```
CONST
    LINES= 10;                          (*an INTEGER constant*)

VAR
    lines: INTEGER;

lines:=5;                               (*initialize the variable*)
PrintLines(lines);
PrintLines(LINES);
PrintLines(5);
```

Scope and existence of variables

Existence A variable is said to *exist* when it has memory allocated to store its value. So variables defined in modules are often referred to as *global variables* as they exist whilst the program is running. On the other hand a variable defined in a procedure only exists whilst the procedure is actually invoked (called), and ceases to exist once the procedure returns control to its caller. Such variables are often referred to as *local variables*, as they are local to their enclosing procedure.

Scope Given that variables in procedures only exist when the procedure is called it is important that it should be illegal to use such variables when they don't exist! To achieve this the concept of scope is introduced. The scope of a variable defines its visibility from other parts of the program. For example a global variable is visible within the module that defines it, and also to other modules if it is explicitly exported. A local variable of a procedure is only visible within the procedure or from procedures which have declarations nested within it. So scoping is a technique used to ensure that the compiler can detect mistaken references to variables which would simply not exist in particular program contexts.

Example

```
MODULE Visible;
VAR i: INTEGER;

PROCEDURE Outer;
VAR i: INTEGER;

    PROCEDURE Inner;
    VAR i: CHAR;
    BEGIN
        (*here i is local for Inner and of type CHAR*)
    END Inner;

BEGIN
    (*here i is local for Outer and of type INTEGER*)
END Outer;

BEGIN
    (*here i is global in the module and of type INTEGER, and
        different from the variables defined in Inner and Outer*)
END Visible.
```

Although in this example all three variables have the same name "i" they are distinct. The scoping rules built into the compiler ensure that each one is referenced unambiguously. Even so it is strongly recommended that in practice variable names are chosen to be different wherever possible to make programs easy to understand for the reader.

For variables declared inside a procedure, new storage is allocated for its local variables and parameters each time it is called and then released after the procedure has been terminated. So if a procedure should call itself, each level of the procedure call operates with its own local data. It should now be clear why local variables do not retain values from one procedure call to the next!   *Local variables*

Variables that are declared outside all procedures (*global variables in modules*) are created when the program is started, and the corresponding variable storage is only released after the program has been terminated.   *Global variables*

VAR and value parameters

Parameter values may be passed to a procedure in two different ways, either by value or by reference. For a parameter passed by value a *copy of the current actual value* is passed. On the other hand when a parameter is passed by reference *only the location* of the variable holding the actual value is passed.

In Oberon-2, both kinds of parameter are possible: value parameters (*call by value*) and VAR parameters (*call by reference*). Parameters are value parameters unless explicitly declared as VAR parameters.

```
PROCEDURE ParmExample
              (n:INTEGER;VAR a:ARRAY 3 OF CHAR);
```

VAR parameters

Because VAR parameters are passed by location, it becomes possible not only to read the actual value from inside a procedure, but also to permanently modify the original data.

value parameters

With a value parameter a local copy of the value is created for the procedure. Any modifications during the execution of the procedure are lost when the procedure returns as they were not made to the original data but to a copy of it.

Generally, the following rules are suggested:

- If data only needs to be passed to a procedure (so-called input parameters) or must definitely not be changed, a value parameter should be used.

- If data will be modified in the procedure or if calculated values need to be passed back to the caller a VAR parameter should be used.

There are some exceptions to this rule for storage-intensive input parameters such as large arrays, deeply nested records with array types, etc. In this case VAR parameters may be used for reasons of runtime efficiency, because no memory is required to allocate the copy variable at run-time and no time is used for copying the data to it. However, you should take into consideration the danger of unexpected side-effects caused by programming mistakes!

Here are some declarations for the next example:

```
PROCEDURE MaxMin (a,b,c:INTEGER; VAR max,min:INTEGER);

PROCEDURE Cramer (a:ARRAY 2,2 OF REAL;
                  d:ARRAY 2 OF REAL;
                  VAR x:ARRAY 2 OF REAL;
              VAR done:BOOLEAN);
```

The next program converts numbers to strings and prints them in normal and reverse and right order:

Ex15.mod

```
MODULE Ex15;
(*convert numbers to strings*)
IMPORT In,Out,Strings;

TYPE
```
a)
```
    StringT= ARRAY 32 OF CHAR;

(*reversal of characters in a string*)
```
b)
```
PROCEDURE ReverseString (VAR s:StringT);
VAR
    temp: CHAR;
    i,j: LONGINT;
BEGIN
    i:=0;
    j:=Strings.Length(s)-1;
    WHILE i<j DO
```

```
          temp:=s[i];                   (*exchange the character*)
          s[i]:=s[j];
          s[j]:=temp;
          INC(i);                  (*setup for next character position*)
          DEC(j);
       END;
    END ReverseString;

    (*conversion of a positive integer number to a
       string in reverse order of the digits*)
    PROCEDURE ReverseInt (n:LONGINT;VAR s:StringT);              .        c)
    VAR i: INTEGER;
    BEGIN
       i:=0;
       (*n is a value param, it is worked on a copy*)

       REPEAT                   (*copy digits one after the other *)     d)
          (*convert ASCII digit char to equivalent integer*)            e)
          s[i]:=CHR(ORD('0')+(n MOD 10));
          n:=n DIV 10;
          INC(i);
       UNTIL n=0;

       s[i]:=0X;                    (* add end of string sentinel*)
    END ReverseInt;

    (*main program *)
    PROCEDURE ProgMain*;
    VAR
       n: LONGINT;
       s: StringT;
    BEGIN
       In.Echo(TRUE);

       LOOP
          In.Prompt("Enter number: ");
          In.LongInt(n);

          IF In.Done=FALSE THEN
             EXIT;                      (*exit loop, if no input*)
          END;

          Out.String(" -> ");
          ReverseInt(n,s);    (*convert integer to reverse string*)
          Out.String(s);

          Out.String(" -> ");
          ReverseString(s);                       (*reverse string*)
          Out.String(s);

          Out.Ln;
       END                                        (*LOOP*)
    END ProgMain;

END Ex15.
```

a) All procedures of this program work with strings not longer than 31 characters.

Length b) The function *ReverseString* reverses the order of the characters in a string. The string *s* is defined as VAR parameter because the modifications have an effect on the original data. The end of the string is determined by the function *Strings.Length*.

c) *ReverseInt* converts a number *n* to a string s. The variable *n* is modified, but these changes must not be visible to the caller and are therefore made to a copy of *n* (value parameter). On the contrary, the value of *s* has to be returned to the caller of the procedure as a VAR parameter.

d) The number *n* is analyzed by a consecutive division by 10 and storing the remainder in the string. Following this, the number is analyzed starting from the least significant digit. Because the single characters are stored in the string starting from index 0, they automatically appear in reverse order.

e) The remainder of the division is always in the interval between 0 and 9 and has to be converted to the ASCII code for the corresponding characters "0" to "9".

Rules for passing parameters

If *fT* is the type of a formal parameter *f* and *aT* the type of the corresponding current parameter *a* during the procedure call, then

- with a VAR parameter *aT* must be of the same type as *fT* or *fT* must be a record and *aT* an extension of it. In the latter situation, only the projection of the data of *aT* is passed to *fT*.

- *a* must be *assignment compatible* to *f*. To explain this term we refer to the language definition in Appendix B. For the moment it is sufficient to interpret the meaning of this term literally.

Note that the function *ReverseString* only works with arrays of the data type *StringT*. Strings with a declaration of type other than *StringT* would somehow have to be copied to a variable of the type *StringT* first. To avoid this inconvenient restriction the open array type is used.

Open arrays Arrays without any declaration of their length are called *open* arrays. They may be used as types of formal parameters and as element types of other open arrays, and no index boundaries are declared.

```
TYPE
    StringT= ARRAY OF CHAR;
    MatrixT= ARRAY OF ARRAY OF INTEGER;
```

Equipped with this, we can now redefine *ReverseString(s:StringT)* as *ReverseString(s:ARRAY OF CHAR)*. However, we need to define the length of the current parameter inside the procedure.

In this example, the length of the formal parameter is taken. *If VAR s: ARRAY 16 OF CHAR* had been defined, the formal parameter would be given the length of the current parameter (here: 16).

The number of elements of an array can be determined using the predefined *LEN* function *LEN*, the call is *LEN(v,n)* for the array *v* with an optional constant *n* to define the intended dimension.

- If no constant *n* is stated the length of the first dimension of the array *v* is returned (in our example *LEN(s)* returns the value 16).

- *LEN(v,0)* equals *LEN(v)* for arrays of any number of dimensions.

We can now make the program work for any string type by replacing the function *Strings.Length* in a new implementation of the function *ReverseString:*

```
PROCEDURE ReverseString (VAR s:ARRAY OF CHAR);
VAR
    temp: CHAR;
    i,j: LONGINT;
BEGIN
    i:=0;
    j:=0;                   (*instead of j:=Strings.Length(s)-1;*)

    WHILE (j<LEN(s)) & (s[j]#0X) DO
        INC(j);                        (*search for the end of j*)
    END;
    DEC(j);                 (*correct the character count*)

    WHILE (i<j) DO                          (*reverse the string*)
        temp:=s[i];
        s[i]:=s[j];
        s[j]:=temp;
        INC(i);
        DEC(j);
    END;
END ReverseString;
```

The standard function *LEN* always returns a number of the type *LONGINT*. This should be borne in mind if you want to use it in a *FOR* statement. The count variable should also be of type *LONGINT*:

```
VAR
    i: LONGINT;

FOR i:=LEN(array)-1 TO 0 BY -1 DO
    ...
END;
```

If the maximum length of the passed array is known the function *SHORT* can *SHORT* be used to convert the *LONGINT* value to a value of the data type *INTEGER*:

```
VAR
    i: INTEGER;

FOR i:=SHORT(LEN(array)-1) TO low BY -1 DO
    ...
END;
```

It is worth remembering that the effect of the FOR statement is equivalent to the statement

```
WHILE (i<=high) DO
   ...
END;
```

So, in

```
FOR i:=low TO high DO
   ...
END;
```

only *low* is used for an assignment of *i*, as opposed to *high* which is used for the comparison with the upper limit. This is why no explicit type conversion is necessary for *high*. No problem will occur - apart from the length of the array - if you write:

```
VAR
   i: INTEGER;

FOR i:=0 TO LEN(array)-1 DO
   ...
END;
```

In practice it is best to err on the side of caution and define the types of variables carefully.

4.11.3 Functions

We are familiar with the use of functions from expressions in mathematical notation, for example:

$$y = \sqrt{1 + x^2}$$

or converted to the notation of Oberon-2,

```
y:=Sqrt(1+x*x);
```

We have in fact become familiar with this concept already under the topic of "predefined functions". Here are some more examples:

ENTIER • *ENTIER(x)* calculates the nearest smaller whole number to a given real number and returns its value:

```
Out.Int(ENTIER(2.34));                    (*returns 2*)
Out.Int(ENTIER(-2.34));                   (*returns -3*)
```

ODD • *ODD(i)* requires an integer number as a parameter and returns *TRUE*, if *i* is odd, and *FALSE*, if *i* is even:

```
IF ODD(i) THEN
   Out.String("odd");
ELSE
   Out.String("even")
END;
```

Functions always return a result, the value of which can be directly used in an *RETURN*
expression. This result is defined by a *RETURN* statement in the procedure
body. When a *RETURN* statement is reached the execution of the procedure
is terminated and the calling program continues with the next statement after
the procedure call that has just been completed. It is possible to have several
RETURN statements in one procedure body.

When a function is defined the type of the returned value (the type of the *Result type*
result) must be defined as well. The type of the expression stated in the
RETURN statement must be *assignment compatible* with the result type
stated in the procedure header declaration.

If no input parameter is required, the function gets an empty parameter list
" ( ) ".

```
PROCEDURE GetNext (): INTEGER;
```

The result type of a function may only be a basic type; structured types are
not allowed in this context. As we will see later, it is easy to work around this
language restriction by using pointer types.

Mathematical functions

As a first example, here is a function for the approximation of the square root
of a number of type *LONGREAL* (although such a function *Float.Sqrt* already
exists in the *OPAL* library). A parameter is assumed to have a positive value:

```
MODULE Ex16;                                                    Ex16.mod
(*compute the square root of numbers*)
IMPORT In,Out;

(*compute square root of x*)
PROCEDURE SqRoot (x:LONGREAL): LONGREAL;
CONST PRECISION= 0.000001;                    (*result resolution*)
VAR xold,xnew: LONGREAL;
BEGIN
    IF x<0 THEN (*check if value negative*)
        Out.String("negative value! ");
    END;

    x:=ABS(x);
    IF x<PRECISION THEN RETURN 0.0;           (*x is too small*)
    ELSIF x=1.0 THEN RETURN 1.0;              (*special case!*)
    ELSE
        xold:=x;
        xnew:=x;
        REPEAT                                (*iteration using*)
            xold:=xnew;
            xnew:=((xold+(x/xold))/2.0);      (*Newton's formula*)
        UNTIL (ABS(xnew-xold)<PRECISION);
        RETURN xnew;
    END;
END SqRoot;

(*main procedure*)
PROCEDURE ProgMain*;
VAR r: LONGREAL;
```

```
BEGIN
    In.Echo(TRUE);

    In.Prompt("Enter value: ");
    In.LongReal(r);
    WHILE In.Done DO
        Out.String(", square root= ");
        Out.LongReal(SqRoot(r),10);
        Out.Ln;
        In.Prompt("Enter value: ");
        In.LongReal(r);
    END;
END ProgMain;

END Ex16.
```

Horner-scheme Another example is the implementation of the Horner function, which calculates the value of a polynomial expression using Horner's algorithm

$$y = a_n*x^n + a_{n-1}*x^{n-1} + ... + a_1*x + a_0$$

by converting it to an Oberon-2 expression

```
y:=(((a[n-1]*x+a[n-2])*x+...))+a[1]*x)+a[0]
```

```
PROCEDURE Horner (a:ARRAY OF REAL;x:REAL): REAL;
VAR
    i,degr: INTEGER;
    y: REAL;
BEGIN
    y:=0.0;
    degr:=SHORT(LEN(a)-1);           (*find the number of terms*)
    FOR i:=degr TO 0 BY -1 DO         (*calculate the sum then*)
        y:=y*x+a[i];
    END;
    RETURN y;                         (*return the result value*)
END HORNER;
```

If, for example, you define

```
VAR
    p: ARRAY 3 OF REAL;
    w: REAL;

p[0]:=3;
p[1]:=5;
p[2]:=7;
```

function calls of the form *w:=Horner(p,1)* are possible as well as calls like *w:=Horner(p,2*SqRoot(4.0))*. They would return the values 15 and 135 respectively.

Boolean functions

Functions are not just used in formulating arithmetic expressions. They are also used with other result types and can increase the readability of programs.

Let us suppose that we have the problem to check whether all elements of an *INTEGER* array have the value 0:

IF "all elements of array list equal zero" THEN ... ELSE ... END;

The following function solves this problem:

```
PROCEDURE IsZero (f:ARRAY OF INTEGER): BOOLEAN;
VAR n: LONGINT;
BEGIN
    FOR n:=0 TO LEN(f)-1 DO            (*for each element ...*)
        IF f[n]#0 THEN
            RETURN FALSE;             (*any non-zero element found*)
        END;
    END;
    RETURN TRUE;                       (*all elements were 0*)
END IsZero;
```

and we can now write:

```
VAR
    list: ARRAY 10 OF INTEGER;

IF IsZero(list) THEN
    ...
ELSE
    ...
END;
```

4.11.4 Procedure variables

A procedure variable is a variable that can hold a value, which is a reference to a procedure. By using procedure variables it becomes possible to control, which procedure of several alternatives to call from a particular place in a program.

If a procedure has been defined as

```
PROCEDURE DoThis;
BEGIN
END DoThis;
```

it will be executed by calling its name: *DoThis* or *DoThis()*. Normally two actions now happen: *Procedure call*

1) Saving the state of the calling procedure's context, especially all local data and the current value of the program counter in a special data area (its *runtime stack*) as well as setting up the new run-time context for the called procedure.

2) Branching to the first executable instruction of the called procedure. (The computer's program counter is assigned the address of this statement.)

From an internal point of view a procedure name is not much more than the   *Address*
bearer of a location address within the program storage area. Addresses in Oberon-2 are internally represented as equivalent to the type *LONGINT*. This provides the basis for a simple programming mechanism to call a procedure *via a variable* and it also introduces a new type of variable which contains the location of a procedure. Such variables are called procedure variables and

can be assigned the locations of procedures. Subsequently the procedure
referenced by the procedure variable can be called in the normal way.

PROCEDURE

```
VAR
    doSomething: PROCEDURE;        (*declare a procedure variable*)

    doSomething:=DoThis;                  (*assigns the procedure name*)
    doSomething;                    (*the procedure DoThis is called*)
```

For procedures with parameters the definition and consistency of data types
is especially important and a potential source of errors. Here are some type
declarations:

```
TYPE
    DoThisProcT= PROCEDURE;
    DoThatProcT= PROCEDURE (i:INTEGER);
    DoOtherProcT= PROCEDURE (VAR r:LONGREAL): LONGREAL;
```

Procedure
variable

Now procedure variables can be declared:

```
VAR
    do: DoThatProcT;

(*every procedure whose procedure header is identical to
    the type DoThatProcT may be assigned,
    the names of the parameters may vary. For example ...*)

PROCEDURE Write (value:INTEGER);
BEGIN
    Out.Int(value,0);
END MyProc;
```

Procedure call

Thus, the statement sequences

```
Write(76);
```

and

```
do:=Write;
do(76);
```

have the same effect.

Functions

Furthermore, functions may be used in procedure variables, as the following
program fragment illustrates:

```
TYPE
    CalculateT= PROCEDURE (r:LONGREAL): LONGREAL;
    ConvertT= PROCEDURE (c:CHAR): CHAR;

VAR
    calc: CalculateT;         (*declare the procedure variables*)
    convert: ConvertT;
    cube, square: LONGREAL;            (*declare data variables*)
    letter: CHAR;

PROCEDURE Square (r:LONGREAL): LONGREAL;
BEGIN
    RETURN r*r;
END Square;
```

```
PROCEDURE Cube (r:LONGREAL): LONGREAL;
BEGIN
    RETURN r*r*r;
END Cube;

PROCEDURE AsItIs (c:CHAR): CHAR;
BEGIN
    RETURN c;
END AsItIs;

PROCEDURE LowerCase (c:CHAR): CHAR;
BEGIN
    IF (c>='A') & (c<='Z')
        RETURN CHR(ORD(c)+ORD('a')-ORD('A'));
    ELSE
        RETURN c;
END LowerCase;

...
calc:=Square;
square:=calc(7.0);

calc:=Cube;
cube:=calc(9.0);

IF ... THEN
    convert:=LowerCase;      (*convert character to lower case*)
ELSE
    convert:=AsItIs;         (*or effectively leave it as is*)
END;
letter:=convert('a');        (*call the appropriate procedure*)
```

Example

The following example is rather detailed. We will prepare for it by describing some background. The task is to design a general program which can be used to browse through all entries of a directory defined as *ARRAY OF EntryT*:

```
TYPE
    EntryT= RECORD
        used: BOOLEAN;
        name: ARRAY 8 OF CHAR;
    END;

VAR
    dict: ARRAY 16 OF EntryT;
```

A function *ScanDict* executes a certain "activity" for each element. We specify this activity by a parameter of the data type *PROCEDURE*. Of course the current parameter must be of the type of the formal parameter, which means that only procedures with a compatible type declaration may be called.

```
TYPE
    WorkT= PROCEDURE (VAR e:EntryT);

PROCEDURE ScanDict (VAR a:ARRAY OF EntryT; work:WorkT);
```

The procedures *MakeCap* (changes the name of an entry to upper case characters) and *PrintEntry* (prints an entry) are used for demonstration purposes.

Code reuse   This is all what is needed to understand the complete demonstration program. Before getting into details we mention two more keywords from object-oriented programming: *reusability and inheritance*. Note that the features of the procedure *ScanDict* may be used in many ways. Only the functionality varies, due to the procedure formally stated in the parameter list when it is called. On inserting, the current parameter *work* becomes overwritten by the current value (here: *PrintEntry* or *MakeCap*). So the ScanDict algorithm can be reused and its behaviour tailored by providing the "plug-in" procedures to do the detailed work.

Ex17.mod
```
MODULE Ex17;
(*collect entries in a dictionary*)
IMPORT Out;

TYPE
    EntryT= RECORD
        used: BOOLEAN;
        name: ARRAY 8 OF CHAR;
    END;

    WorkT= PROCEDURE (VAR e:EntryT);

(*scan through the array 'a' and calls the given procedure,
  wherever an entry is in use*)
PROCEDURE ScanDict (VAR a:ARRAY OF EntryT; work:WorkT);
VAR n:LONGINT;
BEGIN
    FOR n:=0 TO LEN(a)-1 DO
        IF a[n].used THEN
            work(a[n]);
        END;
    END;
END ScanDict;

(*print a single element*)
PROCEDURE PrintEntry (VAR entry:EntryT);
BEGIN
    Out.String(entry.name);
    Out.Ln;
END PrintEntry;

(*convert any lower case letters in 'name' to upper case*)
PROCEDURE MakeCap (VAR entry:EntryT);
VAR n: LONGINT;
BEGIN
    FOR n:=0 TO LEN(entry.name)-1 DO
        entry.name[n]:=CAP(entry.name[n]);
    END;
END MakeCap;
```

```
PROCEDURE ProgMain*;
VAR
   n: LONGINT;
   dict: ARRAY 16 OF EntryT;
BEGIN
   (*initialize directory entries to 'not-in-use'*)
   FOR n:=0 TO LEN(dict)-1 DO
      dict[n].used:=FALSE;
   END;

   (*generate test arrays*)
   dict[0].used:=TRUE; dict[0].name:="one";
   dict[1].used:=TRUE; dict[1].name:="two";
   dict[2].used:=TRUE; dict[2].name:="three";

   (*convert all entries to capital letters*)
   ScanDict(dict,MakeCap);

   (*print entries*)
   ScanDict(dict,PrintEntry);
END ProgMain;

END Ex17.
```

4.11.5 Forward declaration of procedures

The purpose of a *forward declaration* is to define the procedure header calling interface for a procedure, which will be fully specified later in the text. In this way it becomes possible to arrange source code more clearly, i.e. use the procedure name already in calls, although the corresponding implementation is located further on in the program. As we shall see later some program designs rely on the use of this language feature.

A forward declaration is a complete procedure header, with the character "^" in front of the procedure name.

Its typical application is the disentangling of cyclic calls between procedures that are mutually dependent. In the following example the procedure *Proc1* is called by *Proc2* and vice-versa, but *Proc2* is implemented after *Proc1*. To be able to compile this example, *Proc2* has to be declared before Proc1, to ensure that *Proc2* is already known when the procedure call in *Proc1* is compiled:

Cyclic call

```
PROCEDURE ^Proc2 (i:INTEGER);          (*forward declaration*)

PROCEDURE Proc1 (i:INTEGER);
BEGIN
   IF i>0 THEN
      Proc2(i+1);                      (*refers to Proc2 above*)
   END

END Proc1;
```

```
PROCEDURE Proc2 (i:INTEGER);            (*declaration of Proc2*)
BEGIN
   IF i>0 THEN
      Proc1(i-2);
   END;
END Proc2;
```

This concept is called *mutual recursion* and should be treated with great care as it is easy to make disastrous programming errors, which are hard to understand and detect, for example, if the recursion (calling) never stops! The topic is covered in more detail later on.

4.12 Modules

4.12.1 Module concept

Module

A *module* is a collection of declarations for constants, types, variables and procedures. In addition, there is an optional statement sequence for the initialization of the module variables. Every Oberon-2 program created using the *POW!* system consists of at least one module.

Separate compilation

Modules can be compiled separately and are therefore an important tool for structuring, that is, partitioning complex software problems to clearly separated parts. In order for a module to use data or procedures declared in another module, it must *import* the module or parts of it.

Client

By importing a module a *client* can use all constants, data types, variables and procedures, which this module has *exported* (has made visible for other modules to import). So the module concept provides additional ways to control the scope and existence of variables.

Here is the EBNF for modules:

> *Module=   "MODULE" Ident ";" [ImportList] DeclarationSequence*
> *   ["BEGIN" StatementSequence] "END" Ident ".".*
> *ImportList= "IMPORT" Import {"," Import} ";".*
> *Import= [Ident ":="] Ident.*

If a client M imports two modules A and B then it might happen that both A and B export a variable or procedure with identical names. Typically this can happen when several library modules are reused from other projects. For this reason imported items must be made unambiguous. In practice they are *qualified* by putting the name of the corresponding module in front of them, which guarantees that they become unique.

MODULE

When using *POW!* you must save each module in its own file. A module starts with the keyword *MODULE*, followed by the name of the module (this has to be identical with the file name!) and a semicolon.

```
MODULE Mod;
```

The naming of the modules from which we would like to import is achieved   *IMPORT*
by using the *IMPORT* statement at the beginning of each module. It is also
possible to define a shorter way of naming each imported module by defining
an "alias" name for the imported module (often to save typing at the expense
of future program readability!). However, it is very important that programs
are readable by other people; so don't abbreviate names just to save typing!

```
IMPORT Out,S:=Strings;
```

The end of the module is marked by *END*, the module name and a full stop.

```
END Mod.
```

In every module an initialization part can be put just before the end. It is   *Initialization*
automatically executed when the program is started and its purpose is to
ensure that all variables in the module have the intended initial values before
the module is used. This part is introduced with the keyword *BEGIN*. If the
keyword is missing (see above), no initialization is carried out:

```
BEGIN
    ...
    (*any statements, usually used for the initialization of
       global variables and  for calling setup procedures*)
END Mod.
```

Export from modules

It has already been mentioned that the scope of all variables, types, constants,
and procedures defined inside a module is limited to within that module.
Consequently they are invisible to other modules.

Now we would like to define clear interfaces for modules by selectively   *Export*
opening up their scope to define which elements exist and need to be
accessed by other modules. Only chosen elements will be *exported*, i.e., be
visible and available for clients.

The marking of these elements is achieved using *export marks* "*" and "-"   *Markings*
immediately after the relevant qualifier:

* indicates an unrestricted right to read/write for clients. Of course,
  constants exported with this mark cannot be changed.

- means that the variable or component of a structure may only be read   *Read only*
  (*read only*), but not modified.

Please note that fields of structures are not exported automatically together
with marked structures. Each exported field must be marked individually.
This makes it possible to selectively hide structure elements that are used
only internally.

```
MODULE Ex18Mod;                                                    Ex18Mod.
    (*demonstrates the export mechanism, used by ex18.mod*)        mod

CONST
    MAX*= 32;                                    (*exported*)
```

```
TYPE
   ValueT*= INTEGER;                                (*exported*)

   UseT*= RECORD                                    (*exported*)
      readonly-:CHAR;                            (*and read only*)
      readwrite*: INTEGER;                          (*exported*)
      hidden: BOOLEAN
   END;

VAR
   seed-: ValueT;                             (*exported read only*)

PROCEDURE Upper* (c:CHAR): CHAR;                     (*exported*)
BEGIN
   RETURN CAP(c);
END Upper;

PROCEDURE Init;
BEGIN
   seed:=123;
END Init;

BEGIN                        (*called at initialization of module*)
   Init;                 (*to set up default values in variables*)
END Ex18Mod.
```

A client may import the above module and thereby use it:

Ex18.mod

```
MODULE Ex18;
(*client for Ex18Mod.mod, demonstrates module import*)
IMPORT Out,Ex18Mod;

VAR
   c: CHAR;
   value: Ex18Mod.ValueT;
   use: Ex18Mod.UseT;
   field: ARRAY Ex18Mod.MAX OF CHAR;

PROCEDURE ProgMain*;
BEGIN
   use.readwrite:=0;                                (*allowed*)
   c:=use.readonly;                                 (*allowed*)
   c:=Ex18Mod.Upper(c);                             (*allowed*)
   value:=Ex18Mod.seed;                             (*allowed*)

(*
   use.readonly:='1';        (*error, is write-protected*)
   use.hidden:=FALSE;            (*error, not visible*)
   Ex18Mod.seed:=value;      (*error, is write-protected*)
*)

   Out.Int(Ex18Mod.seed,0);
END ProgMain;

END Ex18.
```

Notice that the function *Init* of the module *Ex18Mod* is automatically called by the initialization part of the module and is not exported. As a result it is invisible to the client. This is essential, as the *Init* routine may be concerned with details that are irrelevant to a client and therefore should be inaccessible to it.

The execution of the statements in the module body at import time implies a prohibition of cyclic imports. It is not allowed for a module *M1* to import the module *M2*, where *M2* itself imports *M3* and *M3* again imports *M1*. The compiler checks for such situations and provides a warning message.

Cyclic import

Modules under *POW!*

The concept of *projects* under *POW!* was explained in Chapter 3. It was also mentioned that a project file is not needed for programs that only consist of Oberon-2 modules. The standard project can be used in this case. We are now at a point where it makes sense to describe a project file specially produced to support the next programming example.

Projects

Projects containing only one source file may be generated automatically from the enclosed project *templates* provided with *POW!* Each additional module must be added to the project definition. This is done by calling the dialog **Edit Project** of the menu **Compile**. There, you add all modules of a program to the list of the project files (by selecting the files with a double-click or the **Add** button).

Templates

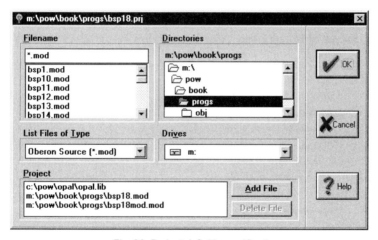

Fig. 36: Project definition ex18.prj

Figure 36 shows the project definition for the program *Ex18*. Note that in all our programs the entry *opal.lib* appears in the project file list, because we use the functions of the *OPAL* library.

The exported interface of every module can be determined separately and displayed with the help of a special tool, the *browser*. Select the command **Module Definition Browser** from the menu **Tools** to display the interface of the currently edited file. The following output is generated for the module *Ex18Mod*:

Browser

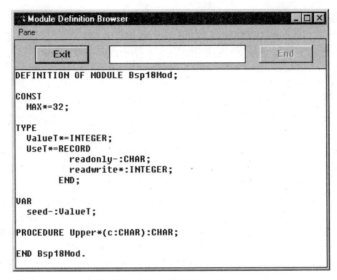

Fig. 37: Module Definition Browser

As an example of blatant misuse of the export mechanism here is a module, which avoids clear parameter passing and relies on the scope rules for the variables instead:

```
MODULE BadStyle;
IMPORT Out;

VAR lines*: INTEGER;            (*declare lines and export it*)

PROCEDURE PrintLines;
VAR i: INTEGER;
BEGIN
    FOR i:=1 TO lines DO     (*could be changed by the client!*)
        Out.Ln;
    END;
END PrintLines;

BEGIN
    lines:=5;                    (*variable initialization*)
END BadStyle.
```

A client may be programmed as follows:

```
MODULE UseBad;
IMPORT BadStyle;
...
BEGIN
    BadStyle.lines:=3;
    BadStyle.PrintLines;
...
END UseBad.
```

This technique would be a throwback to the programming methods of the 60's, because one of the important discoveries in the art of programming is that modules should have a well defined interface for the client and be *designed* to hide and protect information from abuse.

The above example is so simple that the potential danger is not obvious at a glance: if *lines* is assigned, this has a side effect on the behavior of the procedure *PrintLines*. It may happen that *lines* is assigned different values in the course of the program. Furthermore, several different modules might have imported the module with the exported procedure *PrintLines*. In this case the frequent state change of the variable *lines* is hard to control or track.

Now imagine that this programming technique were used in much more complex situations, where several procedures of a module are exported and for each of these procedures you would have to export several variables for data transfer. The problem would be further complicated, because clients of a module must refer to the specific exported names, if such a method is used.

So far we have always used imported modules without mentioning these export mechanisms, for example, when the modules of the *OPAL* library (*Out*, *Strings*, etc.) were used. Before going further the reader is encouraged to read the on-line help of the *POW!* system and so become familiar with the design and interfaces of these modules.

4.12.2 Abstract Data structures

The appreciation and evaluation of a programming language is not only based upon the evaluation of the syntax and the construction of small and simple programs. It is also important to consider how the language can help us with the construction of large programs and how effectively it can be used to help us to engineer the software.

Experience shows that once a problem is understood, the next step is to decide how to solve the problem and then how to partition the solution into smaller parts, each of which can be easily understood, programmed and tested separately. This implies that programming languages must offer a structuring component, which not only enables, but even encourages this partitioning.

In Oberon-2, the partitioning of a solution into manageable parts appears as a separation of the program into separate modules each of which has a purpose. This process is called *modularization*.   *Modularization*

As each module has an interface defined by exporting types, variables, constants, and procedures, the design of interfaces plays a key role. On one hand, it should offer enough information to the client of a module to encourage great flexibility when using the imported module. On the other hand the client should not be overloaded with irrelevant module specific details and internal aspects of implementation. The interface should be designed using a "need to know" philosophy.

For example, if a client wants to sort an array of numbers he or she might wish to use the services provided by a module *Sort*. To do this, he or she must know how to pass on the data, how the sorted data are returned, if the length of the array is limited etc. It should not be important for the client to know which sorting algorithm is used inside the module. It is not necessary to make public the variables, data types and names that have been defined internally. By using the term "make public" we understand the right to read and in particular to write to variables, and call procedures.

Principle of information hiding

The basic strategy for this is suggested in the *principle of information hiding* [Par72]. The client should gain an abstract view of the module, which only provides the exported handling mechanisms defined in the interface. The module interface defines *what* the module provides. The hidden module defines *how* the offered services are provided.

The term module

This leads us to a description and clarification of the term module in software engineering terms:

> *A module is a collection of declarations, data, and procedures which is designed to provide a well defined and cohesive purpose or service. It has a clearly defined export interface through which its clients access and use its data and services. In turn the module may depend on other modules from which it imports, again via an explicitly defined interface.*
>
> *A module in Oberon-2 is also the unit of separate compilation of a program.*

Data encapsulation

The principle of information hiding is intended to prevent unintended access by a module's client to internal data. To achieve this, adequate procedures for data access and manipulation need to be provided. The overall effect is that the data is "encapsulated" in the module; this concept is often referred to as data encapsulation.

The *abstract data structure* is a mechanism for encapsulating data and can be realized as a module with exported access procedures.

Example for an abstract data structure

As an example, we want to implement a buffer for holding data of a specified type. One or more clients can store or fetch the data in it. (Note that to simplify the example we have ignored the complexities introduced by any need for multiple concurrent access.)

FIFO buffer

The data management scheme is based upon the FIFO principle (*first in - first out*). The data is taken from the buffer in the same order that it was stored there in the first place.

In software design terms we proceed *top down* and define the module with the declarations, data structure, and operations on it before defining the details of how it works:

```
MODULE Buffer;

CONST
   QMAX= 100;                          (*maximum number of elements*)

TYPE
   ElemT: INTEGER;      (*data type for the buffered elements*)
```

```
PROCEDURE Insert (e:ElemT): BOOLEAN;
PROCEDURE Remove (VAR e:ElemT): BOOLEAN;
PROCEDURE IsEmpty (): BOOLEAN
PROCEDURE IsFull (): BOOLEAN;

END Buffer.
```

This abstract view provides sufficient information for the client to use it. It includes the maximum buffer capacity $QMAX$, the data type for the elements in the buffer and all procedures for storage and removal and for inquiring about the buffer state. The details of how the data structure is implemented are hidden from the client because the client simply does not need to know them in order to use the module. This is an example of information hiding. *Information hiding*

In order to use this module in a project under *POW!* it is enough to have the compiled code of the module. The source code does not need to be made public apart from the module interface definition. But this is not the real point. It is important that the client can access the buffer *only* by calling the exported functions; in this way the *integrity* of the module and its data cannot be compromised by the client and so the principle of information hiding is realized.

The buffer is implemented at a detailed level as a ring buffer using an array of the length $QMAX$. *Ring buffer*

The ring buffer consists of an array *buffer* which can store a number $QMAX$ of data elements of the defined data type (here: *ElemT*). A new element is stored at the position defined by the index *write* (*write* therefore points to the next element). The variable *read* contains the index of the element to read and is set to the next element after every reading process.

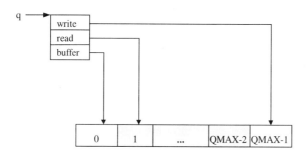

Fig. 38: Principle of a ring buffer

This data structure is called ring buffer because the index variables *read* and *write* are set to the beginning of the buffer (index 0) after the last buffer element (index $QMAX$-1) has been read or written, thus storage is reused after it is no longer required (because of a remove operation). Thus the FIFO principle is always adhered to.

```
MODULE Buffer;                 (*abstract data structure: ring buffer*)

CONST
   QMAX= 100;

TYPE
   ElemT*= INTEGER;                                       (*exported*)

   QueueT= RECORD
      elems: INTEGER;                (*number of stored elements*)
      read,write: INTEGER;                    (*storage indices*)
      buffer: ARRAY QMAX OF ElemT;        (*the buffer storage*)
   END;

VAR
   q: QueueT;

(*checks if structure is empty*)
PROCEDURE IsEmpty* (): BOOLEAN;                           (*exported*)
BEGIN
   RETURN q.elems=0;
END IsEmpty;

(*checks if structure is full*)
PROCEDURE IsFull* (): BOOLEAN;                            (*exported*)
BEGIN
   RETURN q.elems=QMAX;
END IsFull;

(*inserts an element into the data structure*)
PROCEDURE Insert* (elem:ElemT): BOOLEAN;                  (*exported*)
BEGIN
   IF ~IsFull() THEN                    (*ensure its not full*)
      q.buffer[q.write]:=elem;                        (*store it*)
      q.write:=(q.write+1) MOD QMAX;
      INC(q.elems);                        (*update the index*)
      RETURN TRUE;                (*update number of elements*)
   ELSE
      RETURN FALSE;                               (*was full*)
   END;
END Insert;

(*reads an element of the data structure*)
PROCEDURE Remove* (VAR elem:ElemT): BOOLEAN;      (*exported*)
BEGIN
   IF ~IsEmpty() THEN
      elem:=q.buffer[q.read];               (*remove the data*)
      q.read:=(q.read+1) MOD QMAX;       (*update the index*)
      DEC(q.elems);
      RETURN TRUE;
   ELSE
      RETURN FALSE;                    (*buffer was empty*)
   END;
END Remove;

(*initialization of the module*)
BEGIN
   q.read:=0;
   q.write:=0;
   q.elems:=0;
END Buffer.
```

An example of the use of this abstract data structure is shown here:

```
MODULE Ex19;    (*test program for ring buffer data structure*)    Ex19.mod
IMPORT In,Out,Buffer;

PROCEDURE ProgMain*;                                   (*exported*)
VAR
   e: Buffer.ElemT;
   cmd: INTEGER;
BEGIN
   In.Echo(TRUE);

   REPEAT
      (*request the next operation*)
      Out.String("0 or END button=quit, 1=Insert, ");
      Out.String("2=Remove, 3=Empty, 4=Full: ");
      In.Int(cmd);
      Out.Ln;

      CASE cmd OF
         1: (*insert into the structure*)
            In.Prompt("Enter a number: ");
            In.Int(e);
            IF In.Done THEN
              IF ~Buffer.Insert(e) THEN
                Out.String("Error: Buffer is full!");
              END;
            END;
            Out.Ln;

       | 2: (*read from the buffer*)
            IF Buffer.Remove(e) THEN
              Out.String("Element: ");
              Out.Int(e,0);
            ELSE
              Out.String("Error: Buffer is empty!");
            END;
            Out.Ln;

       | 3: (*checks if structure is empty*)
            IF Buffer.IsEmpty() THEN
              Out.String("Buffer is empty");
            ELSE
              Out.String("Buffer is not empty");
            END;
            Out.Ln;

       | 4: (*checks if structure is full*)
            IF Buffer.IsFull() THEN
              Out.String("Buffer is full");
            ELSE
              Out.String("Buffer is not full");
            END;
            Out.Ln;
      ELSE
         (*request to quit or invalid response*)
      END;

      Out.Ln;
   UNTIL (In.Done=FALSE) OR (cmd=0);    (*user wants to quit*)
END ProgMain;

END Ex19.
```

The client can only access the data which is essential to take advantage of the predefined module. However, with this particular design the module is limited to a single data structure (the hidden variable *q*) and is only suitable for use in sequential programs.

4.12.3 Abstract data types

Clearly it would be an advantage if the design could be improved to cope with storing any data type. The data structure *QueueT* defined in Ex19 above limits this possibility. But is it possible to create more than one instance of such a data structure with our module? In fact this would be impossible because data type *QueueT* is not exported!

ADT   This leads us to the quite natural generalization of abstract data structures, i.e. to *abstract data types*. They differ from abstract data structures as they can manage any number of instances of data structures. So an abstract data type is a module which provides services to its client on data instances supplied by the client.

Data encapsulation   Using an Abstract Data Type (ADT), the data manipulation is hidden inside the module and so can only be processed via access procedures also provided by the module. In addition, the module encapsulates the data and is responsible for correctly setting the initial state of the data. Of course the module may service one or more instances of data defined from the ADT by its clients.

The first step consists of the definition and export of the required type declarations. To enforce information hiding only the name of the data type is exported but not the details of its structure.

```
TYPE
   QueueT*= RECORD                              (*exported*)
      elems: INTEGER;
      read,write: INTEGER;
      buffer: ARRAY QMAX OF ElemT;
   END;
```

Now a client of this ADT is in a position to generate one or more buffers:

```
VAR
   q1,q2,q3: Buffer.QueueT;
```

Procedural approach   The next issue to be resolved is how to indicate which buffer should be processed with the modules procedures *(Insert, Remove, ...)*. The most obvious way - the *procedural approach* - is to extend the parameter list of the functions with an explicit parameter which specifies the data instance. For reasons of efficiency, the data structure is usually passed as a *VAR* parameter here as otherwise large data structures would need to be copied literally to and from each procedure.

```
PROCEDURE Insert* (VAR q:QueueT; elem:ElemT): BOOLEAN;
PROCEDURE Remove* (VAR q:QueueT; VAR elem:ElemT): BOOLEAN;
PROCEDURE IsEmpty*(VAR q:QueueT): BOOLEAN;
PROCEDURE IsFull* (VAR q:QueueT): BOOLEAN;
```

There is no need for a global declaration of the instance of the data structure *q* inside the module, as the VAR parameter "q" specifies the data instance to be used.

Instead of the data structure being initialized during initialization of the module a special access procedure *Init* is called explicitly for initializing the particular instance of the buffer. The module containing the definition of the data type *QueueT* takes the following form:

```
MODULE Buffer;                                                          Buffer.mod
(*abstract data type: ring buffer, used by Ex20.mod*)

CONST
   QMAX= 100;

TYPE
   ElemT*= INTEGER;                                      (*exported*)

   QueueT*= RECORD                                       (*exported*)
      elems: INTEGER;
      read,write: INTEGER;
      buffer: ARRAY QMAX OF ElemT;
   END;

(*initialization of a variable of the data type QueueT*)
PROCEDURE Init* (VAR q:QueueT);                          (*exported*)
BEGIN
   q.elems:=0;
   q.read:=0;
   q.write:=0;
END Init;

(*insert an element elem into q*)
PROCEDURE Insert* (VAR q:QueueT;elem:ElemT): BOOLEAN;
BEGIN                                                    (*exported*)
   IF q.elems<QMAX THEN               (*is the buffer full?*)
      q.buffer[q.write]:=elem;            (*store the data*)
      q.write:=(q.write+1) MOD QMAX;      (*update the index*)
      INC(q.elems);                    (*and number of items*)
      RETURN TRUE;
   ELSE
      RETURN FALSE;                              (*buffer full*)
   END;
END Insert;

(*read an element elem from q*)
PROCEDURE Remove* (VAR q:QueueT;
                   VAR elem:ElemT): BOOLEAN;
BEGIN                                                    (*exported*)
   IF q.elems>0 THEN                  (*is the buffer empty?*)
      elem:=q.buffer[q.read];             (*remove the date*)
      q.read:=(q.read+1) MOD QMAX;        (*update the index*)
      DEC(q.elems);                    (*and number of items*)
      RETURN TRUE;
   ELSE
      RETURN FALSE;                             (*buffer empty*)
   END;
END Remove;
```

```
(*check if q is empty*)
PROCEDURE IsEmpty* (VAR q:QueueT): BOOLEAN;        (*exported*)
BEGIN
   RETURN q.elems=0;
END IsEmpty;

(*check if q is full*)
PROCEDURE IsFull* (VAR q:QueueT): BOOLEAN;         (*exported*)
BEGIN
   RETURN q.elems=QMAX;
END IsFull;

END Buffer.
```

An interactive test harness program for a variable *q* of the abstract data type *QueueT* has the following form:

Ex20.mod

```
MODULE Ex20;                      (*test program for module Buffer*)
IMPORT In,Out,Buffer;                       (*import and rename*)

PROCEDURE ProgMain*;
VAR
   e: Buffer.ElemT;
   cmd: INTEGER;
   q: Buffer.QueueT;                  (*create the ADT variable!*)
BEGIN
   In.Echo(TRUE);

   Buffer.Init(q);                          (*initialize queue*)
   REPEAT
      Out.String("0 or END=Quit, 1=Insert, 2=Remove: ");
      In.Int(cmd);;
      Out.Ln;

      CASE cmd OF
         1: (*insert into structure*)
            Out.String("Enter a number: ");
            In.Int(e);
            IF In.Done THEN
              IF ~Buffer.Insert(q,e) THEN
                Out.String("Error: Buffer is full!");
              END;
            END;
            Out.Ln;

       | 2: (*read from the buffer*)
            IF Buffer.Remove(q,e) THEN
              Out.String("Element: ");
              Out.Int(e,0);
            ELSE
              Out.String("Error: Buffer is empty!");
            END;
            Out.Ln;
      ELSE
      END;              (*any other character is ignored here*);

      Out.Ln;
   UNTIL (In.Done=FALSE) OR (cmd=0);   (*user wants to quit*)
END ProgMain;

END Ex20.
```

This is a good point to mention that in Oberon-2 there is a second way to define abstract data types using the *object-oriented approach* which uses the concept of *type-bound procedures*.

Object-oriented approach

In Oberon-2 it is possible to tightly bind access methods to the variables of a type defined by the user. In this case the types and the corresponding procedures are called *classes,* and the procedures themselves *methods*. In Oberon-2 we talk about *type-bound procedures* in this context because of the association between a data type and its corresponding procedure.

Methods

An *instance* of a class is called an *object*.

Instance

Oberon-2 makes it possible to apply this idea to *RECORD* types and this provides great flexibility. The special benefits of classes become obvious if records are extended such that the methods of the base class are inherited, becoming a part of the derived class automatically.

Object

The type binding is explicitly stated between the keyword *PROCEDURE* and the name of the procedure:

```
PROCEDURE (VAR q:QueueT) IsFull* (): BOOLEAN;
```

The application of a method *Proc(...)* to an instance of a class (object) *o* is syntactically formulated as

```
o.Proc(…);
```

These concepts are at the heart of object-oriented programming *(OOP)*. We will go into this subject much more deeply in a later chapter, for now here is the module interface for the abstract data type *QueueT* implemented with type-bound procedures without further comment:

```
MODULE Buffer;
TYPE
   ElemT*= INTEGER;
   QueueT*= RECORD
      elems: INTEGER;
      read,write: INTEGER;
      buffer: ARRAY QMAX OF ElemT;
   END;
PROCEDURE (VAR q:QueueT) Init*;
PROCEDURE (VAR q:QueueT) Insert* (e:ElemT): BOOLEAN;
PROCEDURE (VAR q:QueueT) Remove* (VAR e:ElemT): BOOLEAN;
PROCEDURE (VAR q:QueueT) IsEmpty* (): BOOLEAN;
PROCEDURE (VAR q:QueueT) IsFull* (): BOOLEAN;

END Buffer.
```

4.12.4 Modularization

Modularization is the process of partitioning a problem or its solution into separate parts which localize complexity or kinds of functionality. In Oberon-2 the resulting modules are ordered in a *module hierarchy*.

Modularization

You already have the technical knowledge of how to implement modules and their clients in Oberon-2 but so far we have not discussed how to find the modules for a given problem.

Unfortunately there is no recipe for modularization. There is not even a rational measure for the quality of existing modules because the quality of a set of modules depends on many often conflicting factors. However, if we know what modules need to be used for, there is a better chance to design ones which are valuable for the programs we want to write.

Reasons for implementing modules

• Reuse of code

This is the most intuitive reason for modularization. Instead of developing similar code serveral times, the code can be packaged into a module and then use the functionality of the module for further projects.

All functions in a module should be logically coherent and the name of the module should describe its purpose (e.g. "RandomNumbers").

• Information hiding

The implementation of a module's functionality should be hidden from its clients. There is no need for users of the module *RandomNumbers* to know how the random numbers are generated, they only need procedures to retrieve random numbers. Therefore the programmer has to export only those constants, variables, and data structures which are necessary for clients to use the module.

Implementation details should be hidden because this makes it possible to change the implementation of the module without changing its clients. This technique is often used for stepwise development of a program. In the early stages, a first quick implementation of a module may be implemented and then later optimized for speed or memory consumption.

Abstract data structures and abstract data types are examples of information hiding. In both cases the implementation of the data structure is hidden and only functions for creating, accessing, and removing the data structure are exported.

• Unit testing

Most modules can be tested independent from the rest of the program. Testing of parts of programs (modules) therefore can be done before completing the implementation of the whole program. Special test programs are written for this purpose, which are not bound to a specific client of the module and can be reused later on to verify improved or rewritten implementations of the module.

If the module is well designed then it should be possible to test it via its interface (information hiding). The module is used like a "black box" as its internal workings are hidden from its users.

It is advisable to use different programmers for coding and debugging, because the programmer of a module often tends to generate test patterns that confirm his or her intentions, rather than stressing the module in a practical way.

- **Easily readable programs**

Modular programs are easier to read and therefore more readily understood than programs in single files. You can get a first impression of the program by looking at the main module. This top-level module shows the main structure of the program. Interesting details can then be examined by reviewing the imported modules.

A useful tool which can greatly help in understanding a program is a *module hierarchy diagram* (see Figure 39). It starts with the main module, lists the modules of the program, and displays the dependencies between them. The figure also shows that the modules at the top of the hierarchy describe the project at a higher level of abstraction than the modules at the lower end of the hierarchy.

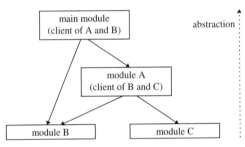

Fig. 39: Module hierarchy diagram

Finding the modules

Now that we have given the most important reasons for using modules, here are some hints for finding the modules for partitioning the solution to a problem (this process is often called *decomposition*):

1. Analyze the problem

This is the most important rule when starting a new software project. *Think through the problem and try to find its structures before writing a single line of code!* It is much easier to implement a program if you really know what you want to implement. It is essential to know the major issues of the project and to be able to imagine how the system could be built.

2. Look for data structures

The key to the structure of the solution to a problem can often be found in the structure of its data. Creating a module for handling this data leads to a good initial modularization almost automatically. Do not forget to implement separate modules for each data structure (information hiding). Always try to generate abstract data types or to reuse ones that already exist!

3. Modularize the user interface

Further good candidates for modules can be found in the user interface of a program. If you have already separated modules by data analysis, you can try to partition the rest of the program according to the program's user interaction tasks: Create a module for each function of the system, but try to keep dependencies between the modules as small as possible.

Problems

The rules suggested above should help for your first programs. Although they are no substitute for experience, we hope they can help you avoid a few problems. There are situations, however, where modularization is difficult or even seems to be impossible:

- **Circular dependencies of modules**

Assume two modules A and B:

Module A	Module B
exports data structure A	exports data structure B
uses data structure B	uses data structure A

This construction would not be possible in Oberon-2 because the language does not allow circular import of modules.

For a correct implementation in Oberon-2, you must either implement both data structures in the same module (loses information hiding between the two and makes the module more complicated to read) or implement generic data structures (with pointers, maybe object-oriented, as explained in Chapter 5).

- **Input and output**

One should be very careful about using input and output procedures liberally from within modules, because this makes the module dependent on the input and output modules and functions used and hence it is less flexible and reusable.

Example: if a module implements an abstract data type *queue*, then exported functions of this module are *Insert*, *Delete*, *Remove*. Including a function *Print* which uses the *Out* module would not be a good idea because the queue module could then only be used together with the module *Out*, even if *Print* were never called.

4.13 Pointer types

4.13.1 Basic ideas

So far we have only been concerned with *static* data structures. The size of data has always been determined by the type definition and their existence by the scope of the variables. *(Static)*

It is therefore essential to think about the number of array elements in advance and then choose the dimension of the variables accordingly. However, when using *open* arrays as parameters to procedures it becomes the clients (procedures) responsibility to define the required dimensions.

But there are many applications where the maximum number of elements is unknown, e.g., a data structure where the number of components is known only at runtime.

As an example, let's discuss the implementation of the ring buffer mentioned in the previous section. There, the maximum capacity of the buffer is limited by the number *QMAX* and this had to be made public by exporting the constant. Even if a smaller buffer were sufficient, space for *QMAX* elements would be reserved, and if a larger buffer were needed the program would need to be changed and recompiled!

What is our goal? It should be possible to reserve space for the buffer *dynamically* based on the current needs of the program: if space is needed for one more element it will be reserved, if an element is deleted the corresponding memory will be released. *(Dynamic)*

There is an alternative: by using abstract data types it becomes possible at least to state the expected maximum number of elements required when an instance of a data structure is initialized.

In general, the scheme works as follows:

A special variable is created which *points* to an object of a certain type. An instance of the desired type is created at runtime and is therefore of definable size; the special variable now points to the newly created instance variable. For this reason, we will call this kind of variable a *pointer* (data type *POINTER*). *(Pointer)*

When we create a pointer the object it will refer to does not yet exist. In this case our pointer has the special value *NIL*. *(NIL)*

There is a predefined function *NEW* which is used to allocate memory for the data on request. *(NEW)*

A pointer does not contain a value in the normal sense of the word, but information about location of the referenced data. A pointer type is declared by putting the keywords *POINTER TO* in front of the definition of the data type as follows *(POINTER TO)*

```
TYPE
   PersonP= POINTER TO PersonT;
   PersonT= RECORD
      name: ARRAY 32 OF CHAR;
      age: INTEGER;
   END;

VAR
   p: PersonP; (*also ... p: POINTER TO PersonT*)

BEGIN
   (*is the pointer assigned NIL automatically?*)
   p:=NIL;

   NEW(p);
   (*a record of the type PersonT is generated in the
     memory and p points at it.*)
```

Initialization In the above example one of the comments contains the question "is a pointer variable automatically assigned the value *NIL* when you start the program?". The answer depends on the state of the setting **Initialize Pointers** in the dialog **Options/Compiler**. If the option is active all pointers are automatically initialized with *NIL*, otherwise the initial value is not defined. To exclude all possibilities for error the following examples are based upon the assumption that the mentioned option need not be set. However, it is always advisable in practice to leave it set just in case you forget to initialize a pointer variable.

Dereferencing So how do we access the data that is hidden in the record of the type *PersonT* generated by a pointer *p*? This is achieved by *dereferencing* the pointer using the syntactic form *p^*.

Note carefully the difference between:

- *p* which is the name of a pointer that is referenced as objects of the type *PersonT* by the following declaration:

```
VAR
   p: POINTER TO PersonT;
```

  It can only point to objects of precisely the declared type. Thus, *NEW(p)* can allocate the required memory and can bind the pointer variable *p* to the dynamically created record of type *PersonT*.

- *p^* which returns the contents of the dynamically created variable that *p* points to.

  So in this case *p^.name* is a variable of the type *ARRAY 32 OF CHAR* and *p^.age* a number of the type *INTEGER*. We can now write statements such as

```
p^.age:=27;
i:=p^.age;
p^.name:="Isaac Newton";
Out.String(p^.name);
```

Let's take another step and create some variables which represent two composers

```
VAR
    p1,p2,temp: POINTER TO PersonT;

NEW(p1);
p1^.name:="W.A.Mozart";
p1^.age:=35;

NEW(p2);
p2^.name:="F.J.Haydn";
p2^.age:=77;

temp:=p1;

Out.String(temp^.name);
```

The string "W.A.Mozart" will be printed when the program is run because *Assignment*
the assignment *temp:=p1* results in the contents of the pointer *p1* (only the pointer, not the data!) being copied to the pointer *temp* which now also points to the same variable in memory. It is important that the pointers *p1* and *temp* reference the same type.

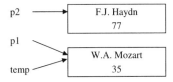

Fig. 39: An example using pointers

From now on we will use the term "pointer" for variables as used in the assignment *temp:=p1*. But it should be noted that no arithmetic operations are possible with variables of the type *POINTER*. The only operations allowed are to check for equality, inequality, or *NIL* and to assign them. The following example illustrates this:

```
temp:=p1;                    (*exchange two pointer references*)
p1:=p2;
p2:=temp;

Out.String(p1^.name);
```

Now *p1^.name* refers to the string "F.J. Haydn" and *p2^.name* to "W.A. Mozart".

If temp is assigned *NIL* then

```
Out.String(temp^.name);
```

would cause the program to terminate. The same thing would happen when attempting to dereference *p1^* without having generated the corresponding data with *NEW* first.

As both *p1^* and *p2^* point to a variable of the type *PersonT* the following assignment is allowed and sensible:

```
VAR
    musician: PersonT;

musician:=p1^;
```

where the difference between the pointer *p1* and the variable *p1^*, which *p1* points to, becomes more obvious. In order to make pointer type clear in the rest of the book the following naming convention will be used: suffix *P* introduces the names of pointer types (as opposed to *T* for other data types).

Address   Pointers contain references to the location of variables (the memory *addresses* of these generated objects). When a dynamic variable is allocated with the function *NEW* then a named pointer to it is used as a reference to an anonymous (unnamed) variable. More precisely, the allocated memory is anonymous (unnamed) and is only accessible via the name of the pointer variable which holds its location. This is in contrast to the explicit declaration of static variables *(VAR x: AnyT)* with a fixed name.

In the spirit of its overall simplicity Oberon-2 only provides the minimum necessary language features for making use of pointers and the operations involving them.

> *Pointer variables may only point to record types or array types. They contain the location reference to the record variable or an array which is dynamically generated. The standard procedure NEW(p) is used for generating variables of the allowed pointer base types.*

> *NEW(p) allocates memory for the variable p^. If no more free memory is available then the pointer p is set to NIL (this is a convention of the Pow! system; in the definition of the programming language this aspect has been left undefined).*

Pointers to arrays

Let's start with some examples by discussing the use of pointers with arrays:

```
CONST
    MAX= 100;

TYPE
    FieldP= POINTER TO FieldT;
    FieldT= ARRAY MAX OF INTEGER;

VAR
    field: FieldP;
    storage: BOOLEAN;
    i,j: INTEGER;

NEW(field);
IF field#NIL THEN
    DoProc(field);
END;
```

The above code declares a pointer variable *field* which can point to data of the type *FieldT*. Hence, because of the type FieldT, every array dynamically produced with *NEW(field)* consists of *MAX* numbers of the type *INTEGER*. The access to the single elements of the *field^* is obtained by dereferencing:

```
field^[0],field^[1],…,field^[MAX-1]
```

Oberon-2 permits a particularly convenient simplification of the syntax by allowing *field^[i]* to be replaced by *field[i]*.

Short form

For the beginner this may sometimes cause some confusion because you must always be aware of the dereferencing hidden in this abbreviation. However, the advantages of the simplification become obvious in procedures where a pointer needs to be passed as a parameter to a dynamically produced array. In the following program fragment the parameter *f* can be declared either as *f: FieldP* or as *VAR f: FieldT* without changing the source code of the procedure:

```
PROCEDURE Sum (f:FieldP): INTEGER;
VAR i,sum: INTEGER;
BEGIN
   sum:=0;
   FOR i:=0 TO LEN(f)-1 DO
      sum:=sum+f[i];                    (*actually sum:=sum+f^[i]*)
   END;
   RETURN sum;
END Sum;
```

This is a good point to review the topic of *VAR* and *value* parameters again.

When parameters were discussed it was explained that with a *VAR* parameter only the address of the current parameter is passed to the procedure. It is therefore possible to work directly with the "original" and modifications can never be lost. With *value* parameters a copy of the parameter's value is made and the changes made to it do not affect the original. Now keep in mind that pointer variables ultimately contain the reference addresses of the data they point at.

VAR and value parameters

For example to write a procedure *Zap* which sets all elements of an array to 0 there are two almost identical alternatives:

```
(*passing the field as a VAR parameter*)
PROCEDURE Zap1 (VAR f:FieldT): INTEGER;
VAR i: INTEGER;
BEGIN
   FOR i:=0 TO LEN(f)-1 DO
      f[i]:=0;
   END;
END Zap1;

(*passing a pointer to the field*)
PROCEDURE Zap2 (f:FieldP): INTEGER;
VAR i: INTEGER;
BEGIN
   FOR i:=0 TO LEN(f)-1 DO
      f[i]:=0; (*actually f^[i]:=0*)
   END;
END Zap2;
```

Pointers to open arrays

Length of an
array

Pointer variables provide a convenient way to access open arrays. They make it possible to declare arrays which will only have their actual length fixed when the function *NEW* is called.

LEN

The actual length of an open array can be found out using the predefined function *LEN*. The result it returns is the number of elements of the array.

```
TYPE
    FieldP= POINTER TO FieldT;
    FieldT= ARRAY OF INTEGER;

VAR
    field,other,temp: FieldP;

...
(*now an array of the type FieldT must be generated
  at the same time the number of elements are fixed*)
NEW(field,32);

(*field now points at 32 INTEGER elements*)
field^[0]:=0;
field[1]:=1;
field[LEN(field)-1]:=2;                          (*the last element*)
```

and once again the advantage of being able to write *field[i]* in place of *field^[i]* becomes clear.

For a little practice try to work out the effect of the following statements:

```
NEW(other,100);
(*points to an open array of 100 elements*)
other:=field;
```

This program fragment illustrates a problem in connection with anonymous variables which can only be referenced by pointers. After the assignment *other:=field* the pointer *other* points to the same array of 32 elements just as *field* does. This assignment is allowed as both pointers are of the type *FieldP*. The array created with *NEW(other,100)* is no longer accessible as its corresponding pointer has been overwritten. To avoid this the pointer should be saved in another variable:

```
NEW(other,100);
temp:=other;    (*save for later use*)
other:=field;
```

Example of pointers to open arrays

Here again is the example, presented earlier, of a data structure used to create a ring buffer. This time a pointer to an open array is used for the implementation of the buffer.

The elements are stored in an open array of the type *BufferT* along with a pointer of the type *BufferP* by declaring the data types.

```
TYPE
   BufferT= ARRAY OF ElemT;
   BufferP= POINTER TO BufferT;
```

The ring buffer (or *queue*) itself is declared as   *Queue*

```
TYPE
   QueueP= POINTER TO QueueT;
   QueueT= RECORD
      elems: INTEGER;
      read,write: LONGINT;
      buffer: BufferP;
   END;
```

If we now write

```
VAR
   queue: QueueP;

NEW(queue);
```

memory for a data structure variable of type *QueueT* will be reserved, however, *queue* does not yet contain fields for storing the elements as the *queue.buffer* field does not yet point to a variable which has been dynamically allocated.

So we add:

```
NEW(queue.buffer,100);
```

and from now on the elements may be accessed with *queue.buffer[i]* or *queue.buffer^[i]*.

In order to make your program robust you should check after each *NEW*   *ASSERT*
statement whether the required memory has in fact been reserved. Its value would be *NIL* if it was not possible to allocate the new variable. This is easily achieved using an *ASSERT* statement which evaluates the result of the expression passed to it as a parameter and terminates the program if it is FALSE; if all is well (i.e., TRUE) it simply returns.

```
ASSERT(queue#NIL);
ASSERT(queue.buffer#NIL);
```

These steps are brought together in the procedure *Init(size:INTEGER)*. When a client calls this procedure, the queue and the open array referencing it by a pointer become accessible:

```
MODULE Queue;                                                    Queue.mod
(*abstract data type: queue*)

TYPE
   ElemT*= INTEGER;

   BufferP= POINTER TO BufferT;
   BufferT= ARRAY OF ElemT;

   QueueP*= POINTER TO QueueT;
   QueueT= RECORD
      elems: INTEGER;
```

```
            read,write: LONGINT;
            buffer: BufferP;
        END;

    (*allocate memory for Queue and Buffer
       Note: queue is a VAR parameter!*)
    PROCEDURE Init* (VAR queue:QueueP; size:INTEGER);
    BEGIN
        NEW(queue);                         (*new queue is allocated*)
        queue.read:=0;                           (*queue^.read:=0*)
        queue.write:=0;                          (*queue^.write:=0*)
        queue.elems:=0;
        NEW(queue.buffer,size);              (*create the buffer*)
    END Init;

    (*insert data into a queue*)
    PROCEDURE Insert* (queue:QueueP; elem:ElemT): BOOLEAN;
    BEGIN
        IF queue.elems<LEN(queue.buffer^) THEN
            queue.buffer[queue.write]:=elem;
            queue.write:=(queue.write+1) MOD
                        LEN(queue.buffer^);
            INC(queue.elems);
            RETURN TRUE;
        ELSE
            RETURN FALSE;
        END;
    END Insert;

    (*read the oldest data of a queue*)
    PROCEDURE Remove* (queue:QueueP; VAR elem:ElemT): BOOLEAN;
    BEGIN
        IF queue.elems>0 THEN
            elem:=queue.buffer[queue.read];
            queue.read:=(queue.read+1) MOD LEN(queue.buffer^);
            DEC(queue.elems);
            RETURN TRUE;
        ELSE
            RETURN FALSE;
        END;
    END Remove;

    (*count the elements of a queue*)
    PROCEDURE Elems* (queue:QueueP): INTEGER;
    BEGIN
        RETURN queue.elems;
    END Elems;

END Queue.
```

The client *Ex21.mod* of this module is almost the same as the version of the previous section and is therefore not printed here, but it is provided on the enclosed disc. Note that the procedure *Init* must be called before you use a variable of the type *QueueP*.

```
VAR
    q: Queue.QueueP;

BEGIN
    Queue.Init(q,10);
```

4.13.2 Linear lists

One particular aspect of the previous example is worth noting: the pointer *queue* points to a variable which itself contains a pointer *buffer* and which in turn points to another object *queue.buffer^*.

This structure can be repeated so that the pointer of the first object of the type *T* can reference another object of the same type *T*, which itself points to a third object, etc. For this to be possible the language must allow such structures to be defined in terms of themselves, i.e., recursively; for example,

```
TYPE
   ListP= POINTER TO ListT;
   ListT= RECORD
      key: KeyT;
      next: ListP;              (*relies on ListP and ListT above*)
   END;

VAR
   first: ListP;
```

Now we have introduced the *linear list* data type. It can be graphically illustrated as follows: *List*

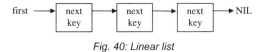

Fig. 40: Linear list

The end of the chain is marked by *NIL* and thus, *first:=NIL* represents an empty list.

Linear lists constitute the basis for *dynamic data types*. The underlying concept of using pointers to recursively reference elements of the same type is developed later for other data types.   *Dynamic data types*

The term "dynamic" reflects the fact that a new element of the list is only created when it is actually needed. The details of what happens to elements which are no longer needed are discussed later.

First we demonstrate the vital step "linking in a new list element" graphically: *Insert*

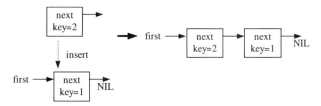

Fig. 41: Insert in a linear list

From the diagram you can see that a new element is inserted at the beginning of the list, just after the *list head*.   *List head*

LIFO buffer   By working in the reverse order, elements can be removed with the result that a dynamic data type following the LIFO principle *(last in - first out)* is created; this is often called a *stack*.

List.mod
```
MODULE List;
(*dynamic data structure: stack *)
(*(last in - first out principle) used in Ex22.mod*)

TYPE
   KeyT*= INTEGER;

   (*data structure ListT is not exported!*)
   ListP= POINTER TO ListT;
   ListT= RECORD
      key: KeyT;
      next: ListP;
   END;

VAR
   first: ListP;                  (*pointer to the first element*)

(*check if list is empty*)
PROCEDURE Empty* (): BOOLEAN;
BEGIN
   RETURN first=NIL;
END Empty;

(*insert new data into the list*)
PROCEDURE Insert* (elem:KeyT): BOOLEAN;
VAR temp: ListP;
BEGIN
   NEW(temp);                     (*generate new list element*)
   IF temp#NIL THEN
      temp.key:=elem;                             (*enter data*)
      temp.next:=first;        (*and insert at the beginning*)
      first:=temp;
      RETURN TRUE;
   ELSE
      RETURN FALSE;             (*allocation failed, no memory*)
   END;
END Insert;

(*remove first element of the list*)
PROCEDURE Remove* (VAR elem:KeyT): BOOLEAN;
VAR temp: ListP;
BEGIN
   IF  Empty() THEN             (*otherwise nothing to remove *)
      temp:=first;
      elem:=temp.key;
      first:=temp.next;
      DISPOSE(temp);       (*memory release, see coming section*)
      RETURN TRUE;
   ELSE
      RETURN FALSE;                          (*list was empty*)
   END;
END Remove;
```

```
(*count list elements*)
PROCEDURE Count* (): INTEGER;
VAR
    temp: ListP;
    count: INTEGER;
BEGIN
    count:=0;
    temp:=first;

    (*sequence through all elements*)
    WHILE temp#NIL DO
        INC(count);                                          (*count*)
        temp:=temp.next;                          (*next element*)
    END;
    RETURN count;
END Count;

(*delete all list elements*)
PROCEDURE Zap*;
VAR
    done: BOOLEAN;
    dummy: KeyT;
BEGIN                       (*assumes the list is correctly formed*)
    REPEAT
        done:=Remove(dummy);
    UNTIL ~done;
END Zap;

(*initialization of the module body*)
BEGIN
    first:=NIL;
END List.
```

For the sake of completeness the output of the browser is shown below. From the parameters to all the procedures, it is evident that this is an example of an *abstract data structure*. Also, there is no procedure available for the client to generate a list.

```
DEFINITION OF MODULE List;

TYPE
    KeyT*=INTEGER;

PROCEDURE Empty*():BOOLEAN;
PROCEDURE Insert*(elem:KeyT):BOOLEAN;
PROCEDURE Remove*(VAR elem:KeyT):BOOLEAN;
PROCEDURE Count*():INTEGER;
PROCEDURE Zap*();

END List.
```

Memory release with *DISPOSE* and garbage collection

The access procedure *Remove* made use of a predefined procedure *DISPOSE(p)* with *p#NIL*. At this point we would like to draw your attention to a significant difference between Oberon-2 with the operating system Oberon and the *POW!* environment under Windows. In the Oberon system there is no *DISPOSE*. This function is provided by an automatic memory

DISPOSE

release (*garbage collection*) which is totally controlled by the system, without the programmer being involved.

It does not make much sense if on the one hand dynamic data types are generated with pointers to meet current demands but on the other hand cannot be released for further use once they are no longer required.

POW! supports both memory release methods, garbage collection and *DISPOSE*:

- It has built-in garbage collection (corresponding linker option must be set!), which becomes active from time to time and in critical situations (when there is not enough memory left for an allocation request).

- In addition to this, the programmer may deallocate memory in the course of the program by using the predefined procedure *DISPOSE*. Although the use of *DISPOSE* is often a good choice - because the programmer knows best, when memory blocks are not needed any more - it is also a dangerous source of errors (memory is freed, but accessed later).

Dangling pointer   We must, however, give a warning: after a *DISPOSE* it is not possible to access the instance of the variable any more, even though the pointer still contains its memory location *(dangling pointer).*

This problem is easy to see, but at the same time can easily cause errors. When dynamic data structures are used in your programs it is very easy to make fatal mistakes, for example:

```
VAR
    p,q: POINTER TO AnyT;

NEW(p);
q:=p;                       (*now q and p point to the same object*)
DISPOSE(p);                         (*the memory is released*)
                    (*q now points to a non-existent structure*)
```

When working with linear lists or similar simple types, it is relatively easy to ensure that all the pointer variables are used correctly. However with more general data structures like directed graphs, where a varying number of pointers of elements may point to each node, there is a serious complication: you must keep track of all the pointer variables and be sure not to use them when the "shared" data structure is disposed of.

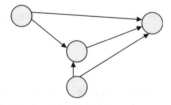

Fig. 42: A complex network data structure

Generally, a garbage collection routine can be written using one of the well established techniques such as introducing a reference counter for every node which is then checked before a desired memory release. If this counter is 0, no other pointers reference this variable and it may therefore be disposed of. Also, the counter must be incremented for each new reference (*NEW*, assignment).

Often a procedure for an automatic memory release is installed so that it is *Heap* called at several points in the program. It checks the memory region reserved for the dynamic memory management (the heap), collects all the bits and pieces of old data structures no longer referenced, and finally disposes of them (this is where the name *garbage collector* originates).

4.13.3 Pointer types and type extensions

When we were discussing record types we introduced the notion of type *Inheritance* extensions and identified them as the basis for the idea of inheritance. The extended type *inherits* the fields of its base type:

```
TYPE
   DateT= RECORD
      year,month,day: INTEGER;
   END;

   TimestampT= RECORD(DateT)
      hour,minute,second: INTEGER;
   END;
```

Such type extensions are consequently applied to pointers:

```
TYPE
   DateP= POINTER TO DateT;
   DateT= RECORD
      year,month,day: INTEGER;
   END;

   TimestampP= POINTER TO TimestampT;
   TimestampT= RECORD(DateT)
      hour,minute,second: INTEGER;
   END;
```

In this example, *TimestampT* is a direct extension of *DateT*, therefore *Extension* *TimestampP* is understood as an extension of *DateP*.

In general, we define:

> If bT *is an extension of* aT *and* aP=POINTER TO aT, *then the pointer type* bP *with* bP=POINTER TO bT *is an extension of* aP. *Conversely,* aP *is the base type of* bP.

Projection with pointers

Assignments make this more interesting, we now know that a *projection* *Projection* takes place when a variable of the base type is assigned a variable of an extended type

```
VAR
    date: DateT;
    timestamp: TimestampT;
```

If we assign the initial values

```
timestamp.second:=48;
timestamp.minute:=12;
timestamp.hour:=10;
timestamp.day:=31;
timestamp.month:=7;
timestamp.year:=1995;
```

the projection *date:=timestamp* has the effect that *date.day, date.month*, and *date.year* are assigned the corresponding values of *timestamp*, i.e. 31, 7, and 1995. The converse assignment *timestamp:=date* is not allowed and impossible, because fields like *hour* are not defined in *date* and would therefore have no defined values.

Now it is quite obvious how to use projection for pointer types:

```
VAR
    date: DateP;
    timestamp: TimestampP;
...
NEW(timestamp);
timestamp.year:=1994;
...
NEW(date);

date^:=timestamp^;
```

At this point, note the crucially important character "^"!

With *date^* and *timestamp^* the referenced data are accessed, and the assignment is executed using the projection rules.

Static and dynamic type

Assignment   The pointer assignment

```
date:=timestamp;
```

requires further explanation and clarification. At the first glance it is easy to explain: the effect is that *date* now points to a structure of the extend type *TimestampT*. Bearing in mind the strict type checking of Oberon-2 and the fact that the pointer of the type *DateP* has been declared as *POINTER TO DateT* we need to know what type *date* is after the assignment.

Static type   The type stated in the variable declaration is called the *static type* of the variable. The static type being the basis for type checking of assignments and operations at compile time.

If a variable of the type *DateT* is assigned a variable of the static type *TimestampT*, some fields are lost. If you assign *date:=timestamp*, no copy of the data structure values is made, it only has the effect that both *timestamp* and also *date* point to a structure of the data type *TimestampT*.

The consequence of the static typing now is that with *date* you only "see" the fields of *timestamp* declared in the static type definition: *date.year, date.month*, and *date.day* (or *date^.year, date^.month, date^.day*) but in contrast to the assignment *date^:=timestamp^* the values *hour, minute*, and *second* are not lost!

On the other hand, *date* was assigned a pointer of the type *TimestampP*. As a consequence we say that *date* is now of the *dynamic type TimestampP*.

Dynamic type

Generally speaking we find that:

Pointers to structures have a dynamic type as well as their static type. The static type is the type stated in the type declaration. Variables of structures have an identical static and dynamic type, the dynamic type of pointer variables is determined by assignments made at runtime. The dynamic type of the pointer depends on the structure referenced at runtime. It may be an extension of the static type according to the rules of assignments and type checks.

Type test

Oberon-2 offers the opportunity to discover the dynamic type of a pointer variable at run-time. This is what the *type test* is for.

IS

```
variable IS TestT
```

The type test returns *TRUE* if the tested variable is of the type *TestT* or an extension of it, otherwise the test returns *FALSE*.

Therefore, after the assignment *date:=timestamp* the test

```
date IS TimestampP
```

returns the value *TRUE* which can be used in a check like

```
IF date IS TimestampP THEN
    ...
ELSE
    ...
END;
```

A test *date IS DateP* always returns *TRUE*, because *date* is either of the type *DateP* initially declared or has been modified to a pointer of a type extended from DateP.

Type guard

Now imagine that we have another pointer variable *p* of the static type *DateP* and in the course of the program assignments such as *p:=date* or *p:=timestamp* have occurred.

The structure *p^* now has to be assigned new values. Assignments such as *p.year:=1995, p.month:=8*, and *p.day:=1* are allowed, as these fields are common to the base type and the extended type. But access to *p.hour, p.minute*, and *p.second* depends on the dynamic type.

However, a reference *p.hour* will not be accepted at compile time as the type check then is based on the static type.

Type guard   To avoid this problem a new concept called the *type guard* is used

```
p(TimeStampP)
```

Type check   Using the type guard compiler is informed that we "know" that the variable *p* will be a pointer of the dynamic type *TimestampP*. The type check is therefore passed over to runtime and the program is terminated with an appropriate error message if a type guard is invalid when it is encountered at run-time.

So we can write:

```
IF p IS TimestampP THEN
    p(TimestampP).hour:=20;
    p(TimestampP).minute:=19;
    p(TimestampP).second:=51;
END;
```

Example for pointers and type extension

The following example makes use of type guards and also leads us deeper into applications of dynamic types. The example goes a small step further and uses output procedures with pointers as parameters.

Keeping in mind that when a procedure is called the formal parameters are replaced by the relevant values of current ones, the same rules apply for this replacement as with an equivalent assignment. So when parameters are passed, the dynamic type of pointer variables needs to be taken into consideration and a type guard used if necessary.

In the next example we define a general list of persons *(PersonT)* who are identified by their names. However, as well as being suitable for administering data about people the list should also have an extended type for car holders *(CarHolderT)*. We therefore start off with the following data types:

```
TYPE
    PersonP= POINTER TO PersonT;
    PersonT= RECORD
        next: OwnerP;
        name: ARRAY 40 OF CHAR;
    END;

    CarHolderP= POINTER TO CarHolderT;
    CarHolderT= RECORD(PersonT)
        cartype: ARRAY 20 OF CHAR;
    END;
```

A concrete example for such a list is the following:

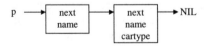

Fig. 43: Linear list with different elements

In principle, we do not know if a list element is of the type *PersonT* or *CarHolderT*. All combinations are allowed. Note that the pointer for the concatenation of the list is always of the base type *PersonP* and that it may be assigned the dynamic type *CarHolderP*.

Thus, for the output we must distinguish if the pointer dynamically shows to a structure of the type *PersonT* or of the type *CarHolderT*.

```
MODULE Ex23;                                                    Ex23.mod
(*simple program demonstrating type extension*)
IMPORT Out;

TYPE
   PersonP= POINTER TO PersonT;             (*base type person*)
   PersonT= RECORD
      next: PersonP;
      name: ARRAY 40 OF CHAR;
   END;

   CarHolderP= POINTER TO CarHolderT;       (*extended type*)
   CarHolderT= RECORD(PersonT)              (*carholder*)
      cartype: ARRAY 20 OF CHAR;
   END;

(*print information for data type PersonT*)
PROCEDURE WritePerson (person:PersonP);
BEGIN
   Out.String(person.name);
   Out.String(", no car");
END WritePerson;

(*print information for data type CarHolderT*)
PROCEDURE WriteCarHolder (carholder:CarHolderP);
BEGIN
   Out.String(carholder.name);
   Out.String(", ");
   Out.String(carholder.cartype);
END WriteCarHolder;

PROCEDURE ProgMain*;
VAR
   first,temp: PersonP;
   second: CarHolderP;
BEGIN
   NEW(first); (*allocate memory for entries*)
   ASSERT(first#NIL);

   NEW(second);
   ASSERT(second#NIL);

   first.name:="Johnson";                   (*first list entry*)
   first.next:=second;

   second.name:="Miller";                   (*second list entry*)
   second.next:=NIL;
   second.cartype:="Trabant";
```

```
(*output of list using a type guard test*)
(*to print the details based on the dynamic type*)
temp:=first;            (* here the dynamic type is OwnerP*)
WHILE temp#NIL DO
    IF temp IS CarHolderP THEN                    (*type guard*)
        WriteCarHolder(temp(CarHolderP));
    ELSE
        WritePerson(temp);
    END;
    Out.Ln;
    temp:=temp.next;
END;
END ProgMain;

END Ex23.
```

4.13.4 Lists with different types of elements

Base type The previous sections have described the use of pointer variables for implementing linear lists, starting with an example of a queue. All the initial examples shared the characteristic that all elements are of the same base type, just as in an array type. Lists containing elements of different types were only introduced in the last example. The necessary precondition was that the data to be chained had to be an extension of the existing base type. Consequently it became possible to declare the pointer necessary for the chaining as a pointer to a base type which also acquires an appropriate dynamic type in the course of the program, according to the rules for the extension of structures.

Consider what happens if we want to work with the following data types:

```
TYPE
    AP= POINTER TO AT;
    AT= RECORD
        next: ????;
        name: ARRAY 16 OF CHAR;
    END;

    BP= POINTER TO BT;
    BT= RECORD
        next: ????;
        year,month,day: INTEGER;
    END;
```

Unfortunately, the variables *a:AP* and *b:BP* cannot be produced by the extension of a common base type and therefore cannot simply be put together in a list.

Abstract data type This situation occurs often in practice and to accommodate it an artificial common base type is defined. As the two original data types have nothing in common, this new common basis is *abstract* and only contains the pointer for the chaining itself. Based on this, the required types are defined by extension to this abstract base type.

It is assumed that we know at least which types may occur. This information is needed, for example, in order to write a corresponding output procedure for each different type.

```
TYPE
   AnyP= POINTER TO AnyT;
   AnyT= RECORD
      next: AnyP;
   END;

   (*and now the extensions*)
   AP= POINTER TO AT;
   AT= RECORD(AnyT)
      name: ARRAY 40 OF CHAR;
   END;

   BP= POINTER TO BT;
   BT= RECORD(AnyT)
      year,month,day: INTEGER;
   END;

VAR
   a: AP;
   b: BP;
   temp: AnyP;
```

Now note: *NEW(a), NEW(b)* allocate memory for data of the type *AT* and *BT*. The assignments *temp:=aptr* and *temp:=bptr* are always possible because of the forced extension of the abstract base type. The chaining can therefore be done just like before.

We do have to program the output procedures for $a^\wedge$ and $b^\wedge$ appropriately as well as the type test together with the necessary type guard before the call.

This design provides a crucial benefit: the types used no longer need to be known in advance. Furthermore for each additional data type the *IF* statements must be completed by a check *IS newtypeP* to provide the branch to the desired "method", i.e., the output procedure. Also, the output procedure together with the corresponding type guard needs to be added. This is exactly where the class concept comes in, providing *type-bound procedures* and the possibility of *overwriting* procedures in the classes.

```
MODULE Ex24;                                               Ex24.mod
(*list with different types of elements*)
IMPORT Out;

TYPE
   AbstractP= POINTER TO AbstractT;
   AbstractT= RECORD                    (*abstract data type*)
      next: AbstractP;
   END;

   AP= POINTER TO AT;
   AT= RECORD(AbstractT)      (*type extension: string type*)
      name: ARRAY 16 OF CHAR
   END;

   BP= POINTER TO BT;
   BT= RECORD(AbstractT)      (*another extension: date type*)
      year: INTEGER;
      month: INTEGER;
      day: INTEGER;
   END;
```

```
(*output procedure data type A*)
PROCEDURE WriteA (VAR p:AP);
BEGIN
   Out.String(p.name);
   Out.String(", no car");
   Out.Ln;
END WriteA;

(*output procedure data type B*)
PROCEDURE WriteB (VAR b:BP);
BEGIN
   Out.Int(b.year,0);
   Out.Int(b.month,4);
   Out.Int(b.day,4);
   Out.Ln;
END WriteB;

(*main procedure*)
PROCEDURE ProgMain*;
VAR
   temp,first: AbstractP;
   a: AP;
   b: BP;
BEGIN
   NEW(a);                           (*create the data structures*)
   ASSERT(a#NIL);

   NEW(b);
   ASSERT(b#NIL);

   first:=a;                         (*load in some test data*)

   a.name:="Johnson";
   a.next:=b;

   b.year:=1996;
   b.month:=7;
   b.day:=31;
   b.next:=NIL;

   temp:=first;                      (*work through the list*)
   WHILE temp#NIL DO
      IF temp IS AP THEN             (*dynamic type test*)
         WriteA(temp(AP));
      ELSIF temp IS BP THEN          (*dynamic type test*)
         WriteB(temp(BP));
      END;
      temp:=temp.next;
   END;
END ProgMain;

END Ex24.
```

4.13.5 Binary trees

Branches   Binary trees are a specific kind of abstract data structure. Instead of *one* successor as in lists, a node of a binary tree has precisely *two* successors, a *left branch* and a *right branch*.

Instead of a formal definition we display a graph and define notions as they occur

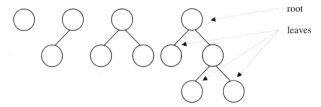

Fig. 44: Structure of binary trees

The uppermost node is called the *root*, and final nodes without further branches are *leaves*. All paths to the leaves are determined in the direction from the root and so the orientation of the edges in the diagrams does not need to be stated.

Root, leaves

Except for the root the nodes of a binary tree share the characteristic that precisely one edge enters them whereas a maximum of two edges may leave them. The root itself has zero, one, or two leaves, and leaves do not have further leaves.

A typical representation of binary trees in programs is based on the use of pointers using the following type declaration:

```
TYPE
   TreeP= POINTER TO TreeT;
   TreeT= RECORD
      key: KeyT;
      left: TreeP;
      right: TreeP;
   END;
```

An important application of binary trees is storing data using the operations *Insert*, *Search*, and *Delete*. For simplicity assume that there are keys *key* of the type *KeyT=INTEGER* stored in the nodes.

Now the data structure needs to be defined. Formally speaking, there is no distinction between a tree and a tree node in this definition, and this has consequences for the algorithms. It does make sense to allow some possibilities, such as a pointer pointing to a tree independently of whether the tree is empty or not. So the representation for an empty tree needs to be agreed. This is important in places where the termination criterion for a procedure is the state "a leaf is reached".

An empty tree, a tree that only consists of the root, and also leaves, are special cases; the following convention is used:

Empty tree

```
VAR
   k: KeyT;
   root: TreeP;
```

Empty tree:

```
root:=NIL;
```

Tree with precisely one node:

```
NEW(root);
root.key:=k;
root.left:=NIL;
root.right:=NIL;
```

Inner node p with a right branch q and without a left branch:

```
p.left:=NIL;
p.right:=q;
p.key:=k;
```

Leaf p:

```
p.left:=NIL;
p.right:=NIL;
p.key:=k;
```

This is one of many possible representations, others might replace the value *NIL* by a pointer to the node itself. In any case, leaves are characterized by the fact that they have empty trees as branches.

Ordered tree   When we name the pointers of a parent node to the left or right branch, we implicitly introduce the concept of an *ordered tree*. As far as mathematics is concerned we need not differentiate between the left and the right branch of a node. However, sometimes it is useful to insert new keys to enable quick and simple searches for already existing keys. This leads us to the term *search tree*, which is a tree structure of nodes organized so that a search for any given key is fast and straightforward.

Search tree   Taking a look at the given node *p* and the key *p.key* of a search tree, all keys accessible via the left branch are smaller than *p.key* whereas all keys reachable via the right branch are bigger than or equal to *p.key*. With this, we have also made the hidden convention that the stored keys *k* form a set, i.e., no key occurs more than once. Also the leaves must contain keys.

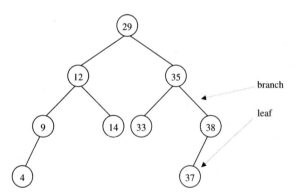

Fig. 45: Example for a search tree

Now we can sketch the first elementary operations:

```
VAR
    k: KeyT;
    root,p: TreeP;
```

- Insert a key *k* into an empty tree:

```
NEW(root);
root.key:=k;
root.left:=NIL;
root.right:=NIL;
```

- Insert a key into a tree which only consists of the root:

```
NEW(p);
p.key:=k;
p.left:=NIL;
p.right:=NIL;

(*assumption: root.key not equal to k*)
IF k<root.key THEN
    root.left:=p;
ELSE
    root.right:=p;
END;
```

Appending a new node *p* to a leaf *q* is implemented in the same way. With tree algorithms it must be decided in advance whether a key is passed to the procedure *Insert* and *NEW* is executed inside of *Insert*, or an already existing node is passed as parameter.

The natural sequence in the discussion of *Insert, Search*, and *Delete* would imply to start with *Insert*, because after this searching and deleting in an existing tree makes sense. However, when we want to insert a key we first have to search for the node that the new node *q* will be appended to. At the same time we need o check if *q.key* is already contained in the search tree.

So we start with the procedure to searching for a key:

```
PROCEDURE Search (p:TreeP; k:KeyT): BOOLEAN;
```

If the tree *p* contains *k, TRUE* is returned, otherwise *FALSE*.

Searching in binary trees

The search procedure starts with *Search(root,k)*, and at every node *p* a decision must be made whether to take the left or right branch. The termination criteria is either the detection of a leaf or finding the key being searched for (this is a typical use of the short circuit evaluation of boolean expressions described earlier in this book).

Search

With *p:=p.right* the right branch of a node *p* is taken and with *p:=p.left* the left one.

```
PROCEDURE Search (p:TreeP; k:KeyT): BOOLEAN;
BEGIN
    (*while no leaf and key not found*)
    WHILE (p#NIL) & (p.key#k) DO
        IF p.key<k THEN
            p:=p.right;
        ELSE
            p:=p.left;
        END;
```

```
    END;
        RETURN p#NIL;
    END Search;
```

Inserting into a binary tree

Insert   When inserting it should be kept in mind that the tree might still be empty. Furthermore, when you reach a leaf you must decide if the new element is to be appended on the right or left. This can be achieved by looking ahead one step.

In our example below this is done secretly by the parameter list of the subroutine *Put*. Note that the pointer to the left or right branch is passed rather than the pointer to the current node and that, more important, the pointer is a VAR parameter!

```
    PROCEDURE Insert (VAR p:TreeP; k:KeyT);
    VAR
        temp: TreeP;

        PROCEDURE Put (VAR node:TreeP; k:KeyT): NodeP;
        BEGIN
            IF node=NIL THEN
                NEW(node);                    (*no node so create one*)
                ASSERT(node#NIL);                (*and initialize it*)
                node.key:=k;
                node.left:=NIL;
                node.right:=NIL;
            END;
            RETURN node;
        END Put;

    BEGIN
        temp:=Put(p,k);
        REPEAT
            IF temp.key<k THEN
                temp:=Put(temp.right,k);
            ELSIF temp.key>k THEN
                temp:=Put(temp.left,k);
            END;
        UNTIL temp.key=k;
    END Insert;
```

Further operations on trees

The procedure for deleting a node from a tree and the explanation of the algorithm are quite demanding. As this subject will be discussed in connection with recursive algorithms it will be described later in the book.

4.14 Recursion

4.14.1 Recursion as a way of thinking

Recursion is the definition or the solution of a problem which involves its own definition. In the context of procedures this means that a procedure which is designed to be recursive may call itself.

Recursive definitions of a problem are quite common and allow short and precise formulation. Such problems can be solved using a recursive style of programming or by developing an equivalent iterative solution.

The factorial of n ($n!$) is defined as $n! = 1 \cdot 2 \cdot 3 \cdot ... \cdot n$, with the special case that $0! = 1$. In an iterative approach we can write:

```
fac:=1;
FOR i:=2 TO n DO fac:=fac*i END;
```

The fact that an arithmetic overflow may occur because of the fast growth of $n!$ does not have to be taken into account.

But we can also express this recursively:

$$n! = \begin{cases} 1 & \text{when } n = 0 \\ n \cdot (n-1)! & \text{when } n \geq 1 \end{cases}$$

and this can be expressed as the following recursive procedure:

```
PROCEDURE Fac(n:LONGINT):LONGINT;
BEGIN
    IF n=0 THEN (*special case and termination criteria*)
        RETURN 1;
    ELSE
        RETURN Fac(n-1)*n;                    (*recursive call*)
    END;
END Fac;
```

From this procedure it is clear that the circularity of the recursive call must be broken by a termination criteria, otherwise it would run on endlessly.

This example is a "direct recursion": a procedure A calls itself. There is another form, an indirect recursion, where a procedure A calls a procedure B and the latter again calls the procedure A (or a sequence of procedures B_1, B_2 ... B_n where B_n calls A again).

Another example is the calculation of x^n (x to the power of n). The preconditions $x \neq 0$ and $n \geq 0$ and n is a whole number help us to concentrate on the essential. Oberon-2 does not provide an exponential operator so we cannot simply write x^2 or generally x^n in an expression. We need an exponentiation function like the one that could be imported from the module *Float*. As an example we will solve this problem ourselves using both iterative and recursive approaches.

A procedure designed using the conventional iterative approach looks like this:

```
PROCEDURE Power(x:LONGREAL; n:INTEGER): LONGREAL;
VAR
    i, result: LONGREAL;
BEGIN
    IF n=0 THEN RETURN 1.0 END;
    result:=x;
    FOR i:=2 TO n DO result:=result*x END;
    RETURN result;
END Power;
```

However, we may also think recursively and define a^n as follows:

$$a^n = \begin{cases} 1 & when\ n = 0 \\ a \cdot a^{n-1} & when\ n \geq 1 \end{cases}$$

Now we get:

```
PROCEDURE Power(x:LONGREAL; n:INTEGER): LONGREAL;
BEGIN
    IF n=0 THEN
        RETURN 1.0;                      (*termination critria*)
    ELSE
        RETURN x*Power(x,n-1);           (*recursive call*)
    END;
END Power;
```

Both of these solutions are simple and direct. When procedures are called recursively you must keep in mind that this requires a great deal of processing. For each procedure call memory needs to be allocated for the return address and for the local variables, as these must be conserved for use as the recursive calls unwind later.

It is usual to store this data in a stack which grows after each call. Generally, the recursive call takes more time, and also requires more memory at run-time than the equivalent iterative scheme. This can be a particular disadvantage if the worst case depth of the recursion cannot be defined before run-time because no guarantee can be given that the program will run to completion. In the previous cases the recursion depth is linearly related to the value of n and the problem of a stack overflow may arise if n is large enough.

Therefore, the selection of the method depends on a subjective trade-off of "elegance" versus "practicality". Most mathematicians consider recursion to be purer and more elegant than iteration, whereas engineers are usually keener on reducing memory needs and increasing performance and so prefer iteration.

When designing a recursive program the essential point is to analyze the problem in terms of partial problems to which the partial solution is applied. Finally the precalculated partial solutions are recombined.

The ideal situation is when the problem can be divided into two halves of about the same size. If the original size of the problem is a power of 2, say $n = 2^i$, then if you divide it you get two problems of size $\frac{n}{2}$, then four of size

$\frac{n}{4}$ and so on, until a trivial problem is reached after i steps with $\frac{n}{2^i}=1$. In such a case the recursion depth is only $\log_2(n)$ and therefore never becomes huge (e.g., $\log_2 1024 = 10$).

This technique is generally called "divide and conquer", and even Julius Caesar was an enthusiastic user of this strategy (*divide et impera*) and used it very effectively. *Divide and Conquer*

If the partial problems gained from a division are identical, it is only necessary to carry out one calculation before reassembling them.

The calculation of x^n provides a good example to demonstrate this idea:

When $n > 0$ and also (*ODD(n)=FALSE*), then

$$x^n = x^{\frac{n}{2}} \cdot x^{\frac{n}{2}}$$

When n is odd (*ODD(n)=TRUE*), then

$$x^n = x \cdot x^{n-1} = x \cdot x^{\frac{n-1}{2}} \cdot x^{\frac{n-1}{2}}$$

Using the relation *for odd n : n DIV 2 = (n-1) DIV 2* leads us to the following program:

```
PROCEDURE Power(x:LONGREAL; n:INTEGER): LONGREAL;
VAR
   result: LONGREAL;
BEGIN
   CASE n OF
      0: result:=1;                      (*termination criteria*)
    | 1: result:=x;
      ELSE
         result:=Power(x,n DIV 2);           (*recursive calls*)
         result:=result*result;          (*cope with odd 'n'*)
         IF ODD(n) THEN result:=result*x END;
      END;
   RETURN result;
END Power;
```

This last version of *Power* contains an important step: by dividing the problem into smaller partial problems, allowance was made for repeated performance of the same calculation, and so the number of recursive calls was drastically reduced.

An extreme example showing how an unfavorable division of the problem can have a catastrophic effect on a recursive solution is the calculation of the Fibonacci numbers. *Fibonacci numbers*

The definition is:

$$Fib(n) = \begin{cases} 0 & when\ n = 0 \\ 1 & when\ n = 1 \\ Fib(n-1) + Fib(n-2) & when\ n > 1 \end{cases}$$

Using this definition, a recursive algorithm can be programmed easily:

```
PROCEDURE Fib(n: INTEGER): LONGINT;
BEGIN
    IF n<2
        THEN RETURN n;                      (*termination criteria*)
        ELSE RETURN Fib(n-1)+Fib(n-2);          (*recursive call*)
    END;
END Fib;
```

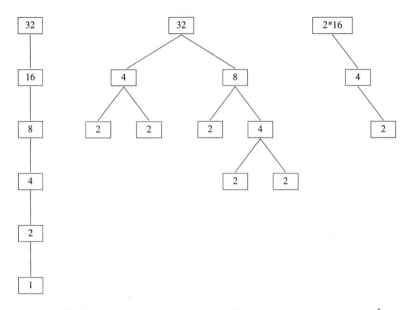

Fig. 45: The recursion levels for the three different recursive solutions of 2^5

Clearly when we use the definition directly for the design of the recursive algorithm we get a division of the problem of size n into one of size $n - 1$ and another of size $n - 2$.

To estimate the further extent of calculation the problem can be simplified to the better case of two problems of size $n - 2$. With every recursion level the number of partial problems doubles, but the size of those problems decreases by the constant value 2. Thus, $\frac{n}{2}$ recursion levels are necessary to reach the abort criterion of $n < 2$, and we get a division of the problem into more than $2^{\frac{n}{2}}$ partial problems. As a consequence the execution time of the recursive Fibonacci algorithm *grows exponentially* with increasing n. For this reason, the recursive solution of the problem is practically useless. In contrast, using an iterative solution the n-th Fibonacci number can be calculated using a simple addition loop:

```
PROCEDURE Fib(n: INTEGER): LONGINT;
VAR
   i:INTEGER;
   alt1,alt2,fib:LONGINT;
BEGIN
   IF n<2 THEN
      RETURN n;                             (*special case*)
   ELSE
      alt1:=1; alt2:=0; fib:=0;
      FOR i:=2 TO n DO
         fib:=alt1+alt2;                    (*iterative loop*)
         alt2:=alt1;
         alt1:=fib;
      END;
      RETURN fib;
   END;
END Fib;
```

This particularly good example demonstrates that recursion and iteration are two different ways of thinking and therefore - in addition to the difference of the definition - often lead to differently structured solutions.

Fortunately many problems have a recursive form that is easy to understand and at the same time leads to a practical algorithmic solution.

An example is the algorithm to find the $n!$ permutations of the n characters of a string $s[0],..., s[n-1]$. This can be done if each character is put in the first position once (i. e., we exchange it with the element there), and then we calculate the permutations for the remaining $(n-1)$ elements. *Permutations of a string*

The length of the string s is detected using the function *Length* of the module *Strings*. Here is the recursive version of the solution.

```
MODULE Ex25;            (*calculate the permutations of a string*)   Ex25.mod
IMPORT Out,Strings;

PROCEDURE PermuteString (s:ARRAY OF CHAR; start:INTEGER);
VAR
   tmp: CHAR;
   i: INTEGER;
BEGIN
   IF start>=Strings.Length(s) THEN    (*invalid parameters*)
      Out.String(s); Out.Ln;
   ELSE
      FOR i:=start TO Strings.Length(s)-1 DO
         tmp:=s[start];                      (*exchange elements*)
         s[start]:=s[i];
         s[i]:=tmp;
         PermuteString(s,start+1);           (*recursive call*)
         s[i]:=s[start];                     (*set up next try*)
         s[start]:=tmp;
      END;
   END;
END PermuteString;

PROCEDURE ProgMain*;
BEGIN
   PermuteString("abc",0);      (*first call of rec. function*)
END ProgMain;

END Ex25.
```

In recursive procedures the significance of the difference between VAR and value parameters is particularly obvious and relevant. With VAR parameters a pointer to the data object is given, and every new recursion passes on a pointer to the original variable, so all references refer to the same data object. This is different from value parameters, where a local copy of the data value is made for each call.

To understand this situation better, take a look at the behavior of the following procedure (we assume *IMPORT Out*):

```
PROCEDURE Demo1 (i:INTEGER);              (*value parameter*)
BEGIN
   DEC(i);
   Out.Int(i,4);
   IF i>0 THEN Demo1(i) END;              (*recursive all*)
   Out.Int(i,4);
END Demo1;
```

We call *Demo1* as follows:

```
Demo1(4);
```

Now this output is generated:

```
       3   2   1   0   0   1   2   3
```

With a VAR parameter, the situation is different:

```
PROCEDURE Demo2 (VAR i:INTEGER);          (*VAR parameter*)
BEGIN
   DEC(i);
   Out.Int(i,4);                          (*i "belongs" to Demo 2*)
   IF i>0 THEN Demo2(i) END;              (*recursive call*)
   Out.Int(i,4);
END Demo2;
```

We call *Demo2* as follows:

```
k:=4;
Demo2(k);
```

to obtain the output:

```
       3   2   1   0   0   0   0   0
```

4.14.2 Some graphical examples of recursion

Computer graphics examples can often expressed recursively and so provide an excellent way to visualize recursion.

These examples provide a good opportunity to introduce some of the procedures from the module *ColorPlane* which is part of the OPAL library. This module provides elementary functions like the drawing of dots, lines, and rectangles, as well as an interface for finding the position of the mouse pointer.

When you import the module with the statement *IMPORT C:=ColorPlane;* it must be initialized by the call of *C.Open()* before any other functions are called. The module *ColorPlane* has been renamed with an alias C just to save typing - not to improve the readability of the program!

Colors are defined as triples (red, green, blue) of integers between 0 and 255. For example, *C.SetForeColor(255,0,0)* sets the foreground color to red with maximum intensity without any green and blue added, and *C.SetBackColor (0,0,255)* changes the background color to blue without any red and green added. Mixed colors are produced by selecting the appropriate colour components, e.g., cyan with (0,255,255). On screens with limited facilities for displaying colors the actual colors produced may deviate from the desired colors quite a bit.

With the library function *C.Box(x,y,x+s-1,y+s-1,f)* you can draw a paraxial square of side *s* with the left bottom corner $a = (x,y)$. With the parameter $f = 1$ it is drawn in the defined foreground color, and with $f = 0$ in the background color, which can also be used for deleting boxes already drawn.

In the following example, we draw a square, and into this we wish to draw another square inset by a tenth of the side length, this second square having two thirds of the initial side length.

```
MODULE Ex26;                                                    Ex26.mod
(*draw squares inside squares, iterative solution*)
IMPORT C:=ColorPlane;

(*draw a single square with width r*)
PROCEDURE SimpleSquare(x,y,r:INTEGER);
BEGIN
    C.Box(x,y,x+r-1,y+r-1,1);
END SimpleSquare;

(*main procedure*)
PROCEDURE ProgMain*;
VAR
    ch: CHAR;
    x,y,r: INTEGER;
BEGIN
    C.Open();                               (*initialization*)
    C.SetForeColor(255,0,0);
    r:=250;
    x:=10;
    y:=10;
    WHILE r>0 DO                            (*iterative loop*)
        SimpleSquare(y,x,r);
        x:=x+r DIV 10;
        y:=y+r DIV 10;
        r:=2*r DIV 3;
    END;
    ch:=C.ReadKey();              (*press any key to quit*)
END ProgMain;

END Ex26.
```

The program draws the following graph:

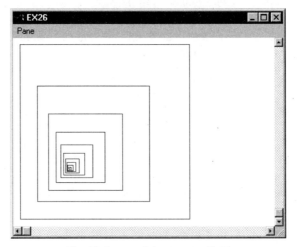

Fig. 46: Output of the program **Ex26**

The inner *WHILE* loop can be replaced more elegantly by a recursive call of the procedure *SimpleSquare* and the termination criterion can be transferred in the recursion. Even though the program is now recursive it has the same behavior. Here is the recursive version.

Ex27.mod

```
MODULE Ex27;
(*draw squares inside squares, recursive solution*)
IMPORT C:=ColorPlane;

(*draw a square, called recursively!*)
PROCEDURE SimpleSquare(x,y,r:INTEGER);
BEGIN
    IF r>0 THEN
        C.Box(x,y,x+r-1,y+r-1,1);
        SimpleSquare(x + r DIV 10, y + r DIV 10,
                     2 * r DIV 3);
    END;
END SimpleSquare;

(*main procedure*)
PROCEDURE ProgMain*;
VAR ch: CHAR;
BEGIN
    C.Open();
    C.SetForeColor(255,0,0);
    SimpleSquare(10,10,250);          (*call recursive procedure*)
    ch:=C.ReadKey();                  (*wait for key pressed*)
END ProgMain;

END Ex27.
```

In one field of computer graphics, the theory of fractals, the problems are usually posed recursively. By the term *fractals* we mean pictures that are composed of smaller partial pictures which are recursively related in some way to the higher level picture.

The components of a fractal often have a physical resemblance to the higher level structure. This characteristic of fractals is also called self-resemblance and can be represented in recursive algorithms very well.

Some examples

The following module draws squares on the screen recursively, and with each recursion the side length and the center of a square are changed relative to its preceding square.

Fig. 47: Square with one recursion level

The core of the module is the procedure *SqFract(x,y,r:INTEGER; col:Color)*. With the help of the basic ColorPlane function *Box* it draws a square with center (*x,y*) and the side length $2 \cdot r$.

The special feature of the program is that *SqFract* calls itself recursively and so in each corner of the drawn square a new square of half the size is drawn. This is continued until the size of the squares reaches a critical limit.

To make the example more interesting and to emphasize the different recursion levels the squares are drawn in different colors at different recursion depths. This is done by *SqFract*: it first draws a single square in the color originally given as a parameter and then changes the color before the next call is effected. You can experiment with different values, if you like.

```
MODULE Ex28;          (*draw squares on the screen recursively*)   Ex28.mod
IMPORT C:=ColorPlane;

TYPE
   Color=RECORD                              (*color data type*)
      r,g,b:INTEGER;                         (*red, green and blue*)
   END;

PROCEDURE SqFract (x,y,r:INTEGER; col:Color);
BEGIN
   (*stop, when width is less than 4 pixels*)
   IF r>3 THEN
      C.SetForeColor(col.r,col.g,col.b);          (*setup*)
      C.Box(x-r,y-r,x+r,y+r,1);              (*parameters for*)
      col.r:=col.r DIV 3;                     (*next level of*)
      col.b:=2*col.b DIV 3;
      SqFract(x-r,y+r,r DIV 2,col);          (*recursive calls*)
      SqFract(x+r,y+r,r DIV 2,col);
      SqFract(x-r,y-r,r DIV 2,col);
      SqFract(x+r,y-r,r DIV 2,col);
   END;
END SqFract;
```

```
(*main procedure*)
PROCEDURE ProgMain*;
VAR
    ch:CHAR;
    col:Color;
BEGIN
    C.Open();
    col.r:=255; col.g:=55; col.b:=255;
    SqFract(200,200,64,col);
    ch:=C.ReadKey();                        (*wait for key pressed*)
END ProgMain;

END Ex28.
```

In the following application we demonstrate the "divide and conquer" strategy with the help of a graphical example. A chess board with any desired number of squares is generated. The board is divided into four smaller chess boards which are in turn divided again until a chessboard consisting of a single square is reached. It is drawn black or white depending on its position.

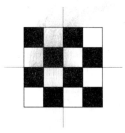

Fig. 48: Division of a chess board into quadrants

Now let's discuss recursion depth. To make things easier, let the initial side length k of the board be a power of 2, then with every recursion level this length is exactly bisected. So the recursion depth will be $\log_2(k)$ because

$$k = 2^{DepthOfRecursion}.$$

From this and from the example with the Fibonacci numbers we can make an important discovery. If the stated problem is divided into several problems at each recursion level, we must try to decrease the problem by an adequate factor (e.g., 0.5) at the same time. If this does not happen and if the problem is decreased only by a constant we get a linear and not a logarithmic dependence with the recursion depth of our problem. Then the execution time and stack memory increase exponentially with the size of the problem, which must be avoided in any practically useful algorithm.

The chess board has been chosen as an example because it provides a good illustration of division into partial problems, regardless of the fact that this problem can also easily be solved iteratively using two nested loops.

```
MODULE Ex29;
(*recursively draw a chess board*)                              Ex29.mod
IMPORT C:=ColorPlane;

CONST
   R= 30;                                   (* width of a field *)

(*draw a chess board, recursive*)
PROCEDURE ChessBoard(x,y,n:INTEGER);
VAR nh: INTEGER;
BEGIN
   IF n>1 THEN (*termination criterion*)
      nh:=n DIV 2;
      ChessBoard(x,     y,    nh);          (*draw partial boards*)
      ChessBoard(x+nh,y,    n-nh);
      ChessBoard(x,     y+nh,n-nh);
      ChessBoard(x+nh,y+nh,n-nh);
   ELSE                                     (*draw a single field*)
      IF (ODD(x) & ~ODD(y)) OR (~ODD(x) & ODD(y)) THEN
         C.Box(x*R,y*R,x*R+R,y*R+R,1);
      ELSE
         C.Bar(x*R,y*R,x*R+R,y*R+R,1);
      END;
   END;
END ChessBoard;

(*main procedure*)
PROCEDURE ProgMain*;
VAR ch:CHAR;
BEGIN
   C.Open();
   ChessBoard(5,5,5);
   ch:=C.ReadKey();                         (*wait for key pressed*)
END ProgMain;

END Ex29.
```

This example highlights another important strategy: the operations for drawing are located together with the termination criterion of the recursion. The complete picture emerges from the sum of the solutions of the trivial problems *at the end* of the recursion as the recursive calls terminate and then "unwind". This feature of our example provides for an automatic recombination of the solutions after the "divide" step. In non-graphical examples explicit program code is usually necessary to execute this step, like for example the "+" in *RETURN Fib(n - 2)+Fib(n - 1)* of the Fibonacci algorithm. This is important for the comprehension of the next example.

This time we want to draw the *Koch curve*, named after the Swedish mathematician *Helge von Koch* who published the principle of its construction in 1904. The curve is constructed as follows:

1) Take a distance (a,b) and divide it into three sections $(a,m_l),(m_l,m_r),$ (m_r,b) of length $|b - a|/3$.

2) The middle section (m_l,m_r) is replaced by an equilateral triangle of side length $|b - a|/3 = |m_r - m_l|$ and corners m_l, c, m_r. The base section (m_l,m_r) of this triangle is removed. Now we have a polygon line that consists of 4 parts: $(a,m_l),(m_l,c),(c,m_r),(m_r,b)$.

3) This procedure is applied to all sections recursively.

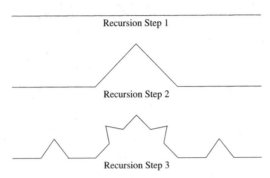

Fig. 49: A Koch curve develops

The core operation is the procedure *EquilaTriangle*. Its task is to draw an equilateral triangle above a line segment defined by the given co-ordinates (a_x, a_y) and (b_x, b_y) and then to remove the base segment. This is what the construction rules specify. We could delete the line by simply redrawing it in the background color. (There is a practical problem here because the line coordinates need to be mapped onto the integer values of the pixels available on the physical screen.)

However, we have already seen from the chess board program that it is advisable to delay the operation "draw" until the end, i.e., to divide until the desired segment length has been reached. For this reason, we do not draw in *EquilaTriangle* but use this procedure only for the analytic calculation of the triangle coordinates. In this program we draw at the position where the termination criterion for the recursion is defined.

By previous analysis based on the rules of analytic geometry we know that the height h of the triangle with base (a,b) is determined by $|b-a| \cdot \dfrac{\sqrt{3}}{2}$ and the co-ordinates of the third vertex c may be calculated as

$$C = (c_x, c_y) = \left(\frac{1}{2} \cdot \left(a_x + b_x + \sqrt{3} \cdot (a_y - b_y) \right) \frac{1}{2} \cdot \left(a_y + b_y + \sqrt{3} \cdot (b_x - a_x) \right) \right)$$

Some data type conversions made in the program are required as a consequence of the rules for the type compatibility and have no relation to the problem itself. The term $\sqrt{3}$ obliges us to use operations with numbers of the type *REAL*, but we later need the type *INTEGER* for the screen coordinates. This is achieved by using the function *ENTIER* in the program, which takes a floating point number as a parameter and returns the nearest whole number as an integer value.

Ex30.mod

```
MODULE Ex30;                              (*draw Koch curves*)
IMPORT Float,C:=ColorPlane;

CONST
  SQRT3=1.7320507;                              (*Sqrt(3)*)
  MINLEN=10;                        (*termination criterion*)
```

```
(*calculate the equilateral triangle*)
PROCEDURE EquilaTriangle(ax,ay,bx,by:INTEGER;
                                VAR cx,cy:INTEGER);
BEGIN
   cx:=SHORT(ENTIER(((ax+bx+SQRT3*(ay-by))/2)));
   cy:=SHORT(ENTIER(((ay+by+SQRT3*(bx-ax))/2)));
END EquilaTriangle;

(*recursively draw Koch curves*)
PROCEDURE KochCurve(ax,ay,bx,by:INTEGER);
VAR mlx,mly,mrx,mry,cx,cy:INTEGER;
BEGIN
   IF Float.Sqrt((ax-bx)*(ax-bx)+(ay-by)*(ay-by))<MINLEN
   THEN                              (*check termination criterion*)
      C.Line(ax,ay,bx,by,1);
   ELSE
      mlx:=(2*ax+bx) DIV 3;
      mly:=(2*ay+by) DIV 3;
      mrx:=(ax+2*bx) DIV 3;
      mry:=(ay+2*by) DIV 3;
      EquilaTriangle(mlx,mly,mrx,mry,cx,cy);
      KochCurve(ax,ay,mlx,mly);              (*recursive calls*)
      KochCurve(mlx,mly,cx,cy);
      KochCurve(cx,cy,mrx,mry);
      KochCurve(mrx,mry,bx,by);
   END;
END KochCurve;

(*main procedure*)
PROCEDURE ProgMain*;
VAR ch:CHAR;
BEGIN
   C.Open;
   C.SetForeColor(255,0,0);
   KochCurve(10,25,500,250);
   ch:=C.ReadKey();                          (*wait for key pressed*)
END ProgMain;

END Ex30.
```

The program for the Koch curve reproduces the construction principle exactly and creates the graphic picture as the recursive calls unwind. It can now be revised by taking into consideration the following aspects:

- The procedure *EquilaTriangle* so far works with floating point numbers. However, the result is an integer, as needed for screen coordinates. The fractional part of $\sqrt{3}$ influences the calculation of

$$\begin{pmatrix} c_x \\ c_y \end{pmatrix} = \begin{pmatrix} \dfrac{\left(a_x + b_x + \sqrt{3} \cdot (a_y - b_y)\right)}{2} \\ \dfrac{\left(a_y + b_y + \sqrt{3} \cdot (b_x - a_x)\right)}{2} \end{pmatrix}$$

Ideally, we would like to avoid floating point arithmetic and use only integer arithmetic in order to speed up calculations, but without losing accuracy from cumulative rounding errors.

If we multiply all components of the equation by a constant X and move X over to the right side, we get the following equation:

$$\begin{pmatrix} c_x \\ c_y \end{pmatrix} = \begin{pmatrix} \dfrac{\left(X \cdot (a_x + b_x) + X \cdot \sqrt{3} \cdot (a_y - b_y)\right)}{X \cdot 2} \\ \dfrac{\left(X \cdot (a_y + b_y) + X \cdot \sqrt{3} \cdot (b_x - a_x)\right)}{X \cdot 2} \end{pmatrix}$$

Of course, nothing has changed from a mathematical point of view, but if we choose $X = 1000$, the three places after the comma are shifted in front of the comma which is again corrected by the division at the end. We can use this "fixed point" arithmetic technique to carry out all calculations with $LONGINT$ values. We can now define the result of $X \cdot \sqrt{3}$ as an integer constant without losing too much accuracy in the calculations. We must not make X too large, because this could cause an overflow of the $LONGINT$ variables. However we need the value of $X \cdot \sqrt{3}$ to be very near to an integer value in order to minimize rounding errors.

The constant X is ideal if the difference between ENTIER $(X*\text{Float.Sqrt}(3))$ and $X*\text{Float.Sqrt}(3)$ is a minimum, because then the error due to rounding will be minimized. If we search for such a constant (e.g., using a little program) we will find 2911 as a possible value for X because $2911 \cdot \sqrt{3} \doteq 5041.999901 \approx 5042$, and with this rather small constant we still achieve a precision of about eight places.

As the integer division with DIV cuts off the fractional part, we must introduce the factor X before the division to achieve a rounding.

If we want to improve the calculation for the segment length we can also use the square

$$(a_x - b_x)^2 + (a_y - b_y)^2 < MINLEN^2$$

instead of the directly equivalent

$$\sqrt{(a_x - b_x)^2 + (a_y - b_y)^2} < MINLEN$$

for comparisons. $MINLEN^2$ can also be predefined as a constant and ultimately determines the resolution of the result.

Now we create the following short program which does not need floating point arithmetic, replacing it with the "fixed point" arithmetic described above.

Ex31.mod

```
MODULE Ex31;
(*draw Koch curves, improved version*)
IMPORT C:=ColorPlane;

CONST
    MINLENQ=100;                        (*termination criterion*)
```

```
(*calculate the equilateral triangle*)
PROCEDURE EquilaTriangle(ax,ay,bx,by:LONGINT;
                        VAR cx,cy:LONGINT);
CONST
   X=2911;                              (*prescaled constants*)
   XSQRT3=5042;
BEGIN
   cx:=(X+(ax+bx)*X+(ay-by)*XSQRT3) DIV (X*2);
   cy:=(X+(ay+by)*X+(bx-ax)*XSQRT3) DIV (X*2);
END EquilaTriangle;

(*recursively draw Koch curves*)
PROCEDURE KochCurve(ax,ay,bx,by:LONGINT);
VAR
   mlx,mly,mrx,mry,cx,cy:LONGINT;
BEGIN
                                   (*termination condition*)
   IF ((ax-bx)*(ax-bx)+(ay-by)*(ay-by))<MINLENQ THEN
      C.Line(SHORT(ax),SHORT(ay),SHORT(bx),SHORT(by),1);
   ELSE          (*prepare for the next level of recursion*)
      mlx:=(2*ax+bx) DIV 3;
      mly:=(2*ay+by) DIV 3;
      mrx:=(ax+2*bx) DIV 3;
      mry:=(ay+2*by) DIV 3;
      EquilaTriangle(mlx,mly,mrx,mry,cx,cy);
      KochCurve(ax,ay,mlx,mly);
      KochCurve(mlx,mly,cx,cy);
      KochCurve(cx,cy,mrx,mry);
      KochCurve(mrx,mry,bx,by);
   END;
END KochCurve;

(*main procedure*)
PROCEDURE ProgMain*;
VAR ch:CHAR;
BEGIN
   C.Open;
   C.SetForeColor(255,0,0);
   KochCurve(10,10,500,212);
   ch:=C.ReadKey();
END ProgMain;                        (*wait for a keypress*)

END Ex31.
```

4.14.3 Sorting by recursive division

To understand the next example we must first understand what the procedure Merge does and how it works.

Let's suppose that we have two array variables a and b of length LEN(a) and LEN(b) and both a and b contain sets of numbers which we assume are already sorted. The procedure *Merge* copies the items from a and b to an array c of length LEN(c) = LEN(a) + LEN(b) in such a way that the numbers of c are then sorted. This process is called *merging*.

```
    a:  7, 9, 16, 25
and
    b:  1, 4, 8, 12
gives
    c:  1, 4, 7, 8, 9, 12, 16, 25
```

The non-recursive algorithm for this is rather simple. If Min($a[0]$, $b[0]$) = $b[0]$ we copy $b[0]$, $b[1]$, ... to $c[0]$, $c[1]$, ... until a $b[i]$ is reached with $a[0] < b[i]$. Then we change sides and transfer $a[0]$, $a[1]$, ... to $c[i]$, $c[i+1]$, ... until we get to an $a[j]$ with $b[i] < a[j]$ and then change again. In the end, one of the two arrays, say b, is completely copied and so we finally copy the remainder of a to c.

It is quite easy now to generalize this problem:

Let p be an array variable which contains numbers and presume we have two partial sequences from $p[lb]$ to $p[mid]$ and from $p[mid+1]$ to $p[ub]$, which we assume are already sorted. The abbreviations lb and ub represent lower bound and upper bound respectively. The function *PROCEDURE Merge (p:FieldP; lb,mid,ub:INTEGER)* merges the array p in such a way that the partial sequence $p[lb]$, $p[lb+1]$, ..., $p[ub]$ is sorted afterwards.

Initial situation with pre-sorted arrays $p[8..11]$ and $p[12..15]$ (therefore lb = 8, ub = 15, and mid = 11):

	0	1	2	3	4	5	6	7	8	9	10	11	12	13	14	15
p	59	14	6	17	3	27	7	35	*2*	*4*	*9*	*25*	*1*	*8*	*11*	*12*

p merged:

	0	1	2	3	4	5	6	7	8	9	10	11	12	13	14	15
p	59	14	6	17	3	27	7	35	*1*	*2*	*4*	*8*	*9*	*11*	*12*	*25*

As an algorithm for the solution outlined above:

```
TYPE
    ElemT= RECORD
        key: INTEGER;
    END;

    FieldP= POINTER TO FieldT;
    FieldT= ARRAY OF ElemT;

PROCEDURE Merge (p:FieldP;
                lb,                    (* starting index, first list*)
                mid,                   (* ending index, first list*)
                ub:INTEGER);           (*ending index, second list*)
VAR
    tmp: FieldP;
    left,right,dest: INTEGER;
BEGIN
    NEW(tmp,ub-lb+1);                  (*temporary sorted array*)
```

```
      dest:=0;
      left:=lb;
      right:=mid+1;
      WHILE dest<ub-lb+1 DO
          IF left>mid THEN          (*left partial array finished*)
              tmp[dest]:=p[right];
              INC(right);
          ELSIF right>ub THEN       (*right partial array finished*)
              tmp[dest]:=p[left];
              INC(left);
          ELSIF p[left].key<=p[right].key THEN
              tmp[dest]:=p[left];       (*left element is smaller*)
              INC(left);
          ELSE                          (*right element is smaller*)
              tmp[dest]:=p[right];
              INC(right);
          END;
          INC(dest);
      END;
      FOR dest:=lb TO ub DO        (*copy the last remaining part*)
          p[dest]:=tmp[dest-lb];
      END;
      DISPOSE(tmp);                (*release the memory for reuse*)
  END Merge;
```

Our goal is to develop a recursive sorting algorithm *MergeSort* which makes use of the subroutine *Merge*. To simplify our situation we assume that p contains exactly $n = 2^m$ elements.

The nature of the process can be understood from the following observations:

- If the array p to be sorted contains only one element, then we do not need to do anything. Otherwise we divide p into two halves p_1 and p_2 of identical size, each with the length 2^{m-1}; thus $\text{len}(p_1) = \text{len}(p_2) = 2^{m-1}$.

- If p_1, p_2 are already sorted $Merge(p_1,p_2)$ returns the desired sorted sequence. Otherwise we bisect p_1 to p_{11}, p_{12} and p_2 to p_{21}, p_{22}, sort p_{11}, p_{12}, and merge them to p_1, and then proceed the same way with p_{21}, p_{22}, etc.

- After $m = \log_2(n)$ steps of bisection we have reached the point where we have two sequences p_a and p_b with a single element each, which can easily be merged to sorted sequences containing two elements. Thus we climb back up, unwinding the recursion again.

Using a kind of meta-language close to Oberon-2 we get the following sorting algorithm:

```
PROCEDURE MergeSort(p:ListOfElemT):ListOfElemT;
VAR q,r,p1,p2:ListOfElemT;
BEGIN
    IF length of p <= 1 THEN RETURN(p);
    bisect p to p1,p2 ;
    q:=MergeSort(p1);
    r:=MergeSort(p2);
    RETURN (Merge(q,r))
END MergeSort;
```

The *MergeSort* program consequently puts into effect the *divide and conquer* strategy already introduced. The initial problem is *divided* into two partial problems of approximately equally size. To each of these we apply our method in a recursive style until we have reached a point where we have small easily *conquered* partial problems. After each step up in the recursion the results are combined with *Merge*.

If we take the number of comparisons of two keys as a measurement for the quality of a sorting algorithm and assume that we want to sort n elements, *MergeSort* does very well compared to simple methods like BubbleSort or sorting by repeated search for the maximum (or minimum). Instead of n^2 comparisons we can do so with only $n*\log_2(n)$.

If n is small the advantage gained is not significant. But if we choose a bigger number for n, like $65536=2^{16}$, then $n^2 \approx 4*10^9$, whereas $n*\log_2 n \approx 1*10^6$. Assuming the other operations of our sorting algorithm consume execution time in proportion to the comparisons the program will run about a thousand times faster!

If n becomes even bigger, the factor moves to a region where the practical application of such algorithms (which have an execution time proportional to n^2) becomes impossible.

The following complete program also contains a generator for random numbers *Random (VAR x:INTEGER): INTEGER*, which produces random numbers in the interval [0...32766]. The quality of the "randomness" of the numbers generated (equal distribution, period length) does not conform rigorously to statistical requirements, but is more than adequate for generating keys for testing purposes.

```
MODULE MSort;      (*this module implements the Mergesort alg.*)

TYPE
   KeyT*= INTEGER;
   ElemT*= RECORD
      key*: KeyT;
   END;

   FieldP*= POINTER TO FieldT;
   FieldT= ARRAY OF ElemT;

(*merge two sequences*)
PROCEDURE Merge (p:FieldP;
                 lb,              (* starting index of first list*)
                 mid,             (* ending index of first list*)
                 ub:INTEGER);     (*ending index of sec. list*)
   … see above
END Merge;

(*sort a part of the field p (indices lb to ub)*)
PROCEDURE MergeSort (p:FieldP; lb,ub:INTEGER);
VAR mid:INTEGER;
BEGIN
   IF lb<ub THEN                     (*termination criterion*)
      mid:=(lb+ub) DIV 2 ;
      MergeSort(p,lb,mid);           (*recursive sort first part*)
      MergeSort(p,mid+1,ub);         (*recursive sort second part*)
      Merge(p,lb,mid,ub);               (*merge both parts*)
   END;
END MergeSort;
```

```
(*sort a field p using the Mergesort algorithm*)
PROCEDURE Sort* (f:FieldP);
BEGIN
   MergeSort(f,0,SHORT(LEN(f^))-1);
END Sort;

END MSort.
```

Here is an example program for testing the MergeSort module:

```
MODULE Ex32;                                                        Ex32.mod
(*test program for the Mergesort module MSort.mod*)
IMPORT In,Out,MSort;

VAR
   rndmSeed: INTEGER;

(*generate pseudo random numbers*)
PROCEDURE Random (): INTEGER;
BEGIN
   rndmSeed:=SHORT(LONG(rndmSeed)*899 MOD 32767);
   RETURN rndmSeed;
END Random;

(*print the elements of an integer array*)
PROCEDURE OutField* (p:MSort.FieldP);
VAR i:INTEGER;
BEGIN
   Out.Ln;
   FOR i:=0 TO LEN(p^)-1 DO
      Out.Int(p[i].key,5);
      IF ((i+1) MOD 10)=0 THEN
         Out.Ln;
      END;
   END;
   Out.Ln;
END OutField;

(*main procedure*)
PROCEDURE ProgMain*;
VAR
   i,max: INTEGER;
   f: MSort.FieldP;
BEGIN
   In.Echo(TRUE);
   In.Prompt("How many elements? ");
   In.Int(max);                (*enter number of elements to sort*)
   IF In.Done THEN
      Out.Ln;

      NEW(f,max);
      FOR i:=0 TO max-1 DO                      (*generate data*)
         f[i].key:=Random() MOD 200;
      END;
      OutField(f);                      (*output of original data*)

      MSort.Sort(f);                               (*sort data*)
      OutField(f);                      (*output of sorted data*)
   END;
END ProgMain;
```

```
BEGIN
   rndmSeed:=564;                          (*module initialization*)
END Ex32.
```

4.14.4 Recursive algorithms for binary trees

Binary trees have already been introduced in connection with the efficient implementation of the operations Insert, Search, and Delete. The algorithms discussed were based on iterations. However, the recursive definition of a binary tree introduces the possibility of formulating the equivalent algorithms in a recursive style. In fact, the type declaration of a tree is already recursive:

```
TYPE
   KeyT= INTEGER;

   NodeP= POINTER TO NodeT;      (*defined in terms of NodeT*)
   NodeT= RECORD                 (*defined in terms of NodeP*)
      key: KeyT;
      left,right: NodeP;
   END;
```

We could also say:

- A tree A is either empty or has a special node w, its root.

- from the root w a pointer points to a right tree and another pointer to a left tree; these are the right or left subtrees of w.

The root of the left (right) subtree is the left (right) child of w and w is the parent *node* of the child nodes.

If we assume the typical application of A is as a search tree we arrive at a recursive algorithm for searching. We suppose that an empty tree is represented by p = NIL and that the pointers (branches) *left* and *right* of the leaves (end nodes) of the tree are assigned NIL. Furthermore we expect that the second pointer of a node with only one child is marked with NIL.

```
PROCEDURE Search(p:NodeP; k:KeyT): BOOLEAN;
VAR ret: BOOLEAN;
BEGIN
   IF p=NIL THEN ret:=FALSE;
   ELSIF k<p.key THEN ret:=Search(p.left,k);
   ELSIF k>p.key THEN ret:=Search(p.right,k);
   ELSE ret:=TRUE;
   END;
   RETURN ret
END Search;
```

The Insert procedure is very similar. First we determine the leaf to which the new node should be appended. However, deleting a node q with a given key k requires much more effort because the balance of the tree with respect to the remaining keys has to be guaranteed. If q is a leaf then we delete directly:

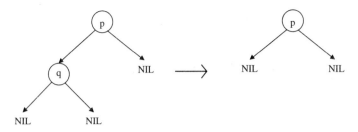

Fig. 50: Deleting a leaf of a binary tree

The situation is just as simple if q is an inner node with only one (left or right) child:

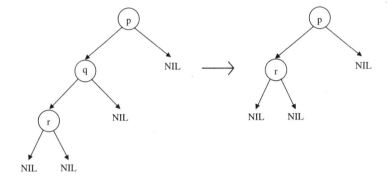

Fig. 51: Deleting an inner node of a binary tree

There is still the case that q has both a left and a right subtree which is non-empty. In this case we must ensure that the criterion for search trees remains consistant: all keys within the left subtree of q are smaller than $q.key$ whilst all keys within the right subtree are bigger than $q.key$.

To do this we go down the left subtree of q and find its biggest key. This is called the *symmetric predecessor* of $q.key$.

This key replaces $q.key$: once it is assigned with its value you can delete the node r. But we must not forget that an existing left subtree will need to be appended to the predecessor of r. The right branch pointer is NIL and does not require any further processing. An equivalent method would be to search for the smallest key in the right subtree of q (the *symmetric successor*), etc.

The procedure *Delete(VAR p:NodeP; k:KeyT)* descends recursively until p points at the node q to be deleted. After a case based test whether it is a leaf or a node with only one child, the procedure *RemoveNode(VAR r:NodeP)* is used for a further descent - if necessary - until the node is reached with the maximum key of the left subtree. Note that when *RemoveNode(q.left)* is first called we branch left whereas later we always call *RemoveNode(r.right)*.

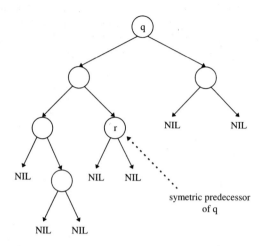

Fig. 52: Symmetric predecessor in a binary tree

```
PROCEDURE Delete (VAR p:NodeP; k:KeyT);
VAR q: NodeP;

    PROCEDURE RemoveNode (VAR r:NodeP);
    BEGIN
        IF r.right#NIL THEN
            RemoveNode(r.right)
        ELSE
            q.key:=r.key;
            q:=r;
            r:=r.left;
        END;
    END RemoveNode;

BEGIN
    IF p=NIL THEN RETURN;
    ELSIF k<p.key THEN Delete(p.left,k);
    ELSIF k>p.key THEN Delete(p.right,k);
    ELSE
        q:=p;
        IF q.right=NIL THEN p:=q.left;
        ELSIF q.left=NIL THEN p:=q.right;
        ELSE RemoveNode(q.left);
        END;
        DISPOSE(q);
    END
END Delete;
```

The above solution is neat and precise as long as we stick to our declared data
types and are not tempted by type extensions. Then $q.key := r.key$ always
works. However, in general we must assume that q and r can be of different
dynamic types. It is then no longer possible to copy the contents of an object
to another object, otherwise data may be lost because of the projection of the
extended type to the base type.

For this reason the following version is recommended because it does not
copy the data, instead it simply rearranges the pointers. The iterative version
given below is preferred on the grounds of efficiency. The program searches
for the symmetric predecessor of the node to be deleted, i.e., the node whose
key is the direct predecessor of *k*. The name "symmetric" stems from the
name of a method for traversing trees which will be discussed later.

```
PROCEDURE Delete (VAR p:NodeP; k:KeyT);
VAR f,h,q,r: NodeP;
BEGIN
   h:=p;
   WHILE (h#NIL) & (h.key#k) DO          (*search tree for key k*)
      f:=h;
      IF k<h.key THEN h:=h.left ELSE h:= h.right END;
   END;

   IF h=NIL THEN
      RETURN;                                      (*key not found*)
   END;

   IF h.left=NIL THEN                   (*remove node h from tree*)
      q:=h.right;
   ELSIF h.left.right=NIL THEN
      q:=h.left;
      q.right:=h.right;
   ELSE
      q:=h.left;
      WHILE q.right#NIL DO
         r:=q;
         q:=q.right;
      END;
      r.right:=q.left;
      q.right:=h.right;
      q.left:=h.left;
   END;

   IF h=p THEN
      p:=q;
   ELSIF f.key>h.key THEN
      f.left:=q;
   ELSE
      f.right:= q;
   END;

   DISPOSE(h);                             (*free allocated memory*)
END Delete;
```

If we want to choose between an iterative and a recursive solution of a tree
algorithm, the advantages of the recursion become obvious for the following
reason: we can visit all nodes of a binary tree in a specified order ("tree
traversal") and process each of the nodes in some way. In our example it is
the value of the key of each node that is significant.

We present the symmetric traversal (*inorder traversal*) of a tree A.

The recursive principle of the symmetric traversal is:

1) view the left subtree,

2) process the root,

3) view the right subtree.

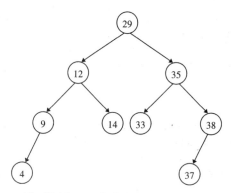

Fig. 53: Traversal of a binary search tree

Figure 53 shows a typical binary tree with the key values marked on it; a symmetric traversal returns the keys in sorted order. Therefore, inorder processing of the nodes in the above search tree would return the following sequence:

```
4, 9, 12, 14, 29, 33, 35, 37, 38
```

Here is the corresponding recursive procedure:

```
PROCEDURE InOrder (p:NodeP);
BEGIN
    IF p#NIL THEN
        InOrder(p.left);
        Display.WriteInt(p.key,4);
        InOrder(p.right);
    END;
END InOrder;
```

As an additional exercise for advanced programmers the problem can be modified as follows: pass over a procedure parameter to redefine the action to be executed on each call.

```
TYPE
    WorkProc=PROCEDURE (key:KeyT);

PROCEDURE InOrder (p:NodeP; proc:WorkProc);
BEGIN
    IF p#NIL THEN
        InOrder(p.left);
        proc(p.key);
        InOrder(p.right);
    END;
END InOrder;
```

Using the same principle, there are also the *preorder traversal* with (root, left subtree, right subtree) and the *postorder traversal* with (left subtree, right subtree, root).

The above tree traversed in postorder returns the following sequence:

```
4, 9, 14, 12, 33, 37, 38, 35, 29
```

To write an equivalent iterative version to these recursive traversal algorithms would take a great deal of work. It is easy to descend from the root to the subtrees because the pointers *p.left* and *p.right* are our signposts. But it is different if you want to ascend from a leaf or, more generally speaking, if you want to return from the child to the parent node. For this we would need to know the sequence of parent nodes along our path, and this chain would have to be established on our way down. Because of the recursive call this information is automatically and implicitly stored in the recursion stack without any effort needed by the programmer. In an iterative version we would have to analyze this awkward problem and explicitly provide data structures to "remember" the paths taken through the branches in the tree.

4.15 Exercises

1. With the following declaration given,

   ```
   VAR
       intVar:INTEGER;
       realVar:REAL;
   END;
   ```

   (a) would

   ```
   realVar:=intVar;
   ```

   be allowed by the compiler? If yes, what is the effect; if no, why not?

   (b) would

   ```
   intVar:=realVar;
   ```

   be allowed by the compiler? If yes, what is the effect; if no, why not?

2. Oberon-2 has several alternative control structures. A structure also called the 1½ loop often occurs in real life, e.g.,

   ```
   OpenFile;
   LOOP
       ReadRecord;
       IF EndOfFile() THEN EXIT END;
       ProcessRecord;
   END;
   ```

(a) How would you recode the same program using a *WHILE* loop?

(b) How would you recode the same program using a *REPEAT* loop?

(c) What are advantages and disadvantages of each style of coding?

3. If a recursive procedure were called and it only contained a call to itself, what would happen?

(a) theoretically?

(b) practically?

4. Write a program to determine whether a given number is prime.

5. Write a program for calculating the coins a vending machine would need to return a certain amount of change. The program should return the combination of coins with the minimum possible number of coins. Design your program in a fashion which allows easy adaptation for different currencies.

6. Write a program which draws the graphs of trigonometric functions like sine, cosine, and tangent. Hint: have a look at the examples in Section 4.13 for drawing dots and lines using the module *ColorPane*.

7. Write a module which supports integers with an arbitrary number of digits. It should be possible to add, subtract, and multiply numbers of that type. To be able to enter numbers and to print them a conversion from and to strings is also needed. Use a separate module to implement an interactive test driver.

Hint: use arrays of *CHAR* for the internal representation of the numbers.

5. Object-Oriented Programming

5.1 Introduction

In contrast to other hybrid languages, such as C++, object orientation has been designed into the syntax and semantics of Oberon-2 right from the start. Consequently, in the preceding chapters all syntactic items needed for object-oriented programming have already been discussed. Fortunately it is not necessary to draw a strict borderline between procedural and object-oriented programming in Oberon-2, because the two programming styles can both be expressed cleanly in the language. It often makes sense to use both elements of procedural programming and object-oriented techniques in one program.

The field of object-oriented programming has established its own terminology. To express things in the conventional "object-oriented" way we need the following "translation" of notions already known:

- Type-bound procedure = method.

- Record type = class; also the type-bound procedures are regarded as part of a class. The output of the Module Definition Browser is effectively a class definition.

- Variable of a record type = object = instance of a class.

- Creating a new record type B by extending an existing record type A = deriving a new subclass B from class A (where B inherits all the properties and methods from A). A is then called the superclass or base class of B.

5.2 From abstract data types to classes

In the earlier section where modules and abstract data types were discussed the terms "abstract data structure" and "abstract data type" were introduced and illustrated by some examples. Let's briefly summarize the results:

data type:

- defines a set of values (the range) that a variable or a constant may contain;

- defines which operations on an instance of the data type are allowed.

abstract data structure:

- generates the data to be manipulated exactly once;
- usually located in a module of its own;
- only the defined interface of exported access procedures and possibly read-only variables are visible to the client. A client knows no details of the implementation.

abstract data type (ADT):

- has a well defined interface and hides its implementation like the abstract data structure does;
- defines a set of objects which all have the same abstract data structure and also the same operations which can be applied to the objects;
- thus enables us to create one or more instances of an abstract data type.

When describing these concepts from an object-oriented viewpoint different terminology is used:

- In the sense of an ADT a class describes a set of objects each of which has the same data structures. Objects of such a class are called *instances* of this class.
- The operations defined on a class are called *methods* of this class. In Oberon-2 we also talk about type-bound procedures.

In general it is recommended that each non-trivial class constructed as a basis for further use and extensions is encapsulated in a separate module. In this case the module name becomes the name of the class.

The object-oriented approach appears to be almost perfectly suited for the implementation of abstract data types. Instead of providing a parameter to define the desired ADT for the access procedures, they are simply bound to the relevant type. So the relation between the access procedures and the abstract data type is also reflected syntactically. In this context it becomes obvious why type-bound procedures are also called methods, because they are *specifically applied to instances of the bound type.*

Also for practical purposes there is a need to provide a well-defined set of methods providing a clear encapsulation of the internal class structure. Type-bound procedures can be defined only in the module where the corresponding type is defined, which reinforces good design practice.

Class A class describes the structure of its objects and also the operations (or methods) that can be applied to these objects.

Object An object is an instance of a class.

None of this changes our concept of the abstract data structure. So anything new or novel about object-oriented programming has its origins elsewhere. But before going further it makes sense get more practice with this approach to programming with the help of some examples.

The implementation of the *Queues* example should be familiar from the Section 4.12.3 describing modules and abstract data types.

We simply rearrange the access procedures and bind them to the type representing the class. After that the externally visible module declarations look like this:

```
MODULE Queues;

TYPE
    ElemT*= INTEGER;
    QueueT* = RECORD END;
PROCEDURE (VAR q:QueueT) Init*;
PROCEDURE (VAR q:QueueT) Insert*(e:ElemT):BOOLEAN;
PROCEDURE (VAR q:QueueT) Remove*(VAR e:ElemT):BOOLEAN;
PROCEDURE (VAR q:QueueT) IsEmpty*():BOOLEAN;
PROCEDURE (VAR q:QueueT) IsFull*():BOOLEAN;

END Queues.
```

The output of the browser for the module *Queues* now has the following form, which also contains the type-bound procedures together with their corresponding structure, exactly in the sense of a class definition:

```
DEFINITION OF MODULE Queues;
TYPE
    ElemT*=INTEGER;
    QueueT*=RECORD
        PROCEDURE (VAR) Init*;
        PROCEDURE (VAR) Insert*(e:ElemT):BOOLEAN;
        PROCEDURE (VAR) Remove*(VAR e:ElemT):BOOLEAN;
        PROCEDURE (VAR) IsEmpty*():BOOLEAN;
        PROCEDURE (VAR) IsFull*():BOOLEAN;
    END;
END Queues.
```

An object is activated using the syntax *object.method*, in contrast to a procedure call, which has the syntax *method (object)*. It is also possible to view a method call as the sending of a message to the object, which then executes the appropriate function. Using this metaphor the object is the *receiver* of the message.

So although the syntax is different the effect is the same: the receiver is a parameter of the method. This is easy to understand if we compare the classic procedural definition for a method of *QueueT* with the object-oriented one:

```
PROCEDURE (VAR q:QueueT) IsEmpty():BOOLEAN;     (*method call*)
```

versus

```
PROCEDURE IsEmpty*(VAR q:QueueT):BOOLEAN;     (*procedure call*)
```

The following example shows the use of an instance of the class *QueueT*:

```
IMPORT Queues;
VAR
    done:BOOLEAN;
    aQueue:Queues.QueueT;

aQueue.Init;
done:=aQueue.Insert(42);
```

So from the declaration *PROCEDURE (VAR q:QueueT) Init*()* it is obvious that *Init* is not a normal procedure but is bound to the type *QueueT*. So *Init* is a method of the class *QueueT* and in the statement *aQueue.Init* the object *aQueue* is the receiver of the message *Init*.

The following example further illustrates the practical application of what we have learned so far. In this example the concept of points and vectors from analytical geometry is modeled to illustrate the application of simple vector algebra. Points and vectors are each represented by a class of their own reflecting their properties and the possible operations on the individual instances of points and vectors.

To highlight the elements of the module we first display the interface definition produced by the browser:

```
DEFINITION OF MODULE Geometry;

TYPE
   PointP*=POINTER TO PointT;
   PointT*=RECORD
              PROCEDURE (VAR) Init*(x, y:REAL);
              PROCEDURE (VAR) AddVector*(v:VectorT);
              PROCEDURE (VAR) SubVector*(v:VectorT);
              PROCEDURE (VAR) Draw*();
           END;
   VectorP*=POINTER TO VectorT;
   VectorT*=RECORD
              PROCEDURE (VAR) Init*(x, y:REAL);
              PROCEDURE (VAR) AddVector*(x:VectorT);
              PROCEDURE (VAR) ScalarMul*(x:REAL);
              PROCEDURE (VAR) Length*():REAL;
              PROCEDURE (VAR) GetUnit*(VAR uv:VectorT);
              PROCEDURE (VAR) GetNormal*(
                                     VAR norm:VectorT);
              PROCEDURE (VAR) DrawFrom*(from:PointT);
           END;

END Geometry.
```

The full implementation of the module is shown below. Note that although the types *PointT* and *VectorT* both have identical record elements, they are differentiated by the sets of operations available on each. The conversion to integer co-ordinates is done by rounding only in the output methods in order to conserve arithmetic precision.

```
MODULE Geometry;
(* This module implements classes which represent points and
   vectors in a plane. *)

IMPORT G:=ColorPlane,F:=Float;

CONST
   ARROWLEN=10;                         (* length of arrow heads *)

TYPE
   PointT*=RECORD (*representing points in Cartesian co-ord.*)
      x,y: REAL;
   END;
   PointP*=POINTER TO PointT;
```

```
VectorT*=RECORD              (* class representing vectors *)
   x,y: REAL;
END;
VectorP*=POINTER TO VectorT;
```

```
(*---- internal functions -------------------------------*)
```

```
(* round the given floating point number and return the
   result*)
PROCEDURE Round(x:REAL):INTEGER;
BEGIN
   RETURN SHORT(ENTIER(x+0.5));
END Round;
```

```
(* draw a line between the two given points *)
PROCEDURE DrawLine(a,b:PointT);
BEGIN
   G.Line(Round(a.x),Round(a.y),
          Round(b.x),Round(b.y),1);
END DrawLine;
```

```
(*---- methods of the class PointT ----------------------*)
```

```
(* initialize the receiver with co-ordinates *)
PROCEDURE (VAR p:PointT) Init* (x,y:REAL);
BEGIN
   p.x:=x;
   p.y:=y;
END Init;
```

```
(* move the receiver by the directed displacement of the given
   vector *)
PROCEDURE (VAR p:PointT) AddVector* (v:VectorT);
BEGIN
   p.x:=p.x+v.x;
   p.y:=p.y+v.y;
END AddVector;
```

```
(* move the receiver in the direction opposite that of the
   given vector *)
PROCEDURE (VAR p:PointT) SubVector* (v:VectorT);
BEGIN
   p.x:=p.x-v.x;
   p.y:=p.y-v.y;
END SubVector;
```

```
(* draw the receiver on the screen *)
PROCEDURE (VAR p:PointT) Draw*;
BEGIN
   G.Dot(Round(p.x),Round(p.y),1);
END Draw;
```

```
(*---- methods of the class VectorT ---------------------*)
```

```
(* initialize the receiver with co-ordinates *)
PROCEDURE (VAR v:VectorT) Init*(x,y:REAL);
BEGIN
   v.x:=x;
   v.y:=y;
END Init;
```

```
(* add a vector to the receiver *)
PROCEDURE (VAR v:VectorT) AddVector* (x:VectorT);
BEGIN
    v.x:=v.x+x.x;
    v.y:=v.y+x.y;
END AddVector;

(* multiply the receiver with a scalar *)
PROCEDURE (VAR v:VectorT) ScalarMul*(x:REAL);
BEGIN
    v.x:=v.x*x;
    v.y:=v.y*x;
END ScalarMul;

(* return the length of the receiver *)
PROCEDURE (VAR v:VectorT) Length* (): REAL;
BEGIN
    RETURN F.Sqrt(v.x*v.x+v.y*v.y);
END Length;

(* obtain a vector with the same orientation as the receiver
   but with length one *)
PROCEDURE (VAR v:VectorT) GetUnit* (VAR uv:VectorT);
VAR
    len: REAL;
BEGIN
    len:=v.Length();
    uv.x:=v.x/len;
    uv.y:=v.y/len;
END GetUnit;

(* obtain the normal vector of the receiver *)
PROCEDURE (VAR v:VectorT) GetNormal* (VAR norm:VectorT);
BEGIN
    norm.x:=v.y;
    norm.y:=-v.x;
END GetNormal;

(* Draw the receiver beginning from the given point on the
   screen. To show the direction of the vector it is drawn
   with an arrow head. *)
PROCEDURE (VAR v:VectorT) DrawFrom*(from:PointT);
VAR
    to,arrowBase,h:PointT;
    nv,hv:VectorT;
BEGIN
    to:=from;
    to.AddVector(v);
    DrawLine(from,to); (* line from starting to ending point *)

    v.GetUnit(hv);
    hv.ScalarMul(ARROWLEN);
    arrowBase:=to;          (* point of intersection of imaginary *)
    arrowBase.SubVector(hv);              (* triangle and vector *)

    v.GetNormal(nv);
    nv.GetUnit(hv);
    hv.ScalarMul(ARROWLEN/4);

    h:=arrowBase;
    h.SubVector(hv);
```

```
    DrawLine(h,to);                          (* arrow-head part 1 *)

    h:=arrowBase;
    h.AddVector(hv);
    DrawLine(h,to);                          (* arrow-head part 2 *)
END DrawFrom;

END Geometry.
```

The program *Ex33* shows the application of the module *Geometry* in a simple example.

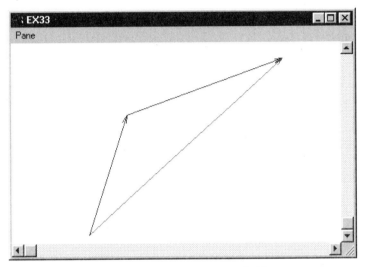

Fig. 54: Output of the program Ex33

```
MODULE Ex33;                                                         Ex33.mod

IMPORT ColorPlane,Geometry;

PROCEDURE ProgMain*();
VAR
    start,p: Geometry.PointT;
    v1,v2,vsum: Geometry.VectorT;
BEGIN
    ColorPlane.Open;
    start.Init(100,10);        (* initialize starting point and *)
    v1.Init(50,150);                          (* two vectors *)
    v2.Init(200,70);

    ColorPlane.SetForeColor(0,0,255);             (* draw first *)
    v1.DrawFrom(start);         (* vector from starting point *)
    p:=start;
    p.AddVector(v1);                     (* draw second vector *)
    v2.DrawFrom(p);             (* from endpoint of first *)

    ColorPlane.SetForeColor(255,0,0);
    vsum.Init(0,0);
    vsum.AddVector(v1);
    vsum.AddVector(v2);        (* calculate sum of both vectors *)
```

```
    vsum.DrawFrom(start);   (*draw result from starting point *)

    REPEAT
    UNTIL ColorPlane.KeyPressed();        (* Press key to exit *)
END ProgMain;

END Ex33.
```

To summarize, classes provide an excellent basis for implementing ADTs: no new concepts are needed and the classic design remains unchanged. However, the object-oriented approach offers the additional benefits of a flexible way to re-use existing classes when a new class with similar properties is needed, as discussed in the next section.

The price that has to be paid to gain this generality is a slight loss of performance. This happens because a method call requires slightly more effort than a normal procedure call. In practice, for an object to know the methods available as a result of inheritance, information about them needs to be held in internal tables. The call is then executed using these "method tables". The execution time lost during the table look-up process can play a role in deciding which programming technique should be used, especially for one-off applications which are not designed or intended for reuse or which are extremely time critical.

5.3 Concepts

One of the fundamental advantages of object-oriented programming is the possibility of reusing existing classes by deriving new classes from existing ones. The new class is usually a more specialized abstraction than the old one. It inherits and thus reuses the properties of the original class and adds or exchanges only the parts which need to behave differently from the super class.

The possibility of extending structures has already been discussed. The type extension mechanism forms the basis for inheritance.

Type-bound procedures can be inherited in a similar way to structure components. If a type T_1 is defined as an extension of T_0, it automatically inherits all components contained in T_0 as well as all procedures bound to T_0.

An important difference is that methods of a derived type can themselves be redefined. In such a case only the implementation will change; the parameter list of the procedure must remain unchanged. When such a method is redefined we say that the method is "overwritten".

The following code fragment forms a small class hierarchy.

```
TYPE
    PersonT=RECORD                            (* base person type *)
        name: ARRAY 32 OF CHAR;
        sex: CHAR;
        age: SHORTINT;
    END;
```

```
PersonP=POINTER TO PersonT;

PersonDataT= RECORD(PersonT)        (* derived from PersonT *)
   salary: REAL;                    (* extension *)
   nationality: ARRAY 3 OF CHAR;    (* extension *)
END;
PersonDataP=POINTER TO PersonDataT;
```

Now we add a method to print the current contents of an object.

```
PROCEDURE (VAR pers:PersonT) Write;
BEGIN
   Out.String("name:"); Out.String(pers.name); Out.Ln;
   Out.String("sex:");  Out.Char(pers.sex);    Out.Ln;
   Out.String("age:");  Out.Int(pers.age,2);   Out.Ln;
END Write;
```

When we derive the class *PersonDataT* from *PersonT* the new class inherits the method *Write* from *PersonT*. *Write* seen as a message sent to an instance of *PersonT* is requesting the object to print its current contents. To keep the semantics of the interface consistent, we "overwrite" the original method with a new one which prints the entire contents of an instance of type *PersonDataT*: *overwriting a method*

```
PROCEDURE (VAR pers:PersonDataT) Write;
BEGIN
   Out.String("name:"); Out.String(pers.name); Out.Ln;
   Out.String("sex:");  Out.Char(pers.sex);    Out.Ln;
   Out.String("age:");  Out.Int(pers.age,2);   Out.Ln;
   Out.String("salary:");
   Out.Real(pers.salary,12);
   Out.Ln;
   Out.String("nationality:");
   Out.String(pers.nationality);
   Out.Ln;
END Write;
```

However, this solution is not ideal because code has been duplicated. What we really want is to reuse the original method and augment it instead of overwriting it completely. For this purpose Oberon-2 has a special syntax for specifically calling the method of the super class: *calling a method of the super class*

```
PROCEDURE (VAR pers:PersonDataT) Write;
BEGIN
   pers.Write^;              (* call method of the super class *)
   Out.String("salary:");
   Out.Real(pers.salary,12);
   Out.Ln;
   Out.String("nationality:");
   Out.String(pers.nationality);
   Out.Ln;
END Write;
```

If the "^" is forgotten, the compiler will still translate the source but the program will run into an endless recursion which eventually causes the program to terminate due to a stack overflow.

In the above example we had to make a choice when we declared the procedure header for the method *Write* because the receiver parameter of a method can be either

- a VAR parameter with a structured type or

- a value parameter with a pointer to a structure.

Thus, we had two possibilities for the declaration:

```
PROCEDURE (VAR pers:PersonT) Write;
```

or

```
PROCEDURE (pers:PersonP) Write;
```

In the first case the receiver parameter is a VAR parameter of type *PersonT,* in the second case it is a pointer to a structure of type *PersonT.* In both cases a reference to the structure is passed rather than the structure itself.

When choosing between a *VAR* parameter or a pointer type for the receiver parameter the following should be considered.

Disadvantages when using a pointer type for the receiver

It is not possible to call a method which needs a pointer as a receiver when no pointer is available. This is the case inside of another method of the same class which has a *VAR* parameter as a receiver or when an object has been declared as a variable and not allocated with *NEW.*

Disadvantages when using a VAR parameter for the receiver

A lot of techniques for handling objects (i.e., maintaining lists of objects) involve storing references to objects. This is only possible if a pointer to an object is available.

So we see that for the above example the choice was arbitrary because the source fragment alone does not contain enough information to make that decision.

How objects can be allocated and the significance of static and dynamic type have already been discussed in Section 4.13.3 "static and dynamic type". One aspect of objects, which still needs to be clarified, is assignment compatibility.

assignment compatibility For an expression *e* of type *Te* to be assigned to a variable *v* of type *Tv* one of the following two conditions must be true:

1. Both *Te* and *Tv* are record types. *Te* is either identical in type to *Tv* or is an extension of *Tv.* Static and dynamic types are always identical. If *Te* is an extension of *Tv,* the contents of *Te* are projected into *Tv* and some part of *Te* is lost in the assignment.

2. Both *Te* and *Tv* are pointer types. *Te* is either identical in type to *Tv* or is an extension of *Tv.* After the assignment the dynamic type of *Tv* is the dynamic type of *Te.*

In Section 4.13.3 we learned how to use type guards to access record fields of the dynamic type which are not part of the static type of a variable, as can also be seen below.

```
VAR
    aPerson:PersonP;
    friend:PersonDataP;

BEGIN
    NEW(friend);
    ...
    aPerson:=friend;            (* dyn. type of aPerson becomes
                                                   PersonDataP *)
    ...
    IF aPerson IS PersonDataP THEN   (*check the dynamic type*)
                              (* now use type guards for access *)
        aPerson(PersonDataP).salary:=7;
        aPerson(PersonDataP).nationality:="OE";
    ELSE
        ...
    END
```

This small example on type guards leads us to the only statement of Oberon-2 which has not been introduced yet, the *WITH* statement.

The *WITH* statement performs one or more type tests on a variable and executes a statement sequence depending on the result. Within the statement sequence the variable can be used as if a type guard was applied to every occurrence of the tested variable.   *WITH*

> *WithStatement = WITH Guard DO StatementSequence*
> *{"|" Guard DO StatementSequence}*
> *[ELSE StatementSequence] END.*
> *Guard = Qualident ":" Qualident.*

Below is the previous example rewritten using a *WITH* statement.

```
VAR
    aPerson:PersonP;
    friend:PersonDataP;

BEGIN
    NEW(friend);
    ...
    aPerson:=friend; (*dyn.type of aPerson is now PersonDataP*)
    ...
    WITH aPerson:PersonDataP DO       (*check the dynamic type*)
    (* aPerson can now be used as if the static type had been
     changed *)
        aPerson.salary:=7;
        aPerson.nationality:="OE";
    ELSE
        ...
    END
```

The next example finally leads us to polymorphism, which is the key to the power of object-oriented programming.

To illustrate this concept an empty base class *BaseT* is declared and several different classes for reading and displaying numbers are derived from it.

The Figure 55 shows the hierarchy of dependencies between the classes.

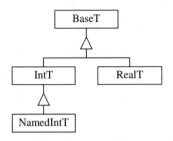

Fig. 55: Class hierarchy of the example

The symbol | A |——▷—| B | means that class A is derived from class B.

```
TYPE
    BaseT= RECORD END;              (* empty base class for entire *)
    BaseP= POINTER TO BaseT;                      (* hierarchy *)

    IntT= RECORD(BaseT)     (* class containing an INTEGER key *)
        key:INTEGER;
    END;
    IntP= POINTER TO IntT;

    RealT= RECORD(BaseT)        (* class containing a REAL key *)
        key:REAL;
    END;
    RealP= POINTER TO RealT;

    NamedIntT= RECORD(IntT)       (* extended IntT class adds *)
        text: ARRAY 32 OF CHAR;                   (* a name *)
    END;
    NamedIntP= POINTER TO NamedIntT;
```

The next step is to define a method for entering data for instances of the classes *IntT* and *NamedIntT*. A boolean *VAR* parameter indicates whether the action was successful. This could also be used to provide a termination criterion for a program.

It would be desirable to have a "suitable variant" of the method for both data types. This procedure should be automatically selected and executed depending on the dynamic type of its receiver parameter without any explicit effort by the programmer. This is exactly what polymorphism makes possible and it can be implemented as follows.

```
PROCEDURE (VAR obj:IntT) Read*(VAR done:BOOLEAN);
BEGIN
    In.Int(obj.key);
    done:=In.Done;
END Read;

PROCEDURE (VAR obj:NamedIntT) Read*(VAR done:BOOLEAN);
BEGIN
    obj.Read^(done);          (* call the method of class IntT *)
    IF done THEN
        In.Int(obj.key);
        done:=In.Done;
    END;
END Read;
```

Now we can see how polymorphism works, here is a little experiment:

```
VAR
    a: IntP;
    b: NamedIntP;
    done:BOOLEAN;
…
NEW(a);
a.Read(done);            (* the method of class IntT is called *)
NEW(b);
a:=b;                    (* the dynamic type of a is changed *)
a.Read(done);    (* the method of class NamedIntT is called *)
```

This example illustrates the concept of polymorphism: although the variable *a* is a single variable with a fixed static type, it references objects of different type at run time. The literal meaning of polymorphism is "of many shapes", which fits rather well.   *polymorphism*

The effective use of polymorphism leads to the concept of the "abstract class".

If we want to create a flexible procedure or method which can handle objects of various types, we need two things:

- a type for the parameter that receives the objects which is assignment compatible with the entire range of types we would like to handle;

- a set of methods which enables us to work with the objects we want to handle and which is available for the objects of all the different types we want to support.

This can be achieved by a common super class of all the classes which should be supported. This super class has to provide all the methods we need for our flexible procedure. All the derived classes have to support at least the interface defined by the super class. Therefore all classes support the interface we need.

Often this common super class does not yet exist. In this case it has to be created and inserted into the class hierarchy so that all the classes we would like to support are derived directly or indirectly from the new super class. Then we need to define the methods necessary to implement our procedure.

Extending the example in that direction we would like to be able to handle lists of objects of the classes *IntT*, *NamedIntT*, and *RealT*. The common super class already exists: it is *BaseT*. *IntT* and *RealT* are derived directly from *BaseT*, *NamedIntT* is derived indirectly from *BaseT*. We would also like to determine the highest value in the list, for which we need to compare objects for lower, equal, or higher value. So we must introduce a method for class *BaseT*, which is capable of comparing two objects. It is important to note that our intention was never to handle instances of class *BaseT* itself. As a consequence the new method *Compare* can be empty, and is just declared to complete the interface. Of course the empty type *BaseT* can be used as a foundation for additional extended types that can be created when needed.

As *BaseT* contains no fields and the method *Compare* no code it would not make sense to create instances of the class *BaseT* itself. Pointers of type *BaseP* are only used to take advantage of polymorphism. This is why it is called an abstract class. An abstract class represents an arbitrary selection of properties, which is usually common to a range of derived classes. Only instances of derived classes exist. In our case the abstract class *BaseT* represents abstract objects which can be ordered according to some magnitude property.

To define an abstract class we declare all the methods which we would later like to apply to the derived classes. The methods directly bound to it may either be empty or print an error message as they are never supposed to be called. It is the implementation of the derived class which provides the useful functionality for a particular application.

Strictly speaking the term "abstract" is reserved for classes which have only methods containing no statements. However, this term is also used quite frequently in connection with classes containing methods that are only partially abstract and therefore not used as instances without being "extended".

For our example we further extend *BaseT* to support *Read* and *Write* (e.g., for printing a sorted list).

What we have discussed so far can now be brought together to create a separate module containing an abstract class as a common basis for extensions.

```
MODULE BaseType;

CONST
   LESS*=-1;                   (* these constants are the possible *)
   EQUAL*=0;                   (* return values of method Compare *)
   GREATER*=1;

TYPE
   BaseT*=RECORD END;
   BaseP*=POINTER TO BaseT;

PROCEDURE (VAR obj:BaseT) Read*(VAR done:BOOLEAN);
BEGIN
   HALT(0); (*HALT box appears, user may choose to continue *)
END Read;

PROCEDURE (VAR obj:BaseT) Write*();
BEGIN
   HALT(0);
END Write;

(* returns LESS     if obj<x,
           EQUAL    if obj=x,
           GREATER if obj>x *)
PROCEDURE (VAR obj:BaseT) Compare*(VAR x:BaseT): INTEGER;
BEGIN
   HALT(0);
END Compare;

END BaseType.
```

A client of the class *BaseT* could have the form:

```
VAR
    a: BaseType.BaseP;
    done: BOOLEAN;
...
(* a^ must already exist *)
a.Read(done);
IF done THEN a.Write END;
```

Any attempt to apply *Read* directly to an instance of *BaseT* will be terminated by *HALT(0)*, or preferably a more meaningful error message, in *a.Read(done)*.

A client defining an extension of the base class has to ensure that the methods of the base class are suitably adapted. If some methods of the base class do not make any sense for the derived class, there is probably some flaw in the design of the class hierarchy.

To adapt the different methods, each must be overwritten by a new method with the same name and an identical parameter list. Only the type of the receiver parameter changes.

The following module shows how the classes *IntT*, *RealT*, and *NamedIntT* are implemented.

```
MODULE Numbers;

IMPORT B:=BaseType,In,Out;

TYPE
    IntT*= RECORD(B.BaseT)   (*class containing an INTEGER key*)
        key-:INTEGER;
    END;
    IntP*= POINTER TO IntT;

    RealT*= RECORD(B.BaseT)    (* class containing a REAL key *)
        key-:REAL;
    END;
    RealP*= POINTER TO RealT;

    NamedIntT*= RECORD(IntT)      (* extended IntT class adds *)
        text-: ARRAY 32 OF CHAR;               (* a name *)
    END;
    NamedIntP*= POINTER TO NamedIntT;

(*---- methods of the class IntT ------------------------*)

PROCEDURE (VAR obj:IntT) Read*(VAR done:BOOLEAN);
BEGIN
    In.Int(obj.key);
    done:=In.Done;
END Read;

PROCEDURE (VAR obj:IntT) Write*();
BEGIN
    Out.Int(obj.key,5);
    Out.Ln;
END Write;
```

```
PROCEDURE (VAR obj:IntT) Compare*(VAR x:B.BaseT):INTEGER;
BEGIN
   ASSERT(x IS IntT);
   IF obj.key<x(IntT).key THEN RETURN B.LESS
   ELSIF obj.key>x(IntT).key THEN RETURN B.GREATER
   ELSE RETURN B.EQUAL
   END;
END Compare;

(*---- methods of the class NamedIntT --------------------*)

PROCEDURE (VAR obj:NamedIntT) Read*(VAR done:BOOLEAN);
BEGIN
   obj.Read^(done);
   IF done THEN
      In.String(obj.text);
      done:=In.Done;
   END;
END Read;

PROCEDURE (VAR obj:NamedIntT) Write*();
BEGIN
   obj.Write^;
   Out.String(obj.text);
   Out.Ln;
END Write;

(*---- methods of the class RealT -----------------------*)

PROCEDURE (VAR obj:RealT) Read*(VAR done:BOOLEAN);
BEGIN
   In.Real(obj.key);
   done:=In.Done;
END Read;

PROCEDURE (VAR obj:RealT) Write*();
BEGIN
   Out.Real(obj.key,12);
   Out.Ln;
END Write;

PROCEDURE (VAR obj:RealT) Compare*(VAR x:B.BaseT): INTEGER;
BEGIN
   ASSERT(x IS RealT);
   IF obj.key<x(RealT).key THEN RETURN B.LESS
   ELSIF obj.key>x(RealT).key THEN RETURN B.GREATER
   ELSE RETURN B.EQUAL
   END;
END Compare;

END Numbers.
```

A small program is used as a first test to combine the different modules into
an executable program:

```
MODULE Ex34;                                                        Ex34.mod

IMPORT B:=BaseType,Numbers,Out;

PROCEDURE ProgMain*;
VAR
   done1, done2: BOOLEAN;
   anInt1,anInt2: Numbers.IntT;
BEGIN
   anInt1.Read(done1);
   anInt2.Read(done2);
   IF done1 & done2 THEN
      anInt1.Write;
      CASE anInt1.Compare(anInt2) OF
         B.LESS:Out.String("is less than");
      |  B.EQUAL:Out.String("is equal to");
      |  B.GREATER:Out.String("is greater than");
      END;
      anInt2.Write;
   ELSE
      Out.String("error in input");
   END;
END ProgMain;

END Ex34.
```

Now let's create a class *ListT* which can hold a list of objects whose dynamic
type is unknown apart from being derived from *BaseT*. It should be possible
to print the list and to determine the maximum value of the list. The *IMPORT*
statement clearly shows that the class *ListT* really just depends on the base
class and is not aware of the available extensions. We could easily create a
StringT extension from *BaseT* and use the module below to find the last
string in alphabetical order in a list of strings without modifying either of the
modules *BaseType* or *Lists*.

```
MODULE Lists;
(* This module implements a list, whose elements are instances
   of the class BaseType.BaseT or derived classes. As a
   special feature the largest element can be determined. *)

IMPORT B:=BaseType;

CONST
   MaxN-= 64;                    (* maximum number of list entries *)

TYPE
   ListT*= RECORD
      k-:ARRAY MaxN OF B.BaseP;            (* holds pointers
                                              to elements *)
      n-:INTEGER;              (* number of elements in list *)
   END;
   ListP*= POINTER TO ListT;
```

```
(* initialize the receiver; must be called prior to any other
   method *)
PROCEDURE (f: ListP) Init*;
BEGIN
   f.n:=0;
END Init;

(* put a new element into the list *)
PROCEDURE (f: ListP) Put* (elem:B.BaseP);
BEGIN
   ASSERT(f.n<MaxN);
   f.k[f.n]:=elem;
   INC(f.n);
END Put;

(* call the Write method of all list elements *)
PROCEDURE (f: ListP) Write*;
VAR
   I: INTEGER;
BEGIN
   FOR I:=0 TO f.n-1 DO f.k[I].Write END;
END Write;

(* determine the largest element in the list; a reference to
   it is returned in max and its position in pos. If the
   list is empty NIL is returned in max and -1 in pos *)
PROCEDURE (f: ListP) Max* (VAR max: B.BaseP;
                           VAR pos: INTEGER);
VAR
   I: INTEGER;
BEGIN
   IF f.n>0 THEN
      pos:=0;
      max:=f.k[0]; (*assume the first element is the largest*)
      FOR I:=1 TO f.n-1 DO
         IF max.Compare(f.k[I]^)=B.LESS THEN      (* current *)
            pos:=I;                          (* element larger? *)
            max:=f.k[I];   (* largest element set to current
                                                         elem. *)
         END;
      END;
   ELSE
      pos:=-1; (* maximum undefined *)
      max:=NIL;
   END;
END Max;

END Lists.
```

A new client of *Lists* just needs to define an extended class of *BaseT* if it is
not already available. In that case the methods of *BaseT* for input, output, and
comparison must be overwritten.

At first glance, the entire scheme appears to be quite a lot of work to find the
maximum of a list. But remember that a very simple example has been
chosen and this tends to make the savings due to re-utilization quite small
relative to the work needed for adaptation.

The following client of *Lists* puts the "search for the maximum" to the test.

```
MODULE Ex35;
(* This is a test module for the module Lists. First integers    Ex35.mod
   are read from input and inserted into a list until the end
   of the input is reached. Then the list and the largest ele-
   ment are printed. *)

IMPORT B:=BaseType,Numbers,Lists,In,Out;

PROCEDURE ProgMain*;
VAR
    list: Lists.ListP;
    item: Numbers.IntP;
    done: BOOLEAN;
    max: B.BaseP;
    pos: INTEGER;
BEGIN
    Out.String("Maximum of a list of elements"); Out.Ln;
    NEW(list);
    ASSERT(list#NIL);
    list.Init;

    LOOP                                    (* build list *)
        NEW(item);
        ASSERT(item#NIL);
        item.Read(done);
        IF ~done THEN EXIT END;
        list.Put(item);
    END;

    Out.String("List: "); Out.Ln;
    list.Write; (* show entire list *)
    Out.Ln;
    list.Max(max,pos);                              (* get maximum *)
    IF pos#-1 THEN                   (* is there a valid result? *)
        Out.F("The maximum is element no. # :",pos+1);
        max.Write;
    END;
END ProgMain;

END Ex35.
```

This concludes our introduction to object-oriented programming as far as the technical use of the language is concerned. Some practice is necessary to take in everything that has been discussed in this section before one can use it naturally and then understand more advanced concepts.

At the level above a specific programming language there exists a wealth of exciting techniques for using standard object and class relationships to help solve demanding problems. These include the notion of "container classes" to gather together objects of similar types which we present later on. Other advanced techniques carry data hiding and encapsulating implementation details even further to hide complete classes. Only the common super class, which defines the available interface, and an "object factory", which can create objects of the hidden classes, are visible for the client. To go into sufficient detail is sadly not possible in this book. A good book for further study is [Gam95].

5.4 Design

The problem of finding an appropriate class hierarchy for a given problem is by no means trivial. Additional requirements like extendability and maintainability make this even more difficult.

The process of designing and defining classes is really about finding abstractions for objects in the domain of the problem. Often it is not even clear what we would like to see as objects.

Lets look at a problem which can be understood intuitively, but for which it might not be trivial to find an object-oriented model, for instance the problem of controlling the traffic lights at a road crossing with several lanes for different directions. It might be obvious to create a class to represent one set of traffic lights, the state of objects being represented by the current color of the lights. It would also be necessary to define the sequence of transitions from one state to another. Another class could represent the entire crossing. It would have to manage all the individual traffic lights for the different lanes. An instance of that class would have to know about the series of states for the entire crossing, and somehow change the state of all the individual traffic lights in order to represent the desired state. A plausibility check might make it necessary to represent lanes and traffic paths as well to be able to detect dangerous or illegal crossings of traffic flow. Soon we meet the limit of the number of classes and their interactions we can handle entirely in our mind. This example illustrates the danger of first implementing one class and then thinking about what could be done next. Without doubt this reduces complexity but is almost bound to fail to produce a useful result unless the whole problem is analysed before starting to implement the solution.

Designing a class hierarchy is a creative process. In many ways it is similar to discovering the mathematical proof of a theorem. It is often easy to appreciate the solution, but not always clear how to arrive there. Fortunately there are some rules and guidelines which can help the developer:

- Design classes by making a drawing of both the class hierarchy and an example of how objects of different classes should interact at runtime. This should clarify issues such as: Which object contains references to other objects of which type? What kind of messages are used between objects? When exchanging messages, are there any protocols (a defined sequence of different messages) used?

- A technique which covers important aspects of object relationships is the OMT notation [Rum91]. It is also used in a later example.

- Do not create isolated classes. A common, possibly empty, super class makes it possible to have methods applicable to all objects while maintaining strict type checking.

- When you think about creating a new subclass B from the existing class A, ask yourself a simple question: "Is an instance of B also a kind of A?" (e.g., "Is an instance of Car also a Vehicle?") This is called an "Is a" relationship. The new class B is a specialisation of class A.

- In other cases there is an obvious connection between two classes, but the above does not work (e.g., A = *Car* and B = *Tyre*). Now we can ask "Has an instance of A an instance of B?" ("Has a *Car* a *Tyre*?") This is called a "Has a" relationship. An instance of class A is an aggregation of instances of other classes.

This is only a very basic introduction to object-oriented design, although it should be a sufficient basis to carry out smaller projects. We feel that a more detailed study of this area, e.g., of one of the more formal design methods like Use Case [Jac92], should be preceded by getting some personal "hands on" experience.

It is crucial to be very thorough when defining classes, including what they should represent and which operations are possible on them, because at that moment we define at which level of abstraction what is possible, and consequently the scope of problems that can be solved at all using those classes. A fundamental change in the class hierarchy later on in the implementation phase could involve modifying all or at least a lot of the source code already developed.

5.5 Application Examples

This section provides some further examples and sometimes a deeper view on the concepts discussed in Section 5.3.

5.5.1 More Lists

The following example makes use of the fact that our data type *BaseT* may be extended in any direction. From *BaseT* we derive a class *ProgramLaunchT*, and a series of instances of this class are inserted into a field of the class *ListT*.

Each instance of class *ProgramLaunchT* manages one string. The corresponding output method, however, not only writes the string to the screen, but also starts a program with this name via a Windows function.

Note that there is a hidden restriction in the example: because the method *Compare* has not been implemented for the class *ProgramT*, the example would stall if the method *Max* of the list were called. Hidden restrictions like this, which appear perfectly sensible at the time the program is written, can cause immense problems in large systems when they are extended over the years. It is therefore vitally important to include hidden restrictions in the documentation of each class.

To implement this example the function *WinExec* from the module *Windows* will need to be called. The first parameter of this procedure is the address of a string that contains the name of the program to be started. To find its address we use *SYSTEM.ADR*. The second parameter indicates whether the program should appear as usual, full screen, or as an icon after the start. The return value of the function indicates whether the program started successfully.

Ex36.mod

```
MODULE Ex36;
(* Assumption: the programs Clock, NotePad and Calc are
   installed on the computer and can be found in the search
   path *)

IMPORT SYSTEM,W:=Windows,BaseType,Lists,Out;

TYPE
   ProgramLaunchP= POINTER TO ProgramLaunchT;
   ProgramLaunchT= RECORD (BaseType.BaseT)
      name: ARRAY 13 OF CHAR;          (* executable to start *)
   END;

VAR
   list: Lists.ListP;    (* global list of programs to start *)

(* Start program and write result of operation on the
   screen *)
PROCEDURE (VAR obj:ProgramLaunchT) Write*;
VAR
   res: INTEGER;
BEGIN
   Out.String("start ");
   Out.String(obj.name);
   Out.String(" : ");
   res:=W.WinExec(SYSTEM.ADR(obj.name),W.SW_SHOWNORMAL);
   IF res=2 THEN
      Out.String("file not found");
   ELSIF res=3 THEN
      Out.String("path not found");
   ELSIF res<32 THEN
      Out.String("error");
   ELSE
      Out.String("successful");
   END;
   Out.Ln;
END Write;

(* Create a new instance of ProgramLaunchT, initialize it with
   the name given and add it to the global list *)
PROCEDURE AddProgramLaunch(name:ARRAY OF CHAR);
VAR
   prg: ProgramLaunchP;
BEGIN
   NEW(prg);
   ASSERT(prg#NIL);        (* basic check of memory allocation *)
   COPY(name,prg.name);
   list.Put(prg);                            (* add to list *)
END AddProgramLaunch;

PROCEDURE ProgMain*;
BEGIN
   AddProgramLaunch("clock.exe");
   AddProgramLaunch("notepad.exe");
   AddProgramLaunch("calc.exe");
   list.Write; (* launch programs in global list *)
END ProgMain;
```

```
BEGIN
   NEW(list); ASSERT(list#NIL);        (* create global list *)
   list.Init;
END Ex36.
```

In the following example we take an in-depth look at some implications that the transition from procedural ADT implementation to the object-oriented style has on the interface design.

In classic procedural programming procedure calls can be executed regardless of the contents of the parameters. However, when working with type-bound procedures the receiver must be a pointer or a VAR parameter (which is also some kind of pointer).

Because methods can be overwritten in derived classes, the dynamic type of the receiver has to be determined internally before a method call can be executed. For example in

```
VAR
obj:BaseP;
...
obj.Write;
```

the choice of the actual method *Write* being called depends on the dynamic type of *obj* at run time. This implies that *obj* must not be *NIL*.

As a consequence an empty list cannot simply be represented by *list=NIL*, but must be represented by an object whose internal state indicates that the list is empty. Otherwise we could not call a method to insert new elements into an empty list.

The following analogy might be interesting for the more mathematically inclined reader. The difference between Ø and {Ø} in set theory is as follows:

Ø is the empty set and Ø is a subset of *every* set M; however M={Ø} is not empty, thus M # Ø.

Applied analogously to pointers this signifies that

NIL has no special type, every pointer may have the value *NIL*. A pointer referring to another pointer with the value *NIL* points to an object that is not empty.

This leads us to the following conclusions:

- For *obj:BaseP* the call *obj.method* selects the method bound to the dynamic type of *obj*.

- But if *obj* is *NIL* no appropriate type-bound method can be selected, so program execution is stopped and an error is reported.

Here is an example which illustrates this clearly.

When introducing lists using the procedural approach the simplest means of implementation was chosen:

```
TYPE
   ListP= POINTER TO ListT;    (* pointer to a list element *)
```

```
ListT= RECORD                              (* list element *)
   key: KeyT;
   next: ListP;
END;

VAR list:ListP;              (*pointer to the first list element*)
```

where the empty list was defined by *list=NIL*.

If we create an ADT for the list we have access procedures such as

```
PROCEDURE NewList (VAR list:ListP);
BEGIN
   list:=NIL;
END NewList;
```

What would happen if *NewList* were implemented as a type-bound procedure?

A call would be of the following form:

```
VAR
   list:ListP;

list.NewList;
```

but this would immediately fail because *list* does not contain a defined value. Even if *NewList* were a normal procedure we could not call any other procedure like *Insert*, as after the initialization with *NewList* a method call would remain impossible because of *list=NIL*.

In addition to this it is worth mentioning that the initialization of objects with methods may be unwise as extended classes may require different parameter lists during the course of the initialization, which is not allowed when overwriting the method *Init*.

Let's concentrate on the essential:

• to be able to execute *list.Insert(...)* we need *list#NIL*,

• for the representation of an empty list an instance of a class must already exist,

• consequently we distinguish between a list and its elements, which is also a more proper abstraction. When we use lists we then have different types for lists and list elements and can therefore clearly specify in a formal parameter list which of the two is required as a parameter.

All this combined together leads us to the following declaration of an abstract class for lists:

```
TYPE
   ListEleP= POINTER TO ListEleT;     (*pointer to list elem.*)
   ListEleT= RECORD                          (* list element *)
      next: ListEleP;
   END;

   ListP= POINTER TO ListT;                (* pointer to a list *)
   ListT= RECORD                                      (* list *)
      head: ListEleP;        (* pointer to first list element *)
   END;
```

```
VAR
    list: ListT;                          (* an instance of ListT *)
```

The following procedure creates and initializes an empty list:

```
PROCEDURE CreateList(VAR list:ListP);
BEGIN
    NEW(list);                (* allocate a new instance of ListT *)
    IF list#NIL THEN (*access list only if allocation worked *)
        list.head:=NIL;              (* initialize empty list *)
    END;
END CreateList;
```

In the following example for a list class it is assumed that the client itself generates an instance of the list to work with.

The client may insert instances of any classes into the list as long as they have been derived from the class used for the parameter of *Put*. This again is an example of the use of polymorphism. Because the dynamic type of the elements is both unknown and not relevant to the list itself, it is the task of the client to create the elements.

The following definition module describes a class *ListT* that has been developed using the design approach just described.

```
DEFINITION OF MODULE GenList;
(* List as an abstract data type; objects are directly
   inserted. It is impossible to insert an object into several
   lists at the same time. *)

TYPE
  ListEleP*=POINTER TO ListEleT;
  ListEleT*=RECORD
                  PROCEDURE (VAR) Write*();
            END;
  ListT*=RECORD
              PROCEDURE (VAR) Put*(ele:ListEleP);
              PROCEDURE (VAR) Get*(VAR ele:ListEleP);
              PROCEDURE (VAR) Write*();
              PROCEDURE (VAR) NrOfElems*():INTEGER;
          END;
  LiFoP*=POINTER TO LiFoT;
  LiFoT*=RECORD (ListT)
          END;
  FiFoP*=POINTER TO FiFoT;
  FiFoT*=RECORD (ListT)
              PROCEDURE (VAR) Put*(ele:ListEleP);
              PROCEDURE (VAR) Get*(VAR ele:ListEleP);
          END;
PROCEDURE NewFiFoL*(VAR list:FiFoT);
PROCEDURE NewLiFoL*(VAR list:LiFoT);

END GenList.
```

Polymorphic elements are directly derived from the abstract base type *ListEleT*. Each element contains a pointer *next* and so may be used as a list element. The structure of the list is shown in Figure 56, where it is easy to see why each element can only be inserted into a single list.

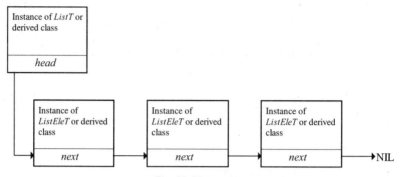

Fig. 56: List structure

The module exports two kinds of lists: a LIFO-list and a FIFO-list. The FIFO-list (First In First Out) retrieves elements in the same order they were inserted. Elements are removed at the beginning (head) and inserted at the end (tail). So the FIFO-list realizes a "waiting queue" having been derived by a type extension of the base type *ListT*. In a LIFO-list elements are both inserted and deleted at the head, which is exactly the principle of a stack. The abstract method *Write* is provided for the processing of the single nodes of the list; this then has to be adapted by the client to support the particular object type to be stored. Both LIFO- and FIFO-lists are created by using procedures. The types are exported so that a client can generate elements with *NEW* as well as type extensions for list elements the pointers. The fact that the list elements contain pointers used for the chaining is kept secret. That is why *ListEleT.next*, *ListT.head*, etc., have no export marks.

It is good design to hide implementation dependent structures like these from the client because it favors an interface design which is driven by logical abstraction rather than the algorithmic choice of the moment. As a consequence the algorithm used in the class can be exchanged later without having to change the interface and thus the clients.

Here is the implementation:

```
MODULE GenList;
(* In this module three classes for lists are implemented. The
   basic list class ListT defines the interface for a list.
   The derived classes LiFoT and FiFoT also define the
   sequence in which elements are retrieved from the list
   depending on the sequence in which they were inserted.*)

IMPORT Out;

TYPE
(* base class for list elements *)
   ListEleP*= POINTER TO ListEleT;
   ListEleT*= RECORD
      next: ListEleP;
   END;

   ListT*= RECORD
      head: ListEleP;
   END;
```

```
(* class implementing a "last in first out" list *)
   LiFoT*= RECORD (ListT) END;
   LiFoP*= POINTER TO LiFoT;

(* class implementing a "first in first out" list *)
   FiFoT*= RECORD (ListT)
              tail: ListEleP;
          END;
   FiFoP*= POINTER TO FiFoT;

(*---- class ListEleT ----------------------------------*)

PROCEDURE (VAR obj:ListEleT) Write*();
BEGIN
END Write;

(*---- class ListT ------------------------------------*)

PROCEDURE InitList*(VAR list:ListT);
BEGIN
   list.head:=NIL
END InitList;

PROCEDURE (VAR list:ListT) Put*(ele:ListEleP);
BEGIN
   ele.next:=list.head;
   list.head:=ele;
END Put;

PROCEDURE (VAR list:ListT) Get*(VAR ele:ListEleP);
BEGIN
   ele:=list.head;
   IF ele#NIL THEN list.head:=ele.next; END;
END Get;

PROCEDURE (VAR list:ListT) Write*();
VAR
   ele:ListEleP;
BEGIN
   ele:=list.head;
   WHILE ele#NIL DO
      ele.Write;
      ele:=ele.next;
   END;
END Write;

PROCEDURE(VAR list:ListT) NrOfElems*():INTEGER;
VAR
   ele:ListEleP;
   I:INTEGER;
BEGIN
   I:=0;
   ele:=list.head;
   WHILE ele#NIL DO
      INC(I);
      ele:=ele.next;
   END;
   RETURN I;
END NrOfElems;
```

```
(*---- class FiFoT --------------------------------------*)

PROCEDURE InitFiFoL*(VAR list:FiFoT);
BEGIN
   InitList(list);
   list.tail:=NIL;
END InitFiFoL;

PROCEDURE (VAR list:FiFoT) Put*(ele:ListEleP);
BEGIN
   ele.next:=NIL;
   IF list.head # NIL THEN
      list.tail.next:=ele;
   ELSE
      list.head:=ele;
   END;
   list.tail:=ele;
END Put;

PROCEDURE (VAR list:FiFoT) Get*(VAR ele:ListEleP);
BEGIN
   list.Get^(ele);
   IF list.head=NIL THEN list.tail:=NIL; END;
END Get;

(*---- class LiFoT --------------------------------------*)

PROCEDURE InitLiFoL*(VAR list:LiFoT);
BEGIN
   InitList(list)
END InitLiFoL;

(* Put and Get need not be newly implemented as they are
   inherited from ListT and can be reused without change! *)

END GenList.
```

The following module implements a client and demonstrates how to use *GenList*. Using type extension it defines two different sorts of node types for the list and then inserts corresponding objects. The order is defined arbitrarily so that a polymorphous list is produced, the method *Write* is then selected according to the dynamic type of the current object.

Ex37.mod

```
MODULE Ex37;
IMPORT In,Out,GenList,Strings;

CONST
   STRLEN=80;

TYPE
(* class for list elements containing integers *)
   IntElemT= RECORD(GenList.ListEleT)
      data:INTEGER;
   END;
   IntElemP= POINTER TO IntElemT;

(* class for list elements containing strings *)
   StrElemT= RECORD(GenList.ListEleT)
      data:ARRAY STRLEN OF CHAR;
   END;
```

```
      StrElemP= POINTER TO StrElemT;

PROCEDURE (VAR obj:IntElemT) Write();
BEGIN
   Out.String("int value: ");
   Out.Int(obj.data,1);
   Out.Ln;
END Write;

PROCEDURE (VAR obj:StrElemT) Write();
BEGIN
   Out.String("string: ");
   Out.String(obj.data);
   Out.Ln;
END Write;

PROCEDURE ProgMain*;
VAR
   list: GenList.LiFoT;
   eleP: GenList.ListEleP;
   intElem: IntElemP;
   strElem: StrElemP;
   I: INTEGER;
BEGIN
   GenList.InitLiFoL(list);   (*initialize last in first out *)

   FOR I:=0 TO 3 DO
      NEW(intElem);          (* create an instance of IntElemT *)
      ASSERT(intElem#NIL);
      intElem.data:=I+100;
      list.Put(intElem);                 (* insert into list *)

      NEW(strElem);       (* create an instance of StrElemT *)
      ASSERT(strElem#NIL);
      strElem.data:= "text ";
      Strings.AppendChar(strElem.data,CHR(97+I));
      list.Put(strElem);              (* insert into list *)
   END;

   list.Write; (* print current list *)
   Out.F("$number of elements now: #$", list.NrOfElems());

   list.Get(eleP);         (* retrieve list element by element *)
   WHILE eleP#NIL DO
      eleP.Write;
      list.Get(eleP);
   END;                              (* list should now be empty *)
   Out.F("number of elements now: #$",list.NrOfElems());
END ProgMain;

END Ex37.
```

5.5.2 Container classes

In many applications the following situation occurs: by importing a module just like *BaseType* we have a base type *BaseT* as a foundation from which other classes can be derived. Elsewhere in the program there is a need to insert instances of these classes into a list or a different generic data structure, but without the restriction that an object can only be part of a single data structure.

In order to achieve this it is clear that the variables for chaining can no longer be stored in the object itself. We therefore use separate objects for the chaining, each of which contain a pointer to the object to be held in addition to the fields for the realization of the desired data structure, e.g., a field *next* to chain a list.

We can compare such a container class to a clothesline onto which we fix a series of objects with the help of pegs. Different types of items (shirts, socks, towels, ...) are defined from the base class laundry. The single items are put on the line using pegs, i.e., instances of the class *ListEleT* as shown above. When we remove the items we must also remember to remove the pegs.

The principal idea is now to design a general *container* in the form of a list into which every object derived from *BaseT* may be inserted. So in this design the objects are not constructed in advance for later usage in a list class, but are first described and then stored in a container. The implementation of the list must of course be slightly different from our previous example. Classes based on this design idea are called container classes. The resulting structure now has the following shape:

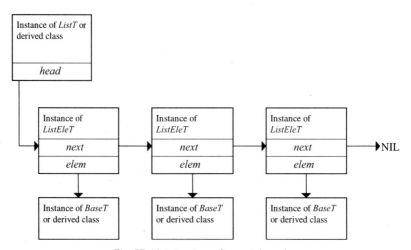

Fig. 57: List structure of a container class

Container classes are the most general case of *genericity*: a module is called *generic* if it can operate different kinds of objects.

The following module implements a list using this structure; the interface looks like this:

```
DEFINITION OF MODULE Container;

TYPE
   WorkProc*=PROCEDURE (obj:BaseType.BaseP);
   ListT*=RECORD
      PROCEDURE (VAR) Init*();
      PROCEDURE (VAR) Put*(obj:BaseType.BaseP);
```

```
        PROCEDURE (VAR) Delete*(obj:BaseType.BaseP);
        PROCEDURE (VAR) ForEach*(proc:WorkProc);
        PROCEDURE (VAR) Zap*();
     END;

 ...

 END Container.
```

Apart from the method *Put* the conventional functions for processing the whole list (*ForEach*) and for deleting a given element (*Delete*) or the whole list (*Zap*) are included. The type *ListEleT* is not contained in the interface as it is only used internally for list management.

In the following implementation the types *ListEleT* and *ListT* are defined following the design shown in Figure 57. A procedure type (*WorkProc*) is defined for the processing of list elements; it is required by the function *ForEach*.

```
MODULE Container;

IMPORT BaseType;

TYPE
    ListEleP=POINTER TO ListEleT;
    ListEleT=RECORD
       next:ListEleP;
       elem:BaseType.BaseP;
    END;

    ListT*=RECORD
       head:ListEleP;
    END;

    WorkProcT*=PROCEDURE (obj:BaseType.BaseP);
```

The method *Init* provides initialization of the empty list before its first use. In this simple implementation without any special features, such as chaining in the form of rings, it is sufficient to set the pointer to the first element to *NIL*.

```
PROCEDURE (VAR list:ListT) Init*;
BEGIN
    list.head:=NIL;
END Init;
```

To add a new element in the list a new "peg" has to be created using *NEW*. It is inserted at the beginning of the list and the element pointer of the peg is set to the object passed as the parameter.

```
PROCEDURE (VAR list:ListT) Put*(obj:BaseType.BaseP);
VAR
    ele:ListEleP;
BEGIN
    NEW(ele);
    ASSERT(ele#NIL);
    ele.elem:=obj;
    ele.next:=list.head;
    list.head:=ele;
END Put;
```

When deleting a list element there is a special case if the first element needs to be removed; in this case *list.head* must be adjusted. If the element is situated anywhere else in the list the peg holding the element on the line must be located first. In both cases, after the modification of the list chaining, a pointer to the peg which is no longer required is stored in *old*. It can be released subsequently using *DISPOSE* (which is only necessary for Oberon implementations without a garbage collector).

```
PROCEDURE (VAR list:ListT) Delete*(obj:BaseType.BaseP;
                                   VAR done:BOOLEAN);
VAR
   ele,old:ListEleP;
BEGIN
   ASSERT(list.head#NIL);
   IF list.head.elem=obj THEN
      old:=list.head;
      list.head:=list.head.next;
      done:=TRUE;
      DISPOSE(old);
   ELSE
      ele:=list.head;
      WHILE (ele.next#NIL) & (ele.next.elem#obj) DO
         ele:=ele.next;
      END;
      IF ele.next=NIL THEN        (* element not found in list *)
         done:=FALSE;
      ELSE
         old:=ele.next;
         ele.next:=ele.next.next;
         done:=TRUE;
         DISPOSE(old);
      END;
   END;
END Delete;
```

ForEach enables the user of a list to execute a given operation on each element without having to write a loop. The desired operation is provided by the user as a procedure supporting the interface defined in the type *WorkProcT*. The procedure can then be passed to *ForEach* as a parameter.

The implementation is pretty simple: a loop is used to run through the list and the processing procedure is called with the current element passed as a parameter.

```
PROCEDURE (VAR list:ListT) ForEach*(proc:WorkProcT);
VAR
   ele:ListEleP;
BEGIN
   ele:=list.head;
   WHILE ele#NIL DO
      proc(ele.elem); ele:=ele.next;
   END;
END ForEach;
```

With *Zap* the list is deleted and all pegs are released. Note that if a garbage collector is present it is enough to set the pointer to the beginning of the list to *NIL*.

```
PROCEDURE (VAR list:ListT) Zap*;
VAR
   old,ele:ListEleP;
BEGIN
   ele:=list.head;
   WHILE ele#NIL DO
      old:=ele;
      ele:=ele.next;
      DISPOSE(old);
   END;
   list.head:=NIL;
END Zap;

END Container.
```

The implementation of the list as container class would now normally be finished. But let's take a look at a typical addition which is often used in practice.

It is not always wise to write a procedure for every operation on all list elements, as currently needed for *ForEach*. This is especially true if the processing of the list elements needs to be stopped before the last element is reached or if local variables that would not be within reach in a separate procedure need to be accessed. Bearing this in mind it would be useful to gain control of the loop which is used for browsing through the list elements.

A simple solution for this situation could be provided by a method *GetNext(VAR obj:BaseType.BaseP)* which returns the next list element each time it is called. The start of such a query could be indicated by calling a method *GetFirst*. This mechanism appears to be straightforward at first sight, but it causes some implementation problems. We could define *GetNext* in a way that the parameter *obj* is not only an output parameter, but also an input parameter. *GetNext* should then return the list element preceded by *obj*. In this case *GetNext* would need to run through the list from the start to search for *obj* on each call. From the point of view of runtime efficiency this would be a disastrous solution, as a second loop would have been hidden inside the user's loop. We could avoid this misery by defining a variable *current: ListEleP* in *ListT* which is set to the list head when calling *GetFirst* and then moves one element forward on every call of *GetNext*. Unfortunately, this approach is not generally applicable because when used in nested loops the call in the inner loop would reposition the current element of the outer loop.

The solution to our dilemma can be found in an additional class specifically *Iterator* designed to support a query for all list elements. A variable *current* is used inside the object for saving the context of the current element. Now the problem of nested calls is solved as a local variable *current* exists for each run through the list.

The interface of the class has the following form:

```
ListRiderT*=RECORD
     PROCEDURE (VAR) BindTo*(VAR list:ListT);
     PROCEDURE (VAR) GetNext*(VAR obj:BaseType.BaseP);
   END;
```

Such a class is also called *iterator* or *rider*.

The *BindTo* method sets the current context to the head of a specific list.

For the implementation the module *Container* is extended by the following fragments:

```
TYPE
    ...
    ListRiderT*=RECORD
        current:ListEleP;
    END;
    ...

    PROCEDURE (VAR rider:ListRiderT) BindTo*(VAR list:ListT);
    BEGIN
        rider.current:=list.head;
    END BindTo;

    PROCEDURE (VAR rider:ListRiderT) GetNext*(
                                    VAR obj:BaseType.BaseP);
    BEGIN
        IF rider.current=NIL THEN
            obj:=NIL;
        ELSE
            obj:=rider.current.elem;
            rider.current:=rider.current.next;
        END;
    END GetNext;

END Container.
```

When using container classes without an automatic garbage collector care must be taken that objects which are still referenced in a list must not simply be released with *DISPOSE*, as this would cause the problem of *dangling pointers* discussed earlier.

5.6 An object-oriented project

With the final example we would like to go a little deeper into the subject. Also we leave the rather abstract world of pure data structures and move on to a more concrete problem which involves a simulated world containing simple robots.

The robots live within a grid of fixed size. Individual cells in the grid can only hold one robot at a time and robots can only move to adjacent cells. Each robot has its own personal color at the beginning. The aim of each robot is to paint all the other robots with its own color. For that purpose each robot can shoot a blob of color on its way, which then travels at the same speed as a robot.

The implementation of many details is deliberately kept simple in order to present the problem as clearly as possible. You are encouraged to experiment with your own extensions such as additional objects for the simulated maze (e.g., obstacles or more complex robots). This will show the advantages of object-oriented programming, such as ease of extensibility. At the same time the example illustrates another point: the attempt to design trivial programs in an object-oriented way often leads to a solution which is much longer than its counterpart developed using the conventional procedural approach. However, when it comes to extending the program it quickly becomes obvious where the true advantages lie. The object-oriented solution appears more elegant and concise only if the problem is of a reasonable size. And of course not every problem is equally well suited to an object-oriented solution.

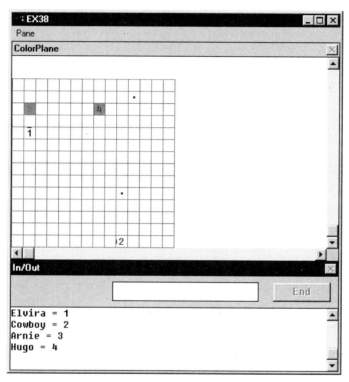

Fig. 58: Four simulated robots in action

At first glance it is obvious that this problem cannot be solved in the same easy fashion as most other small examples, namely by sitting back, thinking briefly, writing about a page of source code, and having a working solution.

Before we start we need to understand the nature of the problem more thoroughly by analyzing it and then producing a more precise description of what the program should do. Then, before writing the program, we need to make design decisions about how to realize a solution and then sketch the structure of the solution. In this way we can find and solve as many flaws in the proposed design as possible before a single line of code is written. These are the reasons why we call this example a project. The individual steps involved are discussed in more detail in the following section.

5.6.1 Projects and problem solving

The basic steps in really solving a problem in a project are

1. Analysis – analysis of the requirements

Clear statement of the problem

This is needed to make sure there is a common understanding of what the problem is between the person who wants the problem solved and whoever is going to solve it.

Analysis of the problem context and of the problem itself.

To fully understand the problem it must be seen in its context, for example to define any interfaces to the outside world.

2. Synthesis – abstract and detailed design

Design at an abstract level

This is basically first partitioning in the large by separating issues, e.g., user interface, command list analyser, simulator. Then for each issue, partitioning in the small is done to determine what the abstract components are (e.g., robots and blobs) and how they relate to each other. Successful partitioning in the large results in finding different parts of the problem which can be implemented separately. They build upon smaller components (found by partitioning in the small) and interface with each other mostly by using common components.

Design at a detailed level

A first draft for the interface of the different components is created. Then a choice of solution techniques can be made. The design of the interface and hidden solution technique of each component should be compatible with the needs of all other parts and components.

Implementation

The common parts are implemented first. This allows testing of basic components before anything is implemented on top of them.

3. Verification – checking the solution

Testing of the solution

This includes testing of the program with selected valid input to check correct behavior and with invalid input to check correct error detection. The test input needs to be chosen so as to constitute a step by step verification of the initial requirements.

Test runs in real life by a variety of users

All the steps from problem description to final laboratory test can contribute errors to the final result. The more complex a problem is the more likely it becomes that some of those errors remain undetected until reality puts software to its ultimate test. Carefully thought out testing carried out in a realistic user environment can provide valuable feedback for improving the quality of the program. In this way almost all faults can be corrected before the program is released for general use.

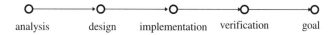

analysis   design   implementation   verification   goal

Fig. 59: Ideal project progress in a completely rational world

The design process is often not as linear as shown here because when improvements in the design are discovered during later stages, it is sometimes necessary to go back to an earlier stage to fix it. The problem solving technique proposed here is generally top-down in the design phase and bottom-up in the implementation phase.

In real life the different project phases seldom follow each other in a clearly separated way. Even at the very beginning of a project the specification usually fails to reflect precisely what people want to achieve and during the project they tend to get new ideas. Therefore it is almost impossible to follow the idealized view as shown in Fig. 59.

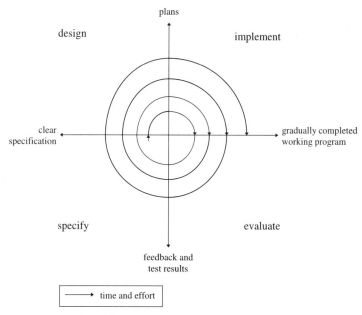

Fig. 60: Incremental development of software

As a matter of fact a project is hardly ever completed when the first solution is presented. The verification of the solution (the final stage when it is used) frequently leads to another cycle of development. This iterative process is illustrated in Fig. 60. The project is completed successfully when the solution reached has proven to be satisfactory for the user. Most successful programs are continually being changed and improved to meet the evolving needs of their users.

5.6.2 Step one: requirements specification

For our project we have chosen to make an informal specification with the goal of creating a sufficiently detailed analysis and description to form the basis of a solution and implementation. One simple quality measurement for a specification is how frequently later in the project an ambiguous situation occurs which cannot be solved without a clarification of the specification.

Formal specification methods have been invented which are especially useful for large projects. For more on specification methods we advise you to study literature specific to that area.

Project context

Sometimes a project has requirements and constraints which are outside the scope of the technical description of the problem. Often this information is not included in the specification because it is generally assumed to be known. Unfortunately this assumption may be wrong and as a result the outcome of a project may be unusable.

To avoid this the constraints and hidden agendas involved are included here although most of them might appear trivial in this case:

- Oberon-2 should be used as the programming language and *POW!* for the development environment.

- Because the program is intended as an example on object-oriented programming in this book an object-oriented approach is to be used throughout.

- The implementation should be easy to understand.

- It should show the advantages of object-oriented design, be easy to extend, and be a good basis for exercises. (This conflicts with the requirements above. In practice compromises are often necessary because of conflicting requirements.)

A closer inspection of the restrictions above reveals that they describe issues from a different viewpoint than the following technical description. They are about the project rather than about the solution to the problem. They define *why* a problem needs to be solved in a particular way instead of just describing *what* the problem is, which might be vital to know for some decisions regarding the design of the program or its future adaption.

Problem description

During a simulation the following items exist: a maze, one or more robots, and zero or more colored blobs. The simulation ends when only one active robot is left.

The following properties describe the maze:

- The maze is square with a size which remains fixed during a simulation.
- Each cell of the maze may be empty or contain one robot or multiple blobs.
- Robots have the following properties:
- Each robot has its own position in the maze, direction of vision, color, and unique id number (which uniquely identifies it and never changes).
- Each robot has a command list which defines its particular strategy. The robot's objective is to paint all the other robots with its own color. In each round of the simulation one command is processed for each robot. It therefore becomes obvious why a robot analyzing its environment moves more slowly than a rival making a getaway.
- As soon as a robot loses its initial color it is deactivated.

The initial conditions of the simulation are as follows:

- The color of each robot is unique.
- There are no active blobs of paint.
- The robots are distributed across the maze so that there is a free adjacent cell for each robot.
- Blobs have the following properties:
- A blob has a color and a fixed direction of movement, either horizontally or vertically.
- A blob moves by one cell during each step of the simulation.
- If a blob hits the border of the maze, it disappears.
- If a blob hits a robot of its own color, the blob disappears and nothing happens.
- If a blob hits a robot of a different color, the robot is painted in the color of the blob and becomes deactivated. (Therefore there may be two or more robots with the same color at the end.) The blob then disappears.

A command list is used to define the behavior of a robot. It may be composed of simple statements, branches and conditional branches.

A command list begins with the word "ROBOT" followed by the name of the robot, the end of the list is terminated with the word "END". In front of each command there is a label. If a command is appended with a colon then it becomes also a branch command and a label defines where the program branches for the next command. Commands followed by a question mark represent a conditional branch.

The following table lists the available robot commands and explains their meaning.

GO	move to the adjacent cell in the direction of vision
BLOB	send a color blob in the direction of vision
TURNLEFT	turn left 90°
TURNRIGHT	turn right 90°
TURNBACK	turn back 180°
SEE?	branch to a label if there is another robot in the line of vision
WALL?	Branch to a label if there is an obstacle in the adjacent cell in the line of vision

An example for such a command list:

```
ROBOT Hugo
  A GO
  - SEE?: B
  - WALL?: C
  - : A
  B BLOB: A
  C TURNLEFT: A
END
```

A more precise description of the robots command syntax can be achieved by using EBNF:

RobotDef = "ROBOT" ident <CR> CmdList "END" <CR>.
CmdList = CmdLine { CmdLine }.
CmdLine = label Cmd <CR>.
Cmd = CondBranchCmd ":" label | StdCmd [":" label] | ":" label.
CondBranchCmd = "WALL?" | "SEE?".
StdCmd = "GO" | "TURNLEFT" | "TURNRIGHT" | "TURNBACK" | "BLOB".

User interface

The description of all robots participating in the simulation is defined in a single text file.

During the simulation all robot and blob movements are displayed. The maze is shown graphically with each robot visible as its unique identification (id) number, with an indication of the current direction of vision (e.g., "3" means that the current direction of the robot with id 3 is downwards).

The association of robot names with their assigned ids should be visible during the simulation.

After the simulation ends the name of the winning robot should be displayed.

5.6.3 Step two: design

Analysis and abstract design

At first we try to reduce the complexity of the problem by dividing it into logically cohesive parts which can be considered separately (partitioning in the large).

A generally good approach is to separate the computational problems from the user interface. In this case we can further partition the user interface into a visible part and the part which analyzes the user input in the form of the robot definition file.

This leaves us with three parts of the problem:

- the analysis of the input file for the initialization of the simulation,

- a graphical user interface which also displays the current state of the objects in the simulation and

- the computation of the simulation itself.

Now we try to find components which can be used to compose a system to solve the different issues. We start with the part of the problem which is regarded as the key issue. This is the simulation itself.

The components we are trying to design are the classes in an object-oriented model for the problem. We try to find this by defining classes which serve as a model of items (which need not necessarily be of physical nature) in the real world. Then we define the methods of the classes by looking at what is done with or to those items in the real world. We must take care that all the essential relationships between items in the real world have a proper analogy in our model.

The obvious items in the simulation are the maze, robots, and blobs. First of all we evaluate their behavioral requirements and then we represent them in our model by defining classes for each. Apart from the command list for robots the properties of the items seem to be simple enough to be represented by basic types. For the representation of commands lists and individual commands it makes sense to define classes as well.

After we have determined which items should probably be represented by classes we need to decide whether they exist independently from each other or whether there are any "is a" or "has a" relationships between them. Also we might think about creating an abstract base class when we find classes with common properties which are also logically a specialisation of an abstract general concept.

Some of the proposed classes "possess" or "consist of" other objects: robots possess a command list, the command list consists of commands, and the maze contains robots and blobs.

Both robots and blobs exist within a maze. This and the common property of a position within a maze leads us to propose a design with an abstract base class for the two which represents objects existing within a maze in general. So far we have defined:

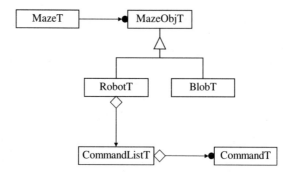

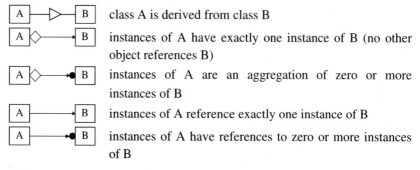

Fig. 61:Relationships of proposed classes

Symbols used for class relationships:

A ▷ B	class A is derived from class B
A ◇ B	instances of A have exactly one instance of B (no other object references B)
A ◇●B	instances of A are an aggregation of zero or more instances of B
A B	instances of A reference exactly one instance of B
A ●B	instances of A have references to zero or more instances of B

This graphical representation of class relationships is based on the Object Modeling Technique (OMT) [Rum91].

Now we look at the remaining issues.

The user interface is limited to obtaining the robots definition file from the user; from then on it just displays the progress of the simulation, which cannot be influenced by the user once it has been started. So the main task here is to create a visual representation based on the state of the objects we have already defined. To clearly separate the screen handling from the internal structure of the simulation objects we could define a corresponding viewer class for each (e.g., *RobotViewerT* for *RobotT*, ...). This would force us to define access methods precisely in the simulation classes to get all the information needed for display. However, we feel that this would introduce too much overhead for the benefits achieved, though it would become practical for extensions allowing interactive manipulation of simulation objects. Therefore, at this point we decide only that each of the simulation objects can create its own screen representation.

The task of the analysis of the input file is basically the conversion of the text based representation of the robots definition into a directly equivalent structure of objects which we have just described. So this particular part of the problem is mainly an algorithmic one involving traditional structured programming and data structures defined elsewhere.

Detailed design

Now we need to:

- look at which operations need to be done on the various different kinds of objects,

- define an interface accordingly, and

- design an internal data structure which should be a suitable basis for an efficient implementation.

Firstly we try to establish the relationships between all the classes which form the environment for the simulated objects. We try to keep this general enough to make it easy to add new objects (different kinds of robots,...) later on.

A word about class names: If one takes the approach of first designing the classes and their relationships and then partitioning them into modules, it is likely that some of the names will need to be changed at that point to make better sense when combined with the module name. To match the actual implementation, the class names in the following text already contain the module name where necessary, although the modules are defined later. Therefore the name of the proposed class *MazeObjT* now changes to *MazeBase.ObjectT* and *CommandListT* to *Commands.ListT*.

Class *MazeT*

A maze must be able to provide information on its contents. Therefore we need a rider which can retrieve the entire contents of a maze by repeated calling. We also sometimes need to know the contents of a specific cell. Because in some cases more than one object may occupy the same cell (blobs passing through the same cell in their path) we also need a rider for the contents of a specific cell.

Another important task of a maze is to show its current status on the screen. To break up the problem we define that each object within a maze must be capable of displaying itself. The maze itself can then display itself by requesting all objects contained in the maze to display themselves, including the empty cells.

After considering the abstract design of the maze and its tasks we can now draw up the following interface. It is important to define the interface of a class before making a final decision on how to implement it because the interface should represent the abstraction yet hide the internal implementation details.

```
MazeT*=RECORD
  (* initialise maze *)
  PROCEDURE (VAR) Init*();
  (* check whether co-cordinates are within range *)
  PROCEDURE (VAR) IsWithin*(x, y:INTEGER):BOOLEAN;
  (* put a new object into the maze *)
  PROCEDURE (VAR) Put*(obj:MazeBase.ObjectP);
```

```
(* delete an object from the maze *)
PROCEDURE (VAR) Delete*(obj:MazeBase.ObjectP;
                        VAR done:BOOLEAN);
(* show the contents of one cell on the screen *)
PROCEDURE (VAR) ShowCell*(x, y:INTEGER);
(* show the maze and all the objects within on the
   screen *)
PROCEDURE (VAR) Show*();
END;
```

A simple way to manage the contents of the maze is to use a container list, which we discussed in Section 5.5.2. We define that a maze owns a list which contains references to all objects within the maze. A rider is then easy to implement by using a list rider. Note that a maze is not logically a list, and thus is not derived from the list class but has an instance of a list. Hence a maze rider is not a list rider and should not be derived from a list rider. The rider for an individual cell is a specialization of the rider for the entire contents of the maze. Consequently we derive the cell rider from the maze rider (see Figure 62).

Class *MazeBase.ObjectT*

This class reflects the common properties of all objects which can exist in a maze. The interface can be easily derived from what we have discussed so far:

```
ObjectT*=RECORD (BaseType.BaseT)
    x-, y-:INTEGER;                    (*position within maze*)
    color*:ColorT;                     (*current color of object*)
    (* initialize object with position and color *)
    PROCEDURE (VAR) InitMazeObj*(x, y:INTEGER; col:ColorT);
    (* abstract method; called when object may do something *)
    PROCEDURE (POINTER) Action*();
    (* move the object to a new position *)
    PROCEDURE (VAR) MoveTo*(x, y:INTEGER);
    (* draw the object on the screen *)
    PROCEDURE (VAR) Show*();
END;
```

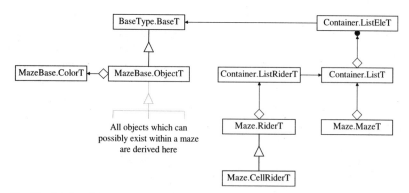

Fig. 62: Relationships of all classes except for those specific to concrete maze objects

Class *BlobT*

This class represents the blobs of color which a robot can fire off in a defined direction. Clearly instances of this class exist within a maze and are consequently derived from *MazeBase.ObjectT*. Because of the simple nature of a blob the interface defined by the base class is sufficient, we just add an initialization method to hide its internal variables.

```
BlobT*=RECORD (MazeBase.ObjectT)
    (* initialize blob with position, heading and color *)
    PROCEDURE (POINTER) InitBlob*(x, y, dx, dy:INTEGER;
                              col:MazeBase.ColorT);
    (* move the blob and paint any robot which has been hit *)
    PROCEDURE (POINTER) Action*();
    (* draw the blob on the screen *)
    PROCEDURE (VAR) Show*();
END;
```

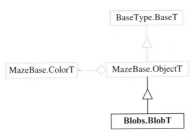

Fig. 63: Location of the blob class in the hierarchy

Class *RobotT*

This class represents the robots we want to simulate. It is derived from *MazeBase.ObjectT*. Apart from the methods inherited from there we define the method *ReadDefinition* which can read the definition of a robot from the input. The method *InitRobot* is added which allows the initialization of the aspects of a robot which are not defined by its definition.

```
RobotT*=RECORD (MazeBase.ObjectT)
    name-:ARRAY MazeBase.MAXSTR OF CHAR;     (*name of robot*)
    active-:BOOLEAN;            (*TRUE if robot is still active*)
    (* initialize robot with position, color and id number *)
    PROCEDURE (POINTER) InitRobot*(x, y:INTEGER;
                              col:MazeBase.ColorT;
                              id:INTEGER);
    (* execute the next command in the command list *)
    PROCEDURE (POINTER) Action*();
    (* read the robots command list from input *)
    PROCEDURE (VAR) ReadDefinition*(VAR done:BOOLEAN);
    (* draw the robot on the screen *)
    PROCEDURE (VAR) Show*();
END;
```

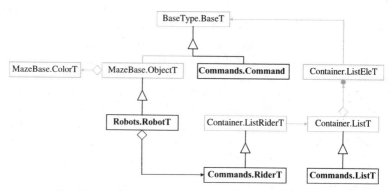

Fig. 64: Location of the robot specific classes in the hierarchy

Class *CommandT*

Instances of this class represent individual robot commands.

```
CommandT*=RECORD (BaseType.BaseT)
    label-:ARRAY MAXSTR OF CHAR;                        (*jump label*)
    code-:INTEGER;                                      (*command code*)
    goTo-:ARRAY MAXSTR OF CHAR;              (*jump target if any*)
    (* initialize the command with a label, a command code and
        a jump target; the command is translated from string to
        an integer code at the same time *)
    PROCEDURE (VAR) InitCommand*(label,
                                cmd, to:ARRAY OF CHAR);
END;
```

Class *Commands.ListT*

This class is used to store robot commands. For simplicity we derive it from *Container.ListT*. It has the same interface as the original class. A special class for command lists is needed only because the order of the commands is important for execution and is not retained by the original class.

```
ListT*=RECORD (Container.ListT)
    (* put a new command into the list and keep the list in the
        same order as the commands are put in *)
    PROCEDURE (VAR) Put*(obj:BaseType.BaseP);
END;
```

Class *Commands.ListRiderT*

This rider is an extended list rider which also makes it possible to change the rider position in the list. For this the method *GoTo* has been introduced, which looks for a list element with a defined jump label. It is assumed that all list elements are instances of *Commands.CommandT*.

```
RiderT*=RECORD (Container.ListRiderT)
    (* bind the rider to a specific list *)
    PROCEDURE (VAR) BindTo*(VAR list:Container.ListT);
```

```
(* set the rider position to the command with the defined
   label *)
PROCEDURE (VAR) GoTo*(label:ARRAY OF CHAR;
                      VAR done:BOOLEAN);
END;
```

Some details, like specific export marks in the proposed class definitions, probably were not obvious from the preceding problem analysis. In real life, minor modifications to the initial concept during implementation are inevitable, because it is impossible to anticipate all consequences of a design in advance.

Decomposition into modules

The attempt to hide the internal structure of all classes from the other parts of the implementation leads to an approach where every class is encapsulated in a separate module. However, this is not always desirable, for example there might be a number of small classes which form a logical group. It would not be wise to complicate the internal interfaces by having both a module and a class name for each class as little would be gained. A more compelling reason to have several classes in one module is a close coupling between two or more classes. In that case each member of a group of classes has to know about the others in order to be able to interact with them. A consequence of this can be quite annoyingly huge modules when the classes in question are non-trivial.

We face a situation like this with the classes *RobotT* and *BlobT*. Both of them are logically at the same level, and describe concrete objects which exist within a maze. Instances of those classes need to be able to interact with each other when they meet in the maze, thus they somehow have to "know" about each other's existence.

Of course there is a cure to this problem. A common abstract super class can be created, in which all possible interactions between instances of the different classes are explicitly specified in the form of methods. We already have the common super class *MazeBase.ObjectT*. All we need to do is to extend the interface as shown below and implement the methods both for blobs and robots.

```
ObjectT*=RECORD (BaseType.BaseT)
   ...
   (* abstract method; return TRUE if an object can be painted
      (e.g. by a blob) *)
   PROCEDURE (VAR) IsPaintable*():BOOLEAN;
   (* abstract method; return TRUE if no other object can
      share a cell with the receiver *)
   PROCEDURE (VAR) OccupiesCellExclusively*():BOOLEAN;
   (* abstract method; only needs to be implemented if
      IsPaintable returns TRUE; repaints the receiver using
      the defined color *)
   PROCEDURE (POINTER) Paint*(col:ColorT);
END;
```

The only remaining interdependence which cannot be resolved so elegantly involves the ability of robots to create a new instance of a blob. But as there is no longer any dependence in the opposite direction, the module *Robots* can now simply import the module *Blobs*.

Now we propose to partition the system into the following modules:

BaseType	contains an empty abstract base type which is used for container classes (as introduced in Section 5.2)
Container	contains a list class for storing arbitrary objects and a matching rider (as introduced in Section 5.5.2)
Commands	contains the robots command class and a list for managing robot commands
MazeBase	defines abstract maze elements
Maze	implements the maze itself
Global	all instances of objects which determine the global environment for simulated objects are in here
Blobs	contains the blob class
Robots	contains the robots class
Ex38	the main program

This design leads to the hierarchy of module dependencies shown in Fig. 65.

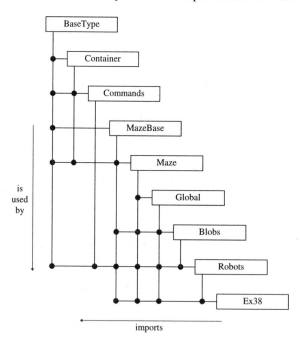

Fig. 65: Module dependencies

5.6.4 Step three: implementation

The solution presented here relies on the existence of a garbage collector which detects objects that are no longer referenced and destroys them to recycle the memory they occupy.

Now we come to the code, which is interleaved with text to explain what is being done and how it works.

```
MODULE MazeBase;                                                      MazeBase
(* This module defines the basic types for the simulation. *)

IMPORT BaseType, C:=ColorPlane;

CONST
   GRID*=16;        (*cell width on display in co-ordinates*)
   MAXSTR*=30;  (*maximum length for strings read from input*)

TYPE
```

MazeBase.ColorT provides for the representation of the colors in terms of red, green, and blue intensity.

```
   (*represents the color of maze objects*)
   ColorT*=RECORD
      r,g,b:INTEGER;
   END;
```

All objects that may be found inside the maze are derived from the class *MazeBase.ObjectT*, which always has a position mark. The method *Action* is abstract. It must be overwritten for each derived class and determines how an object may become active in the maze. The second method of the base class *Show(x,y:INTEGER)* sets the position *(x,y)* of the receiver to where it should be displayed. Instances of the base class are displayed as an empty field. So this method can be used for drawing the background for the derived classes.

```
   (*abstract base class for all objects existing within
     maze*)
   ObjectT*=RECORD (BaseType.BaseT)
      x*,y*:INTEGER;                        (*position within maze*)
      color*:ColorT;                   (*current color of object*)
   END;
   ObjectP*=POINTER TO ObjectT;

(*---- class ColorT -------------------------------------*)

PROCEDURE (VAR c:ColorT) SetTo*(r,g,b:INTEGER);
BEGIN
   c.r:=r; c.g:=g; c.b:=b;
END SetTo;

PROCEDURE (VAR c:ColorT) Set*;
BEGIN
   C.SetForeColor(c.r,c.g,c.b);
END Set;
```

```
PROCEDURE (VAR c:ColorT) Equal*(VAR x:ColorT):BOOLEAN;
BEGIN
    RETURN (c.r=x.r) & (c.g=x.g) & (c.b=x.b);
END Equal;

(*---- class ObjectT -------------------------------------*)

PROCEDURE (VAR obj:ObjectT) InitMazeObj*(x,y:INTEGER;
                                         col:ColorT);
BEGIN
   obj.x:=x;
   obj.y:=y;
   obj.color:=col;
END InitMazeObj;

PROCEDURE (VAR obj:ObjectT) MoveTo*(x,y:INTEGER);
BEGIN
   obj.x:=x; obj.y:=y;
END MoveTo;

PROCEDURE (VAR obj:ObjectT) Show*;
VAR
   posx,posy:INTEGER;
BEGIN
   C.SetForeColor(100,100,100);
   posx:=obj.x*GRID; posy:=obj.y*GRID;
   C.Box(posx,posy,posx+GRID,posy+GRID,1);
   C.SetForeColor(255,255,255);
   C.Bar(posx+1,posy+1,posx+GRID-1,posy+GRID-1,1);
END Show;

PROCEDURE (obj:ObjectP) Action*;
BEGIN
END Action;

PROCEDURE (VAR obj:ObjectT) IsPaintable*():BOOLEAN;
BEGIN
END IsPaintable;

PROCEDURE (VAR obj:ObjectT) OccupiesCellExclusively*():
                                             BOOLEAN;
BEGIN
END OccupiesCellExclusively;

PROCEDURE (obj:ObjectP) Paint*(col:ColorT);
BEGIN
END Paint;

END MazeBase.
```

The class *Maze.MazeT* stores objects using a list. Obviously, it would be easier in this context to use a two-dimensional array instead. However, two blobs could not be situated at the same position, which may well occur if two trajectories cross and this reason alone justifies the design decision.

Instances of the class *Maze.CellRider* may be used to check if and what object is currently at a certain position, and instances of the class *Maze.Rider* can iterate through all objects in a maze.

```
MODULE Maze;                                                              Maze
(* This module implements the maze class and some riders to
   query the contents of a maze *)

IMPORT BaseType, Container, MazeBase;

CONST
   SIZE*=14;                    (* maze width and height in cells *)

TYPE
   (* represents a maze *)
   MazeT*=RECORD
      objList:Container.ListT;
   END;

   (* a rider for retrieving all objects in a maze *)
   RiderT*=RECORD
      listRider:Container.ListRiderT;
   END;
   RiderP*=POINTER TO RiderT;

   (* for retrieving all objects at a certain position in
      a maze *)
   CellRiderT*=RECORD (RiderT)
      x,y:INTEGER;
   END;
   CellRiderP*=POINTER TO CellRiderT;

(*---- class RiderT -------------------------------------*)

PROCEDURE (VAR rider:RiderT) BindTo*(VAR maze:MazeT);
BEGIN
   rider.listRider.BindTo(maze.objList);
END BindTo;

PROCEDURE (VAR rider:RiderT) GetNext*(
                                   VAR obj:MazeBase.ObjectP);
VAR
   ele:BaseType.BaseP;
BEGIN
   rider.listRider.GetNext(ele);
   IF ele=NIL THEN
      obj:=NIL
   ELSE
      obj:=ele(MazeBase.ObjectP)
   END;
END GetNext;

(*---- class CellRiderT -------------------------------*)

PROCEDURE (VAR rider:CellRiderT) BindToCell*(VAR maze:MazeT;
                                             x,y:INTEGER);
BEGIN
   rider.BindTo(maze);
   rider.x:=x;
   rider.y:=y;
END BindToCell;
```

```
PROCEDURE (VAR rider:CellRiderT) GetNext*(VAR
                                         obj:MazeBase.ObjectP);
BEGIN
   REPEAT
      rider.GetNext^(obj);
   UNTIL (obj=NIL) OR
         ((obj.x=rider.x) & (obj.y=rider.y));
END GetNext;

(*---- class MazeT ---------------------------------------*)

PROCEDURE (VAR maze:MazeT) Init*;
BEGIN
   maze.objList.Init;
END Init;

PROCEDURE (VAR maze:MazeT) IsWithin*(x,y:INTEGER):BOOLEAN;
BEGIN
   RETURN (x>=0) & (y>=0) & (x<SIZE) & (y<SIZE);
END IsWithin;

PROCEDURE (VAR maze:MazeT) Put*(obj:MazeBase.ObjectP);
BEGIN
   maze.objList.Put(obj);
END Put;

PROCEDURE (VAR maze:MazeT) Delete*(obj:MazeBase.ObjectP;
                                   VAR done:BOOLEAN);
BEGIN
   maze.objList.Delete(obj,done);
END Delete;

PROCEDURE (VAR maze:MazeT) ShowCell*(x,y:INTEGER);
VAR
   rider:CellRiderT;
   obj:MazeBase.ObjectP;
   empty:MazeBase.ObjectT;
BEGIN
   rider.BindToCell(maze,x,y);
   rider.GetNext(obj);
   IF obj#NIL THEN
      obj.Show
   ELSE
      empty.MoveTo(x,y);
      empty.Show;
   END;
END ShowCell;

PROCEDURE (VAR maze:MazeT) Show*;
VAR
   i,j:INTEGER;
BEGIN
   FOR i:=0 TO SIZE-1 DO
      FOR j:=0 TO SIZE-1 DO
         maze.ShowCell(i,j);
      END;
   END;
END Show;

END Maze.
```

The global data structure *Global.maze* is a "container" for all objects operating in the maze.

```
MODULE Global;                                                    Global
(* In this module all simulation global data representing the
   environment for simulated objects is made accessible *)

IMPORT Maze;

VAR
    maze*:Maze.MazeT; (*global, contains all simulated objects*)

END Global.
```

Instances of the class *Blobs.BlobT* represent the blobs fired by the robots. It travels across the maze in a predefined direction until it reaches either a robot or the borders of the maze. In addition to its position each blob is defined by its color and its direction.

```
MODULE Blobs;                                                     Blobs
(* This module implements the class for the Blobs *)

IMPORT C:=ColorPlane, MazeBase, Maze, Global;

CONST
    GRID=MazeBase.GRID;

TYPE
    BlobP*=POINTER TO BlobT;
    BlobT*=RECORD (MazeBase.ObjectT)
        dx,dy:INTEGER;
    END;

PROCEDURE (VAR obj:BlobT) IsPaintable*():BOOLEAN;
BEGIN
    RETURN FALSE;
END IsPaintable;

PROCEDURE (VAR obj:BlobT) OccupiesCellExclusively*():
                                              BOOLEAN;
BEGIN
    RETURN FALSE;
END OccupiesCellExclusively;


PROCEDURE (blob:BlobP) InitBlob*(x,y,dx,dy:INTEGER;
                          col:MazeBase.ColorT);
BEGIN
    blob.InitMazeObj(x,y,col);
    blob.dx:=dx; blob.dy:=dy;
END InitBlob;
```

In *Show* the position and color of the blob are set up and the background is cleared, the blob is now located within a square in the maze.

```
PROCEDURE (VAR blob:BlobT) Show*;
VAR
    posx,posy:INTEGER;
BEGIN
    blob.Show^;
```

```
    blob.color.Set;
    posx:=blob.x*GRID+GRID DIV 2;
    posy:=blob.y*GRID+GRID DIV 2;
    C.Bar(posx-1,posy-1,posx+1,posy+1,1);
END Show;
```

In the method *Action* a blob is moved to the new position and drawn if it is still inside the maze and has not yet hit a robot. If the blob hits a robot, the robot takes on the blob's color unless it is already that color. In that case, or if the blob would leave the maze, the blob disappears.

```
PROCEDURE (blob:BlobP) Action*;
VAR
    rider:Maze.CellRiderT;
    anObj:MazeBase.ObjectP;
    kill,done:BOOLEAN;
BEGIN
    blob.MoveTo(blob.x+blob.dx,blob.y+blob.dy);
    Global.maze.ShowCell(blob.x-blob.dx,blob.y-blob.dy);
                                    (*redraw previous position*)
    IF Global.maze.IsWithin(blob.x,blob.y) THEN
        rider.BindToCell(Global.maze,blob.x,blob.y);
        rider.GetNext(anObj);
        kill:=FALSE;
        WHILE (anObj#NIL) & ~kill DO
            IF anObj.IsPaintable() THEN
                IF ~blob.color.Equal(anObj.color) THEN
                    anObj.Paint(blob.color)
                END;
                kill:=TRUE;
            ELSIF anObj.OccupiesCellExclusively() THEN
                kill:=TRUE;
            END;
            rider.GetNext(anObj);
        END;
        IF kill THEN
            Global.maze.Delete(blob,done);
            ASSERT(done);
        ELSE
            blob.Show;
        END;
    ELSE
        Global.maze.Delete(blob,done);
        ASSERT(done);
    END;
END Action;

END Blobs.
```

Commands

```
MODULE Commands;
(* The classes for robot commands, command lists, and riders
    for command lists are implemented in here *)
IMPORT Container,BaseType;

CONST
    MAXSTR=30;                       (* maximum length of jump labels *)

    INSERTOK*=0;                         (* result codes for Insert *)
    INSERTLISTFULL*=1;
    INSERTUNKNOWNCMD*=2;
```

```
NOP*=0;                              (* command codes *)
GO*=1;
TURNLEFT*=2;
TURNRIGHT*=3;
TURNBACK*=4;
WALL*=5;
SEE*=6;
BLOB*=7;
```

Commands.CommandT represents a command which contains fields that define its actions. The *label* field contains the commands identifier, the *cmd* field contains its main action, and the field *goto* contains the label at which the execution of the robot program continues if a branch is taken.

```
TYPE

   (*This class represents robot commands. Each instance of
     this class corresponds to one line in a robot program.*)
   CommandT*=RECORD (BaseType.BaseT)
      label-:ARRAY MAXSTR OF CHAR;     (*label of the command *)
      code-:INTEGER;                   (* command code *)
      goTo-:ARRAY MAXSTR OF CHAR;      (* jump label if any *)
   END;
   CommandP*=POINTER TO CommandT;
```

Commands.ListT is used for the management of the whole command list of a robot.

```
   ListT*=RECORD (Container.ListT)
   END;

   RiderT*=RECORD (Container.ListRiderT)
         (* pointer to first list element; needed for GoTo *)
      listHead:Container.ListEleP;
   END;
```

The following methods are used for establishing and managing the command lists. *Put* had to be overwritten because the implementation inherited from *Container.ListT* did not preserve the ordering of the list, which is crucial when dealing with command lists.

```
   (*---- class ListT --------------------------------------*)

PROCEDURE (VAR list:ListT) Put*(obj:BaseType.BaseP);
VAR
   newEle,ele:Container.ListEleP;
BEGIN
   NEW(newEle);
   ASSERT(newEle#NIL);
   newEle.elem:=obj;
   newEle.next:=NIL;
   IF list.head=NIL THEN
      list.head:=newEle;
   ELSE
      ele:=list.head;
      WHILE ele.next#NIL DO ele:=ele.next END;
      ele.next:=newEle;
   END;
END Put;
```

The next command can be queried using *GetNext* which has been inherited from *Container.ListRiderT*. *GoTo* sets the current position in the list to a command with the defined label. The method *BindTo* had to be overwritten because *GoTo* needs to know about the first element of the list, which is remembered here.

```
(*---- class RiderT -------------------------------------*)

PROCEDURE (VAR rider:RiderT) BindTo*(
                              VAR list:Container.ListT);
BEGIN
   rider.BindTo^(list);
   rider.listHead:=list.head;
END BindTo;

PROCEDURE (VAR rider:RiderT) GoTo*(label:ARRAY OF CHAR;
                              VAR done:BOOLEAN);
BEGIN
   rider.current:=rider.listHead;
   WHILE (rider.current#NIL) &
         (rider.current.elem(CommandP).label#label) DO
      rider.current:=rider.current.next;
   END;
   done:=rider.current#NIL;
END GoTo;
```

In *InitCommand* the the robot definition input is used to initialize a *Commands.CommandT* object. The command code is transformed from the initial string to an equivalent integer representation, and the commands are stored numerically in the list. The constants *TURNLEFT*, etc., define the values which represent these commands at the beginning of the module.

```
(*---- class CommandT -------------------------------------*)

PROCEDURE (VAR command:CommandT) InitCommand*(label,
                              cmd,to:ARRAY OF CHAR);
BEGIN
   COPY(label,command.label);
   COPY(to,command.goTo);
   IF cmd="GO" THEN command.code:=GO
   ELSIF cmd="TURNLEFT" THEN command.code:=TURNLEFT
   ELSIF cmd="TURNRIGHT" THEN command.code:=TURNRIGHT
   ELSIF cmd="TURNBACK" THEN command.code:=TURNBACK
   ELSIF cmd="WALL?" THEN command.code:=WALL
   ELSIF cmd="SEE?" THEN command.code:=SEE
   ELSIF cmd="BLOB" THEN command.code:=BLOB
   ELSE command.code:=NOP END;
END InitCommand;

END Commands.
```

Robots
```
MODULE Robots;
(* In this module the class is implemented which represents
   the robots *)

IMPORT Strings,In,Out,C:=ColorPlane,
       BaseType,MazeBase,Maze,Global,Blobs,Commands;
```

```
CONST
   GRID=MazeBase.GRID;
   (* width of a cell in the maze in screen co-ordinates *)

   (* constants for robot headings *)
   LEFT=0;
   UP=1;
   RIGHT=2;
   DOWN=3;

TYPE
   RobotT*=RECORD (MazeBase.ObjectT)
      cmdRider:Commands.RiderT;
      name-:ARRAY MazeBase.MAXSTR OF CHAR;
      heading:INTEGER;
      id:LONGINT;
      active-:BOOLEAN;
   END;
   RobotP*=POINTER TO RobotT;

PROCEDURE (VAR robo:RobotT) IsPaintable*():BOOLEAN;
BEGIN
   RETURN TRUE;.   (* determines that a robot can be painted *)
END IsPaintable;

PROCEDURE (VAR robo:RobotT) OccupiesCellExclusively*():
                                                    BOOLEAN;
BEGIN
   RETURN TRUE; (*This determines that no other object must
                  occupy the same cell together with a robot *)
END OccupiesCellExclusively;

PROCEDURE (robo:RobotP) Paint*(col:MazeBase.ColorT);
BEGIN
   robo.active:=FALSE;
   robo.color:=col;
   robo.Show;
END Paint;
```

On initializing a robot its name and its identifying symbol for the maze are displayed using the module *Out.* Initially the viewing direction of all robots is set to *LEFT.*

```
PROCEDURE (robo:RobotP) InitRobot*(x,y:INTEGER;
                                   col:MazeBase.ColorT;
                                   id:INTEGER);
BEGIN
   Out.String(robo.name); Out.String(" = ");
   Out.Int(id,1); Out.Ln;
   robo.InitMazeObj(x,y,col);
   robo.id:=id;
   robo.heading:=LEFT;
   robo.active:=TRUE;
END InitRobot;
```

The method *ReadDefinition* reads the description of the robot. It begins with the designator "ROBOT", followed by the name of the robot. Then a list of commands is appended. In front of each command there is a label. If the command terminates with a colon a label is expected at which the execution will be continued. Thus the commands "SEE?" and "WALL?" are actually conditional branches.

```
(* This method reads the definition for a robot from the
   input. It assumes that the word "ROBOT" has already been
   read. This allows the caller to recognise the type of
   object definition before deciding which method needs to be
   called for reading a particular object. *)
PROCEDURE (VAR robo:RobotT) ReadDefinition*(
                                         VAR done:BOOLEAN);
VAR
   label,cmd,to:ARRAY MazeBase.MAXSTR OF CHAR;
   command:Commands.CommandP;
   list:Commands.ListT;
BEGIN
   list.Init;
   In.Name(robo.name);
   LOOP
      In.Name(label);
      IF (label="END") OR ~In.Done THEN EXIT END;
      In.Name(cmd);
      IF cmd[Strings.Length(cmd)-1]=":" THEN
         cmd[Strings.Length(cmd)-1]:=0X;
         In.Name(to);
      ELSE
         to:="";
      END;
      NEW(command);
      ASSERT(command#NIL);
      command.InitCommand(label,cmd,to);
      list.Put(command);
   END;
   robo.cmdRider.BindTo(list);
   done:=In.Done;
END ReadDefinition;
```

Depending on the viewing direction of a robot *GetDir* returns values which can be added to the position in order to move it in the direction needed.

```
PROCEDURE (robo:RobotP) GetDir(VAR dx,dy:INTEGER);
BEGIN
   IF    robo.heading=RIGHT THEN dx:=1;  dy:=0;
   ELSIF robo.heading=LEFT  THEN dx:=-1; dy:=0;
   ELSIF robo.heading=UP    THEN dx:=0;  dy:=1;
   ELSIF robo.heading=DOWN  THEN dx:=0;  dy:=-1;
   END;
END GetDir;
```

The following method executes the command "GO". First a check is made to ensure that the next position in viewing direction is still inside the maze and then whether there is an object at this position. If another robot is present the current position remains unchanged.

```
PROCEDURE (robo:RobotP) Go;
VAR
   nx,ny,dx,dy:INTEGER;
   anObj:MazeBase.ObjectP;
   rider:Maze.CellRiderT;
BEGIN
   robo.GetDir(dx,dy);
```

```
    nx:=robo.x+dx; ny:=robo.y+dy;
    IF Global.maze.IsWithin(nx,ny) THEN
        rider.BindToCell(Global.maze,nx,ny);
        REPEAT
            rider.GetNext(anObj);
        UNTIL (anObj=NIL) OR
              anObj.OccupiesCellExclusively();
        IF anObj=NIL THEN
            robo.MoveTo(nx,ny);
            robo.Show;
            Global.maze.ShowCell(nx-dx,ny-dy);
                                    (*redraw previous position*)
        END;
    END;
END Go;
```

The following method implements the command "WALL?". The return value of this function is *TRUE* if a robot or the borderline of the maze is detected at the next position in viewing direction of the robot.

```
PROCEDURE (robo:RobotP) Wall():BOOLEAN;
VAR
    nx,ny,dx,dy:INTEGER;
    anObj:MazeBase.ObjectP;
    rider:Maze.CellRiderT;
BEGIN
    robo.GetDir(dx,dy);
    nx:=robo.x+dx;
    ny:=robo.y+dy;
    IF ~Global.maze.IsWithin(nx,ny) THEN
        RETURN TRUE;
    ELSE
        rider.BindToCell(Global.maze,nx,ny);
        REPEAT
            rider.GetNext(anObj)
        UNTIL (anObj=NIL) OR
              anObj.OccupiesCellExclusively();
        RETURN anObj#NIL;
    END;
END Wall;
```

The following method implements the command "SEE?". The return value of the function is *TRUE* if an object other than a blob is recognized in the viewing direction from the robot to the limit of the maze. In this basic version of the simulation this object can only be a robot.

```
PROCEDURE (robo:RobotP) See():BOOLEAN;
VAR
    dx,dy,x,y:INTEGER;
    anObj:MazeBase.ObjectP;
    rider:Maze.CellRiderT;
BEGIN
    robo.GetDir(dx,dy);
    x:=robo.x; y:=robo.y;
    REPEAT
        x:=x+dx; y:=y+dy;
        rider.BindToCell(Global.maze,x,y);
        REPEAT
            rider.GetNext(anObj);
        UNTIL (anObj=NIL) OR (anObj IS RobotP);
```

```
     UNTIL (anObj#NIL) OR ~Global.maze.IsWithin(x,y);
     RETURN (anObj#NIL) &
            (anObj IS RobotP) & (anObj(RobotP).active);
END See;
```

The following method executes the command "BLOB". It generates a blob in the viewing direction of the robot, moving in the same direction as the robot. To ensure that it is still alive in the next round of the simulation it is entered in the list of active objects *objList*.

```
PROCEDURE (robo:RobotP) CreateBlob;
VAR
    blob:Blobs.BlobP;
    dx,dy:INTEGER;
BEGIN
    robo.GetDir(dx,dy);
    NEW(blob);
    ASSERT(blob#NIL);
    blob.InitBlob(0,0,dx,dy,robo.color);
    Global.maze.Put(blob);
    blob.MoveTo(robo.x,robo.y);
    blob.Action;              (* move blob away from its creator *)
END CreateBlob;
```

In each round of the simulation the activity of a robot consists of executing the next command on its command list. Subsequently the possible labels in the commands are considered and conditional branches are treated appropriately.

All commands are executed by calling separate corresponding methods, in order to limit the size of *Action*, apart from those used for changing the viewing direction. The four possible viewing directions are defined numerically in such a way that the preceding direction modulo 4 is equivalent to turning left whereas the following direction modulo 4 corresponds to turning right.

```
PROCEDURE (robo:RobotP) Action*;
VAR
    obj:BaseType.BaseP;
    command:Commands.CommandP;
    doGo:BOOLEAN;
    done:BOOLEAN;
BEGIN
    IF ~robo.active THEN RETURN END;
    robo.cmdRider.GetNext(obj);
                            (* robot program has terminated? *)
    IF obj=NIL THEN RETURN END;
    command:=obj(Commands.CommandP);
    doGo:=TRUE;
    CASE command.code OF
       Commands.NOP:
    |  Commands.GO: robo.Go;
    |  Commands.TURNLEFT:
       robo.heading:=(robo.heading-1) MOD 4;
       robo.Show;
    |  Commands.TURNRIGHT:
       robo.heading:=(robo.heading+1) MOD 4;
       robo.Show;
```

```
    |  Commands.TURNBACK:
       robo.heading:=(robo.heading+2) MOD 4;
       robo.Show;
    |  Commands.WALL:  doGo:=robo.Wall();
    |  Commands.SEE:   doGo:=robo.See();
    |  Commands.BLOB: robo.CreateBlob;
    END;
    IF doGo & (command.goTo#"") THEN
        robo.cmdRider.GoTo(command.goTo,done);
        IF ~done THEN
            Out.String("jump label not found:");
            Out.String(command.goTo);
            Out.Ln;
        END;
    END;
END Action;
```

In *Show* the background is cleared by using the base class. The robot itself is represented by its symbol at the center of a cell. If it is inactive, this is indicated by a gray background. A small indicator marks the viewing direction.

```
PROCEDURE (VAR robo:RobotT) Show*;
VAR
    t:ARRAY 10 OF CHAR;
    h1,h2:INTEGER;
    posx,posy:INTEGER;
BEGIN
    robo.Show^;
    posx:=robo.x*GRID; posy:=robo.y*GRID;
    IF ~robo.active THEN
       C.SetBackColor(130,130,130);
       C.Bar(posx+1,posy+1,posx+GRID-1,posy+GRID-1,0);
    END;
    robo.color.Set;
    Strings.Str(robo.id,t);
    C.GotoXY(posx+(GRID-C.TextWidth(t)) DIV 2,
             posy+(GRID+C.TextHeight()) DIV 2);
    C.WriteStr(t);
    IF ~robo.active THEN
       C.SetBackColor(255,255,255);
    ELSE
       h1:=GRID DIV 3; h2:=2*GRID DIV 3;
       CASE robo.heading OF
          UP:   C.Line(posx+h1,posy+GRID-1,
                       posx+h2,posy+GRID-1,1);
       |  DOWN: C.Line(posx+h1,posy+1,posx+h2,posy+1,1);
       |  LEFT: C.Line(posx+1,posy+h1,posx+1,posy+h2,1);
       |  RIGHT:C.Line(posx+GRID-1,posy+h1,
                       posx+GRID-1,posy+h2,1);
       END;
    END;
END Show;

END Robots.
```

At last we come to the main module.

At the beginning of the simulation in *InitSimulation*, first the global data structures are initialized, then robots are created as long as it is possible to

read the command lists without error, and finally the graphics window is
opened and the empty maze displayed.

ex38.mod

```
MODULE Ex38;
(* This is the main module of the robots project *)

IMPORT Strings,Process,W:=Windows,
       In,Out,C:=ColorPlane,
       MazeBase,Maze,Global,Robots;

CONST
    DELAY=100;                      (* number of timer ticks to wait
                                       between simulation rounds *)

(* Initializes the maze, reads the input and creates initial
   robot colors, ids, and positions. *)
PROCEDURE InitSimulation;
VAR
    robo:Robots.RobotP;
    color:MazeBase.ColorT;
    x,y,i:INTEGER;
    done:BOOLEAN;
    txt:ARRAY MazeBase.MAXSTR OF CHAR;
BEGIN
    Global.maze.Init;
    i:=0;
    REPEAT
        In.Name(txt);
        IF txt="ROBOT" THEN
            NEW(robo);
            ASSERT(robo#NIL);
            robo.ReadDefinition(done);
            IF done THEN
                Global.maze.Put(robo);
                CASE i MOD 4 OF
                  0:x:=i; y:=i;
                | 1:x:=Maze.SIZE-i; y:=0;
                | 2:x:=0; y:=Maze.SIZE-i;
                | 3:x:=Maze.SIZE-i; y:=Maze.SIZE-i;
                END;
                color.SetTo((i*63) MOD 256, (*an arbitrary way to*)
                            (i*27) MOD 256,    (*obtain different*)
                            (255-i*127) MOD 256); (*robot colors*)
                INC(i);
                robo.InitRobot(x,y,color,i);
            END;
        ELSIF txt="" THEN
            (*skip empty lines between objects*)
        ELSE
            Out.String("unknown maze object:");
            Out.String(txt); Out.Ln;
        END;
    UNTIL ~In.Done;
    C.Open;
    Global.maze.Show;
END InitSimulation;
```

Simulate contains the main loop of the program; the simulation loops round
and round from here as follows:

- first, the action method is called for all active objects,
- the number of active robots is checked, and the name of the first active robot found is remembered.

The simulation terminates as soon as no robot is active.

The local procedure *Wait* is used to control the speed of the simulation. It is based upon the function *GetTickCount* of the Windows programming interface which returns the number of time intervals of an internal clock since the start of the system. The time at the beginning of a simulation round is stored in *startTime*. At the end of each round the program waits until a defined period of time has passed. Thus the loop should run at the same speed on all computers, unless the computer is too slow for this application.

```
(* This procedure contains the main loop of the simulation *)
PROCEDURE Simulate(VAR winner:Robots.RobotP);
VAR
    anObj:MazeBase.ObjectP;
    nActive:INTEGER;
    startTime:LONGINT;
    rider:Maze.RiderT;

    (* wait until a specified amount of time has elapsed *)
    PROCEDURE Wait;
    BEGIN
        REPEAT
            Process.Yield;
        UNTIL W.GetTickCount()-startTime>DELAY;
    END Wait;

BEGIN
    REPEAT
        startTime:=W.GetTickCount();
        rider.BindTo(Global.maze);
        LOOP
            rider.GetNext(anObj);
            IF anObj=NIL THEN EXIT END;
            anObj.Action;
        END;
        nActive:=0;
        winner:=NIL;
        rider.BindTo(Global.maze);
        LOOP                        (* determine an active robot and
                                       the number of active robots   *)
            rider.GetNext(anObj);
            IF anObj=NIL THEN EXIT END;
            IF (anObj IS Robots.RobotP) &
                anObj(Robots.RobotP).active THEN
                winner:=anObj(Robots.RobotP);
                INC(nActive);
            END;
        END;
        Wait;
    UNTIL nActive<=1;
END Simulate;
```

The main program now only has to start the simulation after the initialization and to announce the winner when the simulation is complete.

```
PROCEDURE ProgMain*;
VAR
   winner:Robots.RobotP;
BEGIN
   Out.String("selct 'read input from...' in the menu");
   Out.Ln;
   Out.String("and use the file 'robots.txt' as input");
   Out.Ln; Out.Ln;
   InitSimulation;
   Simulate(winner);
   IF winner#NIL THEN
      Out.Ln; Out.String(winner.name);
      Out.String(" has won!");
   ELSE
      Out.Ln;
      Out.String("draw game");
   END;
END ProgMain;

END Ex38.
```

5.7 Retrospective and summary

In large software systems there are many inter-relationships and dependencies between the separate components. These relations between the classes, modules, and their internal structures determine the complexity of software. To fully understand a whole system it is necessary to comprehend all these relations, structures, and interactions. This is why modern software engineering concentrates on reducing and simplifying the number of interfaces, on describing them and on the idea of re-using of existing modules.

The aim of re-usability is quite obvious: it saves development effort and avoids both new and repeated mistakes. The idea of re-usability is not new; it has its roots in the textual replacement of code (*macros*) and in program libraries for various applications.

Nowadays, however, the emphasis is on ease of re-engineering, adaptation, and the possibility of extending the functionality of these existing components.

Object-oriented programming (OOP) focuses on these tasks: *reduction of complexity* of software as well as *re-usability* and *flexibility* by internalizing the data. These aspects have already been discussed in connection with abstract data types and how they can be implemented and are summarized below:

To support the goals of object-oriented programming a programming language must offer the following features:

- *Interface simplification by the principle of information hiding*

   Data are encapsulated in a way that the user (client) can only see what is necessary. Direct access to data is avoided and access is only provided using procedures or methods instead.

To realize this principle Oberon-2 provides modules with export marks ("*", "-") in addition to procedures.

- *Data abstraction*

   This is a generalization of the possibility of introducing user-defined data types and at the same time declare the exclusively allowed operations (procedures, methods) on them. The abstract data type (ADT) is accessed by the client using a well-defined interface with as many instances as desired being created from the ADT. A further development of the ADT concept leads to the class concept of object-oriented programming. Instances of classes are called objects. The operations to be executed on them (i.e., the messages they can understand) are the methods. Here, Oberon-2 introduces the notion of *type-bound procedures*.

- *Inheritance*

   The idea behind the concept of inheritance is that objects already defined together with their characteristics and their functions/methods can be either used or over-ridden, and extended or partially modified as necessary. Thus, inheritance is a key concept of OOP. If a class is derived from another class (base class) it has the same functionality as the base class. The derived class inherits all the features of its base class.

   Oberon-2 offers the opportunity to extend record types to a new type to realize the principle of inheritance. In this context, the rules of inheritance for type-bound procedures together with the dynamic type of pointers play an important role. Type-bound procedures can be overwritten in the derived class.

- *Dynamic binding*

   In contrast to static binding, with dynamic binding the appropriate method is selected at runtime. This means that the binding of a procedure to the calling statements is effected after the program has been compiled and linked, in fact at runtime. Oberon-2 solves this problem syntactically quite neatly: the receiver parameter of a method is separated from the parameter list and the procedure is bound to the type of the receiver parameter, and therefore the correct binding is obtained even if the dynamic type changes. As the receiver parameter must be either a VAR parameter or an explicit pointer it is always a reference to an object, which is the precondition for making this mechanism effective.

- *Polymorphism*

   By direct translation, the Greek word for polymorphism, πολυ´μορφοσ, means "appearing in different forms" and expresses the possibility that components of certain types may have different shapes. Dynamic binding is the mechanism used to realize polymorphism as it provides the means by which the method suited for the actual type of an object is selected at runtime. This leads to polymorphism in the behavior of an object referenced by a pointer which references a base type. With the operator *IS*, Oberon-2 makes it possible to check whether an object is of a specific type or not; the programmer can then make the resulting decisions based on the dynamic type of the parameter of the type-bound procedure. The right method for processing an object is chosen automatically.

When discussing abstract data types it became clear that the program designer has to decide the most appropriate basis for a solution, i.e., the procedural approach or an implementation using the class concept. This is where a hybrid language like Oberon-2 offers advantages compared to exclusively object-oriented languages. The designer can make decisions freely and is not forced to use a certain technique just because it is fashionably modern or the language being used has limited powers of expression. The choice of programming language should offer freedom of expression to programmers and leave the responsibility for design decisions in their hands. It should not be a question of faith whether or not you choose an object-oriented technique - it should depend on the nature of the problem and on practical and pragmatic considerations.

The programming language determines what can be clearly expressed as a solution. The design of software can be clear and easy to understand and develop if it is based on the basic concepts of software engineering and is expressed in a well-designed language such as Oberon-2.

A simple and flexible programming language is necessary for practical object-oriented programming; however, a language is not enough by itself. A range of typical program structures and design patterns is also essential in order to capture and pass on experience to future programmers and to explain how the language is intended to be used.

5.8 Exercises

- Try to extend the list module in Example 35 with methods for deleting a single element and then all elements.
- Most beginners in object-oriented programming have problems in distinguishing between "is a" relationships (leading to subclasses) and "has a" relationships (leading to instance variables) of classes. To practice this try to analyze (not implement!) classes of an existing real-world system, e.g., a car. Draw a diagram of the relationships of your proposed classes as shown in the robot example.
- Extend the robot description file with an initial position for each robot.
- Invent a new robot command, review its impact on the overall design, and then implement it.
- Extend the robot example with a human-controlled robot. Let the user control the robot with the keyboard and fight against the cyberbots.
- Extend the robot example and introduce the concept of a rock which exclusively occupies one cell of the maze and which acts as an obstacle for both robots and blobs. Rocks cannot be painted, but a blob which hits a rock ceases to exist. Extend the simulation description file to allow the definition of multiple rocks and their position in the maze. Initialize the

maze so that it is surrounded by rocks. Then you can simplify the blob and robot implementation by eliminating the maze boundary checks.

• The simple implementation of the robots simulation has a problem: if two robots try to move to the same cell in one round, which of the robots succeeds depends on the order of execution. So the winner of a simulation may change depending on the order of the robots in the definition file. Try to eliminate the problem by extending the specification to make the behavior of the simulation independent of the order of execution of individual robots and implementing the necessary changes. Hint: use a second maze to "test" all actions tried by all of the robots to detect movement conflicts before all possible movements are carried out after the simulation round; this way robots trying to "see" something in the original maze will also get results independent of the order of execution.

6. Oberon Portable Applications Library

6.1 What is a library?

In the field of software engineering a library is a collection of modules containing procedures which are already compiled and can be linked in as part of a program. Libraries are often specialized, for example for mathematics, graphic displays, and input/output functions.

The Oberon Portable Applications Library (Opal for short) is a general purpose library providing basic functions including output of characters to the screen and file processing. *Opal*

The Opal library takes the form of a Windows dynamic link library or DLL. *DLL* The basic idea is simple: if many different programs make use of the same program code it makes sense to provide this code in one place instead of storing it separately in each program. To achieve this, the code contained in a DLL is not directly copied to the program file, but is separately loaded from its DLL file when the program is started. So programs based on a DLL have the program file and also the DLL file. In the case of the Oberon Portable Applications Library version 2.1 this DLL file has the name *OPAL_201B.DLL*.

When the compiled modules are linked the functions of a DLL need to be known. A table of contents of the DLL is used by the linker which in our case is contained in the file *OPAL.LIB*. This file must be declared in the project definition of all programs using procedures in the library. So far when new projects have been created with the help of templates this has been arranged automatically.

6.2 Overview of the modules

The Opal library contains the following modules.

Basic functions

Float	Mathematical functions like sine, cosine...
Param	Access to command line parameters from program start-up
Process	Functions to control characteristics which influence program execution
Strings	String processing

| *Utils* | General utilities |

User interface

ColorPlane	Graphic-oriented I/O
Display	Text-oriented I/O in a window (80 characters wide and 25 lines high)
Print	Text-oriented output to the printer

File system

| *File* | Read, write and management of files |
| *Volume* | Disk drive-oriented functions |

Compatibility modules which comply with the Oakwood Guidelines[1]

| *In*, *Out* | Text-oriented I/O in a scrollable window |
| *XYplane* | Drawing single dots in a window |

6.3 Notes on the Windows implementation

6.3.1 General notes

The modules *In*, *Out*, *XYPlane*, *ColorPlane*, and *Display* may be used together in the same program. The program window is then automatically divided into several output areas called panes for the different modules.

The contents of the active output area can be copied to the global Windows clipboard Windows by selecting "Copy" from the menu "Pane" or printed on the standard printer by selecting "Print". If the output of the modules *In* or *Out* is selected, an additional menu selection is provided which makes it possible to choose a file as an input medium instead of the keyboard.

6.3.2 Conventions

The following conventions are specific to the implementation of the Robinson Associates Oberon-2 compiler and the *POW!* development environment based on Windows 3.1x.

---

[1] The Oakwood Guidelines [Oak93] are a collection of guidelines for the design of different aspects of Oberon-2 development environments. They were agreed upon by a group of compiler developers in loose co-operation with the ETH.

In the main module every program requires a procedure called "ProgMain". This procedure is the defined starting point for the program execution. First the module is initialized (if necessary) and then the procedure *ProgMain* is called. It is important to use this case-sensitive naming convention even though deviating from it doesn't produce an error during compilation. If you do not consider this requirement Windows will report a memory violation as soon as global variables are accessed and this will immediately lead to program termination.

The following program example writes out the text "Hello world!" using the module *Display*.

```
MODULE Hello;

IMPORT Display;

PROCEDURE ProgMain*;
BEGIN
   Display.WriteStr("Hello world!");
   REPEAT
   UNTIL Display.KeyPressed();    (* Wait for any key press *)
END ProgMain;

END Hello.
```

6.4 The module ColorPlane

6.4.1 Overview

This module eases the design of programs which use simple color graphics.

5.4.2 General notes

All output operations represent their output in a drawing region with fixed resolution. The implementation based on Windows provides an area of 800 x 650 pixels (horizontal by vertical).

The left bottom corner of the output area has the co-ordinate (0,0), the same as for the Cartesian system of co-ordinates.

The definition of colors is based upon a true-color model which defines the colors by their relative concentrations of red, green, and blue. As not every system supports a true-color display the desired colors are mapped to the nearest available equivalent colors.

A cursor is used to indicate the position for input and output of text. It can be positioned by calling the relevant procedures and appears as a flashing mark on the screen. If no input is expected it is not displayed.

6.4.3 Interface

Module definition

```
DEFINITION OF MODULE ColorPlane;

CONST
  BACKSPACE*=8X;          CURSDOWN*=28X;          CURSLEFT*=25X;
  CURSRIGHT*=27X;         CURSUP*=26X;            DELETE*=2EX;
  DRAW*=1;                ENDKEY*=23X;            ENTER*=0DX;
  ERASE*=0;               ESC*= 1BX;              F1* = 70X;
  F2* = 71X;              F3* = 72X;              F4* = 73X;
  F5* = 74X;              F6* = 75X;              F7* = 76X;
  F8* = 77X;              F9* = 78X;              F10*= 79X;
  F11*= 7AX;              F12*= 7BX;              F13*=0D4X;
  F14*=0D5X;              F15*=0D6X;              F16*=0D7X;
  F17*=0D8X;              F18*=0D9X;              F19*=0DAX;
  F20*=0DBX;              F21*=0DCX;              F22*=0DDX;
  F23*=0DEX;              F24*=0DFX;              HOME*=24X;
  INSERT*=2DX;            PAGEDOWN*=22X;          PAGEUP*=21X;
  RESOLUTIONX*=800;       RESOLUTIONY*=650;       TAB*=9X;

PROCEDURE Bar*(x1, y1, x2, y2, mode:INTEGER);
PROCEDURE Box*(x1, y1, x2, y2, mode:INTEGER);
PROCEDURE Clear*();
PROCEDURE Close*();
PROCEDURE CursorOff*();
PROCEDURE CursorOn*();
PROCEDURE Dot*(x, y, mode:INTEGER);
PROCEDURE EditStr*(VAR t:ARRAY OF CHAR;
                   maxLen:INTEGER;
                   VAR resCode:CHAR);
PROCEDURE GetBackColor*(VAR r, g, b:INTEGER);
PROCEDURE GetDot*(x, y:INTEGER; VAR r, g, b:INTEGER);
PROCEDURE GetForeColor*(VAR r, g, b:INTEGER);
PROCEDURE GetMouse*(VAR buttons:SET; VAR x, y:INTEGER);
PROCEDURE GotoXY*(x, y:INTEGER);
PROCEDURE IsCursorOn*():BOOLEAN;
PROCEDURE KeyPressed*():BOOLEAN;
PROCEDURE Line*(x1, y1, x2, y2, mode:INTEGER);
PROCEDURE Open*();
PROCEDURE ReadKey*():CHAR;
PROCEDURE ReadStr*(VAR aString:ARRAY OF CHAR;
                   maxLen:INTEGER; VAR resCode:CHAR);
PROCEDURE SetBackColor*(r, g, b:INTEGER);
PROCEDURE SetForeColor*(r, g, b:INTEGER);
PROCEDURE SetScreenUpdate*(x:BOOLEAN);
PROCEDURE TextHeight*():INTEGER;
PROCEDURE TextWidth*(VAR txt:ARRAY OF CHAR):INTEGER;
PROCEDURE WhereX*():INTEGER;
PROCEDURE WhereY*():INTEGER;
PROCEDURE WriteLn*();
PROCEDURE WriteStr*(txt:ARRAY OF CHAR);

END ColorPlane.
```

Constants

DRAW	required for the parameter *mode* to draw with the foreground color
ERASE	required for the parameter *mode* to draw with the background color
RESOLUTIONX	horizontal resolution of the drawing area
RESOLUTIONY	vertical resolution of the drawing area

Constants for keys

The following constants are designed to be used together with the function *ReadKey* to make it possible to check whether one of the special keys has been pressed. They also are used with the parameter *resCode* of the procedure *EditStr*.

CURSDOWN	Cursor down
CURSLEFT	Cursor left
CURSRIGHT	Cursor right
CURSUP	Cursor up
DELETE	Delete
ENDKEY	End
F1 .. F24	Function keys; The codes for the function keys F13 to F24 are accessed by pressing Shift-F1 to Shift-F12.
HOME	Pos1
INSERT	Insert
PAGEUP	Page up
PAGEDOWN	Page down

The keys enter, escape, tabulator, and backspace are not regarded as special keys, as the corresponding ASCII code is returned in the same way as for the letter keys.

BACKSPACE	Backspace
ENTER	Enter
ESC	Escape
TAB	Tabulator

Management functions

```
PROCEDURE Open();
```
Open

The display area for the graphics is created in the program window.

The function *Open* must be called before any other function in the module as it provides the initialization.

Close   PROCEDURE Close();

The display area for the graphics is closed. The free space in the program window is divided for the remaining output areas (e.g., for the modules *Display* or *Out*).

SetScreen-   PROCEDURE SetScreenUpdate(x:BOOLEAN);
Update

This function inhibits drawing if x is FALSE; if TRUE then drawing is as normal.

In programs that draw many short lines or single dots it can be sensible to inhibit drawing in order to increase the speed of the program.

When the update is enabled again all changes that have taken place in the meantime are displayed automatically.

Drawing functions

Bar   PROCEDURE Bar(x1,y1,x2,y2,mode:INTEGER);

Draws a filled rectangle where the left top corner is defined by the co-ordinate *(x1,y1)* and the right bottom corner by *(x2,y2)*.

mode determines whether the rectangle is drawn in the current foreground or background color. The value *DRAW* represents the foreground color, *ERASE* the background color.

Box   PROCEDURE Box(x1,y1,x2,y2,mode:INTEGER);

Draws a rectangle where the left top corner is defined by the co-ordinates *(x1,y1)* and the right bottom corner by *(x2,y2)*.

Mode determines whether the rectangle is drawn in the current foreground or background color. The value *DRAW* represents the foreground color, *ERASE* the background color.

Clear   PROCEDURE Clear();

The whole drawing area is cleared, or in other words, set to the current background color.

Dot   PROCEDURE Dot(x,y,mode:INTEGER);

Draws a dot at the co-ordinate *(x,y)*. The value *DRAW* for *mode* draws the dot in the current foreground color and *ERASE* selects the background color.

GetDot   PROCEDURE GetDot(x,y:INTEGER; VAR red,green,blue:INTEGER);

The actual color of the point with the co-ordinate *(x,y)* is returned, separated into *red*, *green*, and *blue* components. If the system does not support true-color display the color reported by *GetDot* may deviate from the color values previously passed to *SetDot*.

Line   PROCEDURE Line(x1,y1,x2,y2,mode:INTEGER);

Draws a line starting from the co-ordinate *(x1,y1)* to the co-ordinate *(x2,y2)*.

mode determines whether the line is drawn in the current foreground or background color. The value *DRAW* represents the foreground color, *ERASE* the background color.

Output of text

```
PROCEDURE GotoXY(x,y:INTEGER);
```
GotoXY

The cursor is set to the co-ordinate *(x,y)* position.

```
PROCEDURE TextHeight():INTEGER;
```
TextHeight

The return value of this function is the height of the character set (font) currently in use.

```
PROCEDURE TextWidth(VAR txt:ARRAY OF CHAR):INTEGER;
```
TextWidth

The return value of this function is the width of the string *txt* if it were written with the character set currently in use.

```
PROCEDURE WhereX():INTEGER;
```
WhereX

The return value of this function is the X-co-ordinate of the cursor position.

```
PROCEDURE WhereY():INTEGER;
```
WhereY

The return value of this function is the Y-co-ordinate of the cursor position.

```
PROCEDURE WriteLn();
```
WriteLn

The cursor is moved to the left edge of the drawing region and then one text line down (i.e., the height of the character set in use).

```
PROCEDURE WriteStr(txt:ARRAY OF CHAR);
```
WriteStr

The string txt is written to the screen starting at the cursor position, and results in the cursor being moved to the end of the output. If the left edge of the drawing area is reached then the output is truncated. A carriage return/line feed is not provided automatically.

Color support

```
PROCEDURE GetBackColor(VAR red,green,blue:INTEGER);
```
GetBackColor

The current background color values are returned in *red*, *green*, and *blue*.

```
PROCEDURE GetForeColor(VAR red,green,blue:INTEGER);
```
GetForeColor

The current foreground color values are returned in *red*, *green*, and *blue*.

```
PROCEDURE SetBackColor(red,green,blue:INTEGER);
```
SetBackColor

The new background color is set. The color is defined by the red, green, and blue values contained in *red*, *green*, and *blue*. The color values range from 0 to 255.

If the system cannot provide the desired color then the nearest available color is selected.

SetForeColor   PROCEDURE SetForeColor(red,green,blue:INTEGER);

Sets the new foreground color for all subsequent drawing operations. The color is defined by the red, green, and blue values contained in *red*, *green*, and *blue*. The color values range from 0 to 255.

If the system cannot provide the desired color then the nearest available color is selected.

Input functions

KeyPressed   PROCEDURE KeyPressed():BOOLEAN;

The return value of the function is *TRUE* if a key was pressed; the corresponding code is stored in the keyboard buffer and may be read by calling *ReadKey*.

ReadKey   PROCEDURE ReadKey():CHAR;

This function waits for the next key and returns its character value. This character is not displayed on the screen.

If the key cannot be represented by an ASCII code, the result of the function is initially zero. The next call of the function returns a code which identifies a special key (e.g., the function keys or the cursor keys).

Section 6.5.3 (under "Constants for keys") gives a list of available constants for the special keys.

ReadStr   PROCEDURE ReadStr(VAR aString:ARRAY OF CHAR;
                    maxLen:INTEGER;
                    VAR resCode:CHAR);

The cursor is displayed and the procedure waits for key input. The string that is entered is displayed on the screen.

The maximum length of the input string is limited by the length of the array passed in *aString*. In addition to this, it may be limited by *maxLen*.

The input action can be terminated with either the enter and the escape key. In the first case the value *ENTER* is returned in *resCode*, in the second the value *ESC*.

Mouse support

GetMouse   PROCEDURE GetMouse(VAR buttons:SET; VAR x,y:INTEGER);

The co-ordinates of the current mouse position are returned in *x* and *y*.

The mouse buttons currently pressed are returned in *buttons*. The following coding is used:

0	left button
1	central button
2	right button

The mouse pointer may also be located outside the possible drawing area. In this situation at least one mouse co-ordinate is either less than zero or more than or equal to the corresponding *RESOLUTION* constant.

Example

The following example demonstrates a simple drawing program.

```
MODULE Opal1;                                          Opal1.mod'

IMPORT C:=ColorPlane;

CONST
    LEFT=0;
    RIGHT=2;

PROCEDURE ProgMain*();
VAR
    buttons:SET;
    x,y,ax,ay:INTEGER;
BEGIN
    C.Open;         (* Draw lines whenever the left mouse button *)
    REPEAT          (* is down until the right button is clicked *)
        C.GetMouse(buttons,x,y);
        WHILE LEFT IN buttons DO
            ax:=x; ay:=y;
            C.GetMouse(buttons,x,y);
            C.Line(x,y,ax,ay,1);
        END;
    UNTIL (RIGHT IN buttons);
END ProgMain;

END Opal1.
```

6.5 The module Display

6.5.1 Overview

This module provides a simple, text-oriented user interface which provides an easy-to-understand basis especially for programmers just starting to use Oberon-2. Its main purpose is to make it easy to display text from a Windows program. As far as its features are concerned it is adapted to the possibilities of usual devices operating in the text mode.

In this implementation a window is used for displaying up to 80 characters and 25 lines with a non-proportional font. If the size of the window is reduced any desired section of the whole window can be viewed using scroll bars.

6.5.2 General notes

All procedures for input and output access a virtual text screen with 80 characters and 25 lines. This text screen is called virtual because all functions are described in a way as if they controlled the complete screen operated in text mode. The actual implementation details are hidden from the programmer.

The character positions of the usable area can be directly referenced by their line and column position. The character in the left top corner has the position column one, line one by convention.

For positioning the input and output, a special mark called the cursor may be positioned anywhere by calling the appropriate procedures, and appears as a flashing mark on the screen. It may also be hidden; when invisible its position is still maintained on the virtual screen.

There are two groups of output procedures. One group is characterized by procedure names ending with "XY" and can be used for output at any position. The second group of procedures serves for output at the current cursor position; after the output has taken place the cursor is moved on. When the program is started the cursor is always initialized at the left top corner.

Output that would go over the end of the line is continued on the next line. If this happens in the last line or if a line feed with *WriteLn* is executed in the last line, the whole screen contents is moved up one line. The new "last" line is now empty and may be used for further output, while the old "first" line is lost.

All input procedures expect input typed at the current cursor position. Input functions with a parameter *resCode* return a code which represents the character used to terminate the input (e.g., enter or escape key).

6.5.3 Interface

Module definition

```
DEFINITION OF MODULE Display;

CONST
  BACKSPACE*=8X;          CURSDOWN*=28X;        CURSLEFT*=25X;
  CURSRIGHT*=27X;         CURSUP*=26X;          DELETE*=2EX;
  DRAW*=1;                ENDKEY*=23X;          ENTER*=0DX;
  ERASE*=0;               ESC*= 1BX;            F1*  = 70X;
  F2*  = 71X;             F3*  = 72X;           F4*  = 73X;
  F5*  = 74X;             F6*  = 75X;           F7*  = 76X;
  F8*  = 77X;             F9*  = 78X;           F10*= 79X;
  F11*= 7AX;              F12*= 7BX;            F13*=0D4X;
  F14*=0D5X;              F15*=0D6X;            F16*=0D7X;
  F17*=0D8X;              F18*=0D9X;            F19*=0DAX;
  F20*=0DBX;              F21*=0DCX;            F22*=0DDX;
  F23*=0DEX;              F24*=0DFX;            HOME*=24X;
  INPUTINVALID*=0X;       INSERT*=2DX;          PAGEDOWN*=22X;
  PAGEUP*=21X;            RESOLUTIONX*=800;     RESOLUTIONY*=650;
  TAB*=9X;

PROCEDURE ClrScr*();
PROCEDURE CursorOff*();
PROCEDURE CursorOn*();
```

```
PROCEDURE EditStr*(VAR aString:ARRAY OF CHAR;
                   maxLen:INTEGER;
                   VAR resCode:CHAR);
PROCEDURE FlushKeyBuffer*();
PROCEDURE GetBackColor*(VAR r, g, b:INTEGER);
PROCEDURE GetCharXY*(s, z:INTEGER):CHAR;
PROCEDURE GetForeColor*(VAR r, g, b:INTEGER);
PROCEDURE GetStrXY*(s, z, n:INTEGER;
                    VAR t:ARRAY OF CHAR);
PROCEDURE GotoXY*(s, z:INTEGER);
PROCEDURE IsColorSupported*():BOOLEAN;
PROCEDURE IsCursorOn*():BOOLEAN;
PROCEDURE KeyPressed*():BOOLEAN;
PROCEDURE ReadChar*(VAR x:CHAR);
PROCEDURE ReadInt*(VAR x:INTEGER;
                   maxLen:INTEGER;
                   VAR resCode:CHAR);
PROCEDURE ReadKey*():CHAR;
PROCEDURE ReadLongInt*(VAR x:LONGINT;
                       maxLen:INTEGER;
                       VAR resCode:CHAR);
PROCEDURE ReadLongReal*(VAR x:LONGREAL;
                        maxLen:INTEGER;
                        VAR resCode:CHAR);
PROCEDURE ReadReal*(VAR x:REAL;
                    maxLen:INTEGER;
                    VAR resCode:CHAR);
PROCEDURE ReadStr*(VAR t:ARRAY OF CHAR;
                   maxLen:INTEGER;
                   VAR resCode:CHAR);
PROCEDURE SetBackColor*(r, g, b:INTEGER);
PROCEDURE SetForeColor*(r, g, b:INTEGER);
PROCEDURE SetWindowTitle*(t:ARRAY OF CHAR);
PROCEDURE TerminalBell*();
PROCEDURE WhereX*():INTEGER;
PROCEDURE WhereY*():INTEGER;
PROCEDURE WriteChar*(x:CHAR);
PROCEDURE WriteCharXY*(s, z:INTEGER; x:CHAR);
PROCEDURE WriteInt*(x:LONGINT; len:INTEGER);
PROCEDURE WriteIntXY*(s, z:INTEGER;
                      x:LONGINT;
                      len:INTEGER);
PROCEDURE WriteLn*();
PROCEDURE WriteReal*(x:LONGREAL; len:INTEGER);
PROCEDURE WriteRealXY*(s, z:INTEGER;
                       x:LONGREAL;
                       len:INTEGER);
PROCEDURE WriteSpaces*(n:INTEGER);
PROCEDURE WriteSpacesXY*(s, z:INTEGER;
                         n:INTEGER);
PROCEDURE WriteStr*(t:ARRAY OF CHAR);
PROCEDURE WriteStrXY*(s, z:INTEGER; t:ARRAY OF CHAR);

END Display.
```

Constants

INPUTINVALID   Return code given when an invalid character
                      code or number is input.

Constants for keys

The following constants are designed to be used together with the function ReadKey to manage the special keys. They are also to check the parameter resCode returned from the procedure EditStr.

CURSDOWN	Cursor down
CURSLEFT	Cursor left
CURSRIGHT	Cursor right
CURSUP	Cursor up
DELETE	Delete the character
ENDKEY	End
F1 .. F24	Function keys (the codes for the function keys F13 to F24 are obtained by pressing Shift-F1 to Shift-F12)
HOME	Put the cursor at the origin (1,1)
INSERT	Insert a character
PAGEDOWN	Page down
PAGEUP	Page up

The keys enter, escape, tab, and backspace are not regarded as special keys, as the corresponding ASCII code is returned in the same way as with the letter keys.

BACKSPACE	Backspace
ENTER	Enter
ESC	Escape
TAB	Tabulator

Important functions

ClrScr   `PROCEDURE ClrScr;`

The screen is cleared and set to the current background color (see *SetBackColor*). When the program is started the background color is white.

GotoXY   `PROCEDURE GotoXY(s,z:INTEGER);`

The cursor is moved to column *s* and line *z*. If the stated position is invalid the cursor is positioned at column one, line one.

ReadChar   `PROCEDURE ReadChar (VAR x:CHAR);`

The next key is awaited. The character entered next is returned in *x* and is displayed on the screen at the current cursor position. Keys that do not return an ASCII code are ignored, e.g., all cursor keys and the function keys.

```
PROCEDURE ReadInt (VAR x: INTEGER;
                   maxLen: INTEGER;
                   VAR resCode: CHAR);
```
ReadInt

```
PROCEDURE ReadLongInt (VAR x: LONGINT;
                       maxLen: INTEGER;
                       VAR resCode: CHAR);
```

The cursor is displayed and an input from the keyboard is awaited. The only valid characters are "0" to "9" and the minus symbol.

The length of the input can be limited with *maxLen*.

The input may be terminated using either the enter or the escape key.

If the enter key was used then the input is converted to a value of the type *INTEGER* and returned in *x*. In *resCode* the value *ENTER* is returned. In case the correct conversion of the input to a number is impossible *resCode* is set to *INPUTINVALID*.

If the input is interrupted by the escape key *x* is set to zero and *resCode* returns the value *ESC*.

```
PROCEDURE ReadKey():CHAR;
```
ReadKey

The next key is awaited. The return value of the function is the character entered next; no output on the screen is effected.

If the pressed key does not have an ASCII code the result of the function is initially returned as zero. The next call of this function returns a key code which serves to identify the special key (e.g., the function keys or the cursor keys).

The above section "Constants for keys" gives a list of available constants which define the special keys.

```
PROCEDURE ReadReal(VAR x:REAL;
                   maxLen:INTEGER;
                   VAR resCode:CHAR);
```
ReadReal

```
PROCEDURE ReadLongReal(VAR x:LONGREAL;
                       maxLen:INTEGER;
                       VAR resCode:CHAR);
```

The cursor is displayed and an input from the keyboard is awaited. The only characters accepted are "0" to "9", "." and "-".

The length of the input can be limited by *maxLen*.

The input can be terminated with either the enter or escape key.

If the enter key is used then the input is converted to a value of the type *REAL* and returned in *x*. In *resCode* the value *ENTER* is returned. In case the correct conversion of the input to a number is impossible *resCode* is set to *INPUTINVALID*.

If the input is interrupted by the escape key *x* is set to zero and *resCode* returns the value *ESC*.

ReadStr
```
PROCEDURE ReadStr(VAR aString:ARRAY OF CHAR;
                  maxLen:INTEGER;
                  VAR resCode:CHAR);
```

The cursor is displayed and an input from the keyboard is awaited. The input string is shown on the screen.

The maximum length of the input is limited by the length of the array passed in *aString*. In addition, it may be further limited by *maxLen*.

The input can be terminated using either the enter or escape key. In the first case the value *ENTER* is returned in *resCode,* in the second case *ESC*.

WhereX
```
PROCEDURE WhereX():INTEGER;
```

The return value of this function is the column of the current cursor position.

WhereY
```
PROCEDURE WhereY():INTEGER;
```

The return value of this function is the line of the current cursor position.

WriteChar
```
PROCEDURE WriteChar(x:CHAR);
```

The character contained in x is displayed at the current cursor position. Afterwards the cursor is moved on one character.

WriteInt
```
PROCEDURE WriteInt(x:LONGINT; len:INTEGER);
```

The value contained in x is displayed at the current cursor position. The width of the output is *len* characters or more if this is necessary for the representation of the number. If a representation with *len* characters is possible the number is written right aligned. Then the cursor is moved to the end of the output.

WriteLn
```
PROCEDURE WriteLn;
```

The cursor is moved to the beginning of the next line. If the cursor was already situated in the last available line, then the whole contents of the screen is moved one line up. So the last line is empty and may be used for further output. The former first line is lost.

WriteReal
```
PROCEDURE WriteReal(x:LONGREAL; len:INTEGER);
```

The value contained in x is written at the current cursor position. The width of the output is *len* characters or more if this necessary for the representation of the number. If a representation with *len* characters is possible then the number is written right aligned. Afterwards the cursor is moved to the end of the output.

WriteSpaces
```
PROCEDURE WriteSpaces(n:INTEGER);
```

n blanks are printed at the current cursor position. Then the cursor is moved to the end of the output.

WriteStr
```
PROCEDURE WriteStr(t:ARRAY OF CHAR);
```

The string contained in t is displayed at the current cursor position. Afterwards the cursor is moved to the end of the output.

Each occurrence of the control characters CR, LF, or CR LF is not written out but interpreted as a new line command.

Color support

```
PROCEDURE IsColorSupported():BOOLEAN;
```
IsColor-Supported

The return value of this function is *TRUE* if the system provides colors. In the implementation based on Windows the result of this function is always *TRUE*.

If the system does not support colors then the procedures described in this section have no effect and the return values of *GetForeColor* and *GetBackColor* are always zero.

```
PROCEDURE GetBackColor(VAR red,green,blue:INTEGER);
```
GetBackColor

The background color currently used is returned in *red*, *green*, and *blue* according to their proportions.

```
PROCEDURE GetForeColor(VAR red,green,blue:INTEGER);
```
GetForeColor

The text color currently used is returned in *red*, *green*, and *blue* according to their proportions.

```
PROCEDURE SetBackColor(red,green,blue:INTEGER);
```
SetBackColor

The background for all following output is set to the color defined by *red*, *green*, and *blue*. This defined color is also used for clearing the output region. If the system cannot provide the desired color exactly, the nearest available color is used.

The values for the parameters *red*, *green*, and *blue* must be in the range 0 to 255.

```
PROCEDURE SetForeColor(red,green,blue:INTEGER);
```
SetForeColor

All following output to the screen is drawn in the color defined by the color values given in *red*, *green*, and *blue*. If the system cannot provide the required color exactly, the nearest available color is selected.

The values of the parameters *red*, *green*, and *blue* must be in the range 0 to 255.

Additional functions

```
PROCEDURE CursorOn;
```
CursorOn

The cursor is displayed.

```
PROCEDURE CursorOff;
```
CursorOff

The cursor becomes invisible. Its position and function remain unchanged.

EditStr
```
PROCEDURE EditStr(VAR aString:ARRAY OF CHAR;
                      maxLen:INTEGER;
                      VAR resCode:CHAR);
```

The text passed in *aString* is displayed then the cursor is displayed and an input from the keyboard is awaited. The input line may be edited using the delete, cursor left, and cursor right keys. The entered string is shown on the screen.

The maximum length of the input is limited by the length of the array passed in *aString*. In addition, it may be limited by *maxLen*.

The input may be finished with one of the following keys: enter, escape, cursor up, cursor down, page up, page down, tabulator and the function keys. The code of the terminating key used is returned in *resCode*. See also "Constants for keys".

FlushKey-
Buffer
```
PROCEDURE FlushKeyBuffer;
```

The keyboard buffer is cleared.

This ensures that the next call of *ReadKey* does not return keys that were pressed earlier but not processed.

GetCharXY
```
PROCEDURE GetCharXY(s,z:INTEGER):CHAR;
```

This function returns the value of the character which is currently displayed at column *s*, line *z*.

GetStrXY
```
PROCEDURE GetStrXY(s,z,n:INTEGER; VAR t:ARRAY OF CHAR);
```

Starting at column *s*, line *z*, the following *n* characters displayed on the screen are copied to the array *t*. After the last copied character a character with the code zero is written so that *t* can be used as a string.

If *n* is sufficiently large several lines can be copied with a single call. If *t* is not big enough fewer characters are copied (max. *LEN(t)–1* characters).

IsCursorOn
```
PROCEDURE IsCursorOn():BOOLEAN;
```

The return value of this function is *TRUE* if the cursor is visible.

KeyPressed
```
PROCEDURE KeyPressed(): BOOLEAN;
```

The return value of this function is *TRUE* if a key was pressed and the corresponding code in the keyboard buffer is waiting to be read by a call of *ReadKey*.

SetWindow-
Title
```
PROCEDURE SetWindowTitle(t: ARRAY OF CHAR);
```

The title of the program window is set to the string passed in *t*.

In implementations of Opal on other systems, e.g., on text-oriented systems without any space for displaying a program title, this procedure may have no effect.

TerminalBell
```
PROCEDURE TerminalBell;
```

A short sound is emitted.

```
PROCEDURE WriteCharXY(s,z:INTEGER; x:CHAR);
```
WriteCharXY

The character contained in *x* is printed at the position column *s*, line *z*.

```
PROCEDURE WriteIntXY(s,z:INTEGER; x:LONGINT; len:INTEGER);
```
WriteIntXY

The value of *x* is displayed in column *s*, line *z*.

The width of the output is *len* characters. The number is displayed right aligned. If the number is too big to be represented with *len* characters, the output is widened appropriately.

```
PROCEDURE WriteRealXY(s,z:INTEGER;
                 x:LONGREAL; len:INTEGER);
```
WriteRealXY

The value of *x* is displayed in column *s*, line *z*. The width of the output is *len* characters or more in case this is necessary for the representation of the number. If a representation is possible with *len* characters, the number is written right aligned.

```
PROCEDURE WriteSpacesXY(s,z,n:INTEGER);
```
Write-
SpacesXY

This procedure displays *n* blanks starting at column *s*, line *z*.

```
PROCEDURE WriteStrXY(s,z:INTEGER; t:ARRAY OF CHAR);
```
WriteStrXY

The string passed in *t* is displayed in column *s*, line *z*.

6.6 The module File

6.6.1 Overview

This module provides the functionality needed for working with both files and file management.

6.6.2 General notes

All functions for file processing need a unique reference – a so-called "handle" – which identifies a particular file. To obtain a valid handle a file must be opened with the function *Open*. When all work on a file has been completed the file must be closed with the function *Close*.

Functions that refer to a file as a whole rather than its contents require its file name as an argument instead of a handle.

Files are regarded as a stream of characters without a predefined type; single characters or whole data blocks can be read one after another. To control the current reading position within a file the system provides an internal variable for every open file, the "file pointer", which is also used to define the writing position. Initially the value of the file pointer is zero.

After data has been read or written at the current position, the file pointer is moved on for each read or written character. Additionally, there are functions

Seek and *SeekRel* which make it possible to set the file pointer to a particular position.

6.6.3 Error management

All procedures with a parameter *resCode* return an error code. This code is used to check if the function was successful (*resCode = NOERROR*) or to define a problem which may have occurred.

All errors occurring during file operations are indicated by an appropriate error code. File module errors do not cause a runtime error or program termination. Detecting and coping with errors is the programmer's responsibility. The procedure *GetErrorMessage* provides a message corresponding to every possible error code, which can be used when creating error messages for the user.

During a file operation it is possible that more than one error occurs. For example this happens if the data buffer supplied for the data to be processed is too small (error code *SHORTBUFFER*) and then an additional problem occur sduring the file operation itself. As only a single error code can be returned, the code *SHORTBUFFER* is regarded as being less important and the error code for the error during the file operation is returned. This should be borne in mind when programs are being tested.

6.6.4 Interface

Module definition

```
DEFINITION OF MODULE File;

CONST
  ACCESSDENIED*=5;              ATTRARCHIVE*=5;
  ATTRDIR*=4;                   ATTRHIDDEN*=1;
  ATTRREADONLY*=0;              ATTRSYSTEM*=2;
  ATTRVOLUME*=3;                DENYALL*=10H;
  DENYNONE*=40H;                DENYREAD*=30H;
  DENYWRITE*=20H;               EOFREACHED*=101H;
  FILENOTFOUND*=2;              INVALIDHANDLE*=6;
  MAXFILENAME*=13;              MAXPATH*=100;
  NOERROR*=0;                   READONLY*=0;
  READWRITE*=2;                 SHARINGVIOLATION*=20H;
  SHORTBUFFER*=102H;            WRITEPROTECTED*=13H;
  WRITEONLY*=1;

TYPE
  Handle*=INTEGER;

PROCEDURE AtEnd*(handle:Handle):BOOLEAN;
PROCEDURE Close*(handle:Handle);
PROCEDURE Delete*(name:ARRAY OF CHAR;
                  VAR resCode:INTEGER);
PROCEDURE Exist*(name:ARRAY OF CHAR):BOOLEAN;
```

```
PROCEDURE GetAttributes*(name:ARRAY OF CHAR;
                         VAR attr:SET;
                         VAR resCode:INTEGER);
PROCEDURE GetCreationDate*(handle:Handle;
                           VAR date:ARRAY OF CHAR;
                           VAR resCode:INTEGER);
PROCEDURE GetErrorMessage*(error:INTEGER;
                           VAR message:ARRAY OF CHAR);
PROCEDURE GetModifyDate*(handle:Handle;
                         VAR date:ARRAY OF CHAR;
                         VAR resCode:INTEGER);
PROCEDURE Open*(name:ARRAY OF CHAR;
                create:BOOLEAN;
                deny:INTEGER;
                mode:INTEGER;
                VAR handle:Handle;
                VAR resCode:INTEGER);
PROCEDURE Pos*(handle:Handle;
               VAR pos:LONGINT;
               VAR resCode:INTEGER);
PROCEDURE ReadBlock*(handle:Handle;
                     VAR data:ARRAY OF SYSTEM.BYTE;
                     n:LONGINT;
                     VAR read:LONGINT;
                     VAR resCode:INTEGER);
PROCEDURE ReadChar*(handle:Handle;
                    VAR x:CHAR;
                    VAR resCode:INTEGER);
PROCEDURE ReadLn*(handle:Handle;
                  VAR t:ARRAY OF CHAR;
                  VAR resCode:INTEGER);
PROCEDURE Rename*(oldName, newName:ARRAY OF CHAR;
                  VAR resCode:INTEGER);
PROCEDURE Seek*(handle:Handle; pos:LONGINT;
                VAR resCode:INTEGER);
PROCEDURE SeekRel*(handle:Handle;
                   pos:LONGINT;
                   VAR resCode:INTEGER);
PROCEDURE SetAttributes*(name:ARRAY OF CHAR;
                         attr:SET;
                         VAR resCode:INTEGER);
PROCEDURE SetModifyDate*(handle:Handle;
                         VAR date:ARRAY OF CHAR;
                         VAR resCode:INTEGER);
PROCEDURE Size*(handle:Handle;
                VAR len:LONGINT;
                VAR resCode:INTEGER);
PROCEDURE Truncate*(handle:Handle;
                    VAR resCode:INTEGER);
PROCEDURE WriteBlock*(handle:Handle;
                      VAR data:ARRAY OF SYSTEM.BYTE;
                      n:LONGINT;
                      VAR resCode:INTEGER);
PROCEDURE WriteChar*(handle:Handle;
                     x:CHAR;
                     VAR resCode:INTEGER);
PROCEDURE WriteLn*(handle:Handle;
                   t:ARRAY OF CHAR;
                   VAR resCode:INTEGER);

END File.
```

Constants

MAXFILENAME	the recommended length for strings used for storing the file name
MAXPATH	the recommended length for strings used for storing the path including the file name

Constants for error codes

ACCESSDENIED	The access to the file was denied by the operating system.
EOFREACHED	The end of the file was reached.
FILENOTFOUND	The file could not be found.
NOERROR	The operation was carried out successfully.
SHARINGVIOLATION	The file has already been opened and must not be opened a second time with the requested rights.
SHORTBUFFER	The data buffer supplied is not big enough for the result.
WRITEPROTECTED	An attempt was made to write to a write-protected drive.

The remaining constants are explained in the corresponding procedure descriptions (*Open* and *GetAttributes*).

Types

Handle `Handle`

The type *handle* serves for storing file handles.

Error Handling

GetError- `PROCEDURE GetErrorMessage(error: INTEGER;`
Message   `VAR message: ARRAY OF CHAR);`

The text returned in *message* explains the error code *error*.

If an invalid error code is passed as a parameter a suitable error message is also returned.

Identical constants for error codes defined in the module *Volume* have the same numerical value as their counterparts of the module *File*.

File input and output

AtEnd `PROCEDURE AtEnd(handle:Handle):BOOLEAN;`

The return value of this function is *TRUE* if the file pointer points to the end of the file specified by *handle*.

If it is impossible to determine a correct result (e.g., *handle* does not contain a valid reference to an open file), the return value of the function is *TRUE*.

```
PROCEDURE Close(handle:Handle);                                     Close
```

The file specified by *handle* is closed.

```
PROCEDURE Open(name:ARRAY OF CHAR;                                   Open
              create:BOOLEAN;
              deny,mode:INTEGER;
              VAR handle:Handle;
              VAR resCode:INTEGER);
```

Opens a file.

The file name is passed in *name* along with an optional path. The name must not contain any wildcards like "?" or "*".

If *create* is *TRUE* then the file is created if it does not already exist. Otherwise the code *FILENOTFOUND* is returned and the operation is abandoned.

deny defines whether the file may be used by other programs at the same time and how. The constants used for these parameters are:

DENYALL	No simultaneous access is allowed.
DENYNONE	The file may be read and written by others at the same time.
DENYREAD	The file may be written by others at the same time.
DENYWRITE	The file may be read by others at the same time.

mode defines the required kind of access to the file. The corresponding constants for this parameter are:

READONLY	The file will be read only.
READWRITE	The file will be read from and written to.
WRITEONLY	The file will be written to only.

The parameter *resCode* returns an error code; see Section 6.6.3.

If the file was opened successfully a handle for the open file is returned in *handle* and the file pointer is set to the beginning of the file.

```
PROCEDURE Pos(handle:Handle;                                         Pos
              VAR pos:LONGINT;
              VAR resCode:INTEGER);
```

The position of the file pointer of the file specified by *handle* is returned in *pos*.

The parameter *resCode* returns an error code; see Section 6.6.3.

```
PROCEDURE ReadBlock(handle:Handle;                              ReadBlock
                    VAR data:ARRAY OF SYSTEM.BYTE;
                    n:LONGINT;
                    VAR read:LONGINT;
                    VAR resCode:INTEGER);
```

An attempt is made to read a block of the length *n* from the file specified by *handle*. The number of bytes actually read is returned in *read*.

The file data are written into the region determined by *data.* As *data* is of the type SYSTEM.BYTE any types can be passed. Thus data can be directly written into a structure or an array. If *data* is not large enough to hold *n* bytes the maximum number of bytes possible is read and the return value of the function is set to *SHORTBUFFER.*

The number of bytes actually read is returned in *read.* If an error prevents the reading of data, *read* is set to zero and the error code is returned.

The parameter *resCode* returns an error code; see Section 6.6.3.

Notes on data alignment

When defining the number of the bytes to be read it may be necessary to consider how the data is organized in the main memory, i.e., its alignment. Individual components of structure types are stored consecutively in main memory. Their addresses generally fall on 2 or 4 byte boundaries and this sometimes leaves gaps in the memory between them. For this reason, an elementary data type or an *ARRAY OF CHAR* should be chosen for writing or reading buffers, as these data structures have an alignment which contains no gaps.

ReadChar
```
PROCEDURE ReadChar(handle:Handle;
                   VAR x:CHAR;
                   VAR resCode:INTEGER);
```

A character is read and returned in *x* from the file specified by *handle.*

The parameter *resCode* returns an error code; see Section 6.6.3.

ReadLn
```
PROCEDURE ReadLn(handle:Handle;
                 VAR t:ARRAY OF CHAR;
                 VAR resCode:INTEGER);
```

The file specified by *handle* is regarded as a text file. Starting from the current position of the file pointer a line is read and returned in *t.* A line is terminated either by CR, LF, CR LF, or the end of the file (see the ASCII table in Appendix C).

The parameter *resCode* returns an error code; see Section 6.6.3. If *t* is too short to hold the whole read line the error code *SHORTBUFFER* is returned.

Seek
```
PROCEDURE Seek(handle:Handle;
               pos:LONGINT;
               VAR resCode:INTEGER);
```

The file pointer of the file specified by *handle* is set to *pos.* If this is not possible the file pointer is set to the end of the file.

The parameter *resCode* returns an error code; see Section 6.6.3.

```
PROCEDURE SeekRel(handle:Handle;                                    SeekRel
                  pos:LONGINT;
                  VAR resCode:INTEGER);
```

The file pointer of the file specified by *handle* is transposed by *pos* characters. For example, a value −1 in *pos* would move the file pointer one character back.

If the operation is unsuccessful, the file pointer is set to the end of the file.

The parameter *resCode* returns an error code, see "6.6.3 Error management".

```
PROCEDURE Truncate(handle:Handle;                                   Truncate
                   VAR resCode:INTEGER);
```

The file specified by *handle* is truncated at the current position of the file pointer. With this function the size of a file can be reduced.

The parameter *resCode* returns an error code; see Section 6.6.3.

```
PROCEDURE WriteBlock(handle:Handle;                                 WriteBlock
                     VAR data:ARRAY OF SYSTEM.BYTE;
                     n:LONGINT;
                     VAR resCode:INTEGER);
```

A block *n* bytes long is written to the file specified by *handle*. The data to be written are specified by *data*. The amount of data is determined by the size of *data*, even if *n* is larger.

The parameter *resCode* returns an error code; see Section 6.6.3.

```
PROCEDURE WriteChar(handle:Handle;                                  WriteChar
                    x:CHAR;
                    VAR resCode:INTEGER);
```

The character *x* is written to the file specified by *handle*.

The parameter *resCode* returns an error code; see Section 6.6.3.

```
PROCEDURE WriteLn(handle:Handle;                                    WriteLn
                  t:ARRAY OF CHAR;
                  VAR resCode:INTEGER);
```

The file specified by *handle* is regarded as a text file. The string passed in *t* is written to the file and terminated according to the operating system. Opal for Windows uses the characters CR LF as the mark for the end of a line. (see the ASCII table in Appendix C). The string terminator (0) is not written to the file.

A file written with *WriteLn* can be directly edited with any ASCII editor. Every string written with *WriteLn* appears as a line in the editor.

The parameter *resCode* returns an error code; see Section 6.6.3.

File management

Delete
```
PROCEDURE Delete(name:ARRAY OF CHAR;
                 VAR resCode:INTEGER);
```

The file with the name specified in *name* is deleted. The name may also contain a path. Wildcards such as "*" or "?" are not permitted.

The parameter *resCode* returns an error code; see Section 6.6.3.

Exist
```
PROCEDURE Exist(name:ARRAY OF CHAR):BOOLEAN;
```

This checks whether a certain file exists. The name of the file together with an optional path must be passed in *name*. The return value of the function is *TRUE* if the file exists.

GetAttributes
```
PROCEDURE GetAttributes(name:ARRAY OF CHAR;
                        VAR attr:SET;
                        VAR resCode:INTEGER);
```

The attributes of the directory entry with the name specified by *name* are accessed and returned in *attr*. It is therefore possible to find out if a directory entry is a file or a further directory.

The constants used for attributes are:

ATTRARCHIVE	The file was modified since the last update.
ATTRDIR	The entry is a directory.
ATTRHIDDEN	The directory entry is a hidden entry.
ATTRREADONLY	The file is for reading only.
ATTRSYSTEM	The file is a special file of the operating system.
ATTRVOLUME	This is a special entry defining the drive name.

The parameter *resCode* returns an error code; see Section 6.6.3.

Example:

Check if the file "C:\TEST.DAT" is write-protected:
```
File.GetAttributes("C:\TEST.DAT",attr,resCode);
IF (resCode=File.NOERROR) &
   (File.ATTRREADONLY IN attr) THEN…
```

GetCreation-
Date
```
PROCEDURE GetCreationDate(handle:Handle;
                          VAR date:ARRAY OF CHAR;
                          VAR resCode:INTEGER);
```

The creation date of the file specified by *handle* is returned in *date*. The combination of MS-DOS / Windows 3.1x does not support this information. Thus *date* always returns an empty string.

The parameter *resCode* returns an error code; see Section 6.6.3.

```
PROCEDURE GetModifyDate(handle:Handle;                          GetModifyDate
                    VAR date:ARRAY OF CHAR;
                    VAR resCode:INTEGER);
```

The date of the last modification of the file specified by *handle* is returned in *date*.

The format for the date is "DD.MM.YYYY HH:MM:SS" and the total length of the string is 20 characters (two separating blanks between date and time).

Example: "15. 4.1993 18:06:27"

The parameter *resCode* returns an error code; see Section 6.6.3.

```
PROCEDURE Rename(oldName,newName:ARRAY OF CHAR;                      Rename
                VAR resCode:INTEGER);
```

The file with the name specified in *oldName* is renamed to *newName*. The name may also contain a path. Wildcards such as "*" or "?" are not allowed.

The parameter *resCode* returns an error code; see Section 6.6.3.

```
PROCEDURE SetAttributes(name:ARRAY OF CHAR;                      SetAttributes
                    attr:SET;
                    VAR resCode:INTEGER);
```

The attributes of the file with the name specified by *name* are set to *attr*.

A list of the constants defined for the attributes is defined in the description of *GetAttributes*.

The parameter *resCode* returns an error code; see Section 6.6.3.

```
PROCEDURE SetModifyDate(handle:Handle;                          SetModifyDate
                    VAR date:ARRAY OF CHAR;
                    VAR resCode:INTEGER);
```

The date of the last modification of the file specified by *handle* is set to *date*.

The format for the date is "DD.MM.YYYY HH:MM:SS" and the total length of the string is 20 characters.

The parameter *resCode* returns an error code; see Section 6.6.3.

```
PROCEDURE Size(handle:Handle;                                       Size
            VAR len:LONGINT;
            VAR resCode:INTEGER);
```

The length of the file specified by *handle* is returned in *len*.

The parameter *resCode* returns an error code; see Section 6.6.3.

6.6.5 Examples

Reading and displaying a text file

The following procedure reads a file whose name is passed as a parameter. The output is processed using the module *Out*.

Opal2.mod

```
CONST
    MAXLINE=400;              (* max. length of line in characters *)

PROCEDURE ShowFile(name:ARRAY OF CHAR);
VAR
    t:ARRAY MAXLINE+1 OF CHAR;
    handle:File.Handle;
    res:INTEGER;
BEGIN
    File.Open(name,                          (* open file *)
              FALSE,
              File.DENYNONE,
              File.READONLY,
              handle,
              res);
    IF res=File.NOERROR THEN
        File.ReadLn(handle,t,res);           (* read a line *)
        WHILE res=File.NOERROR DO            (* while no error *)
            Out.String(t);                   (* occurs:        *)
            Out.Ln;                          (* write line and *)
            File.ReadLn(handle,t,res);       (* read next line *)
        END;
        File.Close(handle);                     (* close file *)
    ELSE                                      (* error in open: *)
        File.GetErrorMessage(res,t);    (* get error message *)
        Out.String("Error on opening: ");
        Out.String(t);                        (* and display it *)
    END;
END ShowFile;
```

Conversion of all lowercase letters of a file to uppercase

The following procedure changes all letters of a file to uppercase.

Opal3.mod

```
PROCEDURE UpCaseFile(name:ARRAY OF CHAR);
VAR
    ch,chUp:CHAR;
    handle:File.Handle;
    res:INTEGER;
    t:ARRAY 100 OF CHAR;
BEGIN
    File.Open(name,                          (* open file *)
              FALSE,
              File.DENYALL,
              File.READWRITE,
              handle,
              res);
    IF res=File.NOERROR THEN                  (* no error? *)
        WHILE res=File.NOERROR DO            (* while no *)
                                             (* error:   *)
            File.ReadChar(handle,ch,res);    (* read 1 character *)
            chUp:=Strings.UpCaseChar(ch);       (* convert to *)
                                                (* upper case *)
            IF chUp#ch THEN                  (* character changed? *)
                File.SeekRel(handle,-1,res);    (* one character *)
                                                (* back and *)
                File.WriteChar(handle,chUp,res);   (* write *)
            END;                                (* modification *)
        END;
        IF res#File.EOFREACHED THEN          (* work terminated *)
                                         (* not because of EOF? *)
```

```
        File.GetErrorMessage(res,t);        (* get error message *)
          Out.String("Error during processing: ");
            Out.String(t);                  (* and display it *)
        END;
        File.Close(handle);                      (* close file *)
      ELSE                                  (* error in open: *)
        File.GetErrorMessage(res,t);       (* get error message *)
        Out.String("Error on opening: ");
        Out.String(t);                      (* and display it *)
      END;
    END UpCaseFile;
```

6.7 The module Float

6.7.1 Overview

This module contains the basic trigonometric, exponential, and conversion functions for use with the data types *REAL* and *LONGREAL*.

6.7.2 General notes

For all logarithmic functions a result with an "infinite" value is returned for the value zero. If the argument is less than zero a special code is returned, indicating that the result would be an invalid number. In fact the result would be a complex number and so the code denotes that the real number is not correct.

6.7.3 Error handling

No runtime errors are caused by numerical values out of the range in any of the functions. The result of an invalid operation is a special value instead, which can be tested with the function *KindOfNumber*. If such a special value is used for further calculations a runtime error may well occur.

6.7.4 Interface

Module definition

```
    DEFINITION OF MODULE Float;

CONST
    DENORMAL*=6; e*=2.71828182846;
    ISLONGREAL*=2;                      ISOUTOFRANGE*=4;
    ISREAL*=1;                          NAN*=1;
    NEGINF*=8;                          NORMAL*=2;
    Pi*=3.14159265359;                  POSINF*=3;
    STRINGEMPTY*=5;                     STRINGILLEGAL*=6;
    ZERO*=4;
```

```
PROCEDURE ArcSin*(x:REAL):REAL;
PROCEDURE ArcSinL*(x:LONGREAL):LONGREAL;
PROCEDURE ArcTan*(x:REAL):REAL;
PROCEDURE ArcTanL*(x:LONGREAL):LONGREAL;
PROCEDURE Cos*(x:REAL):REAL;
PROCEDURE CosL*(x:LONGREAL):LONGREAL;
PROCEDURE Exp*(x, y:REAL):REAL;
PROCEDURE ExpL*(x, y:LONGREAL):LONGREAL;
PROCEDURE KindOfNumber*(x:REAL):INTEGER;
PROCEDURE KindOfNumberL*(x:LONGREAL):INTEGER;
PROCEDURE Ln*(x:REAL):REAL;
PROCEDURE LnL*(x:LONGREAL):LONGREAL;
PROCEDURE Log10*(x:REAL):REAL;
PROCEDURE Log10L*(x:LONGREAL):LONGREAL;
PROCEDURE Log2*(x:REAL):REAL;
PROCEDURE Log2L*(x:LONGREAL):LONGREAL;
PROCEDURE Sin*(x:REAL):REAL;
PROCEDURE SinL*(x:LONGREAL):LONGREAL;
PROCEDURE Str*(x:LONGREAL; VAR t:ARRAY OF CHAR);
PROCEDURE StrF*(x:LONGREAL;
                n1,n2:INTEGER;
                VAR t:ARRAY OF CHAR);
PROCEDURE StrL*(x:LONGREAL;
                n:INTEGER;
                VAR t:ARRAY OF CHAR);
PROCEDURE Sqrt*(x:REAL):REAL;
PROCEDURE SqrtL*(x:LONGREAL):LONGREAL;
PROCEDURE Tan*(x:REAL):REAL;
PROCEDURE TanL*(x:LONGREAL):LONGREAL;
PROCEDURE Val*(VAR t:ARRAY OF CHAR):LONGREAL;
PROCEDURE ValResult*(t:ARRAY OF CHAR):INTEGER;

END Float.
```

Numerical constants

```
Pi = 3.14159265359
e  = 2.71828182846
```

Exponential functions

Exp
```
PROCEDURE Exp (x, y: REAL): REAL;
PROCEDURE ExpL (x, y: LONGREAL): LONGREAL;
```

The return value of the function is x to the power of y.

If the value is too big for the exact representation in the floating point format a special code for the result infinity is returned.

The valid range for x comprises only positive numbers. If x is negative a special code is returned indicating that the result is an invalid number.

Ln
```
PROCEDURE Ln (x: REAL): REAL;
PROCEDURE LnL (x: LONGREAL): LONGREAL;
```

The return value of the function is the natural logarithm (base e) of x.

```
PROCEDURE Log2 (x: REAL): REAL;                                    Log2
PROCEDURE Log2L (x: LONGREAL): LONGREAL;
```

The return value of the function is the logarithm base 2 of x.

```
PROCEDURE Log10 (x: REAL): REAL;                                  Log10
PROCEDURE Log10L (x: LONGREAL): LONGREAL;
```

The return value of the function is the logarithm base 10 of x.

```
PROCEDURE Sqrt (x: REAL): REAL;                                   Sqrt
PROCEDURE SqrtL (x: LONGREAL): LONGREAL;
```

The return value of the function is the square root of x.

If x is smaller than zero a special code is returned indicating that the result is an invalid number.

Trigonometrical functions

```
PROCEDURE ArcSin (x: REAL): REAL;                                 ArcSin
PROCEDURE ArcSinL (x: LONGREAL): LONGREAL;
```

The return value of the function is the arc sine of x in radians. The arc cosine is not implemented as a separate function as it can be easily calculated using $\frac{\pi}{2} - \arcsin(x)$.

```
PROCEDURE ArcTan (x: REAL): REAL;                                 ArcTan
PROCEDURE ArcTanL (x: LONGREAL): LONGREAL;
```

The return value of the function is the arc tangent of x in radians.

```
PROCEDURE Cos (x: REAL): REAL;                                    Cos
PROCEDURE CosL (x: LONGREAL): LONGREAL;
```

The return value of the function is the cosine of x in radians.

```
PROCEDURE Sin (x: REAL): REAL;                                    Sin
PROCEDURE SinL (x: LONGREAL): LONGREAL;
```

The return value of the function is the sine of x in radians.

```
PROCEDURE Tan (x: REAL): REAL;                                    Tan
PROCEDURE TanL (x: LONGREAL): LONGREAL;
```

The return value of the function is the tangent of x in radians.

Error treatment

```
PROCEDURE KindOfNumber (x: REAL): INTEGER;                        KindOfNumber
PROCEDURE KindOfNumberL (x: LONGREAL): INTEGER;
```

This function checks if x is a normal number or if it contains a special value.

The following constants are intended to be compared with the return values of the function:

NORMAL   a normal number

ZERO   zero

DENORMAL   a number whose representation is not as precise as the data type used (*REAL* or *LONGREAL*) would suggest; this is due to restrictions of the internal representation of floating point numbers.

POSINF   + infinity

NEGINF   – infinity

NAN   invalid real number (NAN = Not A Number)

Note that the return value of the function may also be a value different from the defined constants. In this case a numerical error has occurred which was not expected in that form. The parameter *x* does not contain a valid numerical value in this case.

Conversions

Str   PROCEDURE Str(x: LONGREAL; VAR t: ARRAY OF CHAR);

The number *x* is converted to a string and the result is returned in *t*.

If *t* is not large enough to hold all characters of the number, *t* is filled with "$" characters.

Examples for *Str(x,t)*:

4	"1e0"
-125	"-1.25e2"
3300790	"3.30079e6"
0.1	"1e-1"
33007000	"3.3007e7"
Log2(0)	"-infinity"
KindOfNumber(x)=NAN	"error"

StrF   PROCEDURE StrF(x: LONGREAL;
                    n1,n2:INTEGER;
                    VAR t: ARRAY OF CHAR);

The number *x* is converted to a string and the result is returned in *t*. The representation is effected with a fixed number of digits before (*n1*) and after (*n2*) the decimal point.

If *t* is not large enough to hold the selected output format or if the number cannot be represented with *n1* digits before the comma, *t* is filled with "$" characters.

The length of the result totals *n1* + *n2* + 2 characters: digits for the integral part + digits for the fractional part + decimal point + sign.

Examples for *StrF(x,4,2,t)*:

1	" 1.00"
-125	" -125.00"
3300790	"$$$$$$$$"
0.1	" 0.10"
33007	"$$$$$$$$"
5887.009	" 5887.01"

```
PROCEDURE StrL(x: LONGREAL;                                               StrL
              n:INTEGER;
              VAR t: ARRAY OF CHAR);
```

The number *x* is converted to a string of length *n* and the result is stored right aligned in *t*. If necessary the number of digits is reduced and the number is rounded.

The minimum value for *n* is five characters. Smaller values are ignored.

If *t* is not large enough to hold all characters of the number, it is filled with "$" characters. Even though the result is reduced to *n* characters *t* must be of a sufficient size to contain the full number.

Examples for *StrL(x,8,t)*:

```
1                         "      1e0"
-125                      " -1.25e2"
3300790                   "3.3008e6"
0.1                       "      1e-1"
33007000                  "3.3007e7"
```

```
PROCEDURE Val (VAR t: ARRAY OF CHAR): LONGREAL;                           Val
```

The string *t* is converted to a number and returned as the result.

If the character sequence in *t* does not represent an integer number and the conversion fails the smallest negative number *(MIN(LONGREAL))* is returned.

Blanks at the beginning and the end of *t* are ignored. The number must not contain blanks within itself.

```
PROCEDURE ValResult (VAR t:ARRAY OF CHAR): INTEGER;                       ValResult
```

This function checks if the string *t* can be converted to a number and what kind of floating point type is at least required for storing it.

The following constants are possible return values of the function:

ISREAL	*t* contains a number which can be stored in a *REAL* variable.
ISLONGREAL	*t* contains a number which can be stored in a *LONGREAL* variable.
ISOUTOFRANGE	*t* contains a number which is too small or too big to be stored in a *LONGREAL* variable.
STRINGEMPTY	*t* is empty or contains nothing but blanks.
STRINGILLEGAL	*t* contains characters that must not occur in a number.

The constants have a numerical order defined relatively to each other:

ISREAL < ISLONGREAL < ISOUTOFRANGE < (STRINGEMPTY, STRINGILLEGAL)

This definition makes it easier to find out if, for example, a number can be stored in a *LONGREAL* variable.

```
IF Float.ValResult(txt)<=Float.ISLONGREAL THEN …
```
instead of
```
IF (Float.ValResult(txt)=Float.ISREAL) OR
   (Float.ValResult(txt)=Float.ISLONGREAL) THEN …
```

6.8 The module In

6.8.1 Overview

This module supports simple, data-stream-oriented input. The source of input can be from the keyboard or from a file. The input from a file is especially useful for the program development as input test data can be prepared and saved in a file. This file is then selected as input source after each program start to run a complete test.

6.8.2 General notes

The interface of this module is call-compatible with the standard stated in the Oakwood Guidelines [OAK93] for a data-stream-oriented input module.

If the input is made from a file the latter can be selected in a pop-up dialog. This file is then read character by character, according to the input functions that are called. As this must be a text file an input file can be created with any text editor. In case of input functions like *LongInt* the procedure reads from the file until a character is detected that does not conform to the rules defined in the EBNF syntax. Leading blanks, tabulators, and CR and LF characters are neglected, with the sole exception of *Char*.

6.8.3 Operation

When the program is started the keyboard is the default input medium. With the menu "Pane" it is possible to switch to a file as input source at any time.

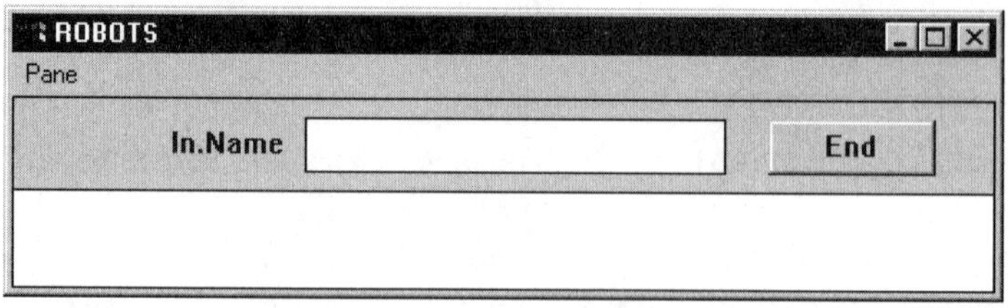

Fig. 66: A program using the modules In and Out

The end of a keyboard string is indicated by pressing the "End" key. When using a file as input source the end of the input stream is signalled by the end of file.

6.8.4 Interface

Module definition

```
DEFINITION OF MODULE In;

VAR
   Done*:BOOLEAN;

PROCEDURE Char*(VAR ch:CHAR);
PROCEDURE Echo*(x:BOOLEAN);
PROCEDURE Int*(VAR i:INTEGER);
PROCEDURE LongInt*(VAR l:LONGINT);
PROCEDURE LongReal*(VAR x:LONGREAL);
PROCEDURE Name*(VAR nme:ARRAY OF CHAR);
PROCEDURE Open*();
PROCEDURE Prompt*(t:ARRAY OF CHAR);
PROCEDURE Real*(VAR x:REAL);
PROCEDURE String*(VAR str:ARRAY OF CHAR);

END In.
```

Variables

`Done:BOOLEAN;`   *Done*

This variable indicates whether the previous input operation was successful. On starting the program *Done* is initialized with *TRUE.*

If the input comes from the keyboard the program waits until the input either is entered or terminated with the "End" button. In the latter case *Done* is set to *FALSE.*

If the input is read from a file, *Done* is set to *FALSE* as soon as the end of the file is reached.

Independently from the input source, *Done* is assigned *FALSE* if it is impossible to read from the data stream according to the EBNF syntax rules of the called input function.

Procedures

`PROCEDURE Char(VAR ch:CHAR);`   *Char*

The next character from the data stream is returned in *ch.*

`PROCEDURE Echo(x:BOOLEAN);`   *Echo*

With *x=TRUE* an automatic output of all input can be obtained using the module *Out.* When the program is started this option is not active. The setting can be "changed" during the program execution at any time.

This procedure is not included in the Oakwood Guidelines.

`PROCEDURE Int(VAR i:INTEGER);`   *Int*

Reads from the input data stream according to the EBNF syntax rule
IntConst   =   ["-"] (digit {digit} I digit {hexDigit} "H").
The result is converted to a number and returned in *i.*

LongInt   PROCEDURE LongInt(VAR l:LONGINT);

Reads from the input data stream according to the EBNF syntax rule
IntConst   =   *["-"] (digit {digit} / digit {hexDigit} "H")*.

The result is converted to a number and returned in *l*.

LongReal   PROCEDURE LongReal(VAR x:LONGREAL);

Reads from the input data stream according to the EBNF syntax rule
RealConst   =   *["-"] digit {digit} ["." {digit}]*
["E" ("+" / "-") digit {digit}].

The result is converted to a number and returned in *x*.

Name   PROCEDURE Name(VAR name:ARRAY OF CHAR);

Reads from the input data stream according to the EBNF syntax rule
NameConst   =   *nameChar {nameChar}*.

where *nameChar* denotes any character apart from the blank, the
quotation mark, CR, or LF.

Open   PROCEDURE Open;

The input position is reset to the beginning of the data stream. The
variable *Done* is initialized with *TRUE*. As input from the keyboard is
also buffered internally, previous input can also be recalled.

Prompt   PROCEDURE Prompt(t:ARRAY OF CHAR);

On executing the next input the string *t* is displayed as a prompt instead of
the default text (e.g., "In.Name").

If the input echo was switched on with *Echo(TRUE)*, *t* is also displayed in
the output via the module *Out*.

This procedure is not included in the Oakwood Guidelines.

Real   PROCEDURE Real(VAR x:REAL);

Reads from the input data stream according to the EBNF syntax rule
RealConst   =   *["-"] digit {digit} ["." {digit}]*
["E" ("+" / "-") digit {digit}].

The result is converted to a number and returned in *x*.

String   PROCEDURE String(VAR str:ARRAY OF CHAR);

Reads from the input data stream according to the EBNF syntax rule
StringConst   =   *"" {char} ""*.

If the input medium is the keyboard and no leading quotation mark is
detected, the procedure inserts one at the beginning and one at the end
automatically.

6.9 The module Out

6.9.1 Overview

This module offers a simple sequential output to the screen. A particular advantage is that the whole output is always accessible, even if it is far longer than one screen page.

6.9.2 General notes

The interface of this module is call-compatible with the standard output module in the Oakwood Guidelines.

All output is sequential and the output area is only limited by the available size of the main memory. The visible section can be selected with the help of scroll bars. All new output automatically shifts the visible area to the end of the output.

6.9.3 Interface

Module definition

```
DEFINITION OF MODULE Out;

PROCEDURE Char*(ch:CHAR);
PROCEDURE F*(t:ARRAY OF CHAR; x1:LONGINT);
PROCEDURE F2*(t:ARRAY OF CHAR; x1, x2:LONGINT);
PROCEDURE F3*(t:ARRAY OF CHAR; x1, x2, x3:LONGINT);
PROCEDURE F4*(t:ARRAY OF CHAR; x1, x2, x3, x4:LONGINT);
PROCEDURE Int*(i, n:LONGINT);
PROCEDURE Ln*();
PROCEDURE LongReal*(x:LONGREAL; n:INTEGER);
PROCEDURE Open*();
PROCEDURE Real*(x:LONGREAL; n:INTEGER);
PROCEDURE String*(str:ARRAY OF CHAR);

END Out.
```

Procedures

```
PROCEDURE Char(ch:CHAR);
```
Char

The character *ch* is printed on the screen.

```
PROCEDURE F (t:ARRAY OF CHAR; x1:LONGINT);
PROCEDURE F2(t:ARRAY OF CHAR; x1, x2:LONGINT);
PROCEDURE F3(t:ARRAY OF CHAR; x1, x2, x3:LONGINT);
PROCEDURE F4(t:ARRAY OF CHAR; x1, x2, x3, x4:LONGINT);
```
F

The *F*-procedures are an extension suggested by Prof. H. Mössenböck to the interface defined in the Oakwood Guidelines. They serve for an easy formatted output of one, two, three, or four integer values (*F*, *F2*, *F3*, or *F4*).

A string is passed in *t* for the output of which two replacement rules are valid:

1. Each occurrence of the character "*#*" is replaced from left to right by the numbers passed in *x1*, *x2*, *x3* and *x4*.

2. Each occurrence of the character "*$*" is replaced by CR and LF.

Example:

```
F2("The co-ordinates for the$center: (#,#)",45,-6);
```

causes the output

```
The co-ordinates for the
center: (45,-6)
```

Int PROCEDURE Int(i, n:LONGINT);

The number contained in *i* is displayed right aligned at least *n* characters wide.

Ln PROCEDURE Ln();

The output is continued at the beginning of the next line.

LongReal PROCEDURE LongReal(x:LONGREAL; n:INTEGER);

The number contained in *x* is displayed right aligned at least *n* characters wide.

Open PROCEDURE Open();

This procedure has no effect and exists only for reasons of compatibility. The output area is automatically initialized when importing the module *Out*.

Real PROCEDURE Real(x:LONGREAL; n:INTEGER);

The number contained in *x* is displayed right aligned at least *n* characters wide.

To increase consistency with respect to the modules *Display* and *Print*, numbers of the type *LONGREAL* may also be passed.

String PROCEDURE String(str:ARRAY OF CHAR);

The string *str* is displayed.

6.10 The module Param

6.10.1 Overview

This module offers access to the command line which was used to start the program. It is possible to access the command line as a whole or only single parameters. It is assumed that the single parameters of the command line are separated either by blanks, commas or both.

6.10.2 Interface

Module definition

```
DEFINITION OF MODULE Param;

PROCEDURE CompleteStr*(VAR cmdLine:ARRAY OF CHAR);
PROCEDURE Count*():INTEGER;
PROCEDURE Str*(paramNr:INTEGER;
               VAR paramTxt:ARRAY OF CHAR);

END Param.
```

Procedures

```
PROCEDURE CompleteStr(VAR cmdLine:ARRAY OF CHAR);
```
CompleteStr

The complete command line is copied to the parameter *cmdLine*.

```
PROCEDURE Count():INTEGER;
```
Count

The return value of the function is the number of parameters in the command line that are separated by blanks or commas.

```
PROCEDURE Str(paramNr:INTEGER;
              VAR paramTxt:ARRAY OF CHAR);
```
Str

A single parameter of the command line is copied to *paramTxt*. The parameter is selected by *paramNr,* starting with one. If a non-existent parameter is selected an empty string is returned.

Parameters containing commas, or even blanks, can be stated between quotation marks. The quotation marks are removed automatically.

Examples:

Command line	Parameter	
/a /b *.txt	1: "/a"	
	2: "/b"	
	3: "*.txt"	
"this is a text", 5,, 7	1: "this is a text"	
	2: "5"	(2nd parameter)
	3: ""	(blank 3rd parameter)
	4: "7"	(4th parameter)

6.11 The module Print

6.11.1 Overview

This makes it easy to obtain printouts on the standard printer.

6.11.2 General notes

The printer is regarded as a sequential line-oriented output medium.

At the beginning of a printout a virtual output cursor is set to the top left corner of the first page. After data has been output this position is moved right by the width of the output; if necessary a CR LF is included. It is also possible to force an immediate change of line or page.

Before starting a printout the module must be initialized by calling *Start*. After the last output on the printout the procedure *Finished* must be called. In a multi-user environment the procedures *Start* and *Finished* ensure that all output in between is managed as a single job.

6.11.3 Interface

Module definition

```
DEFINITION OF MODULE Print;

PROCEDURE Char*(x:CHAR);
PROCEDURE Finished*();
PROCEDURE Int*(i, n:LONGINT);
PROCEDURE Ln*();
PROCEDURE Page*();
PROCEDURE Real*(x:LONGREAL; n:INTEGER);
PROCEDURE RemainingLines*():INTEGER;
PROCEDURE SetLeftMargin*(marg:INTEGER);
PROCEDURE SetTopMargin*(marg:INTEGER);
PROCEDURE Start*();
PROCEDURE Str*(t:ARRAY OF CHAR);

END Print.
```

Management

Finished   `PROCEDURE Finished();`

This procedure is called at the end of the current printout. In a network environment the document is released for printing in the printer queue.

Remaining-   `PROCEDURE RemainingLines():INTEGER;`
Lines

The return value of the function is the number of lines that may still be printed on the current page using the current font.

```
PROCEDURE SetLeftMargin(marg:INTEGER);
```
SetLeftMargin

The left page margin is set to *marg* millimeters. If the current output cursor is situated to the left of the new margin it is automatically adjusted to the new margin.

Bear in mind that paper feeder tolerances and printer driver inaccuracies may give rise to irregularities.

```
PROCEDURE SetTopMargin(marg:INTEGER);
```
SetTopMargin

The top page margin is set to *marg* millimeters. If the current output position is situated above the new margin it is automatically adjusted to the new margin.

Bear in mind that paper feeder tolerances and printer driver inaccuracies may give rise to irregularities.

```
PROCEDURE Start();
```
Start

The module is initialized for the start of a new printout. This procedure must be called before any of the other modules procedures are called. In a network environment the system is indicated the start of a new printer job.

Output

```
PROCEDURE Char(x:CHAR);
```
Char

The character *x* is printed.

```
PROCEDURE Int(i, n:LONGINT);
```
Int

The number passed in *i* is printed right aligned *n* characters wide. If the number cannot be represented in the desired width the stated width is extended.

```
PROCEDURE Ln();
```
Ln

The output cursor is set to the beginning of the next line.

```
PROCEDURE Page();
```
Page

The output cursor is set to the beginning of the next page.

```
PROCEDURE Real(x:LONGREAL; n:INTEGER);
```
Real

The number passed in *x* is printed right aligned *n* characters wide. If the number cannot be represented in the desired width the stated width is extended.

```
PROCEDURE Str(t:ARRAY OF CHAR);
```
Str

The string contained in *t* is printed.

6.12 The module Process

6.12.1 Overview

This module helps to control the execution of a program.

The user can terminate the program execution by pressing ALT-F4 or by using the menu at any time. Also it is possible to define a procedure which is guaranteed to be called on exiting the program (an "exit procedure").

6.12.2 Interface

Module definition

```
DEFINITION OF MODULE Process;

TYPE
  ExitProc*=PROCEDURE ();

PROCEDURE GetExitProc*(VAR proc:ExitProc);
PROCEDURE SetBreak*(x:BOOLEAN);
PROCEDURE SetExitProc*(proc:ExitProc);
PROCEDURE Yield*();

END Process.
```

Types

ExitProc `ExitProc = PROCEDURE ();`

The procedure type for exit procedures has no parameters.

Functions

GetExitProc `PROCEDURE GetExitProc(VAR proc:ExitProc);`

The currently set exit procedure is returned in *proc*.

A combined use of *GetExitProc* and *SetExitProc* supports a concatenation of several exit procedures.

If *GetExitProc* is called before *SetExitProc* the system returns an internal empty exit procedure, which does not need to be called explicitly.

SetBreak `PROCEDURE SetBreak(x:BOOLEAN);`

The user can terminate the program execution by pressing ALT-F4 or using the menu command. If *x* is *TRUE* the user can exit the program at any time. If *FALSE* the key combination ALT-F4 has no effect and the menu item "Exit" is inactive and therefore appears gray.

```
PROCEDURE SetExitProc(proc:ExitProc);
```
SetExitProc

The procedure specified by *proc* is called before the program is terminated. The procedure is not called if the program is terminated due to a system error, a *HALT*, or an *ASSERT* which is not valid.

If *SetExitProc* is called the exit procedure previously selected is overwritten. When used with the function *GetExitProc* the previous setting can be saved and a concatenation of procedures can be implemented.

```
PROCEDURE Yield();
```
Yield

In co-operative multi-tasking systems like Windows 3.x this procedure can be used for processor sharing. During time-consuming calculations other programs may be granted processor time to ensure that the remaining system can still operate promptly.

In systems with pre-emptive multi-tasking this procedure has no effect.

6.13 The module Strings

6.13.1 Overview

This module provides functions for string processing. This includes combining strings, copying parts of a string, the conversion of a string to a number or vice-versa, etc.

6.13.2 General notes

Strings are represented by arrays of characters, where the size of the array determines the maximum length of the string. However, a string may be considerably shorter than the array it is stored in and so to define the length of a string the character (with the code zero) is appended at the end of the string. This implies that a string must not contain a character with the code zero.

For example, if the variable *x* is declared as

```
VAR
   x:ARRAY 10 OF CHAR;
```

x may contain a string of a maximum length of 9 characters. The 10th element of the array $(x[9]=0X)$ is the character with the code zero indicating the end of the string. If $x[0]=0X$, then the string is empty and does not contain any characters.

In an assignment such as x:="Test" the end of the string is marked automatically and all functions for string processing respect this mark. Only if single characters in a string are manipulated individually (e.g.,

$x[4]:="!"$) must the programmer arrange for a correct termination (e.g., $x[5]:=0X$).

All functions of this module start to count the character positions at one, i.e., the first character of a string has position one.

6.13.3 Error handling

All functions tolerate errors in character position. However, strings must always be terminated by a character with the code zero in order to be processed correctly, otherwise runtime errors may occur.

6.13.4 Interface

Module definition

```
DEFINITION OF MODULE Strings;

CONST
  ISINTEGER*=2;
  ISLONGINT*=3;
  ISOUTOFRANGE*=4;
  ISSHORTINT*=1;
  STRINGEMPTY*=5;
  STRINGILLEGAL*=6;

PROCEDURE Append*(VAR dest:ARRAY OF CHAR;
                  t:ARRAY OF CHAR);
PROCEDURE AppendChar*(VAR dest:ARRAY OF CHAR; t:CHAR);
PROCEDURE Copy*(VAR from, to:ARRAY OF CHAR;
                pos, n:LONGINT);
PROCEDURE Delete*(VAR t:ARRAY OF CHAR; pos, n:LONGINT);
PROCEDURE HexStr*(x:LONGINT; VAR t:ARRAY OF CHAR);
PROCEDURE Insert*(src:ARRAY OF CHAR;
                  VAR dest:ARRAY OF CHAR;
                  pos:LONGINT);
PROCEDURE InsertChar*(x:CHAR;
                      VAR dest:ARRAY OF CHAR;
                      pos:LONGINT);
PROCEDURE LeftAlign*(VAR t:ARRAY OF CHAR; n:LONGINT);
PROCEDURE Length*(VAR t:ARRAY OF CHAR):LONGINT;
PROCEDURE Pos*(pattern:ARRAY OF CHAR;
               VAR t:ARRAY OF CHAR;
               start:LONGINT):LONGINT;
PROCEDURE PosChar*(x:CHAR; VAR t:ARRAY OF CHAR;
                   start:LONGINT):LONGINT;
PROCEDURE RemoveTrailingSpaces*(VAR t:ARRAY OF CHAR);
PROCEDURE RemoveLeadingSpaces*(VAR t:ARRAY OF CHAR);
PROCEDURE RightAlign*(VAR t:ARRAY OF CHAR; n:LONGINT);
PROCEDURE Str*(x:LONGINT; VAR t:ARRAY OF CHAR);
PROCEDURE UpCase*(VAR t:ARRAY OF CHAR);
PROCEDURE UpCaseChar*(x:CHAR):CHAR;
PROCEDURE Val*(VAR t:ARRAY OF CHAR):LONGINT;
PROCEDURE ValResult*(VAR t:ARRAY OF CHAR):INTEGER;

END Strings.
```

Important functions

```
PROCEDURE Append (VAR dest:ARRAY OF CHAR; t:ARRAY OF CHAR);
```
Append

The string *t* is appended to the string *dest*.

```
PROCEDURE AppendChar (VAR dest:ARRAY OF CHAR; t:CHAR);
```
AppendChar

The character *t* is appended to the string *dest*.

```
PROCEDURE Copy (VAR from,to:ARRAY OF CHAR; pos,n:LONGINT);
```
Copy

A section of the string *from* is copied to the string *to*. The former contents of *to* are overwritten and therefore lost.

The copied section in *from* starts at the position *pos* and is *n* characters long.

If *to* is not large enough to hold the copied string then only the part that fits in *to* is copied.

```
PROCEDURE Length (VAR t:ARRAY OF CHAR):LONGINT;
```
Length

The return value of the function is the number of characters of the string *t*.

```
PROCEDURE Str (x:LONGINT; VAR t:ARRAY OF CHAR);
```
Str

The number *x* is converted to a string and the result is stored in *t*.

If *t* is not large enough to hold all characters of the number, *t* is filled with "$" characters.

```
PROCEDURE Val (VAR t:ARRAY OF CHAR):LONGINT;
```
Val

The string *t* is converted to a number and returned as result of the function.

If the character sequence in *t* does not represent a number and thus the conversion to a number fails the smallest negative number *(MIN(LONGINT))* is returned.

Blanks at the beginning and the end of *t* are ignored. The number must not contain blanks.

```
PROCEDURE ValResult (VAR txt:ARRAY OF CHAR):INTEGER;
```
ValResult

This function can be used to discover whether the string *txt* can be converted to a number, and which is the least kind of integer necessary for storing it.

The following constants define the possible return values of the function:

ISSHORTINT	*txt* contains a number which can be stored in a *SHORTINT* variable.
ISINTEGER	*txt* contains a number which can be stored in an *INTEGER* variable.
ISLONGINT	*txt* contains a number which can be stored in a *LONGINT* variable.
ISOUTOFRANGE	*txt* contains a number which is too big or too small to be stored in a *LONGINT* variable.

STRINGEMPTY   *txt* is empty or contains nothing but blanks.

STRINGILLEGAL   *txt* contains characters that must not be part of a number.

The constants have a numerical order defined relative to each other:

ISSHORTINT < ISINTEGER < ISLONGINT < ISOUTOFRANGE < (STRINGEMPTY, STRINGILLEGAL)

This definition makes it easier to find out whether, for example, a number is small enough to be stored in a *INTEGER* variable.

```
IF Strings.ValResult(txt)<=Strings.ISINTEGER THEN …
```

instead of
```
IF (Strings.ValResult(txt)=Strings.ISSHORTINT) OR
   (Strings.ValResult(txt)=Strings.ISINTEGER) THEN …
```

Additional functions

Delete   PROCEDURE Delete (VAR t:ARRAY OF CHAR; pos,n:LONGINT);

Starting at the position *pos*, *n* characters of the string are deleted.

HexStr   PROCEDURE HexStr (x:LONGINT; VAR t:ARRAY OF CHAR);

The number *x* is converted to a string in hexadecimal format and the result is stored in *t*. At the end of the string an "h" is appended to indicate the hexadecimal representation of the number.

If *t* is not large enough to hold all characters of the number, *t* is filled with "$" characters.

Example: 0 becomes "0h", 15 becomes "Fh", 16 becomes "10h".

Insert   PROCEDURE Insert (src:ARRAY OF CHAR;
                     VAR dest:ARRAY OF CHAR; pos:LONGINT);

The string *src* is inserted into the string *dest* at the position *pos*. If the maximum length of *dest* is insufficient to store the result only the part of *src* fitting in *dest* is inserted.

InsertChar   PROCEDURE InsertChar (x:CHAR;
                         VAR dest:ARRAY OF CHAR;
                         pos:LONGINT);

The character *x* is inserted into the string *dest* at the position *pos* if *dest* provides space for it.

LeftAlign   PROCEDURE LeftAlign (VAR t:ARRAY OF CHAR; n:LONGINT);

The length of *t* is increased to *n* characters by appending blanks. If *t* has already the appropriate length or is longer, *t* remains unchanged.

Pos   PROCEDURE Pos (pattern:ARRAY OF CHAR;
                 VAR t:ARRAY OF CHAR;
                 start:LONGINT):LONGINT;

This function returns the position of the string *pattern* in the string *t*.

If *pattern* does not occur in *t* zero is returned. If the *pattern* occurs several times, the position of the first occurrence is returned.

start indicates the position starting from which the search shall be carried out. If *start* is less than one, it is set to one. If *start* denotes a position beyond the end of *t*, the function returns zero.

```
PROCEDURE PosChar (x:CHAR;
                   VAR t:ARRAY OF CHAR;
                   start:LONGINT):LONGINT;
```
PosChar

This function returns the position of the character *x* in the string *t*.

If *x* does not occur in *t* zero is returned. If *x* occurs several times the position of the first occurrence is returned.

start indicates the position starting from which the search is to be carried out. If *start* is less than one it is set to one. If *start* denotes a position beyond the end of *t* the function returns zero.

```
PROCEDURE RemoveLeadingSpaces (VAR t:ARRAY OF CHAR);
```
Remove-Leading-Spaces

All blanks at the beginning of *t* are removed.

```
PROCEDURE RemoveTrailingSpaces (VAR t:ARRAY OF CHAR);
```
Remove-TrailingSpaces

All blanks at the end of *t* are removed.

```
PROCEDURE RightAlign (VAR t:ARRAY OF CHAR; n:LONGINT);
```
RightAlign

The length of *t* is increased to *n* characters by inserting blanks at the beginning. If *t* has already the appropriate length or is longer, *t* remains unchanged.

```
PROCEDURE UpCase (VAR t:ARRAY OF CHAR);
```
UpCase

All lowercase letters in *t* are converted to uppercase. (German umlauts are also converted.) All other characters remain unchanged.

```
PROCEDURE UpCaseChar (x:CHAR):CHAR;
```
UpCaseChar

For all lowercase letters the corresponding capital letter is returned. (This also applies to German umlauts.)

All other characters are returned unchanged. The difference between this function and the Oberon-2 function `CAP(x:CHAR): CHAR` is that the return values for characters other than lowercase letters of the latter function depend on the implementation.

6.14 The module Utils

6.14.1 Overview

The functions discussed here tend to be system dependent. Therefore the module Utils is a relative of the module SYSTEM. The import of Utils is an indicator that the program is non-portable.

6.14.2 General notes

For all type conversions it is assumed that the sizes of the elementary types are defined as follows:

INTEGER :   2 byte,
LONGINT :   4 byte,
CHAR : 1 byte.

6.14.3 Error management

All functions are designed so that runtime errors due to invalid parameters can be avoided.

In normal use only the procedure MsDos may lead to errors when applied with invalid parameters. In some cases the resulting runtime errors cannot always be recognised and so this may lead to a program crash. Great care should be taken to only pass valid parameters.

6.14.4 Interface

Module definition

```
DEFINITION OF MODULE Utils;

PROCEDURE BitAnd*(a, b:INTEGER):INTEGER;
PROCEDURE BitAndL*(a, b:LONGINT):LONGINT;
PROCEDURE BitNot*(a:INTEGER):INTEGER;
PROCEDURE BitNotL*(a:LONGINT):LONGINT;
PROCEDURE BitOr*(a, b:INTEGER):INTEGER;
PROCEDURE BitOrL*(a, b:LONGINT):LONGINT;
PROCEDURE BitXor*(a, b:INTEGER):INTEGER;
PROCEDURE BitXorL*(a, b:LONGINT):LONGINT;
PROCEDURE GetDate*(VAR day, month, year, dayOfWeek:INTEGER);
PROCEDURE GetDateStr*(VAR t:ARRAY OF CHAR);
PROCEDURE GetTime*(VAR sec, min, hour:INTEGER);
PROCEDURE GetTimeStr*(VAR t:ARRAY OF CHAR);
PROCEDURE HiByte*(x:INTEGER):CHAR;
PROCEDURE HiWord*(x:LONGINT):INTEGER;
PROCEDURE LoByte*(x:INTEGER):CHAR;
PROCEDURE LoWord*(x:LONGINT):INTEGER;
PROCEDURE MakeLong*(hi, lo:INTEGER):LONGINT;
PROCEDURE MakeWord*(hi, lo:CHAR):INTEGER;
PROCEDURE MsDos*(VAR ax, bx, cx, dx:INTEGER);

END Utils.
```

Conversions

HiByte   PROCEDURE HiByte (x:INTEGER):CHAR;

The return value of *HiByte* is the most significant byte of the two-byte value *x*.

```
PROCEDURE HiWord (x:LONGINT):INTEGER;
```
HiWord

The return value of *HiWord* is the most significant half of the four-byte value *x*.

```
PROCEDURE LoByte (x:INTEGER):CHAR;
```
LoByte

The return value of *LoByte* is the least significant byte of the two-byte value *x*.

```
PROCEDURE LoWord (x:LONGINT):INTEGER;
```
LoWord

The return value of *LoWord* is the least significant half of the four-byte value *x*.

```
PROCEDURE MakeLong (hi,lo:INTEGER):LONGINT;
```
MakeLong

The two-byte values *hi* and *lo* are combined to a four-byte value by concatenation and returned as result of the function. *hi* becomes the most significant and *lo* the least significant part of the result.

```
PROCEDURE MakeWord (hi, lo:CHAR):INTEGER;
```
MakeWord

The one-byte values *hi* and *lo* are combined to a two-byte value by concatenation and returned as result of the function. *hi* becomes the most significant and *lo* the least significant part of the result.

Example: *MakeWord(1X,50X) = 150H*

Binary operations

```
PROCEDURE BitAnd (a,b:INTEGER):INTEGER;
PROCEDURE BitAndL(a,b:LONGINT):LONGINT;
```
BitAnd

A bitwise AND is applied to the values *a* and *b*, and the result returned.

bit of *a*	bit of *b*	*a* AND *b*
0	0	0
0	1	0
1	0	0
1	1	1

```
PROCEDURE BitNot (a:INTEGER):INTEGER;
PROCEDURE BitNotL(a:LONGINT):LONGINT;
```
BitNot

The value of *a* is bitwise negated, and the result returned.

bit of *a*	NOT *a*
0	1
1	0

BitOr
```
PROCEDURE BitOr (a,b:INTEGER):INTEGER;
PROCEDURE BitOrL(a,b:LONGINT):LONGINT;
```

A bitwise OR is applied to the values *a* and *b* are, and the result returned.

bit of *a*	bit of *b*	*a* OR *b*
0	0	0
0	1	1
1	0	1
1	1	1

BitXOr
```
PROCEDURE BitXOr (a,b:INTEGER):INTEGER;
PROCEDURE BitXOrL(a,b:LONGINT):LONGINT;
```

A bitwise XOR is applied to the values *a* and *b*, and the result returned.

bit of *a*	bit of *b*	*a* XOR *b*
0	0	0
0	1	1
1	0	1
1	1	0

Miscellaneous

GetDate
```
PROCEDURE GetDate (VAR day,month,year,dayOfWeek:INTEGER);
```

The current date is read from the system's real-time clock and returned in the parameters *day, month, year*, and *dayOfWeek*.

The year is stated including the century.

In addition, in *dayOfWeek* a value between 1 and 7 is returned, where 1 denotes Monday and 7 Sunday.

GetDateStr
```
PROCEDURE GetDateStr (VAR t:ARRAY OF CHAR);
```

The current date is read from the system's real-time clock and returned as a string in *t*. The result is 10 characters long and has the format "dd.mm.yyyy". If *t* cannot hold a string of 10 characters length, a completely empty string is returned.

GetTime
```
PROCEDURE GetTime (VAR sec,min,hour:INTEGER);
```

The current time is read from the system's real-time clock and returned in the parameters *sec*, *min*, and *hour*.

GetTimeStr
```
PROCEDURE GetTimeStr (VAR t:ARRAY OF CHAR);
```

The current time is read from the system's real-time clock and returned as a string in *t*. The result is 8 characters long and has the format

"HH.MM.SS". If *t* cannot hold a string of 8 characters length, a completely empty string is returned.

```
PROCEDURE MsDos (VAR ax,bx,cx,dx:INTEGER);                    MsDos
```

An MsDos system function is executed via a call of interrupt 21h. The values from parameters ax, bx, cx, dx are copied into the processor registers AX, BX. CD, DX and the interrupt 21H call is then made. After the execution of the system function the resulting register values are returned in the parameters.

6.15 The module Volume

6.15.1 Overview

The Volume module provides facilities for creating, searching, and modifying file directories.

6.15.2 General notes

The module interface is designed to be applicable to different systems. The following notes refer exclusively to the file system of MS-DOS.

Drives are identified by letters.

The letter "A" refers to the first floppy disk, drive, "B" to the second, and "C" to the first hard disk drive.

All letters down to "Z" may be used, but the settings vary from system to system. A drive is specified using a single letter or a letter followed by a colon passed as parameter. No distinction between uppercase and lowercase is made. For example, "a", "A:" and "A" have the same meaning.

A colon must be put after the drive identification when a path is defined, a path being a combination of a drive name and a file name. The backslash "\" serves as a separating symbol between directory names. For compatibility with other systems the forward slash "/" may also be used. For example, a path statement "C:\" refers to the root directory of the drive C.

For access to the current drive the drive identification may be omitted in path statements. If the only the drive identification is given as a parameter then a blank is passed as a reference to the current drive.

File names are passed through to the operating system without any modification. Therefore the rules for creating valid directory and filenames under MS-DOS must be adhered to.

6.15.3 Error handling

All procedures with a parameter *resCode* return an error code. This code can be used to check if the function was carried out successfully (*resCode* = *NOERROR)* or indicate more details about the cause of the error.

All errors occurring during file or drive operations are indicated by an appropriate error code there should be no cases where a runtime error is reported or the program is terminated. It is the programmer's responsibility to arrange for an error handling and to avoid further errors. The procedure *GetErrorMessage* provides an equivalent message for every possible error code and can be used for building error diagnostic dialogs.

6.15.4 Interface

Module definition

```
DEFINITION OF MODULE Volume;

CONST
   ATTRARCHIVE*=5;        ATTRDIR*=4;
   ATTRHIDDEN*=1;         ATTRREADONLY*=0;
   ATTRSYSTEM*=2;         ATTRVOLUME*=3;
   CANNOTMAKE*=52H;       INVALIDDRIVE*=0FH;
   MAXFILENAME*=13;       MAXPATH*=100;
   MAXVOLUME*=3;          NOERROR*=0;
   NOMOREFILES*=12H;      PATHNOTFOUND*=3;
   SHORTBUFFER*=102H;     WRITEPROTECTED*=13H;

TYPE
   Scan*=RECORD
     PROCEDURE (VAR) First*(name:ARRAY OF CHAR;
                          VAR resCode:INTEGER);
     PROCEDURE (VAR) GetAttr*():SET;
     PROCEDURE (VAR) GetCreationDate*(
                                  VAR t:ARRAY OF CHAR);
     PROCEDURE (VAR) GetModifyDate*(VAR t:ARRAY OF CHAR);
     PROCEDURE (VAR) GetName*(VAR name:ARRAY OF CHAR);
     PROCEDURE (VAR) GetSize*():LONGINT;
     PROCEDURE (VAR) Next*(VAR resCode:INTEGER);
   END;
   ScanP*=POINTER TO Scan;

PROCEDURE ChangeDirectory*(name:ARRAY OF CHAR;
                          VAR resCode:INTEGER);
PROCEDURE CreateDirectory*(name:ARRAY OF CHAR;
                          VAR resCode:INTEGER);
PROCEDURE CurrentDirectory*(drive:ARRAY OF CHAR;
                          VAR name:ARRAY OF CHAR;
                          VAR resCode:INTEGER);
PROCEDURE FreeSpace*(drive:ARRAY OF CHAR;
                   VAR space:LONGINT;
                   VAR resCode:INTEGER);
PROCEDURE GetErrorMessage*(error:INTEGER;
                          VAR message:ARRAY OF CHAR);
PROCEDURE RemoveDirectory*(name:ARRAY OF CHAR;
```

```
                           VAR resCode:INTEGER);
PROCEDURE TotalSpace*(drive:ARRAY OF CHAR;
                      VAR space:LONGINT;
                      VAR resCode:INTEGER);

END Volume.
```

Constants

MAXFILENAME	The maximum recommended length of strings used for storing file names
MAXPATH	The recommended length of strings used for storing file names including a path
MAXVOLUME	The recommended length of strings used for storing drive identifications

Constants for error codes

CANNOTMAKE	It was impossible to create the desired directory.
INVALIDDRIVE	The indicated drive could not be found.
NOERROR	The operation was successful.
NOMOREFILES	No further suitable files could be found.
PATHNOTFOUND	The stated path could not be found.
SHORTBUFFER	The data buffer in use is not large enough to contain the result.
WRITEPROTECTED	Attempted write to a write-protected drive

Types

```
ScanP=POINTER TO Scan;
```
ScanP

A pointer to a *Scan* object

Error handling

```
PROCEDURE GetErrorMessage(error:INTEGER;
                         VAR message:ARRAY OF CHAR);
```
GetError-
Message

The text returned in *message* describes the error code *error*.

All return values for all functions in this module may be passed as an error code. Under certain circumstances an error code might be reported which is different from all predefined constants. Even in this case *GetErrorMessage* will provide an appropriate text.

Identical constants for error codes defined in the module *Volume* have the same numerical value as their counterparts in the module *File*.

Drive functions

FreeSpace
```
PROCEDURE FreeSpace(drive:ARRAY OF CHAR;
                    VAR space:LONGINT;
                    VAR resCode:INTEGER);
```

The available space on the drive specified by *drive* is returned in *space*. The amount of available storage is defined in bytes.

The parameter *resCode* returns an error code; see Section 6.6.3.

TotalSpace
```
PROCEDURE TotalSpace(drive:ARRAY OF CHAR;
                     VAR space:LONGINT;
                     VAR resCode:INTEGER);
```

The full drive capacity of *drive* in bytes is returned in *space*.

The parameter *resCode* returns an error code; see Section 6.6.3.

Directory functions

Change-
Directory
```
PROCEDURE ChangeDirectory(name:ARRAY OF CHAR;
                          VAR resCode:INTEGER);
```

The current directory is changed to the one stated in *name*. If the path in *name* contains a drive identification, the current directory of this drive is selected, otherwise the directory of the current drive if it exists. The current drive remains unchanged.

The parameter *resCode* returns an error code; see Section 6.6.3.

Create-
Directory
```
PROCEDURE CreateDirectory(name:ARRAY OF CHAR;
                          VAR resCode:INTEGER);
```

The directory specified by *name* is created. Only one directory and not a whole path can be created per call. For example, if you want to create the path "C:\PRODUCT\EXAMPLE\A" it is necessary to call
```
CreateDirectory("C:\PRODUCT",resCode);
CreateDirectory("C:\PRODUCT\EXAMPLE,resCode);
CreateDirectory("C:\PRODUCT\EXAMPLE\A",resCode);
```

The parameter *resCode* returns an error code; see Section 6.6.3.

Current-
Directory
```
PROCEDURE CurrentDirectory(drive:ARRAY OF CHAR;
                           VAR name:ARRAY OF CHAR;
                           VAR resCode:INTEGER);
```

The current directory of the drive *drive* is returned in *name*. The path stated in *name* always contains a drive identification. If a blank is passed in *drive*, the current drive the current path is returned in *name*.

The parameter *resCode* returns an error code; see Section 6.6.3.

Remove-
Directory
```
PROCEDURE RemoveDirectory(name:ARRAY OF CHAR;
                          VAR resCode:INTEGER);
```

The directory stated in *name* is removed.

The parameter *resCode* returns an error code; see Section 6.6.3.

Objects

```
Scan                                                                      Scan
```

Serves for searching for directory entries which match some given searching criteria.

```
PROCEDURE (VAR anObj:Scan) First(name:ARRAY OF CHAR;         First
                                 VAR resCode:INTEGER);
```

The first directory entry that matches the stated searching pattern given in *name* is searched. This method must be called before any other method.

In *name* any path may be stated; wildcards like "*" and "?" are permitted in the file name.

"*" stands for any number and combination of characters and "?" for precisely one character.

Example for *name*:

"C:\DOS*.COM" starts a search for all files with the extension "COM" in the directory "C:\DOS".

If the value *NOERROR* was returned in *resCode* the search was successful and the name and other characteristics of the matching directory entry may then be obtained using the other methods of the scan object.

The parameter *resCode* returns an error code; see Section 6.6.3.

```
PROCEDURE (VAR anObj:Scan) Next(VAR resCode:INTEGER);        Next
```

On each call of this method the next matching directory entry is searched for until no more entries are available. If the value *NOERROR* is returned in *resCode* the search was successful and the name and other characteristics of the found entry may be obtained using the corresponding methods. If an error occurs then the methods *GetName*, *GetSize*, *GetAttr*, *GetCreationDate*, and *GetModifyDate* must not be applied.

The parameter *resCode* returns an error code; see Section 6.6.3.

```
PROCEDURE (VAR anObj:Scan) GetName(VAR name:ARRAY OF CHAR);  GetName
```

The name of the last matching entry is returned in *name*. If the size of *name* is not sufficient to hold the result an empty string is returned.

The array for the parameter *name* should be sized using the constant *MAXFILENAME*.

```
PROCEDURE (VAR anObj:Scan) GetSize():LONGINT;               GetSize
```

The return value of the function is the size of the last detected file.

```
PROCEDURE (VAR anObj:Scan) GetAttr():SET;                   GetAttr
```

The return value of the function is the number of attributes of the last detected directory entry.

The constants described together with the procedure *GetAttributes* in module *File* are also defined in module V*olume*.

GetCreation-
Date

```
PROCEDURE (VAR anObj:Scan) GetCreationDate(VAR date:
                                      ARRAY OF CHAR);
```

The creation date of the found file is returned in *date*. MS-DOS does not support this information and always returns an empty string in *date*.

GetModifyDate

```
PROCEDURE (VAR anObj:Scan) GetModifyDate(VAR date:
                                    ARRAY OF CHAR);
```

The date of the last modification of the found file is returned in *date*.

The format of the date is "DD.MM.YYYY   HH:MM:SS" with two separating blanks. The total length of the string is 20 characters. If *date* cannot hold a string of length 20 the result is truncated.

Example: "15. 4.1993 18:06:27"

Example using a scan object:

Opal4.mod

```
IMPORT Volume,Out;

PROCEDURE ShowDosDir();
VAR
    scan:Volume.Scan;
    result:INTEGER;
    aString:ARRAY 100 OF CHAR;
BEGIN
    scan.First("C:\DOS\*.*",result);    (*Set search criteria*)
    WHILE result=Volume.NOERROR DO      (*Search the directory*)
        scan.GetName(aString);
        Out.String(aString);                (*Output the matches*)
        Out.Ln;
        scan.Next(result);
    END;
                                    (*Show reason for termination*)
    IF result#Volume.NOMOREFILES THEN
        Volume.GetErrorMessage(result,aString);
        Out.String(aString);
        Out.Ln;
    END;
END ShowDosDir;
```

6.16 The module XYplane

6.16.1 Overview

This module supports very simple monochrome graphics.

6.16.2 General notes

The interface of this module is call-compatible to the standard for the simple graphics module defined in the Oakwood Guidelines.

The drawing area uses a Cartesian system of co-ordinates with the (0,0) origin in the bottom left hand corner. Dots can be drawn in either a foreground or background color.

6.16.3 Interface

Module definition

```
DEFINITION OF MODULE XYplane;

CONST
  erase*=0;
  draw*=1;

VAR
  W-, H-:INTEGER;
  X-, Y-:INTEGER;

PROCEDURE Clear*();
PROCEDURE Close*();
PROCEDURE Dot*(x, y, mode:INTEGER);
PROCEDURE IsDot*(x, y:INTEGER):BOOLEAN;
PROCEDURE Key*():CHAR;
PROCEDURE Open*();

END XYplane.
```

Constants

drawdraw   Used for the parameter mode when the foreground color should be used

erase   Used for the parameter *mode* when the background color should be used

Variables

`W,H:INTEGER;`   *W, H*

These write-protected variables contain the width (*W*) and the height (*H*) of the drawing area.

`X,Y:INTEGER;`   *X, Y*

These write-protected variables contain the position of the bottom left corner of the drawing area. In some implementations of this module the drawing area does not create its own local system of co-ordinates. If this is the case then all drawing operations must compensate (x,y) values with the required offsets.

In the Windows implementation the drawing area creates its own system of co-ordinates with an origin at (0,0).

Procedures

Clear   PROCEDURE Clear;

The drawing area is cleared to the background color.

Close   PROCEDURE Close;

The drawing area is closed and the space released on the screen is used for the output of other modules (*Display*, *Out*, *ColorPlane*).

This procedure is not defined in the Oakwood Guidelines.

Dot   PROCEDURE Dot(x, y, mode:INTEGER);

A dot is drawn at the co-ordinates (*x,y*) if *mode* has the value *draw* or erased if *mode* has the value *erase*.

IsDot   PROCEDURE IsDot(x, y:INTEGER):BOOLEAN;

The return value of the function is *TRUE* if the dot with the co-ordinate (*x,y*) is set.

Key   PROCEDURE Key():CHAR;

The return value of the function is *0X*, if no key was pressed, otherwise it is the key code. Keys that are not assigned an ASCII code are ignored.

Open   PROCEDURE Open;

The module is initialized and the drawing area is created on the screen. *Open* must be called before any other procedure of the module is called.

7. Programming with the Windows API

7.1 Overview

In this chapter we want to show you how to write programs with the *POW!* environment which directly access the application programmers interface (API) of Windows. To understand the chapter you should be familiar with the general mechanisms of Windows programming.

Direct use of the Windows interface requires a clear understanding of the Windows programming model and also the concepts of event driven program design. There is a wide variety of publications available on this subject and so a general introduction is not provided in this chapter. The book written by Charles Petzold and listed in the literature section is recommended as an introduction to Windows programming.

7.2 Language extensions

On the whole, three Oberon-2 language extensions are required to allow access to the programming interface of Windows.

- The character "_" is permitted in symbols
- Structures and procedures may be marked by the keyword "[WINDOWS]". So structures become compatible with Windows (or C) as far as the memory alignment and calling conventions are concerned. In this case an appropriate linker symbol suitable for Windows (or C) is created for these procedures.
- In a definition module the interface of Windows-compatible Dynamic Link Libraries (DLLs) can be defined. For procedures only declarations, without code, are declared. The whole Windows API is accessed using this mechanism, as well as all other DLLs.

These three language extensions are provided by the Robinson Oberon-2 compiler which is supplied with the *POW!* environment for Windows.

7.3 Interfaces to "foreign" DLLs

7.3.1 Definition module

To use a DLL written in a language other than Oberon-2 it is necessary to define a compatible module interface for it. Once this is done the DLL can be used just like a normal Oberon-2 module.

The interface of a "foreign" DLL must be defined in an Oberon-2 definition module. Structures must be declared with the suffix *[WINDOWS]* to avoid differences in the memory representation due to the alignment of Oberon-2. Procedures must declared as *[WINDOWS]* to enable the creation of a linker symbol without the module name at the beginning.

The following example shows a drastically shortened version of the interface definition for the Windows API:

```
DEFINITION Windows;

CONST
    WM_CHILDACTIVATE        =  22H;
    WM_CLOSE                =  10H;
    WM_COMMAND              =  111H;

TYPE            (* Define "C" types in terms of Oberon-2 types *)
    WORD = INTEGER;             DWORD = LONGINT;
    BOOL = INTEGER;             ADR = LONGINT;
    FARPROC = LONGINT;          UINT = WORD;
    HANDLE = UINT;              HDC = UINT;
    HWND = UINT;

    BITMAP = RECORD [WINDOWS]
        bmType: INTEGER;
        bmWidth: INTEGER;
        bmHeight: INTEGER;
        bmWidthBytes: INTEGER;
        bmPlanes: BYTE;
        bmBitsPixel: BYTE;
        bmBits: ADR;
    END;

PROCEDURE [WINDOWS] GetTickCount (): DWORD;
PROCEDURE [WINDOWS] GetTimerResolution (): DWORD;
PROCEDURE [WINDOWS] ShowWindow (a: HWND; b: INTEGER): BOOL;

END Windows.
```

7.3.2 Data types

In C far more basic data types are available than in Oberon-2. So when it comes to defining an Oberon-2 interface a direct equivalent cannot always be found. Unsigned integer types are particularly difficult as they do not exist in Oberon. As long as such variables only serve for comparisons with predefined constants, as it is usually the case in the Windows API, no problem occurs. However problems arise if greater or less than expressions are attempted. For example, Oberon-2 understands the value 45000 of the type *unsigned int* as a negative value of the (16 bit) type *INTEGER* which is regarded as being less than zero.

For basic data types the following equivalents are recommended:

char	CHAR or SHORTINT
unsigned char	CHAR or SHORTINT
short int	INTEGER
int	INTEGER
unsigned int	INTEGER
long	LONGINT
unsigned long	LONGINT
far *	LONGINT

Note that C does not define whether a number of the type *int* is represented by 16 or 32 bits. The above table refers to the situation using 16-bit C compilers and is based on the terminology of Windows 3.x. There is a good description of C data types by Microsoft; see Section "Literature" for details.

7.3.3 Call-back procedures

Call-back procedures are procedures that are installed for later use at one point and then called from a different place (e.g., by Windows itself). Typical examples for this are the event handling procedures of the window classes under Windows.

Call-back procedures must be declared as *[WINDOWS]* and denoted by an export mark. They must also be mentioned on the list of the exported procedures in the linker options.

To pass a call-back procedure to Windows its address needs to be known. The function SYSTEM.ADR cannot be used as it cannot be applied to procedures. For this reason, a procedure variable must be assigned the desired procedure which can then be converted to the required type (e.g., Windows FARPROC or simply LONGINT).

7.3.4 Using "foreign" DLLs

A foreign (existing) DLL can only be used if it has a compatible definition module. Both the definition module and the import library of the DLL must be included in your project. The DLL can now be used just like all other modules using the defined module interface.

The import library interface for an undocumented DLL can be discovered and created using the tool "IMPLIB" provided by Microsoft.

7.4 Basic Windows program

The following program creates an empty window with a menu containing an About-box which can be activated. The implementation relies exclusively on commands from the standard Windows API.

Although the example program does not fulfil any particular purpose all the basic elements of a pure Windows program are present. This is why it is called the basic Windows program, as more sophisticated programs can be derived from it.

The procedures described below each represent a typical function block of a Windows program.

WinMain

The execution of the Windows application program starts with this procedure.

The functions for initialization are called and then a loop is entered where the procedure waits for messages to arrive. These messages are then interpreted by the rest of the program.

InitApplication

The window class used by the program is initialized. If several copies of the same program run simultaneously this function is called only when the first copy is started. The initialization executed here is also effective for copies that are started later.

InitInstance

This procedure generates the main window and is called once for the initialization of each program copy. A handle for the program copy, the "instance-handle", is saved for later use.

MainWndProc

This function is a call-back function called by Windows for the processing of messages to the main window. This procedure is installed when the window class for the main window is defined.

About

This procedure is similar to *MainWndProc* and is used for the processing of messages to the "About" dialog box.

```
MODULE Generic;

IMPORT W := Windows, SYSTEM;

CONST
    IDM_ABOUT = 100;
    txt1 = "GenericMenu";
    txt2 = "GenericWClass";
    txt3 = "AboutBox";
    txt4 = "Generic Sample Application";

VAR
    hInst: W.HANDLE;

PROCEDURE [WINDOWS] About*(
    hDlg: W.HWND;           (* window handle of the dialog box *)
    message: W.WORD;                  (* type of the message *)
    wParam: W.WORD;              (* parameter of the message *)
    lParam: LONGINT              (* parameter of the message *)
    ): W.BOOL;
BEGIN
    IF message = W.WM_INITDIALOG THEN
        RETURN W.true
    ELSIF message = W.WM_COMMAND THEN
        IF (wParam = W.IDOK) OR (wParam = W.IDCANCEL) THEN
            W.EndDialog(hDlg, W.true)
        END;
        RETURN W.true
    END;
    RETURN W.false                  (* message not processed *)
END About;

PROCEDURE [WINDOWS] MainWndProc*(
    hWnd: W.HWND;                          (* window handle *)
    message: W.WORD;                   (*type of the message*)
    wParam: W.WORD;               (*parameter of the message*)
    lParam: LONGINT              (*parameter of the message*)
    ): LONGINT;
VAR
    i: INTEGER;
BEGIN
    IF message = W.WM_COMMAND THEN
        IF wParam = IDM_ABOUT THEN    (*command from the menu? *)
            i := W.DialogBox(hInst,            (* instance handle *)
                        SYSTEM.ADR(txt3),    (*resource name*)
                        hWnd,               (* superior window *)
                        About);            (* message handler *)
        ELSE                      (* processing by Windows *)
            RETURN W.DefWindowProc(hWnd, message,
                                wParam, lParam)
        END
    ELSIF message = W.WM_DESTROY THEN      (* window removed *)
        W.PostQuitMessage(0)
    ELSE                          (* processing by Windows *)
        RETURN W.DefWindowProc(hWnd,message,wParam,lParam)
    END;
    RETURN W.NULL
END MainWndProc;
```

```
PROCEDURE InitApplication(hInstance: W.HANDLE): BOOLEAN;
VAR
   wc: W.WNDCLASS;
BEGIN
   wc.style := W.NULL;
   wc.lpfnWndProc := MainWndProc;
   wc.cbClsExtra := 0;
   wc.cbWndExtra := 0;
   wc.hInstance := hInstance;              (* program instance *)
   wc.hIcon := W.LoadIcon(hInstance,         (* program icon *)
                     SYSTEM.ADR("GENERICICON"));
   wc.hCursor := W.LoadCursor(W.NULL, W.IDC_ARROW);
   wc.hbrBackground := W.GetStockObject(W.WHITE_BRUSH);
   wc.lpszMenuName := SYSTEM.ADR(txt1);        (* name of the *)
                     (* program menu in the resource file *)
   wc.lpszClassName := SYSTEM.ADR(txt2);     (* name of the *)
                              (* new window class *)
   RETURN W.RegisterClass(SYSTEM.ADR(wc)) # 0
END InitApplication;

PROCEDURE InitInstance(hInstance:W.HANDLE;
                     nCmdShow: INTEGER): BOOLEAN;
VAR
   r: INTEGER;
   hWnd: W.HWND;                 (* handle of the main window *)
BEGIN
   hInst := hInstance;              (* save instance handle *)
   hWnd:=W.CreateWindow(SYSTEM.ADR(txt2),     (*window class *)
                     SYSTEM.ADR(txt4),      (*window title *)
                     W.WS_OVERLAPPEDWINDOW,
                     W.CW_USEDEFAULT,
                     W.CW_USEDEFAULT,
                     W.CW_USEDEFAULT,
                     W.CW_USEDEFAULT,
                     W.NULL,
                     W.NULL,
                     hInstance,     (*holder of the window *)
                     W.NULL);
   IF hWnd = 0 THEN RETURN FALSE END;
   r := W.ShowWindow(hWnd, nCmdShow);
   W.UpdateWindow(hWnd);
   RETURN TRUE
END InitInstance;

PROCEDURE [WINDOWS] WinMain*(
     hInstance: W.HANDLE;      (* instance handle of program *)
     hPrevInstance: W.HANDLE;   (* inst. handle of prev. pr. *)
     lpCmdLine: W.LPSTR;      (* pointer to the command line *)
     nCmdShow: INTEGER         (* display mode for program *)
     ): INTEGER;
VAR
   r: LONGINT;
   msg: W.MSG;
BEGIN
   IF hPrevInstance=0 THEN       (* additional program copy? *)
     IF ~InitApplication(hInstance) THEN RETURN 0 END;
   END;
   IF ~InitInstance(hInstance, nCmdShow) THEN
     RETURN 0;
   END;
```

```
    WHILE W.GetMessage(SYSTEM.ADR(msg),
                       W.NULL,W.NULL,W.NULL) # 0 DO
        r := W.TranslateMessage(SYSTEM.ADR(msg));
        r := W.DispatchMessage(SYSTEM.ADR(msg))
    END;
    RETURN msg.wParam
  END WinMain;

END Generic.
```

Normally, Windows programs consist not only of executable program code but also of "resources", which are data structures used to define such things as text strings, menus, and dialog boxes. These are usually embedded into the program's executable file using a special tool.

Pow! provides an integrated tool which creates a resource file from a resource definition. This file can then be embedded into the .EXE-file. As direct programming with the Windows API is not expected to be the main application of *Pow!* the integrated resource compiler does not support all resource types defined by Windows, though it does support all the most frequently needed ones.

The following resource description defines the program icon, the menu, and the contents of the dialog box for our example Generic. A more precise description of the syntax is defined in the following section.

The contents of the resource file Generic.RC:

```
DEFINITION resource;

INCLUDE "C:\POW\SRC\WINDOWS.MOD"
INCLUDE "GENERIC.MOD"

RESOURCE

ICON GenericIcon "RA.ICO"

MENU GenericMenu
  POPUP "&Help"
    MENUITEM "&About Generic...", IDM_ABOUT
  END
END

DIALOG AboutBox
  22, 17, 144, 75
  STYLE DS_MODALFRAME OR WS_CAPTION OR WS_SYSMENU
  CAPTION "About Generic"
  FONT 15, "Arial"
BEGIN
  CTEXT "Microsoft Windows",    -1, 0,  5, 144,  8
  CTEXT "Generic Application",  -1, 0, 14, 144,  8
  CTEXT "Version 3.0",          -1, 0, 34, 144,  8
  DEFPUSHBUTTON "OK", IDOK, 53, 50,  32, 14, WS_GROUP
END

END resource.
```

7.5 The Mini-resource compiler

7.5.1 General notes

The Mini-resource compiler integrated into *POW!* provides a way to declare the most important resources for a program with the minimum effort and to manage them consistently with the rest of the project. However, not all resource types defined by Windows are supported.

The resource compiler is automatically started by *POW!* for all files of the project which have the extension ".RC".

If the resources are created with another tool, for example "AppStudio" from Microsoft, then the ".RES" file produced can simply be added to the *POW!* project.

7.5.2 Structure of resource files

The syntax for the Mini-resource compiler ".RC" files is similar to the Oberon-2 syntax and therefore deviates from the syntax defined by Microsoft, which is closely related to C.

Resource files consist of three sections, the first two of which are optional.

In the first section, definition modules can be included using the *INCLUDE* statement. This provides access to the definition module "Windows.MOD" containing the constants required for resources. Nevertheless there is a restriction: all constant declarations of a definition module must comply with the syntax of the resource compiler.

In the second section constants can be declared. All constants must be numerical and integer. It is also possible to define constants using the operators +, –, *, /, DIV and MOD.

In addition, the operators OR and & may be used to define numerical constants.

The third section contains the resources themselves. The start of this section is indicated by the keyword *RESOURCE*. The syntax of the resource statements is defined in EBNF notation.

7.5.3 Available kinds of resources

Menus

Purpose

A menu bar with all sub-menus can be defined and given a name.

Syntax

MenuDecl	=	*MENU ident { MenuItem } END.*
MenuItem	=	*MENUITEM string "," ConstExpr |*
		POPUP string { MenuItem } END.

Semantics

MENU MenuName

POPUP "popup text"

MENUITEM "item text", itemIdNumber

END

END

Example

```
CONST
  IDM_ABOUT = 100;
  IDM_OPEN  = 101;
  IDM_CLOSE = 102;

RESOURCE

MENU TestMenu
  POPUP "&File"
    MENUITEM "&Open",   IDM_OPEN
    MENUITEM "&Close",  IDM_CLOSE
  END
  POPUP "&About"
    MENUITEM "&About Test", IDM_ABOUT
  END
END
```

Icons

Purpose

Icons in the form of an ".ICO" file can be embedded into the executable file as a resource and they can be assigned a name.

Syntax

IconDecl	=	*ICON ident string.*

Semantics

ICON IconName "iconfilename"

Example

```
ICON TestIcon "C:\POW\TEST\ICON.ICO"
```

Dialogs

Purpose

A dialog box together with the corresponding elements such as text and buttons can be defined and assigned a name.

Syntax

DialogDecl	=	*ident ConstExpr "," ConstExpr "," ConstExpr ","*
		ConstExpr [STYLE ConstExptr] [CAPTION string]
		[FONT ConstExptr "," string] BEGIN {DialogItem}
		END.
DialogItem	=	*TextItem	ButtonItem	ControlItem.*
TextItem	=	*CTEXT string "," ConstExpr "," Position.*
ButtonItem	=	*DEFPUSHBUTTON string "," ConstExpr ","*
		Position "," ConstExpr.
ControlItem	=	*CONTROL string "," ConstExpr "," string ","*
		ConstExpr "," Position.
Position	=	*ConstExpr "," ConstExpr "," ConstExpr "," ConstExpr*

Semantics

DIALOG DialogName

    x, y, width, height

    STYLE styleFlags

    CAPTION "captionText"

    FONT fontSize, "fontName"

BEGIN

    CTEXT...

    DEFPUSHBUTTON...

    CONTROL...

END

The dialog generated has the attributes *LOADONCALL* and *MOVEABLE*.

x	The horizontal distance from the left edge of the dialog box to the left edge of the enclosing window. The distance is not stated in points or pixels, but in "dialog units".
y	The vertical distance from the upper edge of the dialog box to the upper edge of the enclosing window. The distance is stated in dialog units.
width	The width of the dialog box in dialog units.
height	The height of the dialog box in dialog units.

A horizontal dialog unit is a quarter of the average character width of the character set used, a vertical dialog unit is an eighth of the character height. If no special character set is defined for the dialog the normal system character set is used.

Example

```
DIALOG AboutBox
  22, 17, 144, 75
  STYLE DS_MODALFRAME OR WS_CAPTION OR WS_SYSMENU
  CAPTION "About Test"
BEGIN
  CTEXT "Test Application", -1,  0,  5, 144,  8
  DEFPUSHBUTTON "OK", IDOK, 53, 50,  32, 14, WS_GROUP
END
```

Centered text

Purpose

This defines a text centered with reference to a defined position as a component of a dialog.

Syntax

TextItem   =   *CTEXT string "," ConstExpr "," Position.*
Position   =   *ConstExpr "," ConstExpr "," ConstExpr "," ConstExpr*

Semantics

CTEXT "text", id, x, y, width, height

All co-ordinates are stated in dialog units.

Default buttons

Purpose

The default button can be defined as a component of a dialog. It is displayed using a thicker frame and is automatically activated whenever the enter key is pressed.

Syntax

ButtonItem   =   *DEFPUSHBUTTON string "," ConstExpr ","*
                   Position "," ConstExpr.
Position   =   *ConstExpr "," ConstExpr "," ConstExpr "," ConstExpr*

Semantics

DEFPUSHBUTTON "text", id, x, y, width, height, styleFlags

styleFlags: A combination of the attributes *BS_DEFPUSHBUTTON*,
               WS_TABSTOP, *WS_GROUP* and *WS_DISABLED*.

All co-ordinates are stated in dialog units.

Standard controls

Purpose

A dialog element of any class provided by Windows can be defined.

Syntax

```
ControlItem  =  CONTROL string "," ConstExpr ","
                string "," ConstExpr "," Position.
Position     =  ConstExpr "," ConstExpr "," ConstExpr "," ConstExpr
```

Semantics

CONTROL "text", id, "class", styleFlags, x, y, width, height

class: One of the classes of dialog elements *BUTTON*, *COMBOBOX*,
              EDIT, *LISTBOX*, *SCROLLBAR* or *STATIC*.

All co-ordinates are stated in dialog units.

7.5.4 The syntax for resources

The EBNF syntax for resources is as follows:

```
ResourceModule =  DEFINITION ident ";" [IncludeSequ] [DeclSeq]
                  RESOURCE ResourceSeq END ident ".".
IncludeSequ  =  Include ; { Include ; }.
Include      =  INCLUDE Filename.
Filename     =  string.
DeclSeq      =  CONST { ConstDecl ";" }.
ResourceSeq  =  { IconDecl | MenuDecl | DialogDecl }.
ConstDecl    =  ident "=" ConstExpr.
ConstExpr    =  ["+" | "-"] Term { AddOp Term }.
Term         =  Factor { MulOp Factor }.
Factor       =  ident | number | "(" ConstExpr ")".
AddOp        =  "+" | "-" | OR.
MulOp        =  "*" | "/" | DIV | MOD | "&".
IconDecl     =  ICON ident string.
MenuDecl     =  MENU ident { MenuItem } END.
MenuItem     =  MENUITEM string "," ConstExpr |
                POPUP string { MenuItem } END.
```

DialogDecl	=	*ident ConstExpr "," ConstExpr "," ConstExpr ","*
		ConstExpr [STYLE ConstExptr] [CAPTION string]
		[FONT ConstExptr "," string] BEGIN {DialogItem}
		END.
DialogItem	=	*TextItem	ButtonItem	ControlItem.*
TextItem	=	*CTEXT string "," ConstExpr "," Position.*
ButtonItem	=	*DEFPUSHBUTTON string "," ConstExpr ","*
		Position "," ConstExpr.
ControlItem	=	*CONTROL string "," ConstExpr "," string ","*
		ConstExpr "," Position.
Position	=	*ConstExpr "," ConstExpr "," ConstExpr "," ConstExpr*

Appendix A: Oberon-2 for Pascal programmers

The syntax of Oberon-2 is very similar to Pascal and particularly Modula-2. Therefore, Oberon-2 programs can be read very easily if two differences are considered: in constructs such as

```
IF a<b THEN a:=b; b:=c; END;
```

no *BEGIN ... END* blocks occur and some operators have changed, e.g., "~" for "NOT" and "#" (unequal) for "<>". The language is *case sensitive*: upper- and lowercase letters are treated as different characters in identifiers.

Operators

The following sections review the syntax for important cases briefly, illustrated by examples. It is assumed that the reader already has some experience of using Pascal or Modula-2 or similar programming languages. Sometimes constructs are used before they are explained but this has been avoided wherever possible. Most emphasis is given to the language elements that are common in these language families. Other constructs, including those used for object-oriented programming (OOP), such as type extensions and particularly type-bound procedures, are only touched on. Type-bound procedures correspond more or less to "methods of classes", a concept initially introduced by Smalltalk which is now also part of C++ and of some extensions of Pascal and Modula-2.

Fore-knowledge

A.1 Constants

The syntax is almost identical to Pascal. Constants may also be written as constant expressions:

```
CONST
    N= 100;
    LIMIT= 2*(N-1);
```

String constants:

```
"test", 'test', 'Press"a"'
```

Character constants:

```
"y", "5", 20X, 0X
```

Set constants:

```
{5}, {1,2,3}, {1..5}, {}
```

A.2 Operators

Boolean operators

boolean or	OR
boolean and	&
negation	~

Arithmetic operators

+, –, *, /, DIV, MOD

Set operators

+ , – ,*, as well as the symmetric difference x/y with x/y= (x–y)+(y–x)

Relational operators

<, <=, >, >=	used as usual, not defined on sets
IN	checks if contained in a set
=	equality
#	inequality
IS	used for a type check

A.3 Data types

The basic date types are *BOOLEAN* for boolean values, *CHAR* for characters, and *SHORTINT, INTEGER, LONGINT, REAL, LONGREAL* for numerical types. Furthermore, *SET* is used as type for numerical sets.

Type inclusion Oberon-2 does not have hidden conversion rules that are applied during the evaluation of numerical expressions and assignments. Instead a practical hierarchy called *type inclusion* is introduced:

$$\text{LONGREAL} \subseteq \text{REAL} \subseteq \text{LONGINT} \subseteq \text{INTEGER} \subseteq \text{SHORTINT}$$

Type conversion A "bigger" type may be used instead of a "smaller" type at any time. In the other direction an explicit conversion must be carried out so that range violations can be checked at runtime.

```
VAR
    i: INTEGER;
    l: LONGINT;
    s: SHORTINT;
BEGIN
    i:=1;
    l:=i;              (* possible because of type inclusion *)
    s:=SHORT(i);          (* explicit conversion necessary *)
```

A.4 Arrays

Arrays are available, and are similar to Pascal arrays. However there is a major restriction in Oberon-2: the index of arrays always starts with zero. This facilitates the type declaration as the brackets are omitted.

Array index

Example:

```
VAR
    c: ARRAY 3 OF CHAR;
    i: ARRAY 10,15 OF INTEGER;
```

With the declaration of the variable *c* three elements $y[0]$, $y[1]$, and $y[2]$ are declared so that an assignment of the form $y[0]:="a"$ is allowed. The variable *i* stands for a two-dimensional array with one index 0..9 and another index 0..14. The indexing remains as usual: $i[i,j]:=7$. Note the index limits: $i[10,15]$ is not defined whereas $i[0,0]$ and $i[9,14]$ are allowed.

A.5 Strings

There is no explicit data type for character strings in Oberon-2. They are represented by arrays of character *(ARRAY OF CHAR)*.

Strings

```
TYPE StringT = ARRAY 10 OF CHAR;
```

The end of a string is defined by the character with the code 0, in Oberon-2 syntax *0X*.

End of string

```
CONST
    EMPTY1= "";
    EMPTY2= 0X;
    ASTR= "A";
    BSTR= "four";

TYPE
    EmptyT= ARRAY 1 OF CHAR;
    AstrT= ARRAY 2 OF CHAR;
    BstrT= ARRAY 8 OF CHAR;

VAR
    emptystr: EmptyT;
    onechar: AstrT;
    morechars: BstrT;

BEGIN
    emptystr:=EMPTY1;
    onechar:=ASTR;
    morechars:=BSTR;
    ...
```

The relational operators =, #, <, etc., are defined for character sequences and can therefore be applied to arrays of character if the latter contain *0X* as a terminal symbol.

A.6 Open Arrays

If the dimensions of an array are not yet known at compile time, *open arrays* may be used. These are arrays defined without any upper limit for the indices. Open arrays can be used as parameters for procedures as well as in situations where pointers to arrays are needed.

Example:

```
PROCEDURE Length (s:ARRAY OF CHAR): INTEGER;
...
END Length;

PROCEDURE UseIt;
VAR
    txt: ARRAY 20 OF CHAR;
    i: INTEGER;
BEGIN
    txt:="Test";
    i:=Length(txt);
    ...
END UseIt;
```

A.7 Pointer types

A *POINTER* is a pointer to an object in the memory. Pointers are always bound to a certain type. However, there are only pointers to records and arrays, and not, e.g., *POINTER TO BOOLEAN* as is possible in Modula-2.

```
TYPE
    InxListT= ARRAY 99 OF LONGINT;
    InxListP= POINTER TO InxListT;
```

NIL Every pointer can be assigned the special value *NIL*. This value stands for "pointer does not reference any data at the moment".

If used with pointers as operands, the symbol "^" indicates the value pointed at rather than the value of the pointer itself.

Be

```
VAR list: InxListP;
```

this implies

```
list        .. pointer to an array of the type InxList
list^       .. the array itself
list^[0]    .. the first element of the array
```

Selectors of array and record elements imply a dereferencing with pointer types and so the "^" is optional, as an ambiguity is impossible in this case.

This is why *list[0]* is equivalent to *list^[0]* as well as in structures

```
TYPE
   UnionP= POINTER TO UnionT;
   UnionT= RECORD
       s: SHORTINT;
       c: CHAR
   END;
VAR
   union: UnionP;
```

union.s is equivalent to *union^.s*!

To avoid ambiguity it is advisable to include the "^" characters.

A.8 Memory management

There are substantial differences in the area of the memory management between Pascal and Modula-2. There is also a difference between Oberon-2 under the Oberon system compared to the implementation under *POW!* and Windows.

The standard procedure *NEW* is used to create instances of objects in the memory.

NEW

```
VAR list: InxListP;
BEGIN
   list[0]:=3; (* illegal access *)
   NEW(list);
   list[0]:=5; (* valid access *)
```

Deallocation of memory is not necessarily so straightforward.

The ETH Oberon operating system and compiler have an integrated *garbage collector* which automatically releases allocated objects in memory once they are no longer referenced by any pointers, in between execution of commands.

Garbage collector

With *POW!* the programs that are developed are regarded as normal Windows programs (EXE-files) by the operating system. Consequently *POW!* requires an additional function *DISPOSE* to release memory reserved by *NEW*.

DISPOSE

When open arrays are used memory is allocated with *NEW* to reflect the arrays need for memory space. The predefined procedure *LEN(array)* or *LEN(array,i)* can be used to determine the current size of the array *array* or the size of the dimension at any time.

LEN

```
TYPE
   InxListT= ARRAY OF LONGINT;
   InxListP= POINTER TO InxListT;
VAR
   list: InxListP;
BEGIN
   NEW(list,50);          (* creating an array of 50 elements *)
```

A.9 Compound data types

RECORD The well-proven *RECORD* data type is very similar to that in Pascal and Modula-2, for example

```
TYPE
   DateT= RECORD
      day,month,year: INTEGER;
   END;

   PersonT= RECORD
      name: ARRAY 40 OF CHAR;
      age: INTEGER;
      weight: INTEGER;
   END;
```

A.10 Extensions of record types

Records can be used just like in Pascal, but in addition they can also be extended dynamically. This is substantially different from most implementations of Pascal, which tend to have an inheritance mechanism added to the initial language definition by means of new constructs such as *object* or *class*. However, Pascal's variant records are particularly susceptible to errors when programs are ported and should be avoided. When an Oberon-2 record is declared only the base type is defined, and is then extended subsequently. The record derived from it automatically contains all elements of the base type.

```
TYPE
   BirthdayT= RECORD(DateT)
      name: ARRAY 40 OF CHAR;
   END;
```

Projection Variables of the base type can be assigned variables of a derived type. In this case a *projection* of the data is effected.

```
PROCEDURE Print (d:DateT);
...
END Print;

VAR day: BirthdayT;
BEGIN
   ...
   Print(day);
```

Dynamic type If there are pointers rather than variables a projection is not necessary (the space for all elements having already been reserved). This brings us to the term *dynamic type* which denotes the data type of the object referenced by a pointer.

```
TYPE
   DateP= POINTER TO DateT;
   BirthdayP= POINTER TO BirthdayT;
```

```
PROCEDURE Print (d:DateP);
BEGIN
    IF d IS BirthdayP THEN … ELSE … END;
END Print;

VAR
    day: BirthdayP;
BEGIN
    NEW(day);
    day.name:="Arthur";
    …
    Print(day);
```

In the function *Print* of this example· *d* is of the *static* type *DateP* and becomes of the *dynamic* type *BirthdayP*.

The dynamic type of an object can be tested with the operator *IS* and in this way the program can be designed to cope with the result. On the other hand, the elements of a structure referenced by a pointer are checked at compile time and therefore determined by the static type. *IS*

To provide safe access to the elements of a known dynamic (extended) type, *type guards* are used to check the validity of the type before the extended record fields are accessed. *Type guard*

```
PROCEDURE Print (d:DateP);
BEGIN
    IF d IS BirthdayP THEN
        Out.String(d(BirthdayP).name)
    END;
    Out.Int(d.day,3);
    …
END Print;
```

Stating the date after the variable – here *d(BirthdayP)* – guarantees that the variable is of the mentioned type. Thus, all methods and variables of the extended type can be used. If the runtime system detects that the assumption of the type given in the type guard is wrong, the program is terminated and a runtime error is reported.

A.11 Procedure types

Procedure types make it possible to describe classes of procedures with identical parameter lists.

```
TYPE
    InitProcedure= PROCEDURE (i:INTEGER);
```

A variable of this type can then be assigned to all procedures with an equivalent parameter list.

```
PROCEDURE InitXyz (i:INTEGER);
BEGIN
    …
END InitXyz;
```

```
PROCEDURE DoSomething();
VAR
   doInit: InitProcedure;
BEGIN
   doInit:=InitXyz;

   (* The procedure call with a procedure variable
      happens in the same way as a "normal" procedure
      call *)
   doInit(45);
END DoSomething;
```

Another possible application would be

```
PROCEDURE DoSomething (proc:InitProcedure; i:INTEGER);
BEGIN
   proc(i);
END DoSomething;
```

Procedure call:

```
DoSomething(InitXyz,45);
```

A.12 Control structures

For Pascal programmers basic statements have a slightly modified syntax. The control structures comprise *IF*, *CASE*, *WHILE*, *REPEAT*, *FOR*, and *LOOP*.

For a brief description we use the following EBNF notation:

[]   the contained expression may occur once or not at all,

{}   the contained expression may occur several times or not at all.

IF   • *IF boolean expression THEN statements*
{ ELSIF boolean expression THEN statements }
[ELSE statements]
END.

```
IF i=j THEN
   i:=j+1;
ELSEIF i=k THEN
   i:=k+2;
ELSE
   i:=2*i;
   j:=2*j;
END; (* if *)
```

CASE   • *CASE expression OF*
constant list : statements
{ | constant list : statements }
[ELSE statements]
END.

```
CASE c OF
   "a".."z": Out.String("lower case");
```

```
|  "A".."Z": Out.String("upper case");
ELSE Out.String("no letter");
END; (* case *)
```

- *WHILE boolean expression DO statements END.*   *WHILE*

```
i:=0;
In.Char(c);
WHILE In.Done DO
    INC(i);
    In.Char(c);
END; (* while *)
```

- *REPEAT statements UNTIL boolean expression.*   *REPEAT*

```
REPEAT
    In.Char(c);
UNTIL In.Done=FALSE;
```

- *FOR variable := expression TO expression [BY constant]*   *FOR*
  DO statements END.

```
FOR i:=0 TO 2*n BY 2 DO
    y[j]:=i;
    INC(j);
END; (* for *)
```

- *LOOP statements END.*   *LOOP*

  The *LOOP* loop is exited with the command *EXIT* inside the loop.

```
LOOP
    In.Int(i);
    IF In.Done=FALSE THEN
        EXIT;
    END;
    Out.Int(i,0);
END; (* loop *)
```
EXIT

- The meaning of the *WITH* statement is different in Oberon-2 and Pascal.   *WITH*
  In Oberon-2 *WITH* is used to facilitate the use of type guards:

WITH
> *variable x:Typ DO statements*
> *{ | variable x:Typ DO statements}*
> *[ELSE statements]*
END.

```
WITH d:BirthdayP DO
    WriteStr(d.name);
    d.name:="";
ELSE
    ...
END;
```

is equivalent to

```
IF d IS BirthdayP THEN
   WriteStr(d(BirthdayP).name;
   d(BirthdayP).name:="";
ELSE
   ...
END;
```

A.13 Procedures

Procedures in Oberon-2 are almost identical to those of Pascal. The differences are illustrated by the following Oberon-2 examples.

```
PROCEDURE WriteInt (l:LONGINT;in:INTEGER);
VAR j:INTEGER;
BEGIN
   ...
END WriteInt;
```

Functions   Example for a function:

```
PROCEDURE IsPrime (l:LONGINT): BOOLEAN;
VAR val:LONGINT;
BEGIN
   IF (l MOD 2)=0 THEN
      RETURN FALSE;
   END;
   ...
   RETURN (l MOD val)#0;
END IsPrime;
```

A.14 Type-bound procedures

In the implementation of abstract data types all access procedures of a data type have one common parameter which identifies the structure to be processed. Together with extensible structures, type-bound procedures are the key features of object-oriented programming when programming in Oberon-2.

Here is an example demonstrating the procedural approach, based on Pascal:

```
TYPE
   ListP= POINTER TO ListT;
   ListT= RECORD
      elem: INTEGER;
      next: ListP
   END;

PROCEDURE InitList (VAR l:ListT);
PROCEDURE InsertList (VAR l:ListT; i:INTEGER);
```

or

```
PROCEDURE InitList (p:ListP);
PROCEDURE InsertList (p:ListP; i:INTEGER);
```

In Oberon-2 the concept of *abstract data types* (ADT) is also supported syn-   *ADT*
tactically by a binding of procedures to a certain data type (*methods, type-
bound procedures*). Note that this is done by stating the declared data type in
parentheses in front of the method name:

```
PROCEDURE (VAR l:ListT) Init ();
PROCEDURE (VAR l:ListT) Insert (i:INTEGER);
```

or

```
PROCEDURE (p:ListP) Init ();
PROCEDURE (p:ListP) Insert (i:INTEGER);
```
   Methods

The traditional approach using procedure calls might be

```
VAR l: ListT;
BEGIN
    InitList(l);
    InsertList(l,42);
    ...
```

in contrast to a solution with type-bound procedures:

```
VAR l: ListT;
BEGIN
    l.Init();
    l.Insert(42);
    ...
```

The message "apply the method *Init* or *Insert*" is applied to the object defined
by *VAR l:ListT*. This also explains why we write *l.Init()*.

Abstract data types and formation of classes, when used in connection with
type-bound procedures, are treated in detail in the introduction to Oberon-2
and illustrated by complete examples (see Chapter 4).

In the context of OOP and its principles of *inheritance* and *polymorphism*   *Inheritance*
Chapter 4 also explains when it is more sensible to use a pointer *VAR p:ListP*
rather than a variable *VAR l.ListT*. The same reasoning is also valid when
considering whether objects referenced by a pointer should be created with
NEW rather than by using a separate method.

A.15 Modules

Modules are more or less equivalent to "units" used in many Pascal
extensions.

Modules can provide

- the encapsulation of the solution to a specific problem so that the imple-   *Data*
  mentation may be changed without significant changes to the rest of the   *encapsulation*
  program.
- a grouping of a set of related functions, e.g., a module for file
  management functions, module for string processing functions, etc.

- dividing programs into smaller parts which are logically cohesive and so easier to understand and maintain.

This is the form of a module in Oberon-2:

```
MODULE M;
[IMPORT list of items from used modules]

[CONST
    constant declarations]

[TYPE
    type declarations]

[VAR
    variable declarations]

[procedures]

[BEGIN
    initialization part]
END M.
```

IMPORT   A module *M* is *imported* if its name is included in another module's *IMPORT* statement. All constants, types, variables, and procedures exported by *M* then become available.

Oberon-2 also makes use of the concept of the *qualified identifier:* if an identifier from an imported module is used it must be combined with the module name.

Example:

```
IMPORT Out;
Out.Ln();
```

This makes it possible to avoid ambiguity if procedures with the same name are imported from different modules.

A.16 Export of identifiers

Export mark   Constants, types, variables, and procedures which are to be exported from a module are marked with a suffix "*". They can be identified for the importing module, the *client*, and may be accessed there.

```
PROCEDURE Init* (i:INTEGER);
BEGIN
    ...
END Init;
```

Read only   For variables and elements of structure it is also possible to define a restricted write-protected export (*read only*). The symbol for this suffix is "-".

Example:

```
VAR
    i-: INTEGER;
```

If data types are exported this does not affect individual fields, which must be marked separately. This provides a precise mechanism for defining partial export of records as some elements may be private to the module.

```
MODULE Staff;
TYPE
    InfoT*= RECORD
        age-: INTEGER;
        size-: INTEGER;
        index: LONGINT;
    END;
...
```

Other modules may use the type *Staff.InfoT* if they import *Staff*. From the viewpoint of the importing module variables of this type do not appear to have an element *index*, and the elements *age* and *size* cannot be modified.

A.17 Programs in Oberon-2

Initially, there were no classic compilers for Oberon-2 that produced single executable programs.

Oberon-2 was available only together with the Oberon system where all procedures of a module without parameters can be called as a command. There are no single, independent programs available ([Rei93], [Moe93]).

Thus, outside the Oberon system an additional convention is required to define a starting point for the program execution. In *POW!* the procedure containing the main Windows program is called *ProgMain*. The export mark "*" is needed to support the linkage of Oberon-2 programs into the *Windows* system.

ProgMain

```
MODULE Hello;

IMPORT Out;

PROCEDURE ProgMain*;
BEGIN
    Out.String("Hello World!");
END ProgMain;

END Hello.
```

A.18 Object-oriented programming

Type binding   The extensible records of Oberon-2 have characteristics similar to those of objects in Turbo Pascal. The *type-bound procedures* correspond to the *methods* of Turbo Pascal.

Oberon-2	Turbo Pascal
```TYPE Simple*= RECORD hidden: INTEGER; common*: INTEGER; END;```	```TYPE Simple= OBJECT PRIVATE hidden: INTEGER; PUBLIC common: INTEGER; END;```

The declarations of *Simple* given above have exactly the same meaning. All identifiers in Turbo Pascal stated in the *PRIVATE* section correspond to record elements in Oberon-2 that are not exported, all identifiers of the *PUBLIC* section correspond to the identifiers exported with "*". Turbo Pascal does not support write-protected export.

Oberon-2	Turbo Pascal
```TYPE Complex*=RECORD(Simple) END;```	```TYPE Complex= OBJECT(Simple) PUBLIC CONSTRUCTOR Init; DESTRUCTOR Done; PRIVATE PROCEDURE Action; VIRTUAL; END;```
```PROCEDURE (VAR c:Complex) Init*; BEGIN c.hidden:=0; ...```	```CONSTRUCTOR Complex.Init; BEGIN hidden:=0; ...```
```PROCEDURE (VAR c:Complex) Action; ...```	```DESTRUCTOR Complex.Done; ...```
```PROCEDURE (VAR c:Complex) Done*; ...```	```PROCEDURE Complex.Action; ...```

The definitions of the class *Complex* given above have the same purpose in both languages but the declaration of methods involves several important differences:

- In Turbo Pascal all methods must be stated together with the declaration of the object.

- Turbo Pascal also requires that methods carry the keyword *VIRTUAL* to make sure that they are correctly applied to the objects in all situations. There is no need for this in Oberon-2.

- To ensure that methods declared as *VIRTUAL* work properly in Turbo Pascal it is necessary to call a special method declared as *CONSTRUCTOR* before another method may be applied. If this is forgotten unpleasant crashes are the consequence. Oberon-2 does not distinguish different categories of methods. This also applies to Turbo Pascal's destructors.

- In Turbo Pascal the variables and methods of an object are directly known inside a method (see above assignment to *hidden* in the method *Init*). In Oberon-2 the object the method is applied to is given a name. In our example this name is simply *c*:

```
PROCEDURE (VAR c:Complex) …
```

All variables and methods of the object may be referenced using this name. This increases the readability and avoids naming conflicts.

The object variable of Oberon-2 corresponds to the special variable *SELF* of Turbo Pascal which serves for passing the object itself as a parameter or for solving name conflicts.

Example

Oberon-2	Turbo Pascal

`PROCEDURE Work (c:Complex);`
 …
 	
 `PROCEDURE (VAR c:Complex) Init*;`
 `BEGIN`
 `  Work(c);`
 …
	`PROCEDURE Work (c:Complex);`
	 …
	
	 `CONSTRUCTOR Complex.Init;`
	 `BEGIN`
	 `  Work(SELF);`
	 …

The usage of objects is again very similar in both languages:

Oberon-2	Turbo Pascal

`VAR`
 `   c: Complex;`
 `BEGIN`
 `   c.Init;`
 `   c.Action;`
 `   c.common:=7;`
 …
	`VAR`
	 `   c: Complex;`
	 `BEGIN`
	 `   c.Init;`
	 `   c.Action;`
	 `   c.common:=7;`
	 …

Only the use of pointers shows up real differences because in Oberon-2 it is possible to omit the "^" dereferencing symbol.

Oberon-2	Turbo Pascal
```VAR p: POINTER TO Complex; BEGIN NEW(p); p.Init; p.Action; p.common:=7; p.Done; DISPOSE(p); (* optional *) ...```	```VAR p: ^Complex; BEGIN NEW(p,Init); p^.Action; p^.common:=7; DISPOSE(p,Done); ...```

Note:

In implementations of Oberon-2 which do have an automatic *garbage collector* the call of *DISPOSE* is superfluous. A *garbage collector* automatically releases memory that was allocated with *NEW* as soon as it is no longer referenced by any pointers.

A version of the *POW!* Oberon-2 runtime system which provides automatic garbage collection is now available as an option. This makes it possible to use Oberon-2 with or without explicit garbage collection. This can be an advantage for teaching about garbage collection and also in preparing for using languages such as C++ which lack automatic garbage collection.

Appendix B:
The Programming Language Oberon-2

B.1 Introduction*

Oberon-2 is a general-purpose programming language in the tradition of Pascal and Modula-2. Its most important features are block structure, modularity, separate compilation, static typing with strong type checking (also across module boundaries), and type extension with type-bound procedures.

block structure, modular

Type extension makes Oberon-2 an object-oriented language. An *object* is a variable of an abstract data type consisting of private data (its *state*) and *procedures* that operate on this data. Abstract data types are declared as extensible records. Oberon-2 covers most terms of object-oriented languages by the established vocabulary of imperative languages in order to minimize the number of notions for similar concepts.

type extension

This report is not intended as a programmer's tutorial. It is intentionally kept concise. Its function is to serve as a reference for programmers, implementors, and manual writers. What remains unsaid is mostly left so intentionally, either because it can be derived from stated rules of the language, or because it would require commitment to the definition when a general commitment appears unwise.

B.12 defines some terms that are used to express the type checking rules of Oberon-2. Where they appear in the text, they are written in italics to indicate their special meaning (e.g., the *same type*).

B.2 Syntax

An Extended Backus-Naur Formalism (EBNF) is used to describe the syntax of Oberon-2. Alternatives are separated by |. Brackets [and] denote optionality of the enclosed expression, and braces { and } denote its repetition (possibly 0 times). Non-terminal symbols start with an uppercase letter (e.g., *Statement*).

EBNF

---

* This chapter is based on the Oberon-2 language report [MW91] written by Prof. Wirth and Prof. Mössenböck. It has been adapted to the concrete Oberon-2 compiler implementation in *POW!*.

Terminal symbols either start with a lowercase letter (e.g., *ident*), or are written in uppercase letters (e.g., *BEGIN*), or are denoted by strings (e.g., "*:=*").

B.3 Vocabulary and Representation

The representation of (terminal) symbols in terms of characters is defined using the ASCII set. Symbols are identifiers, numbers, strings, operators, and delimiters. The following lexical rules must be observed:

- Blanks and line breaks must not occur within symbols (except in comments, and blanks in strings). They are ignored unless they are essential to separate two consecutive symbols.

- Capital and lowercase letters are considered as distinct.

identifier 1. *Identifiers* are sequences of letters and digits. The first character must be a letter.

> *ident = letter {letter | digit}.*

Examples:

```
x       Scan      Oberon2     GetSymbol     firstLetter
```

number 2. *Numbers* are (unsigned) integer or real constants. The type of an integer constant is the minimal type to which the constant value belongs (see B.6.1). If the constant is specified with the suffix H, the representation is hexadecimal; otherwise it is decimal.

A real number always contains a decimal point. Optionally it may also contain a decimal scale factor. The letter E (or D) means "times ten to the power of". A real number is of type *REAL*, unless it has a scale factor containing the letter D. In this case it is of type *LONGREAL*.

> | | |
> |---|---|
> | *number* | *= integer | real.* |
> | *integer* | *= digit {digit} | digit {hexDigit} "H".* |
> | *real* | *= digit {digit} "." {digit} [ScaleFactor].* |
> | *ScaleFactor* | *= ("E" | "D") ["+" | "-"] digit {digit}.* |
> | *hexDigit* | *= digit | "A" | "B" | "C" | "D" | "E" | "F".* |
> | *digit* | *= "0" | "1" | "2" | "3" | "4" | "5" | "6" | "7" | "8" | "9".* |

Examples:

```
1991                INTEGER        1991
0DH                 SHORTINT       13
12.3                REAL           12.3
4.567E8             REAL           456700000
0.57712566D-6       LONGREAL       0.00000057712566
```

character 3. *Character constants* are denoted by the ordinal number of the character in
constant hexadecimal notation followed by the letter X.

> *character = digit {hexDigit} "X".*

4. Strings are sequences of characters enclosed in single (') or double (")   *string*
quote marks. The opening quote must be the same as the closing quote and
must not occur within the string. The number of characters in a string is
called its length. A string of length 1 can be used wherever a character
constant is allowed and vice versa.

> *string* = ' " ' *{char}* ' " ' | " ' " *{char}* " ' ".

Examples:

```
"Oberon-2"     "Don't worry!"      "x"
```

5. Operators and delimiters are the special characters, character pairs, or   *operator,*
reserved words listed below. The reserved words consist exclusively of   *delimiter*
capital letters and cannot be used as identifiers.

+	:=	ARRAY	IMPORT	RETURN
–	^	BEGIN	IN	THEN
*	=	BY	IS	TO
/	#	CASE	LOOP	TYPE
~	<	CONST	MOD	UNTIL
&	>	DIV	MODULE	VAR
.	<=	DO	NIL	WHILE
,	>=	ELSE	OF	WITH
;	..	ELSIF	OR	
|	:	END	POINTER	
(	)	EXIT	PROCEDURE	
[	]	FOR	RECORD	
{	}	IF	REPEAT	

6. Comments may be inserted between any two symbols in a program. They   *comments*
are arbitrary character sequences opened by the bracket (* and closed by *).
Comments may be nested. They do not affect the meaning of a program.

B.4 Declarations and scope rules

Every identifier occurring in a program must be introduced by a declaration,
unless it is a predeclared identifier. Declarations also specify certain
permanent properties of an object, such as whether it is a constant, a type, a
variable, or a procedure. The identifier is then used to refer to the associated
object.

The *scope* of an object *x* extends textually from the point of its declaration to   *scope*
the end of the block (module, procedure, or record) to which the declaration
belongs and hence to which the object is local. It excludes the scopes of
objects with the same name which are declared in nested blocks. The scope
rules are:

1. No identifier may denote more than one object within a given scope (i.e.,
    no identifier may be declared twice in a block);

2. An object may only be referenced within its scope;

3. A type T of the form *POINTER TO T1* (see B.6.4) can be declared at a point where *T1* is still unknown. The declaration of *T1* must follow in the same block to which *T* is local;

4. Identifiers denoting record fields (see B.6.3) or type-bound procedures (see B.10.2) are valid in record designators only.

export mark   An identifier declared in a module block may be followed by an export mark (" * " or " - ") in its declaration to indicate that it is exported. An identifier *x* exported by a module *M* may be used in other modules, if they import M (see B.11). The identifier is then denoted as *M.x* in these modules and is called a *qualified identifier*. Variables and record fields marked with " - " in their declaration are read-only in importing modules.

> Qualident   = *[ident "."] ident.*
> IdentDef   = *ident [" * " | " - "].*

predeclared
identifiers   The following identifiers are predeclared; their meaning is defined in the indicated sections:

ABS	(B.10.3)	LEN	(B.10.3)
ASH	(B.10.3)	LONG	(B.10.3)
BOOLEAN	(B.6.1)	LONGINT	(B.6.1)
CAP	(B.10.3)	LONGREAL	(B.6.1)
CHAR	(B.6.1)	MAX	(B.10.3)
CHR	(B.10.3)	MIN	(B.10.3)
COPY	(B.10.3)	NEW	(B.10.3)
DEC	(B.10.3)	ODD	(B.10.3)
ENTIER	(B.10.3)	ORD	(B.10.3)
EXCL	(B.10.3)	REAL	(B.6.1)
FALSE	(B.6.1)	SET	(B.6.1)
HALT	(B.10.3)	SHORT	(B.10.3)
INC	(B.10.3)	SHORTINT	(B.6.1)
INCL	(B.10.3)	SIZE	(B.10.3)
INTEGER	(B.6.1)	TRUE	(B.6.1)

B.5 Constant declarations

A constant declaration associates an identifier with a constant value.

> ConstantDeclaration=   *IdentDef "=" ConstExpression.*
> ConstExpression   =   *Expression.*

A constant expression is an expression that can be evaluated by a mere textual scan without actually executing the program. Its operands are constants (see B.8) or predeclared functions (see B.10.3) that can be evaluated at compile time. Examples of constant declarations are:

```
N = 100
limit = 2*N - 1
fullSet = {MIN(SET) .. MAX(SET)}
```

B.6 Type declarations

A data type determines the set of values which variables of that type may   *data type*
assume, and the operators that are applicable. A type declaration associates
an identifier with a type. In the case of structured types (arrays and records) it
also defines the structure of variables of this type. A structured type cannot
contain itself.

TypeDeclaration =   *IdentDef "=" Type.*
Type   =   *Qualident | ArrayType | RecordType |*
                    PointerType | ProcedureType.

Examples:

```
Table = ARRAY N OF REAL
Tree = POINTER TO Node
Node =  RECORD
    key : INTEGER;
    left, right: Tree
END
CenterTree = POINTER TO CenterNode
CenterNode = RECORD (Node)
    width: INTEGER;
    subnode: Tree
END
Function = PROCEDURE(x: INTEGER): INTEGER
```

B.6.1 Basic types

The basic types are denoted by predeclared identifiers. The associated operators are defined in B.8.2 and the predeclared function procedures in B.10.3.
The values of the given basic types are the following:

1. BOOLEAN   the truth values TRUE and FALSE
2. CHAR   the characters of the extended ASCII set (0X .. 0FFX)
3. SHORTINT   the integers between MIN(SHORTINT) and
               MAX(SHORTINT)
4. INTEGER   the integers between MIN(INTEGER) and
               MAX(INTEGER)
5. LONGINT   the integers between MIN(LONGINT) and
               MAX(LONGINT)
6. REAL   the real numbers between MIN(REAL) and
               MAX(REAL)

7. LONGREAL   the real numbers between MIN(LONGREAL) and
                MAX(LONGREAL)

8. SET   the sets of integers between 0 and MAX(SET)

type hierarchy   Types 3 to 5 are integer types, types 6 and 7 are real types, and together they
are called *numeric types*. They form a hierarchy; the larger type includes (the
values of) the smaller type:

LONGREAL >= REAL >= LONGINT >= INTEGER >= SHORTINT

B.6.2 Array types

An *array* is a structure consisting of a number of *elements* which are all of
the same type, called the element type. The number of elements of an array is
called its *length*. The elements of the array are designated by indices, which
are integers between 0 and the length minus 1.

ArrayType   = ARRAY [Length {"," Length}] OF Type.
Length   = ConstExpression.

A type of the form

```
ARRAY L0, L1, ..., Ln OF T
```

is understood as an abbreviation of

```
ARRAY L0 OF
    ARRAY L1 OF
    ...
        ARRAY Ln OF T
```

open arrays   Arrays declared without length are called *open arrays*. They are restricted to
pointer base types (see B.6.4), element types of open array types, and formal
parameter types (see B.10.1).

Examples:

```
ARRAY 10, N OF INTEGER
ARRAY OF CHAR
```

B.6.3 Record types

record fields   A *record type* is a structure consisting of a fixed number of elements, called
fields, with possibly different types. The record type declaration specifies the
name and type of each field. The scope of the field identifiers extends from
the point of their declaration to the end of the record type, but they are also
visible within designators referring to elements of record variables (see
B.8.1).

public,   If a record type is exported, field identifiers that are to be visible outside the
private   declaring module must be marked. They are called *public fields*; unmarked
elements are called *private fields*.

RecordType = *RECORD ["("BaseType")"] FieldList {";" FieldList} END.*
BaseType   = *Qualident.*
FieldList   = *[IdentList ":" Type].*

Record types are extensible, i.e. a record type can be declared as an extension   *type extension*
of another record type. In the example

```
T0 = RECORD x: INTEGER END
T1 = RECORD (T0) y: REAL END
```

T1 is a *(direct) extension* of *T0* and *T0* is the *(direct) base type* of *T1* (see   *base type*
B.12). An extended type *T1* consists of the fields of its base type and of the
fields which are declared in *T1*. Identifiers declared in the extension must be
different from the identifiers declared in its base type(s).

Examples of record type declarations:

```
RECORD
    day, month, year: INTEGER
END

RECORD
    name, firstname: ARRAY 32 OF CHAR;
    age: INTEGER;
    salary: REAL
END
```

B.6.4 Pointer types

Variables of a pointer type P assume as values pointers to variables of some
type T. T is called the pointer base type of P and must be a record or array
type. Pointer types adopt the extension relation of their pointer base types: if
a type $T1$ is an extension of T, and $P1$ is of type *POINTER TO T1*, then $P1$ is
also an extension of P.

PointerType = POINTER TO Type.

If p is a variable of type $P=POINTER TO T$, a call of the predeclared proce-   *NEW*
dure *NEW(p)* (see B.10.3) allocates a variable of type T in free storage
(*heap*). If T is a record type or an array type with fixed length, the allocation
has to be done with *NEW(p)*; if T is an n-dimensional open array the
allocation has to be done with *NEW(p, e0, ..., en-1)* where T is allocated with
lengths given by the expressions *e0, ..., en-1*. In either case a pointer to the
allocated variable is assigned to p. p is of type P. The referenced variable $p^\wedge$
(pronounced "p-referenced") is of type T.

Any pointer variable may assume the value *NIL*, which points to no variable   *NIL*
at all. All pointer variables are initialized to *NIL*, if this is enabled in the
compiler options dialog.

Allocated memory can be freed by using the function $DISPOSE^*$ and can   *DISPOSE*
then again be allocated by further calls of *NEW*. The pointer p does not

---

[*] The original Oberon-2 has no *DISPOSE* statement, which is an extension of the *POW!* Oberon-
2 compiler.

change its value after *DISPOSE(p)*, but access to a memory object is not possible after *DISPOSE*.

B.6.5 Procedure types

Variables of a procedure type *T* have a procedure (or *NIL*) as value. If a procedure *P* is assigned to a variable of type *T*, the formal parameter lists (see B.10.1) of *P* and *T* must match (see B.12). *P* must not be a predeclared or type-bound procedure nor may it be local to another procedure.

> *ProcedureType = PROCEDURE [FormalParameters].*

B.7 Variable declarations

Variable declarations introduce variables by defining an identifier and a data type for them.

> *VariableDeclaration = IdentList ":" Type.*

dynamic type   Record and pointer variables have both a *static type* (the type with which they are declared – simply called their type) and a *dynamic type* (the type of their value at run time). For pointers and variable parameters of record type the dynamic type may be an extension of their static type. The static type determines which fields of a record are accessible. The dynamic type is used to call type-bound procedures (see B.10.2).

Examples of variable declarations (refer to examples in B.6):

```
i, j, k: INTEGER
x, y: REAL
p, q: BOOLEAN
s: SET
F: Function
a: ARRAY 100 OF REAL
w: ARRAY 16 OF RECORD
      name: ARRAY 32 OF CHAR;
      count: INTEGER
   END
t, c: Tree
```

B.8 Expressions

operands,   *Expressions* are constructs denoting rules of computation whereby constants
operators   and current values of variables are combined to compute other values by the application of operators and function procedures. Expressions consist of operands and operators. Parentheses may be used to express specific associations of operators and operands.

B.8.1 Operands

With the exception of set constructors and literal constants (numbers, *designators* character constants, or strings), operands are denoted by *designators*. A designator consists of an identifier referring to a constant, variable, or procedure.

This identifier may possibly be qualified by a module identifier (see B.4 and *selector* B.11) and may be followed by *selectors* if the designated object is an element of a structure.

> *Designator*   = *Qualident {"." ident | "[" ExpressionList "]" | "^" |*
>   *"(" Qualident ")"}.*
> *ExpressionList* = *Expression {"," Expression}.*

If *a* designates an array, then *a[e]* denotes that element of *a* whose index is the current value of the expression *e*. The type of *e* must be an integer type. A designator of the form *a[e0, e1, ..., en]* stands for *a[e0][e1]...[en]*.

If *r* designates a record, then *r.f* denotes the field *f* of *r* or the procedure *f* bound to the dynamic type of *r* (see B.10.2). If *p* designates a pointer, *p^* denotes the variable which is referenced by *p*. The designators *p^.f* and *p^[e]* may be abbreviated as *p.f* and *p[e]*, i.e., record and array selectors imply dereferencing. If *a* or *r* are read-only, then also *a[e]* and *r.f* are read-only.

A *type guard* *v(T)* asserts that the dynamic type of *v* is *T* (or an extension of *type guard* *T*), i.e., program execution is aborted, if the dynamic type of *v* is not *T* (or an extension of *T*). Within the designator, *v* is then regarded as having the static type *T*. The guard is applicable, if

1. *v* is a variable parameter of record type or *v* is a pointer, and if
2. *T* is an extension of the static type of *v*

If the designated object is a constant or a variable, then the designator refers to its current value. If it is a procedure, the designator refers to that procedure unless it is followed by a (possibly empty) parameter list in which case it implies an activation of that procedure and stands for the value resulting from its execution. The actual parameters must correspond to the formal parameters as in proper procedure calls (see B.10.1).

Examples of designators (refer to examples in B.7):

```
i                              (INTEGER)
a[i]                           (REAL)
w[3].name[i]     (CHAR)
t.left.right     (Tree)
t(CenterTree).subnode          (Tree)
```

B.8.2 Operators

Four classes of operators with different precedences (binding strengths) are syntactically distinguished in expressions. The operator ~ has the highest precedence, followed by multiplication operators, addition operators, and relations. Operators of the same precedence associate from left to right. For example, *x-y-z* stands for *(x-y)-z*.

Expression	=	*SimpleExpression [Relation SimpleExpression].*
SimpleExpression	=	*["+"	"-"] Term {AddOperator Term}.*
Term	=	*Factor {MulOperator Factor}.*
Factor	=	*Designator [ActualParameters]	number	*
character |		
		*string	NIL	Set	"(" Expression ")"	"~"*
Factor.		
Set	=	*"{" [Element {"," Element}] "}".*
Element	=	*Expression [".." Expression].*
ActualParameters	=	*"(" [ExpressionList] ")".*
Relation	=	*"="	"#"	"<"	"<="	">"	">="	IN	IS.*
AddOperator	=	*"+"	"-"	OR.*
MulOperator	=	*"*"	"/"	DIV	MOD	"&".*

expression compatible The available operators are listed in the following tables. Some operators are applicable to operands of various types, denoting different operations. In these cases, the actual operation is identified by the type of the operands. The operands must be *expression compatible* with respect to the operator (see B.12).

Logical operators

OR	logical disjunction	p OR q	"if p then TRUE, else q"
&	logical conjunction	p & q	"if p then q, else FALSE"
~	negation	~ p	"not p"

These operators apply to *BOOLEAN* operands and yield a *BOOLEAN* result.

Arithmetic operators

+	sum
−	difference
*	product
/	real quotient
DIV	integer quotient
MOD	modulus

The operators +, −, *, and / apply to operands of numeric types. The type of the result is the type of that operand which includes the type of the other operand, except for division (/), where the result is the smallest real type which includes both operand types. When used as monadic operators, − denotes sign inversion and + denotes the identity operation.

DIV, MOD The operators DIV and MOD apply to integer operands only. They are related by the following formulas defined for any *x* and positive divisors *y*:

```
x = (x DIV y) * y + (x MOD y)
0 <= (x MOD y) < y
```

Examples:

x	y	$x\ DIV\ y$	$x\ MOD\ y$
5	3	1	2
−5	3	−2	1

Set operators

+	union
−	difference $(x - y = x * (-y))$
*	intersection
/	symmetric set difference $(x\ /\ y = (x{-}y) + (y{-}x))$

Set operators apply to operands of type *SET* and yield a result of type *SET*. *SET*
The monadic minus sign denotes the complement of x, i.e. $-x$ denotes the set
of integers between 0 and MAX(SET) which are not elements of x.

Set operators are not associative $((a{+}b){-}c\ \#\ a{+}(b{-}c))$.

A set constructor defines the value of a set by listing its elements between
curly brackets. The elements must be integers in the range 0..MAX(SET). A
range a..b denotes all integers in the interval [a, b].

Relations

=	equal
#	unequal
<	less
<=	less or equal
>	greater
>=	greater or equal
IN	set membership
IS	type test

Relations yield a *BOOLEAN* result. The relations =, #, <, <=, >, and >= apply
to the numeric types, *CHAR*, strings and character arrays containing 0X as a
terminator. The relations = and # also apply to *BOOLEAN* and *SET*, as well
as to pointer and procedure types (including the value *NIL*).

x *IN* s stands for "x is an element of s". x must be of an integer type, and s of *IN*
type *SET*.

v *IS* T stands for "the dynamic type of v is T (or an extension of T)" and is *type test*
called a *type test*. It is applicable if

1. v is a variable parameter of record type or v is a pointer, and if

2. T is an extension of the static type of v

Examples of expressions (refer to examples in B.7):

1991	INTEGER
i DIV 3	INTEGER
~p OR q	BOOLEAN
(i+j) * (i–j)	INTEGER
s – {8, 9, 13}	SET
i + x	REAL
a[i+j] * a[i–j]	REAL
(0<=i) & (i<100)	BOOLEAN
t.key = 0	BOOLEAN
k IN {i..j–1}	BOOLEAN
w[i].name <= "John"	BOOLEAN
t IS CenterTree	BOOLEAN

B.9 Statements

elementary statements

Statements denote actions. There are elementary and structured statements. *Elementary statements* are not composed of any parts that are themselves statements. They are the assignment, the procedure call, the return, and the exit statement. *Structured statements* are composed of parts that are themselves statements.

They are used to express sequencing and conditional, selective, and repetitive execution. A statement may also be empty, in which case it denotes no action. The empty statement is included in order to relax punctuation rules in statement sequences.

Statemen = [*Assignment* | *ProcedureCall* | *IfStatement* |
CaseStatement | *WhileStatement* | *RepeatStatement* |
ForStatement | *LoopStatement* | *WithStatement* |
EXIT | *RETURN [Expression]].*

B.9.1 Assignments

assignment compatible

Assignments replace the current value of a variable by a new value specified by an expression. The expression must be *assignment compatible* with the variable (see B.12). The assignment operator is written as ":=" and pronounced "becomes".

Assignment = *Designator ":=" Expression.*

If an expression *e* of type *Te* is assigned to a variable *v* of type *Tv*, the following happens:

1. if *Tv* and *Te* are record types, only those fields of *Te* are assigned which also belong to *Tv* (*projection*); the dynamic type of *v* must be the same as the static type of *v* and is not changed by the assignment;

2. if *Tv* and *Te* are pointer types, the dynamic type of *v* becomes the dynamic type of *e*;

3. if *Tv* is *ARRAY n OF CHAR* and *e* is a string of length $m<n$, *v[i]* becomes e_i for $i = 0..m-1$ and *v[m]* becomes 0X.

Examples of assignments (refer to examples in B.7):

```
i := 0
p := i = j
k := log2(i+j)
F := log2                              (*see B.10.1*)
s := {2, 3, 5, 7, 11, 13}
a[i] := (x+y) * (x-y)
t.key := i
w[i+1].name := "John"
t := c
```

B.9.2 Procedure calls

A procedure call activates a procedure. It may contain a list of actual parameters which replace the corresponding formal parameters defined in the procedure declaration (see B.10). The correspondence is established by the positions of the parameters in the actual and formal parameter lists. There are two kinds of parameters: variable and value parameters.

If a formal parameter is a variable parameter, the corresponding actual *variable* parameter must be a designator denoting a variable. If it denotes an element *parameter* of a structured variable, the component selectors are evaluated when the formal/actual parameter substitution takes place, i.e., before the execution of the procedure.

If a formal parameter is a value parameter, the corresponding actual *value* parameter must be an expression. This expression is evaluated before the *parameter* procedure activation, and the resulting value is assigned to the formal parameter (see also B.10.1).

ProcedureCall = Designator [ActualParameters].

Examples:

```
WriteInt(i*2+1)                        (*see B.10.1*)
INC(w[k].count)
t.Insert("John")                       (*see B.11*)
```

B.9.3 Statement sequences

Statement sequences denote the sequence of actions specified by the compo-   *statement* nent statements which are separated by semicolons.   *sequence*

StatementSequence = Statement {";" Statement}.

B.9.4 If statements

IfStatement   =   *IF Expression THEN StatementSequence*
                     {ELSIF Expression THEN StatementSequence}
                     [ELSE StatementSequence]
                     END.

If statements specify the conditional execution of guarded statement sequences. The Boolean expression preceding a statement sequence is called its guard. The guards are evaluated in sequence of occurrence, until one evaluates to *TRUE*, whereafter its associated statement sequence is executed. If no guard is satisfied, the statement sequence following the symbol *ELSE* is executed, if there is one.

Example:

```
IF (ch >= "A") & (ch <= "Z") THEN ReadIdentifier
ELSIF (ch >= "0") & (ch <= "9") THEN ReadNumber
ELSIF (ch = " ' ") OR (ch = ' " ') THEN ReadString
ELSE SpecialCharacter
END
```

B.9.5 Case statements

case labels   Case statements specify the selection and execution of a statement sequence according to the value of an expression. First the case expression is evaluated, then that statement sequence is executed whose *case label* list contains the obtained value. The case expression must either be of an integer type that includes the types of all case labels, or both the case expression and the case labels must be of type *CHAR*. Case labels are constants, and no value must occur more than once.

ELSE   If the value of the expression does not occur as a label of any case, the statement sequence following the symbol *ELSE* is selected, if there is one, otherwise the program is aborted.

CaseStatement   =   *CASE Expression OF Case {"|" Case}*
                      [ELSE StatementSequence] END.
Case   =   *[CaseLabelList ":" StatementSequence].*
CaseLabelList   =   *CaseLabels {"," CaseLabels}.*
CaseLabels   =   *ConstExpression [".." ConstExpression].*

Example:

```
CASE ch OF
    "A" .. "Z": ReadIdentifier
|   "0" .. "9": ReadNumber
|   " ' ", ' " ': ReadString
ELSE SpecialCharacter
END
```

B.9.6 While statements

While statements specify the repeated execution of a statement sequence *while* the Boolean expression (its guard) yields *TRUE*. The guard is checked before every execution of the statement sequence.

repeated execution

> *WhileStatement = WHILE Expression DO StatementSequence END.*

Examples:

```
WHILE i>0 DO i:=i DIV 2; k:=k+1 END
WHILE (t#NIL) & (t.key#i) DO t:=t.left END
```

B.9.7 Repeat statements

A repeat statement specifies the repeated execution of a statement sequence until a condition specified by a Boolean expression is satisfied. The statement sequence is executed *at least once*.

> *RepeatStatement = REPEAT StatementSequence UNTIL Expression.*

B.9.8 For statements

A for statement specifies the repeated execution of a statement sequence for a fixed number of times while a progression of values is assigned to an integer variable called the control variable of the for statement.

control variable

> *ForStatement =   FOR ident ":=" Expression TO Expression [BY ConstExpression]*
> *DO StatementSequence END.*

The statement

```
FOR v:=low TO high BY step DO statements END
```

is equivalent to

```
v:=low; temp:=high;
IF step>0 THEN
    WHILE v<=temp DO statements; v:=v+step END
ELSE
    WHILE v>=temp DO statements; v:=v+step END
END
```

low must be *assignment compatible* with *v* (see B.12), high must be *expression compatible* (i.e. comparable) with *v*, and *step* must be a nonzero constant expression of an integer type. If *step* is not specified, it is assumed to be 1.

Examples:

```
FOR i:=0 TO 79 DO k:=k+a[i] END
FOR i:=79 TO 1 BY -1 DO a[i]:=a[i-1] END
```

B.9.9 Loop statements

EXIT   A loop statement specifies the repeated execution of a statement sequence. It is terminated upon execution of an exit statement within that sequence (see B.9.10).

> *LoopStatement = LOOP StatementSequence END.*

Example:

```
LOOP
    ReadInt(i);
    IF i<0 THEN EXIT END;
    WriteInt(i)
END
```

Loop statements are useful to express repetitions with several exit points or cases where the exit condition is in the middle of the repeated statement sequence.

B.9.10 Return and exit statements

RETURN   A return statement indicates the termination of a procedure. It is denoted by the symbol *RETURN*, followed by an expression if the procedure is a function procedure. The type of the expression must be *assignment compatible* (see B.12) with the result type specified in the procedure heading (see B.10).

Function procedures must be left via a return statement indicating the result value. In proper procedures, a return statement is implied by the end of the procedure body. Any explicit return statement therefore appears as an additional (probably exceptional) termination point.

EXIT   An exit statement is denoted by the symbol *EXIT*. It specifies termination of the enclosing loop statement and continuation with the statement following that loop statement. Exit statements are contextually, although not syntactically, associated with the loop statement which contains them.

B.9.11 With statements

With statements execute a statement sequence depending on the result of a type test and apply a type guard to every occurrence of the tested variable within this statement sequence.

> *WithStatement*   =   *WITH Guard DO StatementSequence*
> *{ "|" Guard DO StatementSequence}*
> *[ELSE StatementSequence] END.*
> *Guard*   =   *Qualident ":" Qualident.*

If *v* is a variable parameter of record type or a pointer variable, and if it is of a static type *T0*, the statement

```
WITH v:T1 DO S1 | v:T2 DO S2 ELSE S3 END
```

has the following meaning: if the dynamic type of *v* is *T1*, then the statement sequence *S1* is executed where *v* is regarded as if it had the static type *T1*; else if the dynamic type of *v* is *T2*, then *S2* is executed where *v* is regarded as if it had the static type *T2*; else *S3* is executed. *T1* and *T2* must be extensions of *T0*. If no type test is satisfied and if an else clause is missing the program is aborted.

Example:

```
WITH t:CenterTree DO i:=t.width; c:=t.subnode END
```

B.10 Procedure declarations

A procedure declaration consists of a *procedure heading* and a *procedure body*. The heading specifies the procedure identifier and the formal parameters. For type-bound procedures it also specifies the receiver parameter. The body contains declarations and statements. The procedure identifier is repeated at the end of the procedure declaration.   *heading, body*

There are two kinds of procedures: *proper procedures* and *function procedures*. The latter are activated by a function designator as a constituent of an expression and yield a result that is an operand of the expression. Proper procedures are activated by a procedure call. A procedure is a function procedure if its formal parameters specify a result type. The body of a function procedure must contain a return statement which defines its result.

All constants, variables, types, and procedures declared within a procedure body are local to the procedure. Since procedures may be declared as local objects too, procedure declarations may be nested.   *local*

The call of a procedure within its declaration implies recursive activation.   *recursion*

Objects declared in the environment of the procedure are also visible in those parts of the procedure in which they are not concealed by a locally declared object with the same name.

ProcedureDeclaration   = *ProcedureHeading ";" ProcedureBody ident.*
ProcedureHeading   = *PROCEDURE [Receiver] IdentDef*
[FormalParameters].
ProcedureBody   = *DeclarationSequence [BEGIN*
StatementSequence] END.
DeclarationSequence   = *{CONST {ConstantDeclaration ";"} |*
                            TYPE {TypeDeclaration ";"} |
                            VAR {VariableDeclaration ";"} }
                            {ProcedureDeclaration ";" |
                            ForwardDeclaration ";"}.

$$ForwardDeclaration \quad = \quad PROCEDURE\ "\wedge"\ [Receiver]$$
$$IdentDef\ [FormalParameters].$$

type-bound If a procedure declaration specifies a receiver parameter, the procedure is
procedures considered to be *bound to a type* (see B.10.2).

forward A *forward declaration* serves to allow forward references to a procedure
declaration whose actual declaration appears later in the text. The formal parameter lists
of the forward declaration and the actual declaration must match (see B.12).

B.10.1 Formal parameters

Formal parameters are identifiers declared in the formal parameter list of a
procedure. They correspond to actual parameters specified in the procedure
call. The correspondence between formal and actual parameters is established
when the procedure is called. There are two kinds of parameters, value and
variable parameters, indicated in the formal parameter list by the absence or
presence of the keyword *VAR*.

Value parameters are local variables to which the value of the corresponding
actual parameter is assigned as an initial value. Variable parameters correspond to actual parameters that are variables, and they stand for these
variables.

scope The scope of a formal parameter extends from its declaration to the end of the
procedure block in which it is declared.

A function procedure without parameters must have an empty parameter list.
It must be called by a function designator whose actual parameter list is
empty too. The result type of a function procedure can be neither a record nor
an array.

$$FormalParameters \quad = "("\ [FPSection\ \{";"\ FPSection\}]\ ")"\ [":"\ Qualident].$$
$$FPSection \quad = [VAR]\ ident\ \{","\ ident\}\ ":"\ Type.$$

Let Tf be the type of a formal parameter f (not an open array) and Ta the type
of the corresponding actual parameter a. For variable parameters, Ta must be
the same as Tf, or Tf must be a record type and Ta an extension of Tf. For
value parameters, a must be *assignment compatible* with f (see B.12).

If Tf is an open array , then a must be *array compatible* with f (see B.12). The
lengths of f are taken from a.

Examples of procedure declarations:

```
PROCEDURE ReadInt (VAR x:INTEGER);
VAR
    i: INTEGER;
    ch: CHAR;
BEGIN
    i:=0;
    Read(ch);
    WHILE ("0"<=ch) & (ch<="9") DO
        i:=10*i+(ORD(ch)-ORD("0"));
        Read(ch)
    END;
```

```
      x:=i
END ReadInt;

PROCEDURE WriteInt (x:INTEGER);                    (*0<=x<100000*)
VAR
    i: INTEGER;
    buf: ARRAY 5 OF INTEGER;
BEGIN
    i:=0;
    REPEAT
        buf[i]:=x MOD 10;
        x:=x DIV 10;
        INC(i)
    UNTIL x = 0;
    REPEAT
        DEC(i);
        Write(CHR(buf[i]+ORD("0")))
    UNTIL i = 0
END WriteInt;

PROCEDURE WriteString (s:ARRAY OF CHAR);
VAR i: INTEGER;
BEGIN
    i:=0;
    WHILE (i<LEN(s)) & (s[i]#0X) DO
        Write(s[i]);
        INC(i)
    END
END WriteString;

PROCEDURE log2 (x:INTEGER): INTEGER;
VAR y: INTEGER;                                    (*assume x>0*)
BEGIN
    y:=0;
    WHILE x>1 DO
        x:=x DIV 2;
        INC(y)
    END;
    RETURN y
END log2
```

B.10.2 Type-bound procedures

Globally declared procedures may be associated with a record type declared in the same module. The procedures are said to be bound to the record type. The binding is expressed by the type of the receiver in the heading of a procedure declaration. The receiver may be either a variable parameter of record type T or a value parameter of type *POINTER TO T* (where T is a record type). The procedure is bound to the type T and is considered local to it.

ProcedureHeading   = *PROCEDURE [Receiver] IdentDef [FormalParameters].*
Receiver   = *"(" [VAR] ident ":" ident ")".*

If a procedure P is bound to a type $T0$, it is implicitly also bound to any type $T1$ which is an extension of $T0$. However, a procedure P' (with the same name as P) may be explicitly bound to $T1$ in which case it *overrides* the binding of *P*. *P'* is considered a *redefinition* of *P* for *T1*. The formal parameters of *P* and *P'* must *match* (see B.12). If *P* and *T1* are exported (see B.4) *P'* must be exported too.

If *v* is a designator and *P* is a type-bound procedure, then *v.P* denotes that procedure *P* which is bound to the dynamic type of *v*. Note that this may be a different procedure than the one bound to the static type of *v*. *v* is passed to *P*'s receiver according to the parameter passing rules specified in B.10.1.

If *r* is a receiver parameter declared with type *T*, *r.P^* denotes the (redefined) procedure *P* bound to the base type of *T*.

In a forward declaration of a type-bound procedure the receiver parameter must be of the *same type* as in the actual procedure declaration. The formal parameter lists of both declarations must match (see B.12).

Examples:

```
PROCEDURE (t:Tree) Insert (node:Tree);
VAR p,father: Tree;
BEGIN
   p:=t;
   REPEAT
      father:=p;
      IF node.key=p.key THEN RETURN END;
      IF node.key<p.key THEN p:=p.left ELSE p:=p.right END
   UNTIL p=NIL;
   IF node.key<father.key THEN
      father.left:=node
   ELSE
      father.right := node
   END;
   node.left:=NIL;
   node.right:=NIL
END Insert;

PROCEDURE (t:CenterTree) Insert (node:Tree);   (*redefinition*)
BEGIN
   WriteInt(node(CenterTree).width);
   t.Insert^(node) (*calls the Insert procedure bound to Tree*)
END Insert;
```

B.10.3 Predeclared procedures

generic
procedure   The following table lists the predeclared procedures. Some are *generic procedures*, i.e., they apply to several types of operands. *v* stands for a variable, *x* and *n* for expressions, and *T* for a type.

Function procedures

Name	Argument type	Result type	Function
ABS(x)	numeric type	type of x	absolute value
ASH(x, n)	x, n: integer type	LONGINT	arithmetic shift (x * 2n)

CAP(x)	CHAR	CHAR	x is letter: corresponding capital letter
CHR(x)	integer type	CHAR	character with ordinal number x
ENTIER(x)	real type	LONGINT	largest integer not greater than x
LEN(v, n)	v: array; n: integer const.	LONGINT	length of v in dimension n (first dim. = 0)
LEN(v)	v: array	LONGINT	equivalent to LEN(v, 0)
LONG(x)	SHORTINT	INTEGER	identity
	INTEGER	LONGINT	
	REAL	LONGREAL	
MAX(T)	T = basic type	T	maximum value of type T
	T = SET	INTEGER	maximum element of a set
MIN(T)	T = basic type	T	minimum value of type T
	T = SET	INTEGER	0
ODD(x)	integer type	BOOLEAN	x MOD 2 = 1
ORD(x)	CHAR	INTEGER	ordinal number of x
SHORT(x)	LONGINT	INTEGER	identity
	INTEGER	SHORTINT	identity
	LONGREAL	REAL	identity (truncation possible)
SIZE(T)	any type	integer type	number of bytes required by T

Proper procedures

Name	*Argument types*		*Function*
COPY(x, v)	x: character array, string; v: character array	v := x	
DEC(v)	integer type		v := v - 1
DEC(v, n)	v, n: integer type		v := v - n
EXCL(v, x)	v: SET; x: integer type	v := v - {x}	
HALT(x)	integer constant		terminate program execution
INC(v)	integer type		v := v + 1

INC(v, n)	v, n: integer type		v := v + n
INCL(v, x)	v: SET; x: integer type	v := v + {x}	
NEW(v)	pointer to record or fixed array	allocate v^	
NEW(v, x0, ..., xn) v: pointer to open array; xi: integer type	allocate v ^ with lengths x0.. xn		

COPY   *COPY* allows the assignment of a string or a character array containing a terminating *0X* to another character array. If necessary, the assigned value is truncated to the target length minus one. The target will always contain a terminating *0X*.

In *HALT(x)*, the interpretation of *x* is left to the underlying system implementation.

B.11 Modules

A module is a collection of declarations of constants, types, variables, and procedures, together with a sequence of statements for the purpose of assigning initial values to the variables. A module constitutes a text that is compilable as a unit.

Module	=	*MODULE ident ";" [ImportList] DeclarationSequence*
		[BEGIN StatementSequence] END ident ".".
ImportList	=	*IMPORT Import {"," Import} ";".*
Import	=	*[ident ":="] ident.*

import list   The *import list* specifies the names of the imported modules. If a module *A* is imported by a module *M* and *A* exports an identifier *x*, then *x* is referred to as *A.x* within *M*. If *A* is imported as *B:=A*, the object *x* must be referenced as *B.x*. This allows short alias names in qualified identifiers. A module must not import itself. Identifiers that are to be exported (i.e., that are to be visible in client modules) must be marked by an export mark in their declaration (see B.4).

module
initialization   The statement sequence following the symbol *BEGIN* is executed when the module is added to a system (loaded), which is done after the imported modules have been loaded. It follows that cyclic import of modules is illegal.

```
MODULE Trees;
(*exports: Tree,Node, Insert, Search, Write, NewTree*)

IMPORT Texts,Oberon;

TYPE
   Tree*= POINTER TO Node;
   Node*= RECORD
      name-: POINTER TO ARRAY OF CHAR;
      left,right: Tree
   END;

   VAR w: Texts.Writer;

   PROCEDURE (t:Tree) Insert* (name:ARRAY OF CHAR);
   VAR p,father: Tree;
   BEGIN
      p:=t;
      REPEAT
         father:=p;
         IF name=p.name^ THEN RETURN END;
         IF name<p.name^ THEN
            p:=p.left
         ELSE
            p:=p.right
         END
      UNTIL p=NIL;
      NEW(p);
      p.left:=NIL;
      p.right:=NIL;
      NEW(p.name,LEN(name)+1);
      COPY(name,p.name^);
      IF name<father.name^ THEN
         father.left:=p
      ELSE
         father.right:=p
      END
   END Insert;

   PROCEDURE (t:Tree) Search*(name:ARRAY OF CHAR): Tree;
   VAR p: Tree;
   BEGIN
      p:=t;
      WHILE (p#NIL) & (name#p.name^) DO
         IF name<p.name^ THEN
            p:=p.left
         ELSE
            p:=p.right
         END
      END;
      RETURN p
   END Search;

   PROCEDURE (t:Tree) Write*;
   BEGIN
      IF t.left#NIL THEN t.left.Write END;
      Texts.WriteString(w,t.name^);
      Texts.WriteLn(w);
      Texts.Append(Oberon.Log,w.buf);
      IF t.right#NIL THEN t.right.Write END
   END Write;
```

```
PROCEDURE NewTree* (): Tree;
VAR t: Tree;
BEGIN
    NEW(t);
    NEW(t.name,1);
    t.name[0]:=0X;
    t.left:=NIL;
    t.right:=NIL;
    RETURN t
END NewTree;

BEGIN
    Texts.OpenWriter(w)
END Trees.
```

B.12 Definition of terms

integer   **Integer types**   SHORTINT, INTEGER, LONGINT

real   **Real types**   REAL, LONGREAL

numeric   **Numeric types**   integer types, real types

same types   Two variables a and b with types Ta and Tb are of the **same type** if

1. Ta and Tb are both denoted by the same type identifier, or
2. Ta is declared to equal Tb in a type declaration of the form $Ta=Tb$, or
3. a and b appear in the same identifier list in a variable, record field, or formal parameter declaration and are not open arrays.

equal types   Two types Ta and Tb are **equal** if

1. Ta and Tb are the same type, or
2. Ta and Tb are open array types with equal element types, or
3. Ta and Tb are procedure types whose formal parameter lists match.

type inclusion   Numeric types **include** (the values of) smaller numeric types according to the following hierarchy:

$$LONGREAL >= REAL >= LONGINT >= INTEGER >= SHORTINT$$

type extension   Given a type declaration $Tb=RECORD (Ta) ... END$, Tb is a **direct extension**
(base type)   of Ta, and Ta is a **direct base type** of Tb. A type Tb is an **extension** of a type Ta (Ta is a **base type** of Tb) if

1. Ta and Tb are the *same types*, or
2. Tb is a *direct extension* of an *extension* of Ta

If $Pa=POINTER\ TO\ Ta$ and $Pb=POINTER\ TO\ Tb$, Pb is an *extension* of Pa (Pa is a *base type* of Pb) if Tb is an *extension* of Ta.

An expression *e* of type *Te* is **assignment compatible** with a variable *v* of type *Tv* if one of the following conditions hold:

assignment compatible

1. *Te* and *Tv* are the *same type*;
2. *Te* and *Tv* are numeric types and *Tv* includes *Te*;
3. *Te* and *Tv* are record types and *Te* is an *extension* of *Tv* and the dynamic type of *v* is *Tv*;
4. *Te* and *Tv* are pointer types and Te is an *extension* of *Tv*;
5. *Tv* is a pointer or a procedure type and *e* is *NIL*;
6. *Tv* is *ARRAY n OF CHAR*, *e* is a string constant with *m* characters, and $m < n$;
7. *Tv* is a procedure type and *e* is the name of a procedure whose formal parameters match those of *Tv*.

An actual parameter a of type *Ta* is **array compatible** with a formal parameter *f* of type *Tf* if

array compatible

1. *Tf* and *Ta* are the same type, or
2. *Tf* is an open array, *Ta* is any array, and their element types are *array compatible*, or
3. *f* is a value parameter of type *ARRAY OF CHAR* and *a* is a string.

For a given operator, the types of its operands are **expression compatible** if they conform to the following table (which shows also the result type of the expression). Character arrays that are to be compared must contain *0X* as a terminator. Type *T1* must be an *extension* of type *T0*:

expression compatible

operator	first operand	second operand	result type
+ − *	numeric	numeric	smallest numeric type including both operands
/	numeric	numeric	smallest real type including both operands
DIV, MOD	integer	integer	smallest integer type including both operands
+ - * /	SET	SET	SET
OR & ~	BOOLEAN	BOOLEAN	BOOLEAN
= # < <= > >=	numeric	numeric	BOOLEAN
	CHAR	CHAR	
	char. array, string	char. array, string	

= #	BOOLEAN	BOOLEAN	BOOLEAN
	SET	SET	
	NIL, pointer type T0 or T1	NIL, pointer type T0 or T1	
	procedure type T, NIL	procedure type T, NIL	
IN	integer	SET	BOOLEAN
IS	type T0	type T1	BOOLEAN

matching formal parameter lists

Two ***formal parameter lists match*** if

1. they have the same number of parameters, and
2. they have either the same function result type or none, and
3. parameters at corresponding positions have equal types, and
4. parameters at corresponding positions are both either value or variable parameters.

B.13 Syntax of Oberon-2

```
Module  = MODULE ident ";" [ImportList] DeclSeq
          [BEGIN StatementSeq] END ident ".".
ImportList  = IMPORT [ident ":="] ident {"," [ident ":="] ident} ";".
DeclSeq   = { CONST {ConstDecl ";" } |
          TYPE {TypeDecl ";"} | VAR {VarDecl ";"}}
          {ProcDecl ";" | ForwardDecl ";"}.
ConstDecl  = IdentDef "=" ConstExpr.
TypeDecl  = IdentDef "=" Type.
VarDecl = IdentList ":" Type.
ProcDecl  = PROCEDURE [Receiver] IdentDef [FormalPars] ";" DeclSeq
          [BEGIN StatementSeq] END ident.
ForwardDecl   = PROCEDURE "^" [Receiver] IdentDef [FormalPars].
FormalPars = "(" [FPSection {";" FPSection}] ")" [":" Qualident].
FPSection   = [VAR] ident {"," ident} ":" Type.
Receiver= ("  [VAR] ident ":" ident ")".
Type    = Qualident | ARRAY [ConstExpr {"," ConstExpr}] OF Type |
          RECORD ["("Qualident")"] FieldList {";" FieldList} END |
          POINTER TO Type | PROCEDURE [FormalPars].
FieldList   = [IdentList ":" Type].
StatementSeq    = Statement {";" Statement}.
Statement   = [Designator ":=" Expr | Designator ["(" [ExprList] ")"]] |
          IF Expr THEN StatementSeq {ELSIF Expr THEN StatementSeq}
          [ELSE StatementSeq] END |
          CASE Expr OF Case {"|" Case} [ELSE StatementSeq] END |
          WHILE Expr DO StatementSeq END |
          REPEAT StatementSeq UNTIL Expr |
          FOR ident ":=" Expr TO Expr [BY ConstExpr]
          DO StatementSeq END |
          LOOP StatementSeq END |
```

```
        WITH Guard DO StatementSeq {"|" Guard
        DO StatementSeq} [ELSE StatementSeq] END |
        EXIT | RETURN [Expr]{SYMBOL 95 \f "Symbol"}].
Case      = [CaseLabels {"," CaseLabels} ":" StatementSeq].
CaseLabels = ConstExpr [".." ConstExpr].
Guard     = Qualident ":" Qualident.
ConstExpr = Expr.
Expr      = SimpleExpr [Relation SimpleExpr].
SimpleExpr = ["+" | "-"] Term {AddOp Term}.
Term      = Factor {MulOp Factor}.
Factor    = Designator ["(" [ExprList] ")"] | number | character | string |
            NIL | Set | "(" Expr ")" | " ~ " Factor.
Set = "{" [Element {"," Element}] "}".
Element = Expr [".." Expr].
Relation    = "=" | "#" | "<" | "<=" | ">" | ">=" | IN | IS.
AddOp  = "+" | "-" | OR.
MulOp  = " * " | "/" | DIV | MOD | "&".
Designator  = Qualident {"." ident | "[" ExprList "]" | " ^ " | "(" Qualident ")"}.
ExprList    = Expr {"," Expr}.
IdentList   = IdentDef {"," IdentDef}.
Qualident   = [ident "."] ident.
IdentDef    = ident [" * " |{SYMBOL 95 \f "Symbol"}"-"].
```

B.14 The module SYSTEM

The module SYSTEM contains certain types and procedures that are necessary to implement low-level operations particular to a given computer and/or implementation. These include for example facilities for accessing devices that are controlled by the computer, and facilities to break the type compatibility rules otherwise imposed by the language definition. It is strongly recommended to restrict their use to specific modules (called low-level modules). Such modules are inherently non-portable, but easily recognized due to the identifier SYSTEM appearing in their import list.

The following specifications hold for the implementation of Oberon-2 in *POW!*.

Module SYSTEM exports a type *BYTE* with the following characteristics: Variables of type *CHAR* or *SHORTINT* can be assigned to variables of type *BYTE*. If a formal variable parameter is of type *ARRAY OF BYTE* then the corresponding actual parameter may be of any type.   *BYTE*

Another type exported by module SYSTEM is the type *PTR*. Variables of any pointer type may be assigned to variables of type *PTR*. If a formal variable parameter is of type *PTR*, the actual parameter may be of any pointer type.   *PTR*

The procedures contained in module SYSTEM are listed in the following tables. Most of them correspond to single instructions compiled as in-line code. For details, the reader is referred to the processor manual. *v* stands for a variable, *x*, *y*, *a*, and *n* for expressions, and *T* for a type.

Function procedures

Name	Argument types	Result type	Function
ADR(v)	any	LONGINT	address of variable v
BIT(a, n)	a: LONGINT	BOOLEAN	bit n of Mem[a]
	n: integer		
CC(n)	integer constant	BOOLEAN	condition n ($0 <= n <= 15$)
LSH(x, n)	x: integer, CHAR, BYTE	type of x	logical shift of x for n bits ($n>0$ ... shift left) ($n<0$ ... shift right)
	n: integer		
ROT(x, n)	x: integer, CHAR, BYTE	type of x	rotation of x for n bits ($n>0$ ... rotate left) ($n<0$ ... rotate right)
	n: integer		
VAL(T, x)	T, x: any type	T	x interpreted as of type T

Proper procedures

Name	Argument types	Function
GET(a, v)	a: LONGINT; v: any basic type, pointer, procedure type	$v := M[a]$
PUT(a, x)	a: LONGINT; x: any basic type, pointer, procedure type	$M[a] := x$
GETREG(n, v)	n: integer constant; v: any basic type, pointer, procedure type	$v :=$ Register n
PUTREG(n, x)	n: integer constant; x: any basic type, pointer, procedure type	Register $n := x$
MOVE(a0, a1, n)	a0, a1: LONGINT; n: integer	$M[a1.. a1+n-1] := M[a0.. a0+n-1]$
NEW(v, n)	v: any pointer; n: integer	allocate storage block of n bytes and assign its address to v

Register numbers[*] for functions *GETREG* and *PUTREG*:   *CPU registers*

```
EAX = 0      ECX = 1
EDX = 2      EBX = 3
ESP = 4      EBP = 5
ESI = 6      EDI = 7
ES  = 8      CS  = 9
SS  = 10     DS  = 11
FS  = 12     GS  = 13
EIP = 14
```

B.15 Windows related language extensions

Oberon-2 has been developed for the operating system Oberon. To access the Windows system the language has been slightly extended:

Keyword [WINDOWS]

Records and procedures, which are declared with the keyword [WINDOWS], are treated specially by the compiler for interfacing to the Windows system:

Records

```
TYPE ... = RECORD [WINDOWS] ... END;
```

Such records are arranged linearly in memory without any gap between the fields.

Records without [WINDOWS] (the default) have a 4-byte alignment. This   *Alignment*
means that all record fields are at an address divisible by 4.

Windows data structures (e.g., the *LOGFONT* structure for defining a logical font) are always packed (without alignment) and so all structures in the module *Windows* are declared as [WINDOWS].

The keyword [WINDOWS] is necessary also for retrieving data from and sending data to programs not written in Oberon-2.

Example:

```
TYPE POINT = RECORD [WINDOWS]
                x: INTEGER;
                y: INTEGER;
             END;
```

---

[*] These numbers are only correct for the Oberon-2 compiler implementation in *POW!*.

Procedures

```
PROCEDURE [WINDOWS] ... ;
```

Procedures which are called from programs not written in Oberon-2 must be declared with the keyword [WINDOWS]. Additionally, these procedures must be exported and listed in the export list of the linker options dialog (see Chapter 3).

The symbol generated by the compiler for a [WINDOWS] procedure is the procedure name alone, whereas the names for standard Oberon-2 procedures consist of the module name followed by an underscore and the procedure name (e.g., *Out_String*).

Examples:

```
PROCEDURE [WINDOWS] CloseWindow (hwnd:HWND);
PROCEDURE [WINDOWS] GetTickCount (): DWORD;
PROCEDURE [WINDOWS] GetTopWindow (hwnd:HWND): HWND;
```

Definition modules

The Windows system consists of many parts, most of them implemented as dynamic link libraries (DLLs).

DEFINITION For interfacing with a DLL it is necessary to inform the compiler about the content of the DLL. This is done in *POW!* by creating a *definition module*.

Definition modules begin with the keyword DEFINITION instead of MODULE, their content is a list of definitions of the exported symbols (variables, data type declarations, and procedures) of the specific DLL. Definition modules contain no code because this is already in the DLL!

Definition modules are treated like Oberon-2 modules. They are imported by the IMPORT statement as usual and then the procedures of the DLL can be called like procedures in Oberon-2 modules.

All symbols in definition modules are exported automatically; they need not be marked with the export mark.

windows.mod Have a look at the file *windows.mod* in subdirectory *src* of *POW!* as example for a definition module. It contains the declaration of all constants, data types, and procedures of the Windows system API. These declarations can be used by simply importing the *Windows* module.

Note that the formal parameters of a procedure in a definition module need not match the real parameters of the corresponding DLL procedure. There is no way for the compiler to check the correctness of declarations inside definition modules. So you need to take great care when designing and typing them!

Appendix C:
Table of ASCII Codes

Basic ASCII code

dec	hex		dec	hex		dec	hex		dec	hex	
0	0	NUL	32	20	SPC	64	40	@	96	60	`
1	1	SOH	33	21	!	65	41	A	97	61	a
2	2	STX	34	22	"	66	42	B	98	62	b
3	3	ETX	35	23	#	67	43	C	99	63	c
4	4	EOT	36	24	$	68	44	D	100	64	d
5	5	ENQ	37	25	%	69	45	E	101	65	e
6	6	ACK	38	26	&	70	46	F	102	66	f
7	7	BEL	39	27	'	71	47	G	103	67	g
8	8	BS	40	28	(	72	48	H	104	68	h
9	9	HT	41	29	)	73	49	I	105	69	i
10	A	LF	42	2A	*	74	4A	J	106	6A	j
11	B	VT	43	2B	+	75	4B	K	107	6B	k
12	C	FF	44	2C	,	76	4C	L	108	6C	l
13	D	CR	45	2D	-	77	4D	M	109	6D	m
14	E	SO	46	2E	.	78	4E	N	110	6E	n
15	F	SI	47	2F	/	79	4F	O	111	6F	o
16	10	DLE	48	30	0	80	50	P	112	70	p
17	11	DC1	49	31	1	81	51	Q	113	71	q
18	12	DC2	50	32	2	82	52	R	114	72	r
19	13	DC3	51	33	3	83	53	S	115	73	s
20	14	DC4	52	34	4	84	54	T	116	74	t
21	15	NAK	53	35	5	85	55	U	117	75	u
22	16	SYN	54	36	6	86	56	V	118	76	v
23	17	ETB	55	37	7	87	57	W	119	77	w
24	18	CAN	56	38	8	88	58	X	120	78	x
25	19	EM	57	39	9	89	59	Y	121	79	y
26	1A	SUB	58	3A	:	90	5A	Z	122	7A	z
27	1B	ESC	59	3B	;	91	5B	[	123	7B	{
28	1C	FS	60	3C	<	92	5C	\	124	7C		
29	1D	GS	61	3D	=	93	5D	]	125	7D	}
30	1E	RS	62	3E	>	94	5E	^	126	7E	~
31	1F	US	63	3F	?	95	5F	_	127	7F	⌂

ANSI
extension

dec	hex		dec	hex		dec	hex	
160	A0		192	C0	À	224	E0	à
161	A1	¡	193	C1	Á	225	E1	á
162	A2	¢	194	C2	Â	226	E2	â
163	A3	£	195	C3	Ã	227	E3	ã
164	A4	¤	196	C4	Ä	228	E4	ä
165	A5	¥	197	C5	Å	229	E5	å
166	A6	¦	198	C6	Æ	230	E6	æ
167	A7	§	199	C7	Ç	231	E7	ç
168	A8	¨	200	C8	È	232	E8	è
169	A9	©	201	C9	É	233	E9	é
170	AA	ª	202	CA	Ê	234	EA	ê
171	AB	«	203	CB	Ë	235	EB	ë
172	AC	¬	204	CC	Ì	236	EC	ì
173	AD	-	205	CD	Í	237	ED	í
174	AE	®	206	CE	Î	238	EE	î
175	AF	¯	207	CF	Ï	239	EF	ï
176	B0	°	208	D0	Ð	240	F0	ð
177	B1	±	209	D1	Ñ	241	F1	ñ
178	B2	^{2}	210	D2	Ò	242	F2	ò
179	B3	^{3}	211	D3	Ó	243	F3	ó
180	B4	´	212	D4	Ô	244	F4	ô
181	B5	µ	213	D5	Õ	245	F5	õ
182	B6	¶	214	D6	Ö	246	F6	ö
183	B7	·	215	D7	×	247	F7	÷
184	B8	¸	216	D8	Ø	248	F8	ø
185	B9	^{1}	217	D9	Ù	249	F9	ù
186	BA	º	218	DA	Ú	250	FA	ú
187	BB	»	219	DB	Û	251	FB	û
188	BC	¼	220	DC	Ü	252	FC	ü
189	BD	½	221	DD	Ý	253	FD	ý
190	BE	¾	222	DE	Þ	254	FE	þ
191	BF	¿	223	DF	ß	255	FF	ÿ

Literature

The following books and publications are referred to in the text:

[Wir71]

    Wirth N.: The Programming Language Pascal.
    Acta Informatica, 1: 35-63, 1971

[Wir82]

    Wirth N.: Programming in Modula-2. Springer-Verlag, 1982

[WG89]

    Wirth N., Gutknecht J.: The Oberon System.
    Software – Practice and Experience, 19: 857-893, 1989

[MW91]

    Mössenböck H., Wirth N.: The Programming Language Oberon-2.
    Structured Programming, 12(4): 179-195, 1991

[Rei91]

    Reiser M.: The Oberon System, User Guide and Programmer's Manual.
    Addison-Wesley, 1991

[Rum91]

    Rumbaugh J., Blaha M., Premerlani W., Eddy F., Lorenson W.: Object-Oriented
    Modelling and Design. Prentice Hall, 1991

[Jac92]

    Jacobson I., Christerson M., Jonsson P., Overgaard G.: Object-Oriented Software
    Engineering – A Use Case Driven Approach. Addison-Wesley, 1992

[Mö93]

    Mössenböck H.: Object Oriented Programming in Oberon-2.
    Springer-Verlag, 1993

[Oak93]

    Kirk B.(ed.): The Oakwood Guidelines for Oberon-2 Compiler Developers.
    Available via FTP from ftp.fim.uni-linz.ac.at, /pub/soft/pow-oberon/oakwood and
    the British Computer Society (BCS), Modular Languages SIG

[MLK95]

    Mühlbacher J. R., Leisch B., Kreuzeder U.: Programmieren mit Oberon-2 unter
    Windows. Carl Hanser Verlag, 1995

[Gam95]

  Gamma E., Helm R., Johnson R., Vlissides J.: Design Patterns – Elements of
  Reusable Object-Oriented Software. Addison-Wesley, 1995

*The following books provide good background reading and are
recommended.*

Petzold C.: Programming Windows Microsoft Press, 1993

  A clearly set book which gradually introduces the beginner in on the secrets of
  Windows programming. Contains many examples on disc (written in C).

Sedgewick R.: Algorithms. Addison-Wesley, 1992

  This is a standard work of computing containing algorithms for a variety of
  subjects (searching, sorting, numerical mathematics, graph theory, geometry, ...).

Sommerville I.: Software Engineering. Addison-Wesley, 1995

  This book contains a very thorough introduction to software engineering. It is
  partitioned in a way which makes it suitable both for beginners and more
  advanced readers.

The Windows Interface. Microsoft Press

  An application design guide.

Index

Springer
und
Umwelt

Als internationaler wissenschaftlicher
Verlag sind wir uns unserer besonderen
Verpflichtung der Umwelt gegenüber
bewußt und beziehen umweltorientierte
Grundsätze in Unternehmens-
entscheidungen mit ein. Von unseren
Geschäftspartnern (Druckereien,
Papierfabriken, Verpackungsherstellern
usw.) verlangen wir, daß sie sowohl
beim Herstellungsprozess selbst als
auch beim Einsatz der zur Verwendung
kommenden Materialien ökologische
Gesichtspunkte berücksichtigen.
Das für dieses Buch verwendete Papier
ist aus chlorfrei bzw. chlorarm
hergestelltem Zellstoff gefertigt und im
pH-Wert neutral.

Springer